African Virtues in the Pursuit of Conviviality: Exploring Local Solutions in Light of Global Prescriptions

Edited by

Yntiso Gebre, Itaru Ohta and Motoji Matsuda

In collaboration

Langaa RPCIG
Mankon Bamenda

CAAS
Kyoto University

Publisher:
Langaa RPCIG
Langaa Research & Publishing Common Initiative Group
P.O. Box 902 Mankon
Bamenda
North West Region
Cameroon
Langaagrp@gmail.com
www.langaa-rpcig.net

In Collaboration with
The Center for African Area Studies, Kyoto University, Japan

Distributed in and outside N. America by African Books Collective
orders@africanbookscollective.com
www.africanbookscollective.com

ISBN-10: 9956764175

ISBN-13: 9789956764174

About the Contributors

Kyoko CROSS is Associate Professor at the College of International Relations, Ritsumeikan University, Japan. Her major research fields are international relations, transitional justice and human security. Her major works include: *Diffusing Post-conflict Reconciliation: The Localization Mechanism of Pluralistic Norms* (Yushindo 2016, in Japanese) and 'The designing of the "reconciliation" process by the South African Truth and Reconciliation Commission: Analytical perspectives on local justice employment and its effects,' *Peace Studies,* Vol. 38 (2012, in Japanese).

Yntiso GEBRE is Professor of Social Anthropolgoy at Addis Ababa University, Ethiopia. He served as department head and college dean. His research interests include civil society organisations, population movement, conflict, violent extremism, and environment and livelihoods. His recent articles include: 'Ethnic boundary making in East Africa: Rigidity and flexibility among the Nyangatom people', *African Study Monographs*, Vol. 37, No. 4 (2016) and 'Pastoral conflicts in East Africa: The unnoticed wars in the Ethiopia-Kenya border', *Ethiopian Journal of Development Research*, Vol. 38, No. 1 (2016). He co-edited *Customary Dispute Resolution Mechanisms in Ethiopia, Volume 1 & 2* (EACC 2011 & 2012) and *Displacement Risks in Africa* (Kyoto University Press 2005).

Senishaw GETACHEW is Assistant Professor of Social Anthropology at Addis Ababa University, Ethiopia. Before joining the university, he worked for the Authority for Research and Conservation of Cultural Heritage of Ethiopia in different capacities: Director of Cultural Heritage Collection and Research Laboratory Service Directorate, Director of Cultural Heritage Research Directorate, and Head of Cultural Anthropology Department. He also served as consultant for various organizations, including UNESCO. His research interests focus on indigenous knowledge, environment, livelihoods and heritage management. His recent publications in proceedings include: 'Indigenous ecological knowledge system and local ecological management in midland Gedeo' (2015) and 'Intangible cultural heritage management' (2010).

Masashi HASEGAWA is a graduate from the Graduate School of International Cooperation Studies, Kobe University, Japan and the Chief Executive Officer of the Grassroots Walkers Ltd. in Kenya.

Morie KANEKO is Associate Professor at the Graduate School of Asian and African Area Studies, Kyoto University, Japan. Her main research topics are the cultural transmission of techniques of body and technological innovation in Africa. Her recent works include: *Emerging Approaches to Understanding Gender-based Knowledge and Techniques in Africa* (co-edited, Kyoto University 2013) and *The Ethnography of Pottery Making* (Showado 2011, in Japanese).

Edward K. KIRUMIRA is Professor of Sociology and the Principal of the College of Humanities and Social Sciences, Makerere University, Uganda. He specialises in population and international health and has carried out research and acted as policy advisory on HIV and AIDS in sub-Saharan Africa. He has published on HIV and AIDS, sexual and reproductive health, and integrated rural development. He co-edited the book *Sharing Water: Problems, Conflicts and Possible Solutions* (Universitetsforlaget 2009) and published in 2015 on deaf identities in a multi-cultural setting. He is a Fellow of the Uganda National Academy of Sciences (UNAS) and Chair of the Partnership for Africa's Next Generation of Academics (PANGeA).

Eisei KURIMOTO is Professor of the Graduate School of Human Sciences, Osaka University, Japan. He is a social anthropologist and has conducted research in South Sudan as well as western Ethiopia. His main interests are Nilotic ethnography, conflict and refugee studies. His major publications include: *Conflict, Age and Power in North East Africa* (co-edited, James Currey 1998) and *Remapping Ethiopia* (co-edited, James Currey 2002).

Augustine Ekitela LOKWANG is currently the County Security Advisor in the Turkana County Government. He has previously worked as a coordinator for various conflict and security projects with Danish Demining Group and Field Security Advisor for Tullow Oil, and also served in the Kenya Defence Forces for 11 years in the command, intelligence, training, personnel, administrative and operations positions. While working with the latter he served in the AMISOM operations as a security analyst supporting the sector commander. His current interests are in peace, conflict and governance.

Motoji MATSUDA is Professor of Sociology and Anthropology, Kyoto University, Japan. His Research fields are Nairobi and Western Kenya. His research topics are urbanisation, migration and conflict. His major works include: *Urbanisation from Below* (Kyoto University Press 1998); *The Manifesto of Anthropology of the Everyday Life World* (Sekai Shisosha 2009, in Japanese); 'The difficulties and potentials of anthropological practice in a globalized world', *Japanese Review of Cultural Anthropology*, Vol. 14 (2012) and 'Communauté et violence de rue à Nairobi', *Diogène*, No. 251-252, Presses Universitaires de France (2015).

Hisashi MATSUMOTO is Associate Professor at the Graduate School of Urban Innovation, Yokohama National University, Japan. His area of specialisation is cultural anthropology. His major research field is the resiliency of traditional rulers in contemporary Nigeria, especially among the Igbos. His works include *The Resilience of Chieftaincy in Postcolonial Nigeria* (Akashishoten 2008, in Japanese). Currently he carries out fieldwork on the Nigerian diaspora in East Asia.

Kennedy MKUTU is Associate Professor in International Relations at United States International University-Africa, on sabbatical with the World Bank where he is a Senior Conflict Sensitivity Consultant. His research interests include pastoralism and security, in particular as it relates to the extractive industry in East Africa, and radicalisation in Kenya. He has been managing the Crime and Violence Prevention Training, a joint collaboration between Kenya School of

Government and USIU-Africa, sponsored by Open Society Initiative in East Africa; which brings together stakeholders from both government and non-government sectors, furthering partnership, understanding and skills for safety and security.

Michael NEOCOSMOS is the Director of the Unit for the Humanities at Rhodes University (UHURU) in South Africa. He is the author of numerous articles in academic journals on different aspects of African studies and of the following books: *Social Relations in Rural Swaziland* (edited, University of Swaziland 1987); *The Agrarian Question in Southern Africa* (Nordic Africa Institute 1993); *From Foreign Natives to Native Foreigners: Explaining Xenophobia in South Africa* (CODESRIA 2006, 2010). His latest book is entitled *Thinking Freedom in Africa: Toward a Theory of Emancipatory Politics* (Wits University Press 2016).

Francis B. NYAMNJOH is Professor of Social Anthropology at the University of Cape Town. He served as the Head of Publications at the Council for the Development of Social Science Research in Africa (CODESRIA), Dakar, Senegal, from July 2003 to July 2009. He has taught sociology, anthropology and communication studies at universities in Cameroon and Botswana. He is: a B1 rated Professor and Researcher by the South African National Research Foundation (NRF); a Fellow of the Cameroon Academy of Science since August 2011; a fellow of the African Academy of Science since December 2014; a fellow of the Academy of Science of South Africa since 2016; and Chair of the Editorial Board of the South African Human Sciences Research Council (HSRC) Press since January 2011. His scholarly books include: *Africa's Media, Democracy and the Politics of Belonging* (Zed Books 2005); *Insiders and Outsiders: Citizenship and Xenophobia in Contemporary Southern Africa* (CODESRIA 2006); *'C'est l'homme qui fait l'homme': Cul-de-Sac Ubuntu-ism in Côte d'Ivoire* (Langaa RPCIG 2015) and *#RhodesMustFall: Nibbling at Resilient Colonialism in South Africa* (Langaa RPCIG 2016).

Itaru OHTA is Professor at the Centre for African Area Studies, and the Dean of the Graduate School of Asian and African Area Studies, Kyoto University, Japan. He has carried out anthropological research among the Turkana in Kenya and the Himba in Namibia. His major publications include: *African Potentials* (Kyoto University Press 2016, editor-in-chief, a set of five volumes in Japanese); *Conflict Resolution and Coexistence: Realizing 'African Potentials'* (co-edited, Kyoto University 2014); *Displacement Risks in Africa* (co-edited, Kyoto University Press 2005); *The Nomads in Africa* (co-edited, Showado 2004, in Japanese) and *Marriage and Bridewealth Negotiations among the Turkana in Northwestern Kenya* (Kyoto University 2007).

Masayoshi SHIGETA is Professor of African Area Studies at the Center for African Area Studies, Kyoto University, Japan. His main research interests cover agricultural science, ethnobiology and anthropology of development. His recent works include: 'Enset (*Ensete ventricosum*) production in Ethiopia: Its nutritional and socio-cultural values', *Agricultural & Food Science Research*, Vol. 3, No. 2 (co-authored, 2016); *Emerging Approaches to Understanding Gender-based Knowledge and Techniques in Africa* (co-edited, Kyoto University 2013) and 'Phylogenetic relationships between "Ensete" and "Musa" species as revealed by the trnT trnF region of cpDNA', *Genetic Resources & Crop Evolution*, Vol. 58 (co-authored, 2011).

Motoki TAKAHASHI is Professor at the Graduate School of Asian and African Area Studies, Kyoto University, Japan. His major research fields are sub-Saharan Africa's socio-economic development and foreign aid to low-income countries. His academic works include: *Towards Renewal of Political Economy of Africa* (Keiso Shobo 2010, in Japanese) and *Contemporary African Economies under Glogalization* (co-edited, Minerva Shobo 2014, in Japanese). He is the President of Japan Society for International Development and former Editor-in-Chief of the *Journal of African Studies* (Japan Association for African Studies).

Samson Samuel WASSARA is Professor of Politics in the University of Juba, South Sudan. He holds PhD from Université de Paris XI-Sceaux (1994). He is currently the Vice Chancellor of the

University of Bahr el Ghazal. His research interests include post-conflict politics, the security sector, state building, and hydro-politics. His most recent publications are: 'Political history of southern Sudan before independence of the Sudan', in (R. Bereketeab, ed.) *Self-Determination and Secession in Africa: The Post-Colonial State* (Routledge 2015) and 'South Sudan: State sovereignty challenged at infancy', *Journal of Eastern African Studies*, Vol. 9, No. 4 (2015).

Table of Contents

Part One

Conceptual and Contextual Issues

Chapter 1

Introduction: Achieving Peace and Coexistence through African Potentials

Yntiso Gebre, Itaru Ohta and Motoji Matsuda

1.1. Defining 'African Potentials'

African societies, like other peoples in the world, have rich histories, cultural heritages, knowledge systems, philosophies and institutions that they shaped and reshaped in due course. In the West, however, the African continent has been portrayed negatively as having a multitude of troubles: famine, conflict, coups, massacres, corruption, disease, illiteracy, refugees, failed states, etc. Even worse, African people are often viewed as incapable of addressing their problems on their own. Based on such erroneous perspectives, Western solutions are prescribed, out of context, for African problems. Against the backdrop of such paternalistic thinking, this book intends to shed light on the positive aspect of African reality under the key concept of 'African potentials'.

The book comprises the results of a research project carried out from 2011 to 2015.[1] During the project period, six other books have been published (one in English and five in Japanese) and this book represents the seventh volume in the series titled 'African Potentials'. The project focused on various issues related to the themes of 'conflict and coexistence.' The notion of African potentials refers to philosophies, knowledge, institutions, values and practices that African societies have developed, modified and utilised in handling conflicts and achieving peaceful coexistence. The term 'potentials' is intentionally accorded a deeper and broader meaning than its literal dictionary definition. Our search for distinct qualities that enable the Africans to overcome challenges duly accounts for the dynamic nature of these qualities and the global interconnectedness.

In the past, researchers in the fields of political science and international relations, peace and security studies, or development economics have often carried out studies on conflict and peace-building. In contrast, our research project has sought to ensure the participation of researchers from these three disciplines and a variety of other disciplines from the perspective of area studies that allows a comprehensive approach. In this project, a total of more than fifty Japanese researchers and in excess of twenty international colleagues, primarily from Africa, have taken part and expanded the discussion in a variety of ways. This is the first project in the history of African Studies in Japan to have marshalled so many researchers to explore the issues of conflict and coexistence in cooperation with African researchers. We take pride in the publication of the results of the project in the African Potentials Series, a testament to and a legacy of our cooperation based on mutual respect and scholarly determination.

Contemporary Africa, particularly since the 1990s, has experienced frequent outbreaks of violence, including civil wars, clan and ethnic conflicts, religious frictions and disputes over resources. The Rwandan genocide, which saw the massacre in a very short time of between 500,000 and 800,000 people, is still fresh in our memories. Civil wars continued for a prolonged period in places like Sierra Leone, Liberia, and Somalia. In South Sudan, which overcame a civil war spanning more than twenty years to achieve independence in July of 2011, civil war broke out once more in December 2013, with few prospects of any path to a resolution to date. Most recently, the civil war in the Central African Republic and the violent acts of Boko Haram mainly in northern Nigeria and Al-Shabaab in Somalia have garnered considerable attention in the mass media. In addition, all manner of conflicts have taken place in Africa, even aside from these large-scale conflicts, including struggles over political power and natural resources, clashes over land use rights between farmers and pastoralists, as well as tensions between local peoples and governments over the establishment of natural parks, resulting in the generation of vast numbers of refugees and internally displaced persons.

With the intention to address such challenges, the international community has become involved in African society in a variety of ways, including armed interventions and support for the signing of cease-fire and peace agreements, cooperation in post-conflict institution building and legal interventions such as through the International Criminal Court. Civil society organisations in the non-profit sector have also instituted various measures to assist in the relief of conflict victims and reconstruction of post-conflict society. Such actions on the part of the international community have been powerfully driven by Western ideological and value norms that have their origin in notions of liberal democracy and retributive legal justice. In other words, this is a line of thinking which holds that peace is realised precisely through efforts to stabilise public order by strengthening state sovereignty and the rule of law, through defending human rights, through the establishment of democratic governance and through extending free market economy. Interventions based on this ideology are referred to as *liberal peace-building* (Newman et al. 2009).

While we will discuss this point in more detail below, such interventions by the international community have a tendency to attempt to resolve conflicts using the same sorts of remedies no matter where these conflicts occur. The argument that conflicts occur in the absence of established democracies, free market economy and state sovereignty leads to the conclusion that these systems should be introduced. Therefore, the international community tends to regard conflict resolution as more than anything a *technical problem*, and assume that they will be able to resolve these problems by sending in external experts to promote peace-building activities. Partially hidden below the surface, this line of thinking hints at the attitude that because African societies lack mechanisms for conflict resolution, and because they do not have the expert technical knowledge for peace-building, the correct measures must be provided by the international community. It follows that peace-building interventions are pervaded with a way of thinking that sees such assistance as a unidirectional flow of knowledge to African people, who are presumed to lack the capabilities (and agency) to clear a path to peace on their own. Africa is treated as being in a state of *deficiency*.

We do not wish to argue that the international community's support of and interventions in Africa are all utter failures. There are certainly many cases that have achieved some degree of success.

Nevertheless, several reports have also suggested that, in fact, failed interventions by the United Nations (UN) and regional agencies far outnumber their successes (Boulden 2003; 2013). Moreover, even if interventions by the international community are successful militarily, politically or economically, they are rarely effective in realising social reconstruction and reconciliation between African neighbours scarred by conflict.

What is needed here is *inspiration from the lived experiences of African people* – in other words, a fundamental shift away from concepts that originated in the West. Rather than viewing Africa as *deficient*, we take a close-up look at the knowledge, institutions and values that Africans have themselves created, accumulated and put into practice for achieving conflict resolution and coexistence. The people of Africa have avoided the escalation of conflict on the basis of their own formulas; where such conflicts have occurred, they have achieved coexistence by seeking strategies for their resolution and carrying out some manner of adjustment or accommodation. In our research project, we characterise such knowledge and institutions as 'African potentials' and have adopted the stance that these have been effective in their own ways and can moreover be leveraged to achieve settlement and reconciliation among people in contemporary conflicts, as well as in the revival of social order and restoration of post-conflict societies.

While endeavouring to be attentive to and learn from practices grounded in the experience of people living in African communities, our project challenges the mainstream Western-centric discourse – implicit within peace-building activities by the international community – that depicts the African people as incapable of achieving peace and coexistence on their own.

1.2. Critiquing the View of Liberal Peace as Self-Evident

Interventions into conflicts by the international community carried out under the banner of 'peace-building' have been taking place since the 1990s. With the end of the Cold War, the worldwide shift in political and social conditions was accompanied by changes in the nature of conflict (Kaldor 1999) as well as the manner in which the international community became engaged in it (UN Secretary General 1992).[2] Since the turn of the millennium, it has been pointed out that these engagements have not had their intended effects, and the interventional methods pursued by the international community have themselves come under close scrutiny in fields such as international relations, political science and peace studies. This discourse has been focused on debates around 'the liberal peace.'

The liberal peace (also referred to variously as 'liberal democratic peace' and 'Western peace') is in effect shorthand for the character of the peace that the international community aims to realise. The focus here is on elements specific to Western concepts, namely ideologies of individual liberalism, open market economy, the establishment of state sovereignty, a multi-party system founded on a mature civil society, elections-based democracy, individual human rights, accountability and the rule of law.

Roland Paris (2002) has indicated that state building based on principles of liberal democracy and market economy has been promoted as a part of peace-building activities implemented by the international community in conflict-stricken countries. Paris (2002, p. 656) sees such activities as having been attempts to transplant specific standards about what might constitute 'norms of appropriate or "civilised" conduct' – which is to say modern Western norms – into other regions; in that sense, he argues, they are similar to the civilising mission advocated by Western society in the colonial era. Paris, however, is not trying to move beyond liberal peace or criticise it in a fundamental sense. Rather, he acknowledges that the critique of liberal peace has, in some cases, gone too far, and that in the absence of any realistic alternatives, the best option is to revise current approaches to peace-building within the liberal framework (Paris 2010).

According to Roger Mac Ginty (2008), advocates and proponents of liberal peace are firm in their belief in its supremacy and universal appeal. Liberal peace is thus always carried out according to standardised formulas (e.g., ceasefire monitoring, peace negotiations, Disarmament, Demobilisation and Reintegration (DDR) programmes, Security Sector Reforms (SSR), civil society capacity building, good governance and economic reorganisation). Although

7

these approaches are grounded in a limited ethos specific to the modern West, they tend to exclude or reject non-Western methods that seek to realise peace (Mac Ginty 2008). Mac Ginty (2014a) also cites technocracy as an issue for liberal peace. Basically, concepts and approaches that have come to be used in the industrial sector have also been adopted in the context of peace-building, such that the problems that must be resolved are regarded as merely technical in nature.[3]

While critically examining liberal peace in this fashion, Mac Ginty also points out the prior existence of conventional peace-building approaches in the regions where the international community has intervened (Mac Ginty 2008; 2010). Thus, in the settings where peace-building is being carried out, he argues that liberal peace approaches have been blended with conventional approaches, resulting in the realisation of a state he calls 'hybrid' or 'composite' peace. Mac Ginty argues for a pragmatic approach that aims at achieving peace while integrating people's conventional institutions and values with those of the modern West; such approaches are more likely to be accepted as legitimate by the people involved, and will thus have the greatest possibility of achieving sustainable peace (Mac Ginty 2010). In other words, this is to emphasise the interaction of 'top-down peace' delivered by the international community with 'bottom-up peace' arising from the local community.[4]

Such criticisms of liberal peace are extremely important in that they serve to illuminate the uncritical assumptions that underlie the concepts – namely the notion that liberal democracy and market economy are a panacea that can be applied in any situation. However, the discussion by Mac Ginty and his colleagues becomes cloudier with respect to the specifics of how these 'top-down' and 'bottom-up' activities might be integrated. For this reason, it has been suggested that criticisms of liberal peace may be ineffective as an analytical lens by virtue of being too broad in scope and lacking in precise focus. There has also been some discussion that they are without benefit even for those working on the ground in the field of peace-building (Zaum 2012). Also, while liberal peace expounds a universal vision of state and society whose construction is its goal, if we cast doubt on the value of this vision, the question of how to establish criteria for evaluating peace-building activities becomes more complicated, making the validation of such efforts difficult (Yamashita 2014).

In response to the critique of liberal peace, doubts have also been raised as to whether liberal institutions and values should be discarded entirely. For the present, however, it lies beyond our scope to formulate an answer to this by grappling with liberal ideology directly. Also, the emphasis given to what is meant, exactly, by liberalism (or libertarianism) can also vary depending on the proponent (Seiyama 2006). The critique of liberal peace has brought light to the universalising concepts on which peace-building activities by the international community are uncritically founded. And while these activities have raised the fundamental problem of imposing standardised formulas while promoting reforms based on neoliberal democratisation and marketisation as the one and only method of resolving conflict, their ultimate destination remains unclear.

1.3. Two Paths to Exploring 'African Potentials'

In this research project, our aim has been to explore African potentials as a means of realising conflict resolution and coexistence. Many of us working on the ground felt that the international community's liberal peace interventions were not very effective or did little to help repair social relations impaired by conflict or achieve coexistence between peoples.[5] Furthermore, we were resolutely opposed to a stance that understood Africa to be in a state of *deficiency*. This was because we had seen in reality that forms of knowledge and institutions for achieving coexistence were alive and well in Africa, created and put into practice by the African people.

We have seen first-hand how people with opposing interests, who embrace differing opinions and beliefs, have come together through various processes to form consensus, and communities in which struggles have been brought under control, where wounded social relations have been repaired. Given these realities, which we call 'African potentials', we feel that it is an area highly worthy of elucidation and we have accordingly explored these 'potentials' as the theme of our research.

In seeking to elucidate the African potentials, our studies have intentionally adopted two separate and complementary approaches. The first approach is to describe African philosophy, knowledge, institutions and practices (empirical and experiential inquiries), while the second explores the concept as an ideology or set of values (philosophical and theoretical inquiries).

1.3.1. Empirical and Experiential Inquiries

The African and Japanese researchers who have taken part in this project have all had a great deal of experience carrying out field studies in Africa, where they sensed the presence of African potentials for themselves. Specifically, the people of Africa have realised reconciliation and coexistence by building close social relationships through the production and distribution of foodstuffs; by pre-emptively avoiding the intensification of confrontation; by overcoming their feelings of resentment and anger or releasing such emotions in public to be shared among members of the community; and by resolving incompatibilities through the involvement of a third-party. Our intention is, therefore, to take careful notes of such knowledge and practices and learn how they might be leveraged in handling ongoing conflicts.

However, it is also true that matters of peace attract little attention. We have also looked for mechanisms that enable the African people to maintain and uphold peace values not only in the presence of conflict but also in its absence with the view to preventing it from ever happening. In this way, the initial direction for our studies was to clarify the practicality and effectiveness of African potentials as a topic for empirical or practical study. To this end, we cast our eyes over the lived realities of African people, and positively evaluate the forms of agency that these entailed.

Some readers might consider the knowledge, practices and institutions that we take up as African potentials to have been 'long-held properties of the people of Africa' and as such, as traditional. The word 'traditional' is sometimes used to denote backwardness and/or absence of change in the form of knowledge or institutions that people have possessed since long ago. In our project, however, we recognise that knowledge, institutions and customs often undergo change. Human beings follow some manners (customs and culture), which are constantly renewed and created anew through transformations arising from within or as a result of contacts with the outside world. In other words, the knowledge and institutions possessed by the African people are not static – they exist in a state of dynamic change.

In order to avoid misunderstanding and confusion, we prefer the term 'indigeneity' rather than 'tradition'. Here, indigeneity refers to customs, culture, ideologies and norms that have been created and used by people in a given society. We believe that the notion of indigeneity is less likely to be confused or associated with backwardness and static existence. As they respond to changes in the ecological and social environments that surround them, and as they make reference to the institutions they have used and knowledge they have appropriated from the outside, people are constantly devising new forms of knowledge and institutions in order to improve their lives. We refer to the things that people have created and adopted for the betterment of their own lives as 'indigeneity'. In other words, the knowledge and institutions that we discuss as African potentials are not immutable or intrinsic entities, but are rather always being formed in the midst of the give-and-take with the outside world.

Therefore, in our research project, we have striven not to succumb to the dualistic trap of either seeing African potentials as self-contained and immutable wisdom or dismissing the interventions by the international community as all imposed and therefore ineffective. To do so is tantamount to the romanticisation and entrenchment of African tradition. Some participants in the project felt that some studies may have excessively glamorised African potentials, and this line of thinking may give blanket praise to Africa-specific traditions as alternatives to modern Western solutions. Others stressed that the continued existence and, in some cases, the growing popularity of some indigeneity in contemporary Africa warrant the need to tell stories without value judgment and self-censorship.

The research team agrees that it would be unethical either to exaggerate the significance of indigeneity or to underrate their functional relevance. In other words, perspectives that excessively

11

glamorise the past and those that arbitrarily dismiss the indigenous practices as backward or uncivilised require fundamental critique. At the same time, legitimate community-driven revivalist movements to re-evaluate or reinvent cultures (see Edward Kirumira's paper in Chapter 13 in this volume) as a protest to global/local injustice or as part of efforts to reclaim what people lost due to historical dominance deserve to be analysed objectively.

Another critical inquiry relates to the handling of conflicts through customary law. Some studies examined how the customary law might differ from or complement the formal law (Fenrich et al. 2011). Yet despite this emphasis, customary law is frequently positioned as something 'used by people living in poverty, without much access to school education on the frontiers where state controls have not sufficiently penetrated'. However, recent studies demonstrated the popularity and widespread use of customary conflict-handling methods in rural and urban areas of Africa (Pankhurst and Getachew 2008; Gebre et al. 2011; Mutisi 2012; Kariuki 2015).

Discussions have also taken place whether conventional methods of conflict resolution are applicable for different occasions and in different social environments. Discussing the international community's intervention into the process of conflict resolution in northern Uganda, Tim Allen (2008) has criticised that international community has decontextualised the use of Acholi rites, because some elements of the original rites have been arbitrarily picked out and utilised in different contexts. The international community has mistakenly claimed that these elements represented Acholi's 'traditional justice'. These interventions could not necessarily obtain the support of the local people, according to Allen (2008). When rituals are decontextualised, it is the nature of things that they lose their original meanings and power.

While recognising the positive roles of African customary law in conflict handling, it is necessary, as Yntiso Gebre pointed out in this volume (Chapter 2) to indicate the common limitations: gender insensitivity, breach of human rights and weak procedural fairness in adjudication and punishment, among others. Some of the injustices against women often overlooked by the customary law include: lack of women's participation in customary courts, denial of women's rights to property, marriage of rape victims to perpetrators, denial of women's rights to divorce and arranged/forced marriage. In some cases, customary courts overstretch their powers to handle hard crimes such as homicide. Sometimes convicted offenders are subjected to harsh physical punishment that violates their bodily integrity. Therefore, the application of conventions that violate the rights and dignity of people should be subjected to critical scrutiny.

1.3.2. Philosophical, Theoretical and Ideological Inquiries

The second direction we adopted in our research project was to explore African potentials as a kind of ideology or set of values to provide philosophical and theoretical explanations on what it means to be human, and what the ideal form of coexistence might look like.

As noted earlier, critics of liberal peace have brought to light and questioned the international community's unconditional adoption of Western-derived concepts when intervening in conflicts that break out around the world, as well as how the interventional methods are predicated on such thinking. This concept assumes autonomous individuals with universal human rights, and is premised on the establishment of sovereign states on the basis of a contract with these individuals. Here, therefore, human beings are treated as independent actors disconnected from the wider community. Liberal peace regards the order produced in this way as the universal, supreme and only possibility.

In contrast, Francis Nyamnjoh (2002), also one of the contributors to this volume, based on the example of Cameroon, argues for the existence of humans as having *domesticated agency*. Here, the term 'domesticated' is used in the sense of *living in the midst of a deep relationship with others*. Human beings, at the same time as being left to fully pursue their own potential, share collective interests with their families and other members of their communities. In other words, it is precisely through their interactive relationships with others that human beings exist as autonomous and independent individuals. It is exactly this relational view of human existence, as being based on mutual and complex networks with others, that serves to provide direction to the studies we carried out. Nyamnjoh (2002)

13

uses the term 'conviviality' to express the practices carried out by human beings in the context of their fundamental relationships with others. Nyamnjoh (2015a) argues that, understood in this way, human existence is characterised by what he describes as 'incompleteness'.

Mac Ginty, whose work we discussed earlier when presenting the critique of liberal peace, advocates a concept that he refers to as 'everyday peace' (Mac Ginty 2014b). This is an attempt to focus on ways of behaving that people adopt in order to avoid direct violence in societies suffering from ruptures due to religious or ethnic differences. Mac Ginty claims that these are not merely passive strategies for avoiding struggles, but lead to active efforts to contain violent confrontation and transform conflict. An edited volume theorising peace as a 'space of living' has recently been published as a response to this discussion (Oda 2015; 2014). All these studies have focused on the forms of subjective agency that can be observed in the midst of everyday life.

In our exploration of African potentials, we wanted to construct a view of the world – an idea of coexistence – that was grounded in the local life-worlds of the day-to-day existence of African people. This is something completely foreign to the concept, derived from Western modernity, that rational order is only achievable through a system of states and the rule of law. In order to exercise our mind to explore outside the conventional ways of thinking through radical discussion and dialogue, we have been holding an annual meeting, called 'African Forum' in different sub-regions of Africa, in which African and Japanese scholars, NGO activists and sometimes politicians gather and exchange different views. In addition, we held two more intensive meetings, inviting African scholars to Kyoto, to enhance our discussions further.

1.4. The Experiences of the Five African Forums

Having noticed the significance of cultural prescriptions for conflict resolution that have been generated in African societies, it behoved us to situate their significance in a wider context through a deeper examination of their specific content. The discussions that took place in the African Forum played a key role in this regard. The goal of our grand project has been the attempt to uncover the potentials generated in African societies for resolving conflict and attaining coexistence and evaluate these as a common heritage of humanity in the 21st century. Through the various discussions exchanged at the Forum and the pluralistic networks that are generated as a result, the initially elusive concept of African potentials has been further refined to evolve into a workable intellectual concept. The African Forum has also been an invaluable opportunity for those of us seeking to grasp African potentials from a social and cultural standpoint and to re-orient it relative to a broader context.

The first African Forum was held in Nairobi, where participating researchers and activists from countries across East Africa reviewed the merits and significance of African potentials as an innovative concept. Specific examples of such potentials proposed at the Nairobi Forum, where inter-ethnic conflict was a principal theme, related to the aspect of the effective operation of customary systems for coping with conflicts that exist in African societies. African methods and ideas for coping with conflict that had previously been disparaged by Western conventional wisdom were instead evaluated positively with a view to demonstrating their effectiveness and versatility using specific examples. In this context, the theme of African potentials became synonymous with traditional and customary methods of conflict resolution that were indigenous to Africa.

However, the Nairobi Forum also contested the fundamental validity of our initial discussions. Namely, it was recognised that finding and unconditionally appreciating putative African potentials amidst African traditions and customs, just as with the blanket rejection of modern Western methods of coping with conflict, amounted to little more than a socially constructed romantic fantasy. It was emphasised that the concept of African potentials, rather than simply an assemblage of indigenous customs specific to Africa, was in fact a dynamic entity produced through contact, negotiation and compromise with state and global political mechanisms in the context of the contemporary world.

The second forum was convened in Harare, Zimbabwe, bringing together practitioners and commentators from various countries across southern Africa. The focus of the Harare Forum, as opposed to the inter-ethnic conflicts discussed in Nairobi, was placed on conflicts as opposition and resistance movements opposed to systems of governance structured by centuries of colonial rule and racist polices as well as the realisation of state formations that inherited such systems. Examples here included the struggles of African peasants over land, movements invoking the rights of veterans of wars of liberation, as well as social experiments to overcome the racism and xenophobia that persisted even after the repeal of apartheid. In this context, the concept of African potentials represented a force that opposed mechanisms leading to global inequality and oppression.

The Harare Forum was open to diverse people of heterogeneous backgrounds and facilitated the process of inclusive interaction among such people. In this sense, perspectives that discussed traditional culture as something fixed were strongly criticised for being completely out of touch with this inherent dynamism. As an example, rituals of reconciliation organised by governments and global NGOs as symbolic observances leading to the mediation of inter-ethnic conflict, the settling of issues and subsequent reconciliation, even if these were to produce scenes of African-style reconciliation, would amount to little more than simple cultural appropriation, with no connection to the practices and wisdom of African societies.

The third African Forum was held in the South Sudan capital of Juba a scant two years after independence was achieved in 2011. In the context of South Sudan, where intermittent civil wars have continued since 1955, spanning more than half a century, the question of how people have suppressed and mitigated these conflicts and moved forward from the cessation of hostilities toward peace and reconciliation generated a mass of discussion on the basis of reports by researchers, local NGOs as well as government officials (including cabinet ministers and legislators involved in these processes).

The salient conflict for the Juba Forum was the Sudanese civil war, and experimental proposals were presented toward social and cultural models for conflict remedies, reconciliation and coexistence in the Sudanese context. The concept of African potentials explicitly raised by the Juba Forum was neither the contemporary forms of indigenous methods of conflict resolution like those discussed in Nairobi nor the forces resisting structural domination regulating the world order brought up at Harare. Here, rather, discourses of religious (Christian) reconciliation, global universal human rights thought, the logics of nation-building, practices of ethnic and cultural advocacy, and other themes including a perspective that moved from the local toward regional and global forms of pragmatic politics, were broken down and recombined into hybrid forms based on the standard of effectiveness in real-life contexts. In this sense, African potentials were presented as something neither static and fixed nor exclusive and unitary.

In 2014, the fourth African Forum was held in Yaoundé, Cameroon, with a focus on researchers living in or native to West Africa. Despite the fact that participation on the part of several countries including Sierra Leone could not take place due to that year's outbreak of the Ebola virus, this meeting saw discussions of African potentials deepen even further. One of the defining features of the Yaoundé Forum was the attempt to situate the intellectual historical pedigree of African potentials, a question that had not previously received any deep consideration at the other forums. These discussions were stimulated by a keynote address by Professor Francis B. Nyamnjoh, a Cameroonian native who teaches at the University of Cape Town in South Africa.

Drawing on examples from *The Palm-Wine Drinkard* by the Nigerian novelist Amos Tutuola, Nyamnjoh argued that a defining feature of African modes of knowledge, as distinct from the modern Western episteme, has been the quality of 'incompleteness'. This refers to something imperfect and monstrous, lacking both the complete body of an able-bodied individual and a spirit constructed by reason and language. African knowledge offers a device for temporarily bracketing the world of modern Western knowledge, and the wisdom and practices that are created out of this practice are tied to African potentials. Accordingly, it has become possible to situate African potentials within the broader context of contemporary thought and philosophy.[6]

The fifth African Forum was held in Addis Ababa in October of 2015. Through studies focusing on cases of indigenous knowledge being re-created in the context of national, regional and global social transformations in fields across Ethiopia, the Forum was unmistakably able to unlock the power to fuse together disparate forms of knowledge and institutions, thought and practices that differed in terms of thought patterns, historical origin, and political and economic foundation. Positing this combinatory power as both a theoretical and empirical feature of African potentials was the largest takeaway from the Addis Ababa Forum. For example, in the case of land issue, despite government policies mandating the state's ownership of all land, those 'influential external parties' seeking to accumulate personal wealth through neoliberal market policies could manage to acquire land in an ingenious manner. This caused serious popular discontent, in most cases, the grievances of local residents. In the claim discourses of communities attempting to raise opposition, the *bricolage* tactics could be activated to skilfully mix up heterogeneous worlds such as Christian discourse, modern scientific knowledge and politically correct logics of civil society, as well as kinship value and 'traditional' belief. This is what these meetings succeeded in elaborately portraying as African potentials.

1.5. Expressions of African Potentials

Over the course of discussions carried out at the five African Forums and the two meetings held in Japan, some key features and expressions of African potentials emerged. These include interface function, pluralism, collective agency, networking, dynamism, resilience and innovativeness. In addition, harmony, sharing, hospitality, faithfulness/truthfulness and respect for the elderly are other cultural values worth mentioning. The centrality of harmony and sharing in African cultures cannot be emphasised better. Age represents another central factor for adulthood is associated with gaining wisdom and transmitting knowledge. Hence, respect is accorded and support is extended to the elderly. Truth is highly valued because the social life of people is built around trust. Since betrayals and lies are seen as exceptions rather than norms, people entrust things to each other without any third party in witness or any record in evidence. Nevertheless, African potentials may be manifested as likely outcomes consistent with values and worldviews or as spontaneous and unexpected responses to new developments and new settings.

1.5.1 Interface Function

Given the complexities and interconnectedness of the world, we believe that African potentials have been generated through encounters, clashes and negotiations with outside influences such as the modern Western traditions and the Arabic-Islamic worldviews. African potentials have been undergoing constant transformation due to global interactions. We call the ability to interweave and forge connections within assemblages of values, thought and practices that belong to disparate dimensions and different historical phases an 'interface function'. In the context of conflict, our effort has been to attempt to discover how distinctive cultures of conflict handling have been generated in the midst of such conditions of fluidity and complexity.

Nyamnjoh (2015a) points out that it is this function itself that represents the nexus point where Africa diverges from the intellectual history of Western modernity. In the encounter with alterity (in the broad sense of 'the other' not only among human beings, but including the ideological, institutional, material, animal and spiritual dimensions), the epistemology of Western modernity has privileged their standards of the self/other and imposed them on Africa through the exercise of physical force, which finally subjected Africa to colonial worldview. He concludes that underlying this is a mentality that defines itself as 'sufficient and complete'. Once we begin to believe in our own completeness, intolerance toward and attacks on 'other' things are legitimised as justice 'for the salvation of the benighted'. In contrast, African society understands the self as 'something incomplete' and has the potential power to create a symbiotic order of interdependence free from the mutual exclusion of others, who are similarly incomplete. He points to this 'convivial' power to link, combine and complement dissimilar things as the kernel of Africa's cultural potential. This conviviality is what we call an *interface function.*

Specific instances of practices based on this interface function have been presented at meetings of the African Forum to date. One such example, reported at the Juba Forum by a Nuer pastor, who also directs a non-governmental peace organisation, can be found in the power to facilitate social approval for peace processes by interweaving traditional Nuer concepts of mediation with Christian forgiveness and the universal human rights discourse of global NGOs.

Another example, presented at the Nairobi Forum, is to be found in the practices by which checks have been applied to the expanding chains of violence in Kenya's coastal region. There, by gathering together under a single roof Christian and Islamic religious leaders preaching peace according to their respective religious beliefs, NGO activists advocating modern civil rights and local community elders emphasising folk practices of hospitality toward strangers, a patchwork was stitched together from each of these claims to build a forum for suppressing violence. This power represents the interface function of African potentials.

The 'Palaver' Forum of South Africa mentioned at the Harare Forum had something of a similar quality. 'Palaver', as free and rambling chatter derided as meaningless babble during the era of apartheid, became the driving force behind the creation of a cooperative forum that freely transcended ethnicity, generation, gender and race. For example, this idea guided the emergence of Durban's Abahlali community movement, which was organised in an instance of direct action 'from below' with the aim of securing public housing. Such practices, in the sense that they are leveraged in the context of contemporary society by creating new forces that blend a variety of pluralistic elements, are a good illustration of the possibilities of the interface function inherent in Africa's cultural potential'.[7]

The power to unite diverse elements from heterogeneous dimensions indicated to have been at the core of the Addis Ababa

Forum might also be considered as an expression of interface function. Motoji Matsuda's paper in this volume (Chapter 10) reveals how the residents of Kangemi in Kenya employed the technique of *bricolage* – the picking and choosing of principles from different models of community policing, and this is another example of interface function.

1.5.2. Aspiration for Pluralism

The second feature of African potentials is the aspiration for pluralism rather than unity. With regard to the implementation of justice, the accepted wisdom in the West is adherence to the formal law and tribunals – acceptance of a single approach and a single school of thought. Although alternative dispute resolution (ADR) is practised, divergent solutions are generally denounced as peripheral, informal, inferior or incorrect. Aspirations for unity, when reduced to the level of dogma, finds eventual culmination in a faith in *purity*. In other words, one's own thoughts, values and approaches are regarded as an absolute good, while the admixture of any other (and therefore impure) thing is stringently denounced as incorrect action that compromises purity and perfection.

In the African contexts, in contrast, it is uncommon to think about a single approach in absolute terms or reject alternative approaches as totally mistaken. African cultural potentials acknowledge the hybrid and mixed property of various elements, and attach value to the character of incompleteness. This signifies a more open and tolerant attitude to thoughts and values that differ from those of one's own worldview. This is what we consider as an aspiration for pluralism, an approach that embraces different values and practices. The phenomenon of legal pluralism (the coexistence of more than one legal system in a given society) throughout Africa is a case in point. The state law, the customary law, religious courts and other legal systems are allowed to operate side by side, although their relations take different forms: complementary, antagonism, avoidance, indifference, arbitrary and inconsistent.

Aspiration for pluralism can also be explained in terms of the management of diversity – a situation where people with different backgrounds (ethnic, religious, language, occupational, etc.) reside in the same neighbourhood and as an integrated community respecting each other's religions, traditions and choices. Although ethnic-based or religiously inspired tensions/conflicts sometimes break out, the modus operandi is to employ African potentials to normalise relations and move on as a plural society, once again cherishing their unity in diversity. It can be argued that cultural pluralism as opposed to the 'melting pot' model ensures harmony through the protection of unique cultural identities, values and practices of smaller groups within a larger society. Today, these longstanding and commonly used African values of cultural pluralism are being globally promoted at workplaces and in classrooms under the new concept of multiculturalism.

1.5.3. Collective Agency and Networking

A growing body of literature adopted the capability approach to understand what an individual is capable of doing/being using his/her freedom and agency (Sen 1990). In recent years, the focus shifted from the analysis of individual capability to the analysis of collective capabilities, which are realised through collective agency and collective action. By virtue of their participation in the collectivity, people are believed to achieve outcomes that they value individually. Therefore, collective capabilities are described as 'new choices that the individual alone would neither have nor be able to achieve unless he/she joins a collectivity' (Ibrahim 2006, p. 398). Collective capabilities are reported to empower communities in poverty reduction, conflict prevention and peace building. From the perspectives of African societies, the new choices are not as such new for collectivity has been the hallmark of the continent. The rediscovery and appreciation of collective capabilities by analysts reconfirm that the African values of cooperation and networking are gaining momentum within the continent and beyond.

Although there is a tendency on the part of many analysts of inter-ethnic relations to assume that ethnic tensions are pervasive and commonplace, other studies reveal that peaceful and cooperative relations are far more common than incidents of conflict (Fearon and Laitin 1996). Many recent writers underline that social capital contributes to communal capacities for resilience and survival

(Blackburn et al. 2014; Galvin 2008). It has been widely recognised that pastoralist communities, in particular, need social ties to access resources and survive environmental stress. In Africa, bond-friendships, reciprocity, marital ties, trade and sharing of resources connect people and ensure peaceful coexistence. Although natural factors and manmade adversities are poised to weaken social networks and erode communality, people often search for solutions in cooperation. The paper by Motoki Takahashi and Masashi Hasegawa (Chapter 6, in this volume) discusses how Kenyans who experienced post-election violence in 2007/8 later embraced cooperation and expressed a sense of belonging to the same nation.

The Western institutional settings focus on individuals, while the African cultures consider the collective as the unit of social organisation. During conflict, offensive actions or retaliatory measures are taken against unsuspecting members of a group, sometimes in the form of collective punishment. Social groups often take the blame for offences perpetrated by their members and the responsibility for the consequences. This sense of collective responsibility urges the wrongdoers' group to take the initiative to make peace and avoid retribution. One might challenge the appropriateness of holding groups responsible for offences committed by individuals. One might also wonder whether sharing of the consequences of wrongdoing would not encourage repeated perpetration. Yntiso Gebre reflects on these pertinent issues in this volume, Chapter 2.

1.5.4. Dynamism and Flexibility

The world has been changing at an increasing pace, and Africa, which is part and parcel of the globalised world, cannot be expected to remain unaffected. The continent has to adapt to changing circumstances and come to terms with new thoughts and practices. The African potentials are characterised by dynamism, which is expressed in flexibility, adaptability, receptivity, proactivity and consensus. The ability to adapt positively to changing environments and stay relevant helps individuals and groups to achieve what they want and avoid risks of getting into trouble. Masayoshi Shigeta and Morie Kaneko explain in this volume (Chapter 11) how the Aari people in Ethiopia resorted to the pursuit of knowledge to understand their oppressors and find amicable ways to coexist. Another manifestation of adaptability is the hybridisation or collaborative approach (the use of traditional and modern conflict-handling principles) that Kennedy Mkutu and Augustine Lokwang discuss in this volume in the context of the Turkana pastoralists in Kenya.

The culture of embracing pluralism (which involves accepting other people and respecting their values) translates into people's openness to new opportunities and challenges. People are aware of the fact that adapting to something new may require forgoing something else. The culture of give-and-take, often expressed in terms of reciprocal exchange and sharing, comes into play when people think about trading something for another. Even when flexibility results in losses, people would normally understand and move on rather than hold grudges or exchange blame. Itaru Ohta's paper in this volume (Chapter 9) shows how Africans arrive at consensus to resolve serious matters mainly by speaking and listening to each other, even without the involvement of a third party.

On the whole, Africa's cultural potentials should be viewed as dynamic and fluid processes rather than a static or fixed assemblage. The vitality of its potentials has enabled Africa to undergo endless transformation. It is equally important not to reduce dynamism or its manifestation (flexibility, adaptability, etc.) to opportunistic actions aimed at taking advantage of circumstances with little regard for principles, ethics or morality. Dynamism should be understood as established cultural mechanism that enables societies to navigate and negotiate in the changing environment.

1.5.5. Resilience and Tolerance

Responses to the changing circumstances or difficult times may not necessarily be adaptation. Keeping composed in the face of difficulties and remaining persistent in the face of unexpected eventualities are also considered as important qualities. Hence, African potentials exhibit such qualities as resilience, tolerance, endurance and patience. Resilience is an expression of strength, which is more than being in a defensive posture to counter or resist

24

intrusion. It is about remaining empowered and being able to thrive despite the onset of setbacks/challenges. African societies have often been overwhelmed by such factors as armed conflicts, environment disasters, population pressure and development-induced displacements.

In worst-case scenarios, such adversities lead to loss of lives, livelihood disruptions and community disintegration. Yet, resilience enables people to reconstitute their lives, move on, and even thrive. Yntiso Gebre and his associates (2014) studied resilience in children living in Merkato (Addis Ababa, Ethiopia), a neighbourhood known for pervasive poverty, prevalent prostitution, sexual offences, drug abuse and trafficking of children. Despite the prevalence of risks and individual vulnerabilities, many children and young people not only remained resilient to adversities but also excelled and succeeded in their lives by employing different protective strategies (Gebre et al. 2014). Senishaw Getachew's paper in this volume (Chapter 7) also points to the resilience of the Gedeo people to ecological problems and extremely high population pressure.

Tolerance is another feature of African potentials, which is expressed in recognition and respect for other people's religions, values and practices by those who do not actually share them. In Africa, cultural pluralism has flourished and the coexistence of diverse groups has been attained because of the culture of tolerance. Tolerance is harmony in difference that makes peace possible. Tolerance, which has positive connotations and elements of unreserved willingness to accept and respect difference, should not be confused with reluctant toleration of social injustice, which is more about patience and endurance (a slightly different form of African potentials).

1.5.6. Innovativeness and Creative Expression

In the West, studies of creativity have focused on personality rather than on social or cultural factors, and this has reportedly hampered understanding of the social nature of creativity (Lebedeva and Grigoryan 2013). The authors further stated that studies in Chinese and Korean cultures and cultures of Islamic countries have demonstrated that there is no universal understanding of creativity.

Hence, creativity should be studied in the context of interaction between individuals and sociocultural factors. Apart from personality, such variables as experience, demographics, scarcity and sociocultural values may have implications for innovativeness. Our intention here is not to join the debate and scrutinise whether African cultural values influence innovative thinking.

Instead, we would like to recognise the role of creative cultural expression, as an aspect of African potentials, in peace building. Innovative artistic and cultural activities can help prevent conflict or facilitate post-conflict reconciliation. In Uganda, for example, creative arts were incorporated into conflict resolution, community reconciliation and psychosocial healing (McClain 2010). Similarly, in Rwanda, creative industries such as film, theatre, music and others played critical roles in post-conflict reconciliation and reconstruction. Although resolving conflict requires political agreements, creative artistic expressions play important parts in rebuilding confidence and preventing a return to conflict. The power of innovative arts lies in making people understand each other better, rediscover the possibility of cooperation and cherish cultural pluralism. Besides the peace-building role, innovativeness as an African potentials takes different forms.

1.6. Organisation of the Book

This book is divided into three parts and 14 chapters, including the introduction. In Chapter 2, Yntiso Gebre examines the roles of customary law in Africa in restoring social order, finding truth, ensuring public participation and transparency, and making legal services accessible, efficient and affordable. However, studies on this important African potentials remain isolated ethnographic accounts without theoretical and policy implications due to lack of conceptual clarity that hinders communication and common understanding; failure to identify the core values and virtues worth appreciating; and lack of comprehensive knowledge to develop theories or influence policies. Moreover, African customary law has been challenged on a number of grounds: gender insensitivity, breach of human rights, ill-defined legal status, lack of uniformity, and incompatibility with state law and international instruments. In order to address all the challenges, Gebre proposes the need to systematise knowledge about customary law through conceptual clarity and the development of a common research strategy.

Kennedy Mkutu and Augustine Lokwang's paper in Chapter 3 examine the new challenges that pastoralists in marginal areas of Kenya, South Sudan, Somalia, Ethiopia, Uganda and even Tanzania are facing as their land becomes valuable to investors. The extractive industries and accompanying developments in Turkana, Kenya, are raising new sources of conflict and straining existing mechanisms for peaceful co-existence amongst pastoralists of the Ateker cluster. Geopolitical forces and external interests are now involved in the competition for land and land-based resources, which is a challenge for pastoralist participation. The proposed plan to create conservancies in Turkana and Pokot to manage security and land threatens to limit pastoral mobility and create rival management structures to the existing legitimate ones. Law and policy to protect pastoralists' interests is currently weak, but encouragingly, in Turkana the pastoralists are uniting and participating in new processes for representation of their own rights to investors and to the county and national government.

In Chapter 4, Samson Wassara and Eisei Kurimoto focus on the crisis of South Sudan that became independent in 2011 after six years of interim period after the Comprehensive Peace Agreement (CPA) of 2005 that put an end to the 22 year long Sudanese civil war. Through in-depth analysis of the armed conflict between the state and rebel groups that quickly devastated the newly born country, which had just started the process of reconstruction and peace building after the civil war, the chapter tries to demonstrate the relevance of African potentials for peace and reconciliation in a situation where they seem to be invalid. Highlighted are the role of civil society, namely faith-based organisations and groups, the ambiguous role of community defence groups and the mediation and intervention by the Intergovernmental Authority for Development (IGAD) and African Union (AU). In them we are able to find evidence of African potentials and it is hoped that they would be effective in restoring peace and achieving reconciliation among various actors, thus realising statehood in an almost collapsed state of South Sudan.

The article by Kyoko Cross in Chapter 5, focusing on a reconciliation process of Sierra Leone, clearly indicates that institutions for national reconciliation have generally not worked as they had been designed. This is quite natural, considering the fact that overcoming the past has never been an easy and short-term task. In this experience of Sierra Leone, however, the limits of institutions have triggered various attempts for overcoming the past among ordinary people. It takes up those initiatives from the below as one of the important actors of the post-conflict institutions for national reconciliation in Sierra Leone. But at the same time it has institutional limitations. Faced with these institutional limitations, national NGOs took initiatives for attempts at a grassroots process of reconciliation.

In Chapter 6, Motoki Takahashi and Masashi Hasegawa examine people's perceptions on politics, resource distribution and ethnic belonging, based on research conducted in two neighbouring villages affected by the 2007–2008 post-election violence in Kenya. The majority of residents living in one village belongs to the Kikuyu and was victimised by the violence. A number of inhabitants in the other village, most of whom are the Nandi (a sub-group of Kalenjin), are suspected to be perpetrators of the attacks. The study solicited the views of household heads on the responsibility of leaders, corruption, ethnic-based distribution of public resources and inter-ethnic relations. According to the findings, the majority of informants in the two villages favoured unbiased resource distribution, disapproved corruption, argued in favour of national integrity and called for inter-ethnic cooperation at times of difficulty. Takahashi and Hasegawa argue that these perceptions could serve as a basis for national integration and inter-ethnic coexistence.

In Chapter 7, Senishaw Getachew states that the relationship between humans and their environment in Gedeo (Ethiopia) is based on people's worldview, environmental values and livelihood practices. The worldview accords great respect for nature and humans – both viewed as the creations of God. The human interaction with the natural environment is governed by environmental values. The Gedeo local ecology has evolved from forestry to agroforestry through livelihood practices guided by a sophisticated local ecological knowledge. Despite the high population pressure with 818 persons/km2 crude density in 2012, the agroforestry remains a major livelihood activity that covered 94.5 per cent of their total landscape. Getachew concludes that local ecological knowledge, livelihood activities, environmental values and worldview are highly intertwined elements that structure human–environment relations among the Gedeo people.

The article by Hisashi Matsumoto in Chapter 8, based on the position of titular chief in Igbo society in Nigeria, reveals how a variety of contemporary meanings are being created for this position in the context of the high mobility that has accompanied globalisation. While African institutions of chieftainship might refer to a traditional and pre-modern political institution, chieftainship in Igbo society did not originally exist as a political institution, but was rather 'invented' in the modern era. In the context of Nigerian society, which generates the highest rate of overseas migration from the entire continent, this title of traditional authority has helped build stable communities among immigrants in host societies and has been more than sufficiently leveraged as collateral for ties and contributions to the homeland. But this process has also involved an ingenious and creative artistry, and it is by virtue of this quality of re-creation that local traditional authority has been fused with global dynamics.

The essay by Itaru Ohta in Chapter 9 shows how two parties to a conflict somehow arrive at a consensus in the face of mutual claims with no seeming common ground at all. Consensus, in the majority of cases, will be achieved through mutual conversation (discussions) without any direct recourse to the power of a third party. Unlike communications based on communicative rationality such as that emphasised in the work of Jürgen Habermas (1987), actors speak enthusiastically with others, listen to their words and arrive at consensus through negotiation. Ohta defines such instances of conflict resolution through the power of conversation as 'palaver', and abstracts the possibility of arriving at consensus while taking full advantage of the powers of speech and listening to maintain social order and reassure coexistence. Ohta's analysis is based on cases from societies in Ethiopia, Kenya and the Democratic Republic of the Congo.

The essay by Motoji Matsuda in Chapter 10 concerns contemporary Kenyan society. The chapter discusses post-election violence, particularly the outbreak from late 2007 to early 2008 that temporarily plunged Kenya into anarchy (civil confusion) and undertakes an analysis of community policing activities by Nairobi slum dwellers during this period of violent confusion. Confronted with a physical and social crisis, the inhabitants of Nairobi's slums spontaneously organised policing activities in the midst of raging violence to protect the lives and property of fellow slum dwellers. However, such vigilante movements tend to be easily leveraged as violent apparatus for the peripheral extension of state power and to devolve into private gang organisations rooted in xenophobic tribalism. Despite such risks, this period also saw the birth of unstable and irregular practices based on expediency and the contingent demands of people's life-worlds. In these slum environments, fraught with the potential threat of imminent violence, these practices came to be wielded and deployed as a force of restraint. Matsuda's paper shows that the concept of African potentials points not only to the wisdom of age, but may also be produced in new settings such as urban slums.

In Chapter 11, Masayoshi Shigeta and Morie Kaneko discuss the adaptive strategies of the Aari people in southwest Ethiopia following their conquest and incorporation into the Ethiopian empire in the late 19th century. In many cases, conflict ensues when repressive powers encroach on the rights of original inhabitants and plunder their resources. In such cases relationships of tension, conflict and hatred are created and strengthened between indigenes and outsiders. Although they were overwhelmed by the new settlers (the occupiers) and experienced impositions, according to Shigeta and Kaneko, the Aari society (after their initial violent resistance failed) resorted to the pursuit of knowledge (embracing an epistemological outlook) to understand the invaders and protect their interests in the new reality of coexistence. The authors methodically narrate the experiences of a father and a son to illustrate the story.

The contribution by Francis Nyamnjoh in Chapter 12 consists of two parts. Part one makes a case exploring African potentials through the lens of incompleteness and conviviality. It explores unique perspectives of Africans as frontier beings and conviviality as a currency. Frontier African's world is characterised by flexibility in mobility, identity, citizenship and belonging, and myriad interconnections, inextricable entanglements and creative interdependencies. The currency of conviviality that skillfully articulates heterogeneous beings of various dimensions could promote diversity, tolerance, trust, equality, inclusiveness and cohabitation. Part two discusses convivial scholarship and international research collaboration. It argues that an approach to research collaboration informed by a recognition of incompleteness as the normal order of being, would foreground conviviality in a manner that allows for Africans and Japanese involved in collaborative research to be more open to possible enrichment with creative, cultural, social and intellectual African potentials derailed or caricatured by the orgy of coercive colonial violence and impulse to monopolise humanity and the world's resources.

In Chapter 13, Edward Kirumira focuses on the conceptualisation of indigeneity. Despite the fact that indigeneity has tended to be applied in reference to what is local and small-scale, revisiting the concept of indigeneity offers potential for broadening the theoretical and methodological frames of African potentials for addressing state and global issues. He shows how indigeneity is used to negotiate with social, philosophical, cultural and environmental issues, lending itself to negotiating trans-local systems of power and knowledge and, emphasises the argument that identity and self-representation are vital elements of the political platform that a conversation on indigeneity must embrace.

Michael Neocosmos' paper in Chapter 14 argues that the idea of 'African potentials' can be understood not so much as a given characteristic of African cultures, but as a political possibility for the construction of an alternative idea of universal humanity. Africans are no different from other humans in having thought the universality of humanity. However, what seems unique to African history is the political possibility of thinking universal humanity outside an exceptional aleatory event. Starting with Alain Badiou's concept of the 'immanent exception', the chapter shows that the potential for exceeding liberal conceptions of universality exist in African popular practices within a creative alternative that must be fought for politically. Neocosmos challenges the historically formed hierarchical structure and intellectual tradition where the West has monopolised universal ideas of humanity.

As we have seen so far, African potentials are endowed with characteristics such as conviviality, plurality, flexibility and innovativeness. Such features constitute the antithesis of a mode of thought characterised by a complete, pure and solitary truth that seeks to occupy the position of absolute victor by opposing, casting aside and dominating all other possibilities in a hostile manner that precludes reconciliation. In that sense, as Nyamnjoh considers in detail from his unique perspective, it is the very quality of incompleteness itself that will be the ideological core of African potentials.

Lastly, we are confident that our attempt to construct African potentials as an idea for fundamental coexistence will provide useful guidance not only for the tumultuous era in which we live at present, but also for future of human society. In the exploration of African potentials, attempts aiming in this direction are only just beginning, and so do not feature very explicitly in this book. However, all of the papers collected here offer rich material that will contribute to such an idea of coexistence.

Notes

[1] The project titled 'Comprehensive Area Studies on Coexistence and Conflict Resolution Realizing "African Potentials"' was financed by the Japan Society for the Promotion of Science (JSPS) Grant-in-Aid for Scientific Research (S), Grant Number 23221012, and the project leader was Itaru Ohta of Kyoto University.

[2] With regard to UN policies relating to intervention and support in the context of African conflicts, the need for comprehensive measures, including support for sustainable development, has been argued in

documents submitted to the Security Council by the UN Secretary-General (UN Secretary General 1998; 2014).

[3] For critiques of liberal peace, see also Belloni (2012), Mac Ginty and Williams (2009) and Richmond and Mac Ginty (2015).

[4] In Japan as well, Kurimoto (2000; 2014) indicated the need to integrate 'top-down peace' with 'bottom-up peace' relatively early on.

[5] Shinoda (2002) states that because reconciliation and the rebuilding of social relationships between the parties to a conflict constitute a difficult challenge, the international community has avoided involving itself in these areas and entrusted such tasks to the parties involved. Rather, the focus of external intervention has been on resolving issues in those areas where visible outcomes can be realised within a specific period of time, namely the establishment of state institutions and the rule of law, and the resolution of issues relating to poverty and economic inequality.

[6] Nyamnjoh formulates the personhood and agency cultivated by African society as *ubuntu*. This concept seeks to derive an alternative humanist, social and historical awareness to that of Western modernity, which Nyamnjoh expresses as being characterised by 'incompleteness' (Nyamnjoh 2015a; 2015b).

[7] The community movement known as Abahlali baseMjondolo ('those who live in shacks') is a joint forum for disenfranchised urban residents in Durban, South Africa open to people of all races and backgrounds. In that Abahlali represents the deployment of a potential that is distinct from Western modernist civic movements, some scholars have understood it to be a modern incarnation of the thought of Frantz Fanon (e.g., Gibson 2014). For a discussion of the inner workings of this forum drawing on an experience of direct participation, see Neocosmos (2007).

References

Allen, T. (2008) 'Ritual (ab) use? Problems with traditional justice in northern Uganda', in N. Waddell and P. Clark (eds.) *Courting Conflict? Justice, Peace and the ICC in Africa*, London: Royal African Society, pp. 47–54.

Belloni, R. (2012) 'Hybrid peace governance: Its emergence and significance', *Global Governance*, No. 18, pp. 21–38.

Blackburn, M., Guzman, A., Lieberman, J. and Sprinkel, A. (2014) *Assessing the Role of Social Capital in Agro-Pastoral Resilience in the Sahel: A System's Perspective.* https://www.humanitarianresponse.info/system/files/documents/files/Mercy%20Corps%20Role%20of%20Social%20Capital%20in%20Agro-pastoral%20Resilience%20in%20the%20Sahel.pdf (Accessed 18 December 2016).

Boulden, J. (ed.) (2003) *Dealing with Conflict in Africa: The United Nations and Regional Organizations*, New York: Palgrave Macmillan.

----------(2013) *Responding to Conflict in Africa: The United Nations and Regional Organizations*, New York: Palgrave Macmillan.

Fearon, J. and Laitin, D. (1996) 'Explaining interethnic cooperation', *American Political Science Review*, Vol. 90, No. 4, pp. 715–35.

Fenrich, J., Galizzi, P. and Higgins, T.E. (eds.) (2011) *The Future of African Customary Law*, New York: Cambridge University Press.

Galvin, K. (2008) 'Responses of pastoralists to land fragmentation: Social capital, connectivity, and resilience', in K. Galvin, R. Reid, R. Behnke and T. Hobbs (eds.), *Fragmentation in Semi-Arid and Arid Landscapes: Consequences for Human and Natural Systems*, Dordrecht, The Netherlands: Springer, pp. 369–89.

Gebre Y., Ayalew, G., Rahel, S. and Hiwot, W. (2014) *Learning from Children Exposed to Sexual Abuse and Sexual Exploitation: Resilience in Children Living in Merkato, Addis Ababa, Ethiopia*, a research report commissioned by Oak Foundation.

Gebre, Y., Assefa, F. and Fekade, A. (eds.) (2011) *Customary Dispute Resolution Mechanisms in Ethiopia*, Addis Ababa: EACC.

Gibson, N.C. (2014) *Fanonian Practices in South Africa: From Steve Biko to Abahlali Basemjondolo*, London: Palgrave Macmillan.

Habermas, J. (1987) *The Philosophical Discourse of Modernity*, Cambridge, MA: The MIT Press.

Ibrahim, S. (2006) 'From individual to collective capabilities: The capability approach as a conceptual framework for self-help', *Journal of Human Development*, Vol. 7, No. 3, pp. 397–416.

Kaldor, M. (1999) *New and Old Wars: Organized Violence in a Global Era*, Stanford, California: Stanford University Press.

Kariuki, F. (2015) 'Conflict resolution by elders in Africa: Successes, challenges and opportunities', *Alternative Dispute Resolution*, Vol. 3, No. 2, pp. 30–53.

Kurimoto, E. (2000) "Top-down peace' and 'bottom-up peace': Remarks on the civil war in Sudan', *NIRA Policy Studies*, Vol. 13, No. 6, pp. 46–9 (in Japanese).

----------(2014) Limits and possibilities for grassroots peace-building in South Sudan', in H. Oda and Y. Seki (eds.) *Anthropology of Peace*, Kyoto: Horitsu Bunkasha, pp. 27–48 (in Japanese).

Lebedeva, N. and Grigoryan, L. (2013) 'Implicit theories of innovativeness: Cross-cultural analysis', *WP5/10 Research Working Paper*. http://www.ub.edu/searchproject/wp-content/uploads/2013/01/WP-5.10.pdf (Accessed 18 December 2016).

Mac Ginty, R. (2008) 'Indigenous peace-making versus the liberal peace', *Cooperation and Conflict*, Vol. 43, No. 2, pp. 139–63.

----------(2010) 'Hybrid peace: The interaction between top-down and bottom-up peace', *Security Dialogue*, Vol. 41, No. 4, pp. 391–412.

----------(2014a) 'Why do we think in the ways that we do?', *International Peacekeeping*, Vol. 21, No. 1, pp. 107–12.

----------(2014b) 'Everyday peace: Bottom-up and local agency in conflict-affected societies', *Security Dialogue*, Vol. 45, No. 6, pp. 548–64.

Mac Ginty, R. and Williams, A. (2009) *Conflict and Development*, New York: Routledge.

McClain, L. (2010) 'The Art of creative conflict resolution: A critical evaluation of approaches to post-conflict reconstruction in northern Uganda', *Pursuit: The Journal of Undergraduate Research at the University of Tennessee*, Vol. 1, Iss. 1. http://trace.tennessee.edu/pursuit/vol1/iss1/9 (Accessed 19 December 2016).

Mutisi, M. (ed.) (2012) *Integrating Traditional and Modern Conflict Resolution Experiences from Selected Cases in Eastern and the Horn of Africa*, Africa Monograph Series, ACCORD.

http://accord.org.za/publications/special-issues/994-integrating-traditional-and-modern-conflict-resolution (Accessed 19 December 2016).

Neocosmos, M. (2007) 'Civil society, citizenship and the politics of the (im)possible: Rethinking militancy in Africa today', *Report for the Codesria MWG on Citizenship*.

Newman, E., Paris, R. and Richmond, O.P. (2009) 'Introduction', in E. Newman, R. Paris and O.P. Richmond (eds.), *New Perspectives on Liberal Peacebuilding*, Tokyo: United Nations University Press, pp. 3–25.

Nyamnjoh, F. (2002) '"A child is one person's only in the womb": Domestication, agency and subjectivity in the Cameroonian Grassfields', in R. Werbner (ed.) *Postcolonial Subjectivities in Africa*, London: Zed Books, pp. 111–38.

---------- (2015a) 'Incompleteness: Frontier Africa and the currency of conviviality', *Journal of Asian and African Studies*, first published online on 23 April 2015.

----------(2015b) *C'est l'homme qui fait l'homme: Cul-de-sac Ubuntu-ism in Cote D'Ivoire*, Bamenda, Cameroon: Langaa RPCIG.

Oda, H. (2014) 'Introduction: The anthropology of peace', in H. Oda and Y. Seki (eds.) *Anthropology of Peace*, Kyoto: Horitsu Bunkasha, pp. 1–23 (in Japanese).

Oda, H. and Fukutake, S. (2015) '"Spaces of living" and peace research from an area studies perspective', *The Emergence of Peace at the Community and Grassroots Levels, Peace Studies* (Waseda Daigaku Shuppanbu), No. 44, pp. i–viii (in Japanese with English abstract).

Pankhurst, A. and Getachew, A. (eds.) (2008) Grass-roots Justice in Ethiopia: *The Contribution of Customary Dispute Resolution*, Addis Ababa: French Center of Ethiopian Studies.

Paris, R. (2002) 'International peace-building and the "mission civilisatrice"', *Review of International Studies*, No. 28, pp. 637–56.

----------(2010) 'Saving liberal peace-building', *Review of International Studies*, No. 36, pp. 337–65.

Richmond, O.P. and Mac Ginty, R. (2015) 'Where now for the critique of the liberal peace?', *Cooperation and Conflict*, Vol. 50, No. 2, pp. 171–89.

Seiyama, K. (2006) *Defining Liberalism: Rawls and the Logic of Justice*, Tokyo: Keiso Shobo (in Japanese).

Sen, A. (1990) 'Development as capability expansion', in K. Griffin and J. Knight (eds.) *Human Development and the International Development Strategy for the 1990s*, London: Macmillan, pp. 41–58.

Shinoda, H. (2002) 'Re-considering the concept of peace-building from strategic perspectives on international peace operations', *Hiroshima Heiwa Kagaku*, No. 24, pp. 21–45 (in Japanese).

UN Secretary General (1992) An Agenda for Peace: Preventive Diplomacy, *Peacemaking and Peace-keeping* (United Nations A/47/277), http://www.un-documents.net/a47-277.htm (Accessed 30 December 2015).

----------(1998) *The Causes of Conflict and the Promotion of Durable Peace and Sustainable Development in Africa* (United Nations A/52/871 – S/1998/318), http://www.un.org/ga/search/view_doc.asp?symbol=A/5 2/871&referer=/english/&Lang=E (Accessed 30 December 2015).

----------(2014) *Causes of Conflict and the Promotion of Durable Peace and Sustainable Development in Africa* (United Nations A/69/162– S/2014/542), http://daccess-ddsny.un.org/doc/UNDOC/GEN/N14/492/90/PDF/N 1449290.pdf?OpenElement (Accessed 30 December 2015).

Yamashita, H. (2014) 'Peace-building and the theory of 'hybrid peace'', *Bosai Kenkyujo Nyusu*, March 2014, No. 185 (in Japanese). http://www.nids.go.jp/publication/briefing/pdf/2014/brie fing_185.pdf (Accessed 24 December 2014).

Zaum, D. (2012) 'Beyond the 'liberal peace'', *Global Governance,* No.18, pp. 121–32.

Chapter 2

The Potentials of African Customary Law: Reflections on Concepts, Values, and Knowledge Generation

Yntiso Gebre

2.1. Introduction

The context. The basic premise of the Japanese research project on 'African potentials' (discussed in the introduction to this book) seems to follow three related lines of argument. First, Africa has increasingly been encountering disruptions of social orders that should be rectified to enhance stability and development in the continent. Second, the formalised national, regional and international conflict handling interventions have achieved only little, mainly because they are based on ideologies, values and processes that are western in origin. Third, there exist knowledge and institutions (the African potentials) developed by African societies that can be employed to handle conflicts perhaps effectively. With these arguments in mind, the author of this chapter suggests that customary law (despite its identifiable gaps) may be considered as African potentials for effective conflict handling and peaceful coexistence of individuals and communities. The chapter discusses pertinent issues relevant to the continent by drawing illustrations from a few countries, mainly from Ethiopia.

The state of customary law. Prior to the 19th century colonialism, customary law governed all affairs of the people of Africa. Following the introduction of the codified modern legal system into Africa from the west during the colonial period, legal pluralism became a key feature of African legal systems. The customary law, one of the plural legal orders, survived colonialism and marginalisation by the formal justice systems (Kariuki 2015; Mutisi 2012). Many studies point to the fact that these deep-rooted and widely accepted institutions have demonstrated resilience and utility in post-conflict situations and they are likely to remain relevant and crucial factors in addressing intra- and inter-group conflicts in the continent (Mutisi 2012). The popularity of customary law may be explained in relation to qualities that make it preferable over the state laws. These include the ability to restore community peace, the ability to discover the truth, transparency, accessibility, efficiency, affordability, flexibility, simplicity and familiarity (Gebre et al. 2012; Ogbaharya 2010; Pankhurst and Getachew 2008; Kane et al. 2005).

Many African states have given constitutional recognition to customary law. For example, in South Africa, section 166(e) of the Constitution and item 16(1) of Schedule 6 recognise the judicial powers of traditional leaders. Likewise, Articles 34(5) and 78(5) of the Ethiopian Constitution make reference to customary law. In Tanzania, the customary law is recognised alongside the state law and attempts have also been made to reconcile customary law with national and international laws (Derman et al. 2013 in Muigua 2015, p. 89). In Rwanda, where the famous *Gacaca* courts handled genocide cases, the integration of the *abunzi* mediation into the legal system (Organic Law No. 31/2006) is one of the recent developments that point to the relevance of customary courts in contemporary Africa (Cuskelly 2011; Kariuki 2015). According to Katrina Cuskelly (2011, p. 6),

> The highest level of recognition of customary law is found in African constitutions, both in terms of the number of countries with relevant provisions and the breadth of aspects of customary law covered. Of 52 African constitutions analysed, 33 referred to customary law in some form … there is a high level of recognition of traditional and customary institutions, as well as a broad recognition of customary law in the courts and relating to land. At the weakest level of recognition of customary law, a large number of African constitutions have provisions relating to the protection of culture or tradition.

Customary institutions of dispute- and conflict-handling mechanisms have also received growing scholarly attention as evidenced by the growing number of studies and publications. The regional level comparative works of Zartman (2000), Ogbaharya (2010), Mutisi (2012) and Kariuki (2015), among others, deserve mention. Country-specific studies and publications are abundant. The edited volumes on the customary conflict-handling mechanisms in Ethiopia by Alula Pankhurst and Assefa Getachew (2008), Yntiso Gebre and his associates (2011, 2012), and Stebek Elias and Muradu Abdo (2013) revealed the breadth of studies in the country. Many researchers today recognise that customary law can effectively be used alongside the state laws thereby providing people alternative options (Zartman 2000; Mutisi 2012; Kariuki 2015; Muigua 2015). Kariuki Muigua (2015, p. 88) wrote,

> It is noteworthy that there is an overlap between the forms of ADR mechanisms and traditional justice systems. The Kenyan communities and Africa in general, have engaged in informal negotiation and mediation since time immemorial in the management of conflicts. ... Effective application of traditional conflict resolution mechanisms in Kenya and across Africa can indeed strengthen access to justice for all including those communities who face obstacles to accessing courts of law, and whose conflicts, by their nature, may pose difficulties to the court in addressing them.

Gaps and challenges. However, many of the studies and publications in Africa remained ethnographic accounts with little theoretical and policy implications due to certain inadequacies. First, concepts borrowed from western alternative dispute resolution (ADR) literature have been used interchangeably and confusingly. Hence, a lack of conceptual clarity has hindered clear communication between scholars and practitioners and common understanding. Second, an absence of efforts to identify and analyse customary law systematically has constrained our ability to identify the core values and virtues worth appreciating. Referring to the Ethiopian context, Gabriele Hoehl (2004, p. 114) wrote, 'lacking systematic knowledge and proper concepts of how to handle conflicts ... entities are mostly unable to coordinate their activities even towards crisis management'. Other scholars have also recognised that lack of systematic knowledge prevented the development of theoretical frameworks and concrete policy ideas. Minneh Kane and others (2005, p. 3) argued in favour of systematic and comprehensive studies on African customary law as follows:

> [I]t is important to note that insufficient research has gone into understanding both the dynamics and the operation of customary law tribunals and into assessing the content and status of most customary law to ensure that they in fact reflect the values and mores of the communities. ... We recommend comprehensive research into the universe of dispute resolution services available to poor and vulnerable people, including surveys to gauge user perceptions and preferences within this universe. ... We recommend that a participatory assessment of the contemporary status and content of customary law be carried out in order to open up knowledge of customary law and ensure that the voices of all stakeholders are actually heard as these laws naturally evolve.

To add to the complication, some African customary law has certain dimensions that are incompatible with national laws and international standards and norms. The customary institutions have been challenged on such grounds as gender insensitivity, discrimination against minorities, breach of other human rights, weak procedural fairness in adjudication and punishment, ill-defined legal status, lack of uniformity and lack of records, among others. In today's world where transnationalism, multiculturalism, and rapid social transformation are bridging the global–local divide, the compatibility of customary law to the new and changing contexts has become an issue that must be addressed. Violation of constitutional and human rights principles would make customary law invalid. There are cases where formal laws weakened and sidelined the traditional legal orders. Hence, the same African Constitutions that have accorded recognition to the customary law have also imposed operational restrictions.

Suggestions for researchers. At the moment, knowledge about the customary law is scattered and seems to lack academic and policy weight. Therefore, it needs to be systematised through conceptual clarity that avoids the confusing usage of the ADR terms, by identifying the values that enhance the legitimacy and popularity of customary law and by promoting comparative studies to pave the way for comprehensive understanding. The present paper is written with the firm conviction that this approach would enable researchers to generate knowledge amenable to comparative analysis, scientific generalisation, theory building, and/or policy application. The author recognises that a comprehensive study of African customary law is difficult or even unrealistic given its immensity and multiplicity. However, systematisation of knowledge as proposed above would help in appreciating the basic communalities and differences, identifying the potentials worth promoting, and evaluating the principles and practices viewed as incongruous in today's Africa.

Research approach. This paper is primarily based on the review of literature on African customary law or customary conflict-handling mechanisms. Apart from the general literature review, the author significantly benefited from the co-editing of two volumes on customary law in Ethiopia (Gebre et al. 2011; 2012). Some limited ethnographic accounts based on the writer's own ethnographic research in Ethiopia have also been used to provide illustration. Between September 1988 and December 1998, he undertook research in the Metekel Zone (Benishangul-Gumuz Region, Ethiopia), which enhanced his knowledge about the customary law of the Gumz people. In 2010 and 2011, he had the opportunity to carry out research on intra- and interethnic dispute- conflict-handling mechanisms in the Omo-Turkana basin, around the border between Ethiopia, Kenya and South Sudan. During the fieldworks, qualitative data were collected through key informant interviews, focus group discussions, observations and document reviews.

Organisation of the chapter. This short introduction is followed by the second section that focuses on conceptual issues related to the interchangeable and confusing usage of terminologies that hinder a common understanding. The commonly used key concepts that need clarity include dispute, conflict, negotiation, mediation, arbitration, conciliation, dispute settlement, conflict resolution, conflict management and conflict transformation. Section three focuses on the major values and practices that contribute to the prominence and/or dominance of customary law in African societies. In this regard, the author identified certain qualities (namely, restoration of order, quest for truth, public participation, collective responsibility, transparency, efficiency and accessibility) that represent virtues worth recognising. Building on section three, the fourth section proposes the need for a comparative research strategy that would capture other salient features of customary law, including their limitations worth interrogating. Issues related to the structures and procedures of customary law, the state of legal pluralism (especially, relations between the formal and informal laws) and the weaknesses of the customary law are discussed in this section, which is followed by the conclusion.

2.2. Towards Conceptual Clarity

The key concepts used to describe the African customary law are the same terms that have been used in the alternative dispute resolution (ADR) literature. The usage of the common terms to describe the two different legal orders may be explained in terms of operational resemblance or an overlap of mechanisms as Muigua (2015, p. 88) noted. However, the application of the ADR methods is different from the customary law practised in African countries. Hence, the interchangeable and reckless use of the concepts has led to misrepresentation, misunderstanding and confusion. Since the terminological usages would have discrete implications for the outcome of a dispute/conflict situation, ensuring conceptual clarity is indispensable.

Half a Century ago, two prominent anthropologists (Paul Bohannan and Max Gluckman) espoused a debate on whether universal categories and terminologies should be used to depict the legal systems of different societies. Bohannan (1969, p. 403) advocated for the use of native terms to be accompanied by ethnographic meaning, arguing that using universal categories act as a barrier to understanding and representing the legal systems in different cultures. Gluckman (1969, p. 535), on the other hand, argued in favour of translating native concepts into English, stating that excessive use of local terms serve as a barrier to cross-cultural comparison of legal practices. As Kevin Avruch (1998, p. 60) rightly stated, the etic approaches that allow comparative analysis and the emic approaches that provide much deeper and contextualised insights are equally important in dealing with dispute/conflict.

Why is ADR different from customary law? ADR refers to a variety of processes that parties use to resolve disputes/conflicts informally and confidentially without a formal court trial. In England, the history of voluntary conciliation and arbitration goes back to 1850 where these methods were used to address industrial disputes with 'the highest hopes of abolishing strikes completely by the most ruthless application of arbitration' (Hicks 1930, p. 26). In the United States, legal practitioners and law professors conceived the ADR with the intention to reform the justice system through the introduction of non-litigant methods (Nader 1993). The early advocates of ADR with the reformist agenda in the US sought the non-litigant model from customary law, which was viewed as more humane, therapeutic and non-adversarial (Avruch 2003, p. 352). Ugo Mattei and Laura Nader (2008, p. 77) argued that ADR was used as a disempowering tool 'to suppress people's resistance, by socializing them toward conformity by means of consensus-building mechanisms, by valorizing consensus, cooperation, passivity, and docility, and by silencing people who speak out angrily'.

The relationship between ADR and customary law can be discussed at two levels: the transferability of the ADR system and the transferability of ADR terminologies. Some researchers sought to explore the ways in which the ADR system can be developed in Africa by integrating the formal legal structures with customary conflict handling systems (Ogbaharya 2010). However, the idea of transplanting ADR from the west to non-west has been challenged on the grounds that ADR, which developed within a given cultural, ideological and political contexts cannot be expected to fit in other contexts (Ogbaharya 2010). For example, the western institutional settings focus on individuals, while the African cultures consider the collective as the unit of social organisation (Grande 1999). Hence, the ADR procedures in the west are closed as opposed to the African procedures, which are open to the public, and therefore transparent. Some writers also expressed concerns that ADR can be used to justify the imposition of western values, protect western economic

45

and political interests and benefit the local elites rather than the masses (Nader and Grande 2002).

According to the proponents of the ADR transfer, non-western states tend to weaken and sideline customary institutions. Therefore, the creation of ADR by revitalising the customary system would lead to a sustainable resolution of communal and intergroup conflicts in Africa (Smock 1997). Edward Torgbor (2015, p. 117) stated, 'with the existence of new African ADR institutions and the ever growing crop of learned and well trained professionals, there can be little excuse for exporting African disputes and conflicts to foreign capitals'. Other writers expressed that ADR has failed to meet expectations in Africa. For example, Kibaya Laibuta (2015, p. 172) wrote,

> [I]t was hoped that ADR would offer practical solutions to the impediments that characterize the administration of civil justice in commonwealth Africa. Indeed, ADR was often viewed as a universal remedy for the afflictions with which our modern-day civil justice systems are identified. However, this supposed panacea has itself fallen ill with multiple wounds, inflicted by ill-fitting policy, legal and institutional frameworks, not to mention the slow pace at which the legal profession and court users move towards internalizing the value of alternatives to litigation. It is true to say that the journey has been long and the Promised Land far from view … arbitral tribunals are transformed into private courts, completely robed in the dilatory conduct, complexity and disproportionate costs, which ADR seeks to purge.

The second issue, the focus of this paper, relates to the borrowing of ADR terms, namely, dispute, conflict, negotiation, mediation, arbitration, conciliation, dispute settlement, conflict resolution, conflict management and conflict transformation to describe processes in the customary law. In the African literature, these concepts are not sufficiently differentiated. A volume edited by Betty Rabar and Martin Karimi (2004) started by defining two key concepts: conflict prevention and conflict management. However, terms like negotiation, mediation, arbitration, reconciliation, conflict resolution and dispute resolution were used in different chapters without explanation. Adeyinka Theresa Ajayi and Lateef Oluwafemi Buhari (2014, p. 149) noted, 'The methods of performing conflict resolution in the traditional African societies are as follows: mediation, adjudication, reconciliation, arbitration and negotiation'. These concepts were used without explanation about their meanings and usage.

For analytical purpose, the terms that require differentiation are categorised into three: types of incompatibility (dispute and conflict), methods of handling incompatibility (negotiation, mediation, arbitration and conciliation), and approaches to ending incompatibility (dispute settlement, conflict management, conflict resolution and conflict transformation). This section attempts to clarify the meanings of these concepts, find out whether they have equivalent practices in Ethiopia and reflect on the aptness of their usage in the African literature. In this paper, as part of the knowledge systematisation effort, the concept of customary law has been used intentionally, avoiding the interchangeable use of such terms as 'indigenous laws', 'traditional laws', 'informal laws' and 'dispute/conflict-resolution mechanisms'. Although there exist some debates on the notion of customary law (Merry 1988), the term has been used widely in the academic literature, legal documents such as African constitutions and law schools. Concepts like 'law', 'court' and 'judge' have been used for describing local institutions and customary practices for lack of better terms.

2.2.1. Types of Incompatibility

In the literature, there exists lack of uniformity in the use of the terms dispute and conflict. While some writers stress differences between the two, others use them interchangeably. In the Ethiopian literature on customary law, the terms 'dispute' and 'conflict' have not been adequately differentiated. In the book 'Grassroots Justice in Ethiopia' (Pankhurst and Getachew 2008), the titles of 10 out of 11 chapters carry the term dispute, but nowhere in the volume it is made clear whether the choice was meant to convey the message that the issues discussed in the book are specifically about disputes and not conflicts. Likewise, the two volumes on 'Customary Dispute

Resolution Mechanisms in Ethiopia' failed to differentiate the usage of the two concepts (Gebre et al. 2011; 2012). Many chapter contributors to these two books and others published in Ethiopia used the terms dispute and conflict without providing any operational definitions and at times interchangeably.

In order to ensure conceptual clarity in the field of dispute/conflict handling research, this paper adopted John Burton's (1990, p. 2), the most widely quoted approach, that describes dispute as a short-term disagreement between two persons or groups over a specific set of facts and/or issues that are negotiable in nature, and conflict as a long-term and deeply rooted incompatibility associated with seemingly 'non-negotiable' issues between opposing groups or individuals. Non-negotiable issues include, among others, denial of basic human rights and deprivation of essential economic resources such as land and water. A specific dispute, if not settled, could turn into conflict, not the other way round. It is beyond the scope of this paper to delve into the argument that conflict is inevitable and useful for change.

2.2.2. Methods of Handling Incompatibility

The common methods employed to address individual or group disputes/conflicts outside of the formal court include negotiation, mediation, conciliation and arbitration. The four methods of alternative dispute resolution, as practised in western societies, vary in their respective meanings and approaches. For example, in the context of western ADR mediators do not suggest a solution, conciliators suggest non-binding agreement ideas, and arbitration results are final and legally binding. Francis Kariuki (2015, p. 13) wrote, 'Conflict resolution amongst African communities has since time immemorial and continues to take the form of negotiation, mediation, reconciliation or arbitration by elders'. Kariuki did not elaborate on the meanings of these terms in the African contexts. It is incumbent on researchers of African customary law to make sure that the concepts that they borrow from the ADR or other international literature adequately represent the local realities.

In the Ethiopian literature, these terms are not sufficiently differentiated from each other and from their usage in the ADR

48

literature. Girshaw Tirsit (2004, p. 49) stated that, 'reconciliation and arbitration are common features of indigenous conflict resolution mechanisms'. Habtie Wodisha (2011, pp. 438–440) noted that negotiation, mediation, and arbitration exist as distinct methods among the Boro-Shinasha. Among the Nuer, according to Tutlam Koang (2011, p. 412), kinsmen and elders arrange mediation to determine the fine and ask the culprit to pay compensation to the victim. These authors did not explain what they meant by these concepts. This section attempts to discuss the meanings of the four concepts and the actual ADR proceedings (private in nature) so that researchers could establish the presence or absence of resemblance with the proceedings of customary law (public in nature) that they are studying.

Negotiation is a mechanism where the parties that are directly involved meet to resolve their differences and reach an agreement on their own without the involvement of a third party (Muigua 2015, p. 84; Assefa 2012, p. 245). If conducted without influence and intimidation, negotiation is known to be the most efficient and cost-effective approach to handle a dispute/conflict. Since it is conducted based on the principle of give-and-take and willingness to ease tension, private negotiators are expected to opt for compromise and enjoy maximum control over the process (Muigua 2015). Apart from this specific and narrow usage, the term negotiation is flexibly and broadly employed to refer to any discussion aimed at finding a middle ground, be it in the context of mediation, conciliation or the early phase of arbitration.

Mediation as dispute/conflict handling method involves an appointment of a neutral and impartial third party (a mediator, often a trained person or a legal expert) to facilitate dialogue between conflict parties and help them reach a mutually acceptable agreement without imposing a biding solution (LeBaron-Duryea 2001, p. 121). Mediation is often preferred over litigation because the former is faster, fair, efficient, cheaper and confidential, and addresses the unique needs of parties. The main principles of mediation are voluntarism, being non-binding, confidentiality and being interest-based (LeBaron-Duryea 2001). The parties are free to accept or withdraw from negotiated agreements.

In order to facilitate the resolution of a conflict, a mediator performs a series of activities. The mediator is expected to understand the perspectives of the parties, set ground rules for improved communication, encourage them to discuss in good faith and articulate their interests or concerns, remind them to make decisions on their own, and convince them to remain committed to a peaceful result. In meditation parties may be represented by lawyers who argue their case, advocate for their clients and negotiate on their behalf. One might wonder whether mediation as practised in the west is consistent with the African customary law where non-professionals handle disputes/conflicts in public.

The 1960 Civil Code of Ethiopia does not clearly recognise mediation procedure. According to Fiseha Assefa (2012, p. 247), it appears that the Ethiopian Civil Code combines mediation and conciliation. Researchers of African customary law should bear in mind the fact that a mediator in the ADR context would not dictate the process, make a judgment or suggest any solution.

Conciliation (or reconciliation) is another dispute/conflict handling method that involves an appointment of a neutral and impartial third party (a conciliator) to assist parties to reach a satisfactory agreement. Conciliators are appointed based on their experiences, expertise, availability, language and cultural knowledge. Louis Kriesberg and Bruce Dayton (2012, p. 305) stated that there are four important dimensions of reconciliation that parties expect for the process to succeed: truth, justice, regard and security. Conciliation and mediation have a lot in common, and sometimes the two terms are used interchangeably. In both methods, the parties retain the power to select their conciliators, the venue, the language, the structure, the content and the timing of the proceedings. Both techniques are flexible, time- and cost-efficient, confidential and interest-based. The parties also retain autonomy to make the final decision without imposition by a third party.

The difference between conciliation and mediation is that a conciliator could play direct/active roles in providing a non-binding settlement proposal. The Ethiopian Civil Code (Articles 3318–3324) duly recognises the conciliation procedure and provides details about, among others, the role of conciliators and the conciliation proceedings.

Arbitration is the fourth major dispute/conflict handling method where parties voluntarily present their disagreement to unbiased third party arbitrators or arbitral tribunals. Arbitrators are expected to apply the law and start the proceedings after receiving a written consensus (arbitration agreement) from the parties on the content of their disagreement and their willingness to accept in advance the 'arbitral award' – the verdict issued after the hearing. Arbitral proceedings are conducted under strict rules of confidentiality (not open to the public). Like mediation and conciliation, arbitration is supposed to be efficient, easier, faster, cheaper and relatively flexible. Parties are free to choose their arbitrators, the venue, the language and the timing of the arbitral proceedings.

Arbitration is different from mediation and conciliation in that (1) arbitrators have the power to administer a legally enforceable award and (2) parties lose control over their ability to make a decision on their own. Arbitral awards are enforced even internationally because of the 1958 New York Convention on the Recognition and Enforcement of Foreign Arbitral Awards. As practised in the West, the decisions of arbitrators are final and binding and cannot be reversed even by the formal courts unless the arbitration agreements were invalid. It would be interesting to know whether customary courts exist in Africa that apply the formal law, require the submission of written arbitration agreements and conduct hearings protected from the public.

Arbitration as an ADR method is legally recognised in Ethiopia and has been used to handle different disputes/conflicts (Tilahun 2007). Although the procedure seems to be similar to western practices, Assefa (2012, p. 25) noted that arbitration in the Ethiopian context is becoming more expensive and that arbitral awards are not necessarily final and binding as courts tend to accept appeals from parties dissatisfied with the decisions of arbitrators. Such court interference is inconsistent with the principles of arbitration and unfairly diminishes the relevance and the credibility of the method.

2.2.3. Approaches to Ending Incompatibility

The ending of a conflict takes four major forms: dispute settlement, conflict management, conflict resolution and conflict transformation. In the Ethiopian literature, the terms dispute settlement, conflict resolution and conflict management are not sufficiently differentiated (sometimes used interchangeably), while conflict transformation is a new concept the local equivalent of which is yet to be found. The following discussions will clarify the common usage of the four approaches and thereby avoiding confusion and interchangeable use.

Dispute settlement is an approach that removes a dispute through negotiation, mediation, conciliation and arbitration. A dispute is settled (rather than resolved, managed or transformed) because it represents an easily addressable short-term problem that has emanated from negotiable interests. Establishing the facts of the dispute and satisfying the interests of disputants are among the basic conditions to be met for successful dispute settlement. Depending on the methods employed, a third party may use persuasion, inducement, pressure or threats to ensure that the disputants arrive at a satisfactory settlement. A dispute settlement strategy aims at ending the dispute through compromises and concessions without addressing the fundamental causes or satisfying the basic demands of the disputants (Burton and Dukes 1990, pp. 83–7). Since it does not change the existing structures and relationships that are causing disputes, the efficacy and durability of the settlement approach (compared to the resolution and transformation approaches) are considered to be limited.

Conflict management refers to the process of mitigating, containing, limiting or controlling conflict temporarily through third party intervention. Conflict management steps are taken with the recognition that conflicts cannot be quickly resolved, and with the conviction that the continuation or escalation of conflicts can be somehow controlled as an interim measure. The conflict management process succeeds only when the conflicting parties have respect for the integrity, impartiality and ability of the third party. However, the strategy neither removes the conflict nor addresses the underlying causes (Lederach 1995, pp. 16–7). As Merton Deutsch

(1973, p. 8) noted, the main intention is to make the situation more constructive and less destructive to the conflicting parties through lose-lose, win-lose or win-win results. Conflict management must soon be followed by other strategies to resolve the problem permanently.

Conflict management as defined in ADR has equivalent cultural and religious practices in Ethiopia. For example, among the Orthodox Christians, a priest can hold the holy cross and pronounce religious injunction on adversaries to temporarily halt offensive actions. In some cultures in Ethiopia, offenders take refuge with individuals and institutions believed to have cultural and religious sanctity to protect them against revenge (Alemu 2011, p. 41).

Conflict resolution is an approach that removes the underlying causes of conflict decisively. Peter Wallensteen (2012, p. 8) defines conflict resolution as 'a situation where conflicting parties enter into an agreement that solves their central incompatibilities, accept each other's continued existence as parties and cease all violent action against each other'. From this definition it is apparent that conflict resolution follows a mutual understanding about a problem to be solved and a firm commitment to address the root causes of conflict. This can be accomplished through changes in behaviours, attitudes, structures and relationships that incite or perpetuate conflict.

The resolution approach leads to a long-term solution. The role of a third party is to facilitate communication and enable conflict parties to achieve a comprehensive agreement. Resolving conflicts, as opposed to settling disputes, demands more than establishing the facts or satisfying the interests of the parties. It is equally important to note that conflict resolution may not remove all differences or may not lead to major structural changes to avoid a future relapse of a conflict.

Conflict transformation may be described as the deepest level of change that results from an improved and accurate understanding of a given conflict. Conflict transformation underlines the need for major structural and relational changes to avoid relapse of conflicts due to similar causes. Apart from the structures and relations, those issues and interests that have been leading to conflicts are expected to change to allow the establishment of a new system and a new environment. In this regard, the transformational approach seems to have an interest in conflict aftermath or post-conflict peace-building processes. John Paul Lederach (1995, p. 17), the leading advocate and proponent of conflict transformation, wrote:

> Transformation provides a more holistic understanding, which can be fleshed out at several levels. Unlike resolution and management, the idea of transformation does not suggest we simply eliminate or control conflict, but rather points descriptively toward its inherent dialectic nature. Social conflict is a phenomenon of human creation, lodged naturally in relationships. It is a phenomenon that transforms events, the relationships in which conflict occurs, and indeed its very creators. It is a necessary element in transformative human construction and reconstruction of social organization and realities.

The gist of Lederach's argument is that conflict (created by people in some kind of relationships) transforms the creators and the relationships. If unchecked or left alone, it could have destructive consequences for the conflicting people. However, such adverse effects (hostile relations and negative perceptions) can be modified through long-term and sustained processes that involve education, advocacy and reconciliation to improve mutual understanding and transform the people, relationships and structures for the better. Hence, conflict transformation is explained in terms of healing and major structural change with positive implications for social transformation and nation building.

2.3. Values and Virtues of Customary Law

The studies undertaken thus far in Ethiopia indisputably reveal that the customary law is deeply rooted in cultural and religious values and widely practised throughout the country. Especially in the countryside, it seems that comparatively fewer cases are taken to the state court (Woubishet 2011, p. 194) and that most plaintiffs (more than 76 per cent according to Dejene 2011, p. 271) withdraw cases filed with formal institutions before proper investigation. It is equally important to acknowledge the fact that the degree to which the local population resists the formal law depends on the intensity of state influence, which gets weaker from the centre to the periphery.

Many professionals and practitioners (informants) in the justice sector acknowledged that the customary courts have been helpful in terms of reducing the workload of the formal courts. In their efforts to address inter-ethnic conflicts, government officials have been openly co-opting influential customary authorities and judges. This section focuses on the core values, perspectives and functions that contribute to the perpetuation, resilience and, in some cases, dominance of the customary law.

2.3.1. Restoration of Social Order

In places where people live in settings of strong networks of kinship, clanship, ethnicity and other social groupings, disputes/conflicts between individuals are likely to engulf much larger groups. Unlike the formal courts that define justice in terms of penalising perpetrators, customary courts focus on larger groups (e.g., families, communities, clans, etc.) that may have been drawn into the trouble from both the perpetrator's and the victim's sides. This is because discords are viewed not only as isolated individual differences to be addressed but also as a disconcerting social disorder to be restored. The restoration of social order is ensured only when the larger groups, far beyond the actual perpetrators and victims, drawn into the dispute/conflict come to grips with it and move forward, leaving the trouble behind them. Hence, the deliberations of customary courts often end with repentance of the perpetrator's group and the forgiveness of the victim's group thereby bridging the social divide and healing the social scar.

In 1999, the author witnessed reconciliation processes between two Gumz families in the presence of their respective relatives and neighbours to resolve an adultery case. When a young married woman admitted to have been impregnated by a young man in the same village, the case was brought to the attention of elders and clan leaders, who immediately summoned the family and relatives of the impregnator and those of the young woman's husband (who was away from the village for education). The problem between the two families was resolved through repentance and forgiveness in the absence of the husband who was expected to agree to the deal upon his return to the village. Generally, families and large groups are involved during the handling of disputes and conflicts initiated by individuals or small groups.

The staging of a forum for group involvement in a customary peace-making process is meant not only to resolve disputes/conflicts but also to avoid possible relapses and spillover effects, and ensure social order and community peace. Hence, justice and peace are served at the same time. It can be argued that in communities with a strong sense of social bonding and group loyalty, the customary law is better suited for the transformation of hostility to solidarity at both individual and group levels. In view of this fact, the customary law provides an indisputable advantage over the formal law, which focuses only on the prosecution of the perpetrator, a measure that does not necessarily lead to community peace.

2.3.2. Quest for Truth

The second important quality of the customary law is its strength in discovering the truth that would otherwise pose challenges for the formal justice system. The police would find offences committed under secrecy and in the absence of any evidence to be difficult or impossible to investigate. In the context of customary law, the victim's side is not expected to open up for discussion and forgiveness before the disclosure of truth. Hence, the primary role of customary judges is to discover the facts through confession or investigation. In closely organised communities, people do not hesitate to expose culprits, and it is not uncommon for family members to testify against their loved ones involved in unlawful acts. Customary courts rarely convict alleged perpetrators based on circumstantial evidence, and offenders rarely get away with wrongdoing for lack of witness/evidence.

Telling the truth is given high value for practical and religious reasons. On the practical side, the social life of people in communities is built around mutual trust. People make agreements and entrust things to each other without any third party in witness or any record in evidence. If the social contract of trust was allowed to crumble, the consequence for individuals and society at large would be grave. For example, untrustworthy individuals risk being dishonoured and disgraced in their own families and communities. A society would become dysfunctional without its basic principles that govern the behaviours and actions of its members. Hence, there exists a great deal of social pressure to tell the truth.

Regarding the religious aspect, telling lies while under oath is associated with a betrayal of faith that might have supernatural consequences. Among the Nuer people of Ethiopia, 'The disputants swear an oath of innocence and the person who doesn't tell the truth is bound to suffer misfortune' (Koang 2011, p. 425). Among the Waliso Oromo, 'Customary courts attempt to prove the truthfulness of cases through the flow of information, directly from the disputants. Both parties are expected to be honest in providing information. … It is believed that the *Waaqa* [God] easily identifies the truthfulness and falsity' (Dejene 2011, pp. 261-2). Customary law employs divine means (fear of supernatural consequences) to make offenders admit guilt or tell the truth. But other superstitious mechanisms of extracting truth (e.g., through divination, sorcery, magic and witchcraft) practised by some customary institutions in Africa are not considered as genuine sources of truth worth discussing.

2.3.3. Public Participation

The notion of public participation in the context of the customary law is explained in terms of the involvement of community members in a dispute/conflict handling process. As opposed to the closed and confidential ADR proceedings of the west, customary law allows people to attend the public deliberations and provide opinion about the validity or falsity of evidence provided and/or the fairness of verdict reached. This was the case, until the 1936 Italian occupation, with the customary justice system of the Government of Ethiopia, where the Imperial Courts invited bystanders and passerby to attend hearings and air their opinion.

According to Fiseha Assefa (2011, pp. 366-7) and Tadesse Abraham (2011, p. 123), public participation in the administration of justice characterises the customary law of Tigray and Sidama respectively. Dejene (2011, pp. 261–76) wrote, 'Apart from direct participation, the community provides information and suggests ideas on the issue under litigation. Such informal discussions and public views are important to arrive at consensus at the end of the day. The final decisions are the outcome of these various views and suggestions from the community. Among the Nuer, the open procedures and participation of the community members in the administration of customary justice tend to limit the possibility for corruption and nepotism (Koang 2011, p. 429).

Why is popular participation so important? First, the involvement of community members as observers, witnesses and commentators increases the credibility and transparency of customary law. Second, non-confidential proceedings help to put public pressure on parties to honour and respect agreements. Non-compliance to a customary court decision is rare mainly because nonconformity is likely to be interpreted as rebellion against community values and interests. Finally, since customary judges pass decisions in the presence of community observers, the possibility for corruption and prejudiced judgment is limited.

2.3.4. Collective Responsibility

Collective responsibility refers to a situation where social groups take the blame for offences perpetrated by their members and the responsibility for the consequences. This principle is widely practised in cultures where group identification and group control mechanisms are strong, and where the idea of individualisation of crimes is not common. In such societies, to redress offences, retaliatory acts are taken against unsuspecting members of a perpetrator, sometimes in the form of collective punishment. Hence, families and relatives of wrongdoers often take the initiative to make peace and avoid retribution. The customary judge(s) may require the perpetrator's family, lineage or clan to take responsibility, express repentance as a group and contribute towards compensation for the victim.

One might challenge the appropriateness of holding communities/groups responsible for offences committed by individuals. The rationale behind blame-sharing may better be understood in some contexts. First, it represents a tacit recognition that the family or the group to which the perpetrator belongs failed to detect, discourage, stop or report unjustified offences, and therefore, should take some responsibility. Second, when the verdict involves costly compensation to the victim's group, the principles of reciprocity, solidarity and sharing are often evoked to help members in trouble. Third, in a situation where the group (rather than the individual offender) is the target of retribution, the cost of not taking collective responsibility could be higher than sharing the blame and the fine.

One might also wonder whether sharing of the consequences of wrongdoing would not encourage repeated perpetration. However, since it is an unpleasant experience for any group to go through such trials and tribulations that tarnish group reputation and image in society, repeated offences may strain the relationship between the perpetrator and his group and lead to harsher measures such as humiliation, ostracism, expulsion from community, capital punishment, etc. In other words, there exist internal mechanisms to discourage and control offenders. On the whole, under an ideal situation, collective responsibility for any wrongdoing is not a virtue worth pursuing. In the contexts discussed above, however, it seems to serve important purposes worth appreciating.

2.3.5. *Accessibility, Efficiency and Affordability*

In Ethiopia, the formal law is inaccessible to a significant proportion of rural communities due to the distance of its institutions, its lack of efficiency and affordability factors, not to mention the popularity deficiency. Most rural communities lack easy physical access to the formal courts because the District Courts are located in the *Woreda* (District) capitals, far away from most villages. Travelling to a Woreda capital to file a case would, undoubtedly, incur costs: money, time and energy. Moreover, it creates inconveniences associated with the following: language barriers (where the local languages are not used in courts), facing unfamiliar and intimidating judges, repeated court appearances and delays. Although the quasi-formal social courts exist in most villages, their mandates are limited to civil cases and petty crimes the punishments for which do not exceed a one-month jail term and a 500 Birr (US$25) fine.

On the other hand, the customary law represents alternatives that fairly adequately address the gaps and challenges. The customary judges, who are sometimes appointed and entrusted by the parties and who speak the local languages, are readily available in every locality and provide speedy services free of charge (or for a nominal fee). Hence, the customary courts are more affordable and more accessible. Unlike the formal courts, which are complicated and known for rigidity, customary courts are characterised by flexibility and simplicity, which make the latter more efficient. Inconveniences and dissatisfactions associated with repeated court appearances, unbearable delays, intimidating court procedures and corruption are limited in customary courts.

2.4. Systematic and Comparative Research

Studies on customary law may be undertaken in a variety of ways depending on their purpose and design. In this section, with the idea of knowledge systematisation in mind, attempts are made to outline and explain salient variables useful for understanding the structures and procedures of customary courts and the state of legal pluralism in Ethiopia, which is unique in some ways. It is assumed that a systematic study of customary law requires a structured research approach that ensures the collection and analysis of comparable data.

2.4.1. The Structure of Customary Courts

This subsection attempts to identify the judicial levels and frameworks, the identity and legitimacy of judges, and their terms of office. Regarding court levels, some customary courts are hierarchically organised and have procedures for appeal, while others lack hierarchy and possibility for appeal. The absence of hierarchical structure does not deter complainants from taking their cases to other parallel levels for rehearing (Debebe 2011, p. 348). Some customary courts such as the Mad'a of the Afar people handle different types of cases (Kahsay 2011, p. 326), while others such as those among the Wolayita are specialised to handle only specific cases (Yilma 2011, p. 106). While the judicial levels and frameworks vary from society to society, flexibility seems to be one of the characterising features of customary law. Among the Tswana of Botswana, customary law runs parallel to the formal justice system (Kariuki 2015, pp. 35–6). The author further noted,

> Dispute resolution starts at the household (lolwapa) level. If a dispute cannot be resolved at the household level, it is taken to the Kgotlana (extended family level) where elders from the extended family sit and listen to the matter. ... If the kgotlana does not resolve the dispute, the disputants take the matter to kgotla, which is a customary court with formal court like procedures. It consists of the chief at the village level and the paramount chief at the regional levels. The chiefs are public officials and handle both civil and criminal matters. ... The decision of the paramount chief is appealable to the customary court of appeal, which is the final court on customary matters and has the same status as the high Court. At every level, a council of elders (bo-ralekgotla) exists to advise the decision maker. Further, village committees exist to support and compliment the dispute resolution process.

Customary court judges are known for their wisdom, impartiality, knowledge of their culture, rhetoric skills or convincing power, and rich experience in dispute/conflict handling. Apart from such well-versed individuals, influential clan leaders, ritual specialists, religious leaders, senior elders, village administrators and lineage heads often participate in customary courts. The power of the customary judges emanates from at least four sources: consent of the parties, administrative position (e.g., clan leaders), participation in rituals as in the case among the Sidama (Abraham 2011) and the Dassanech (Gebre 2012), and in some cases from leadership in religious institutions as in some parts of Amhara (Birhan 2011). The identity of judges as prominent individuals and their power derive from secular and spiritual sources, which contribute to their legitimacy.

The terms of office of judges vary depending on the sources of their authority. The role of those judges appointed by parties in dispute/conflict end the moment the discords are handled. However, judges who acquired authority by virtue of their religious or administrative posts or by performing rituals may continue to serve until their formal replacement unless they are required to step down for legitimate reasons, such as inability to function, poor performance and malpractice. While individuals with excellent records of service are invited to join the panel of judges repeatedly, those who failed to meet expectation are rarely given another chance. It can be noted that judges are under close public scrutiny and this helps to ensure their impartiality and competence for the task.

2.4.2. The Procedures of Customary Courts

This subsection focuses on events/activities that span from the occurrence of an incident to its eventual closure. These include: reporting cases, evidence collection and verification, deliberation and verdict, closing rituals and enforcement mechanisms. Reporting cases to customary courts is a collective responsibility rather than a matter to be left to those directly involved. Family members, relatives, neighbours or anyone who has knowledge about the dispute/conflict is expected to report. In many cases, the culprit or his/her kin would admit guilt and report incidents to ensure quick conciliation. It is also a common practice for the party of the victim to file a case with the judicial body instead of resorting to vengeance.

The ultimate objective of customary courts is genuine conciliation after the disclosure of the truth. The truth is expected to surface through confession or public investigation that may involve review of evidence and witness testimony. Thanks to the high value accorded to truth, serious offences committed under secrecy and in the absence of witness find solution through customary law. The judges remind disputants to restrain themselves from doing things that can derail the process, hurt feelings and exacerbate social disorder. Apart from those directly involved in disputes/conflicts and their witnesses, representatives of the parties (often family members) and ordinary spectators of the deliberation may be asked to air their views and comments in the interest of reconciliation and community peace.

When guilt is admitted or proven with evidence, a case comes to closure, and verdict will be passed often by consensus, although it does not preclude coercion (when persuasion fails). The offender's group may have to pay compensation to the victim's side, and express sincere repentance, which is often reciprocated with forgiveness from the victim's group. Regarding compensation, there exist significant variations across cultures. In some societies, fixed payment regimes exist, while in others judges or the parties specify fines based on the severity of the offence and sometimes the economic capacity of the offender. Compensation may be paid immediately, in piecemeal over a short period of time, or as a long-term debt to be inherited by generations as in the case among the Dassanech (Gebre 2012). In some cases, compensation may not be required, expected, demanded or accepted.

Most customary court rulings end with closing ritual performances that involve sacrificial animals, expression of commitment to agreements, cursing wickedness and nonconformist behaviours, and blessing righteousness and conformity. Such rituals of partly divine content are believed to deter rebellious tendencies and avoid possible relapse to discord. Besides the mystified harm that rituals are believed to inflict on the defiant, social pressure (e.g., defamation, ostracism, etc.) and physical measures (e.g., punishment, property confiscation, etc.) may be used to enforce customary court decisions. Handing an offender to the formal justice system is also viewed as dealing with the disobedient.

2.4.3. Legal Pluralism

Legal pluralism is explained in terms of the co-existence of more than one legal system in a given social field (Merry 1988, p. 870). Sally Merry, who distinguished between 'classical legal pluralism' (that focused on the intersections of the colonial law and customary law of the colonised) and the 'new legal pluralism', argued that the latter 'places at the center of investigation the relationship between the official legal system and other forms of ordering that connect with but are in some ways separate from and depend on it' (Merry 1988, p. 873). Internal diversity within the state system, where various state sectors may be competing for authority also represents legal pluralism. Likewise, the non-state legal systems (of which customary law represents one variant) are characterised by plurality of legal practices. Customary law is also differentiated both within and across ethnic groups. In this paper, therefore, the concept of legal pluralism is employed to refer to (a) the coexistence of and the relationships between the state law and the non-state laws, and (b) the coexistence of and relationships among various legal practices within customary law.

Typology. For analytical purpose, five normative legal regimes (one state law and four non-state laws) have been identified in Ethiopia. These include: (1) the codified law introduced in the 1960s and the subsequent laws issued later in time; (2) the customary law characterised by both commonalities and differences between and within ethnic groups; (3) the Sharia courts that have been in existence for long time, recognised by the last three successive governments, and currently operating with jurisdiction over family and personal issues; (4) the certified commercial arbitration forums that provide arbitration and mediation services in commercial, labour, construction, family and other disputes; and (5) the spirit mediums, believed to operate as mediators between humans and God and accepted by followers as representing dispute/conflict handling institutions. While Sharia courts and the commercial arbitration forums have clear legal grounds to operate, the customary law and spirit mediums largely function based on public acceptance and preference.

Relations. The relationship between the state law and the customary law is an important area of study. The Ethiopian Constitution (Articles 39:2 and 91:1) provides, in broad terms, for the promotion of the cultures of nations, nationalities and peoples of the country. Article 34:5 makes more specific and direct reference to adjudication of disputes relating to personal and family laws in accordance with customary law, with the consent of the parties to the dispute. Article 78:5 also states that the House of People's Representatives and State Councils can give official recognition to customary courts. Thus far, however, neither the particulars of Article 34.5 have been determined by law nor the official recognition stipulated in Article 78:5 has been given. Criminal law is clearly under the jurisdiction of the state law and all cases should be transferred to the formal courts, though in practice variations exist on how criminal cases are actually handled.

The actual interactions between the state law and the customary law are arbitrary, inconsistent, unregulated and quite unpredictable, to say the least. At one extreme, the two legal systems unofficially recognise each other and cooperate to the extent of transferring cases and/or exchanging information (Mamo 2006, pp. 129–31). There are instances where government authorities and customary judges work together in peace-making processes or addressing inter-ethnic conflicts (Birhan 2011; Israel 2011) and there are also situations where the formal and customary courts operate side-by-side exhibiting indifference and tolerance (Wodisha 2011). At the other extreme, both get antagonistic, especially when one intervenes in the domains and activities of the other (Yewondwesen 2011). There is a need to regulate the relationship between the two legal systems and avoid anomalous practices.

Since little is known about the state of legal pluralism in Ethiopia and other African countries, the following questions await answers from researchers. What is the source of legitimacy of each legal order in every society? What are the common features shared by the different legal systems operating in the same social environment? What are their internal and external differences? What kinds of relationships exist amongst the various legal orders? Are there categories of people who prefer certain legal orders to others? What are the criteria employed by people for their choices? What are the strengths and weaknesses of each legal system? The answers to these questions and information on whether each institution is currently getting weaker or stronger and the reasons behind such a trend are expected to enhance knowledge about the state of legal pluralism in Africa.

2.5. Conclusion

The plural legal orders of Africa came into being as a result of three processes: transplantation of foreign laws from western countries into African contexts (both during colonial times and as a result of later transnational processes), imposition of national laws on local areas and derivation from local values and traditions. Compared to the transplanted and imposed laws, the local level customary law seems to enjoy widespread acceptance throughout the continent and especially in rural areas, where the majority of Africans reside. They have also received increasing attention by researchers as evidenced by the growing research reports and some publications. The knowledge generated thus far, however, is not comprehensive and systematic enough to develop social theory or influence public policy. Therefore, this paper suggests the need to systematise knowledge about customary law through conceptual clarity aimed at avoiding distortions and confusions and through comparative studies aimed at generating data amenable to scientific generalisation and/or policy application.

African customary law has faced existential challenges that placed the whole local mechanism at a crossroads. While operating in the context of competing domestic constitutional laws, they are criticised for gender insensitivity, weak procedural fairness in adjudication and punishment, breach of human rights, lack of uniformity and incompatibility with changing contexts. The application of some customary law obviously violates the classic liberal rights such as privacy, personal dignity and bodily integrity. Despite the identifiable gaps, the relevance and influence of customary law in modern Africa cannot be underestimated. At the same time, the relationship between the formal and informal institutions cannot be taken for granted due to contestations and complexities involved. The states try to exert influence on the traditional institutions, which are rendered invalid for violation of formal laws or manipulated to serve the interests of the states. Therefore, research on customary law should clearly spell out the broad spectrum of pros and cons to ensure comprehensive and balanced understanding.

References

Abraham, T. (2011) 'Customary conflict resolution among the Sidama', in Y. Gebre, A. Fekade and F. Assefa (eds.) *Customary Dispute Resolution in Ethiopia*, Addis Ababa: EACC, pp. 121–32.
Ajayi, A.T. and Buhari, L.O. (2014) 'Methods of conflict resolution in

African traditional society', *An International Multidisciplinary Journal*, Vol. 8, No. 2, pp. 138–57.

Alemu, K. (2011) 'Blood feud reconciliation in Lalomama Midir district, North Shoa', in Y. Gebre, A. Fekade and F. Assefa (eds.) *Customary Dispute Resolution in Ethiopia*, Addis Ababa: EACC, pp. 157–80.

Assefa, F. (2012) 'Business-related alternative dispute resolution mechanisms in Addis Ababa', in Y. Gebre, F. Assefa and A. Fekade (eds.) *Customary Dispute Resolution in Ethiopia, Vol. 2*, Addis Ababa: EACC, pp. 241-60.

Avruch, K. (1998) *Culture and Conflict Resolution*, Washington, DC: United States Institute of Peace.

----------(2003) 'Type I and type II errors in culturally sensitive conflict resolution practice', *Conflict Resolution Quarterly*, Vol. 20, No. 3, pp. 351–71.

Birhan, A. (2011) 'Yamare Fird [customary court] in Wogidi and Borena district, South Wollo', in Y. Gebre, A. Fekade and F. Assefa (eds.) *Customary Dispute Resolution in Ethiopia*, Addis Ababa: EACC, pp. 133–56.

Bohannan, P. (1969) 'Ethnography and comparison in legal anthropology', in L. Nader (ed.) *Law in Culture and Society*, Chicago: Aldine, pp. 401–18.

Burton, J. and Dukes, F. (1990) *Conflict: Practices in Management, Settlement and Resolution*, New York: St. Martin's Press.

----------(1990) *Conflict: Resolution and Prevention*, New York: St. Martin's Press.

Civil Code of the Empire of Ethiopia, Proclamation No. 165/1960, *Negarit Gazeta* 19 Year Extra Ordinary Issue No. 2, 5 May 1960, Addis Ababa.

Cuskelly, K. (2011) *Customs and Constitutions: State Recognition of Customary Law around the World*, Bangkok: IUCN.

Debebe, Z. (2011) 'Conflict resolution among the Issa community', in Y. Gebre, A. Fekade and F. Assefa (eds.) *Customary Dispute Resolution in Ethiopia*, Addis Ababa: EACC, pp. 341–69.

Dejene, G. (2011) 'The customary courts of the Waliso Oromo', in Y. Gebre, A. Fekade and F. Assefa (eds.) *Customary Dispute Resolution in Ethiopia*, Addis Ababa: EACC, pp. 251–78.

Deutsch, M. (1973) *The Resolution of Conflict: Constrictive and Destructive Processes,* New Haven: Yale University Press.

Elias, S. and Muradu, A. (eds.) (2013) *Law and Development, and Legal Pluralism in Ethiopia,* Addis Ababa: Justice and Legal Systems Research Institute.

Gebre, Y. (2012) 'Arra: customary conflict resolution mechanisms of the Dassanech', in Y. Gebre, F. Assefa and A. Fekade (eds.) *Customary Dispute Resolution in Ethiopia, Vol. 2*, Addis Ababa: EACC, pp.51–79.

Gebre, Y., Assefa F. and Fekade A. (eds.) (2012) *Customary Dispute Resolution Mechanisms in Ethiopia, Vol. 2*, Addis Ababa: EACC.

Gebre, Y., Fekade A. and Assefa F. (eds.) (2011) *Customary Dispute Resolution Mechanisms in Ethiopia*, Addis Ababa: EACC.

Gluckman, M. (1969) 'Concepts in the comparative study of tribal law', in L. Nader (ed.) *Law in Culture and Society*, Chicago: Aldine, pp. 349–73.

Grande, E. (1999) 'Alternative dispute resolution, Africa and the structure of law and power: The horn in context', *Journal of African Law*, Vol. 43, No. 1, pp. 63–70.

Hicks, J.R. (1930) 'The early history of industrial conciliation in England', *Economica,* No. 28, pp. 25–39.

Hoehl, G. (2004) 'Exploring and understanding conflicts', in *First National Conference on Federalism, Conflict and Peace Building, Organized by the Ministry of Federal Affairs and German Technical Cooperation (GTZ),* Addis Ababa: Ministry of Federal Affairs.

Israel, I. (2011) 'The quest for the survival of the Gada system's role in conflict resolution', in Y. Gebre, A. Fekade and F. Assefa (eds.) *Customary Dispute Resolution in Ethiopia*, Addis Ababa: EACC, pp. 299–320.

Kahsay, G. (2011) 'Mad'a: The justice system of the Afar people', in Y. Gebre, A. Fekade and F. Assefa (eds.) *Customary Dispute Resolution in Ethiopia*, Addis Ababa: EACC, pp. 323–40.

Kane, M., Oloka-Onyango, J. and Tejan-Cole, A. (2005) 'Reassessing customary law systems as a vehicle for providing equitable access to justice for the poor', a paper presented for the Arusha World Bank conference titled '*New Frontiers of Social Policy*', held on 12–15 December.

Kariuki, F. (2015) 'Conflict resolution by elders in Africa: Successes, challenges and opportunities', *Alternative Dispute Resolution*, Vol. 3, No. 2, pp. 30–53.

Koang, T. (2011) 'Dispute resolution mechanisms of the Nuer', in Y. Gebre, A. Fekade and F. Assefa (eds.) *Customary Dispute Resolution in Ethiopia*, Addis Ababa: EACC, pp. 407–34.

Kriesberg, L. and Dayton, B.W. (2012) *Constructive Conflicts: From Escalation to Resolution,* Lanham, Maryland: Rowman & Littlefield Publisher.

Laibuta, K. (2015) 'ADR in Africa: Contending with multiple legal orders for wholesome dispute resolution', *Alternative Dispute Resolution*, Vol. 3, No. 2, pp. 170–80.

LeBaron, M. (2001) *Conflict and Culture: A Literature Review and Bibliography*, Revised edition, Victoria, BC: Institute for Dispute Resolution.

Lederach, J.P. (1995) *Preparing for Peace: Conflict Transformation across Cultures*, Syracuse, NY: Syracuse University Press.

Mamo, H. (2006) *Land, Local Custom and State Policies: Land Tenure, Land Disputes and Dispute Settlement among the Arsii Oromo of Southern Ethiopia*, Kyoto: Shoukado.

Mattei, U. and Nader, L. (2008) *Plunder: When the Rule of Law is Illegal*, Oxford: Wiley-Backwell.

Merry, S. (1988) 'Legal pluralism', *Law & Society Review*, Vol. 22, No. 5, pp. 869–96.

Muigua, K. (2015) 'Empowering the Kenyan people through alternative dispute resolution mechanisms', *Alternative Dispute Resolution*, Vol. 3, No.2, pp. 64–108.

Mutisi, M. (ed.) (2012) *Integrating Traditional and Modern Conflict Resolution Experiences from Selected Cases in Eastern and the Horn of Africa*, Africa Monograph Series, ACCORD. http://accord.org.za/publications/special-issues/994-integrating-traditional-and-modern-conflict-resolution (Accessed 19 December 2016).

Nader, L. and Grande, E. (2002) 'Current illusions and delusions about conflict management: In Africa and elsewhere', *Law & Social Inquiry*, Vol. 27, No. 3, pp. 573–94.

Nader, L. (1993) 'Controlling process in the practice of law: Hierarchy and pacification in the movement to reform dispute ideology', *Ohio State Journal on Dispute Resolution*, Vol. 9, pp. 1–8.

Ogbaharya, D. (2010) 'Alternative dispute resolution (ADR) in sub-Saharan Africa: The role of customary systems of conflict resolution (CSCR)', Paper Presented at the 23rd Annual International Association of Conflict Management Conference Boston, Massachusetts, June 24–27.

Pankhurst, A. and Getachew, A. (eds.) (2008) *Grass-roots Justice in Ethiopia: The Contribution of Customary Dispute Resolution*, Addis Ababa: French Center of Ethiopian Studies.

Rabar, B. and Karimi, M. (eds.) (2004) *Indigenous Democracy: Traditional Conflict Resolution Mechanisms: Pokot, Turkana, Samburu and Marakwet*, Nairobi, Kenya: Intermediate Technology Development Group, Eastern Africa.

Smock, D. (1997) 'Building on locally-based and traditional peace processes', in D. Smock (ed.) *Creative Approaches to Managing Conflicts in Africa: Findings from USIP funded Projects*, Washington, DC: US Institute for Peace.

Tilahun, T. (2007) 'The Legal regime government arbitration in Ethiopia: A synopsis', *Ethiopian Bar Review*, Vol. 1, No. 2, pp. 117–40.

Tirsit, G. (2004) 'Indigenous conflict resolution mechanisms in Ethiopia', in *First National Conference on Federalism, Conflict and Peace Building*, organized by the Ministry of Federal Affairs and German Technical Cooperation, Addis Ababa: Ministry of Federal Affairs, pp. 49–65.

Torgbor, E. (2015) 'Privatization of commercial justice through arbitration: The role of arbitration institutions in Africa', *Alternative Dispute Resolution*, Vol. 3, No. 2, pp. 109–21.

Wallensteen, P. (2012) *Understanding Conflict Resolution*, Third Edition, London: SAGE publications.

Wodisha, H. (2011) 'The Nèèmá: Conflict resolution institution of the Boro-Šinaša', in Y. Gebre, A. Fekade and F. Assefa (eds.) *Customary Dispute Resolution in Ethiopia*, Addis Ababa: EACC, pp. 435–60.

Woubishet, S. (2011) 'Spirit medium as an institution for dispute resolution in North Shoa: The case of Wofa Legesse', in Y. Gebre, A. Fekade and F. Assefa (eds.) *Customary Dispute Resolution in*

Ethiopia, Addis Ababa: EACC, pp. 181–202.

Yewondwesen, A. (2011) 'Yejoka Qic'a: Conflict resolution mechanisms of the seven house gurage', in Y. Gebre, A. Fekade and F. Assefa (eds.) *Customary Dispute Resolution in Ethiopia*, Addis Ababa: EACC, pp. 37-62.

Yilma, T. (2011) 'Mediation and reconciliation among the Wolayita ethnic group', in Y. Gebre, A. Fekade and F. Assefa (eds.) *Customary Dispute Resolution in Ethiopia*, Addis Ababa: EACC, pp. 103–20.

Zartman, W. (ed.) (2000) *Traditional Cures for Modern Conflicts: African Conflict 'Medicine'*, Boulder, Colo: Lynne Rienner Publishers.

Chapter 3

New Challenges for African Potentials in Mediating Conflicts: The Case of Turkana, Northwestern Kenya[1]

Kennedy Mkutu and Augustine E. Lokwang

3.1. Introduction

In many parts of the Greater Horn of Africa which are marginal and underdeveloped, and where states have no capacity to exercise authority, communities have relied on informal systems to protect and adjudicate for conflict management and justice (Menkhaus 2007). Such is the case for the Ateker cluster of pastoralists occupying the borderlands of Uganda, Kenya, South Sudan and Ethiopia, which experience recurrent cycles of resource-based conflict over pastureland and water sources, reciprocal raiding of livestock and pursuit of dominance over neighbours. In the semi-arid savannah, pastoralism or agro-pastoralism are the most sustainable livelihood strategies and rely upon mobility to access pasture and water according to the season (Lamphear 1992). Climatic variability and mobility then become important triggers for resource-based conflict while other contributory factors include the small arms trade, beef trade and state and investor activities (to be explored).

To temper these conflict cycles, many examples can be found of valuable processes to mediate peace and cooperation amongst communities, independent of state mechanisms for law and order. Some of these processes have existed for centuries and serve to limit losses of lives and property, restore peaceful relations, and manage the sharing of land and water resources. Sometimes these processes have been facilitated by civil society organisations in the interests of stabilisation of the areas for development. These processes however, could be challenged by new developments in the Ateker cross-border areas, such as oil exploration and its associated infrastructure, and the recent devolution in Kenya of many functions and budgets to the local level. As the stakes for power and control of the Ateker cluster's oil wealth increase, so locally generated mechanisms for conflict resolution may now be under increased strain.

This work begins by providing a background on existing conflict dynamics in the Ateker cluster; it then examines local conflict resolution mechanisms in general along with their strengths and limitations before looking at the new challenges. The work asks, what could be the impact on local negotiation and conflict resolution mechanisms when political and geo-political forces and powerful external players are at work in Turkana? And if local mechanisms can bring communities together, can this unity help to protect their interests? The work draws on several years of in-depth research in the area, using qualitative methods such as in-depth interviews and focus group discussions with government ministry officials, civil society and faith-based organisation representatives, donor agencies and community members. Media reports have also been used but interpreted with caution, and other documentary sources such as civil society reports have assisted to inform the work. Findings have then been triangulated.

3.2. Background

3.2.1. The Area

The Ateker cluster is composed of interrelated pastoral groups of the borderlands of Kenya, Uganda, South Sudan and Ethiopia. The area traversed by these groups also encompasses the so-called 'Ilemi Triangle', a 10,300–14,000 square kilometre area where Kenya, Ethiopia and South Sudan adjoin and where borders have never been formally agreed. The main livelihood strategy in the arid/semi-arid Ateker cluster area is nomadic livestock herding, which may involve frequent movements across international borders. Mobility may be seen as a finely tuned rational response to ecological patterns but for policy makers it is often viewed as 'backward' and undesirable; hence policy decisions are often insensitive to pastoral livelihoods (Mkutu 2008).

Resource-based conflicts between pastoral groups in the area are frequent and often lethal. Two interacting wider conflict systems involve Turkana pastoralists, namely, the Karamoja (encompassing the Ateker cluster straddling Uganda, Kenya and South Sudan international borders) and the Somali (encompassing the Somali cluster straddling Somalia, Ethiopia and Kenya international borders). Specific current conflicts will be discussed in the sections which follow. Livestock raiding practices and confrontations over land and water have both survival and cultural purposes (such as bride price, establishing one's status and domination over enemy groups). More recently, automatic weapons have been used in conflicts, which have served to increase the scale, frequency and fatality of resource-based conflicts, and to facilitate a commercially driven dimension of raiding livestock for sale on the market (Mkutu 2008). This dynamic makes recovery very difficult because cattle have already been sold, and recovery is an essential part of traditional peace processes between rival groups.

The Kenya section of the Ateker cluster area is Turkana, a large county in the northwest corner of the country. Most of the populations are pastoralist Turkana, closely related to the Jie and Karamojong of Uganda, and numbering around 900,000 (GOK 2011). Many Turkana currently reside in Uganda since migrating in 2006 due to drought. Further, droughts combined with policy failures have made the Turkana perennially dependent upon relief food. In a recent government survey, Turkana ranked the poorest county with 94.3 per cent of the people living in poverty (Omari 2011).[2] Both colonial and postcolonial governments have marginalised Turkana, and formal government administration, and legal and security infrastructure is very thin on the ground, contributing to ongoing reliance upon local or customary mechanisms for law and order, and conflict resolution. Local communities also rely on their own illegally armed community members for policing.

In 2012 Tullow Oil PLC/Africa Oil announced that they had found commercially viable reserves in south Lokichar, Turkana. Exploration activities in this area are the furthest along, and the production phase is expected to start in 2017, with a share in the project now owned by Maersk Oil also. Other Tullow/Africa Oil fields are located in the south and east, while Compañía Española de Petróleos (CEPSA) is exploring in the northwest near the Mogila mountains. Plans for associated infrastructure have been made; those for the oil pipeline are currently suspended but road and rail links are set to transform the Ateker cluster area and other pastoralist areas of northern Kenya, South Sudan and Ethiopia.

3.2.2. Local Conflict Resolution Mechanisms and Pastoral Conflicts

Zartman (2000, p. 7) defines certain cultural conflict resolution practices in the African context which 'have been practiced for an extended period and have evolved within African societies rather than being the product of external importation'. These may be mechanisms for avoiding conflicts, preventing aggressions and tolerating others, and negotiating to attain co-existence, dispute settlements systems such as village and community courts, community-based NGOs and FBOs, and peace initiatives; that is, all knowledge, practices and institutions other than the modern courts. Since most of Africa is rural, where the state has often made little mark on the place or the people, such practices are essential for co-existence.

These practices and structures are rooted in the culture and history of African people and are in one way or another exceptional to each community. Iritongo in Kuria, Njuri Ncheke in Meru, Ekokwa in Bukusu and Turkana, Kokwa in Kalenjin and Monyomiji in Eastern Equatorial west of Kidepo river in South Sudan have been described (Egesa and Mkutu 2000; Heald 2006). In Kuria, Iritongo traditional courts, overseeing *sungusungu* community vigilante was able to reduce rampant cross-border cattle raids and restore peace and trade to the area. Kuria become more 'governable' though the method itself contradicted the structures of modern state (Mkutu 2010). In Eritrea, the community owns land and land tenure is governed by traditional laws and administered under traditional administrative bodies. In the United Republic of Tanzania these mechanisms remain strong and visible in Mara, Iringa, Tabora, and even among the Wasukuma in Mwanza regions as an elder noted. In Rwanda where an estimated 500,000 to one million were killed in the 1994 genocide, the community has revived the *Gacaca*, which has now been domesticated in law to address issues of injustice. Zartman (2000) identifies important elements often common to these mechanisms such as the tradition of forgiveness, respect for elders because of their symbolic authority to enforce decisions and transfer of resources as compensation.

Assefa (2005) notes that African conflict resolution mechanisms quickly respond to crises in terms of time, contribute to the reduction of regular court case loads, save public money, minimise the problem of a shortage of judges who work in the regular courts and overcome budget constraints. They are complementary to modern government structures and are not substitutes or competitors as some government officials think and worry about. They give access to many people who do not find the modern system of conflict resolution comfortable, affordable or suitable to their needs; disputants are satisfied with their operation and view their outcomes as fair, and the like. In the case of Somalia, and in the context of state failure where various powerful players are jostling for position, indigenous mechanisms, some *ad hoc*, others long established, have provided some order where the outsider's eye sees only chaos. In Puntland, Somalia, Sharia courts are enforcing law and order, a welcome novelty for residents who have been deprived of a functioning judicial system for years (Osman 2010).

Local Mechanisms for Peace in Turkana[3]

In times of difficulties (drought or famine) the Ugandan government has often allowed a section of Turkana to move with their livestock into Karamoja District and even further west to the wetlands by the lakes (Lake Alberta) in east central Uganda. It was noted by the member of the county assembly that many Turkana know Uganda as a 'second home' and that this is mainly managed by the elders of Matheniko and Turkana and sanctioned by district administrators through an agreement known as the Lokiriama Accord. The Accord, signed in 1973 has resulted in cooperation between grazing units, marriages and reduction of violence and conflict. Another peace initiative is Nao Day, named after a village south-east of Kotido, Uganda, which involves Kobebe (Matheniko) and Kalosarich (Jie, cousins of the Turkana) in commemoration of a large attack on a Jie *kraal* (a temporary camp of people and cattle) in 1969 in which around 200 people died. In the last two years Turkana,

Jie, Bokora and Matheniko communities have used the anniversary as an opportunity to meet together to promote peace. The governor noted, in a speech in 2014, the existence of other cross-border agreements to promote peace and security.[4]

Civil society and faith-based organisations play an important part in bringing communities together. Administrators and, lately, the Turkana County government have often been involved in cross-border meetings in partnership with civil society and communities.[5] Peace meetings vary in their involvement of communities, however, traditional prayers, community choir performances and dances or exhibitions as well as gifts of produce and crafts are often features of the meetings. Moru Anayeche is one such inclusive function funded by civil society amongst others; in 2014 a choir combined members of different communities and the Turkana County governor washed the feet of the warriors of the Ateker cluster, for purification towards a peaceful future, following which communities washed one another's feet in a curiously biblical act. Moru Anayeche is named after a story of how the Turkana people emerged from the Ateker group; this tells of a girl who ran away from her people and settled in a fertile mountainous area later joined by a man. They were cursed by the community with drought and a nomadic existence and the need to live in caves (*ng'aturkan*) from which the name Turkana is derived. The story is retold to remind Ateker cluster communities of their common ancestry (LOKADO 2014b).

Relations across the internal borders may also be enhanced by intermarriage, trade, shared facilities and individual friendships. The Women Rural Peace Link network in Lorengippi, funded by Practical Action, noted that several Turkana have married in Pokot and, thus, the women try to maintain peace. A trader in *mira* (a mild drug) who travels from Uganda through Turkana to Pokot is sent with greetings and letters to relatives in Pokot. They also sent Kenya Police Reserves (KPRs) (now National Police Reserves known as NPRs) to place green leaves on the road in Pokot as a message to promote peace. Dialogue, sports for peace and exchange visits were other mechanisms noted by the women and others.

3.2.3. Challenges for Local Conflict Resolution Mechanisms

There are different ways in which modern government may interact with traditional institutions and local conflict resolution processes. The former might dominate and squash the latter, or conversely might recognise its value in bringing law and order, particularly in underdeveloped areas. The state might attempt to collaborate with the local systems, which may bring dilemmas in terms of human rights and professionalism as observed amongst the *sungusungu* community vigilante of Kuria (Heald 2006). Collaboration was favoured by former President Moi who frequently consulted with local elders. But as noted by Logan (2008, p. 5) 'Traditional leaders have been banned, disposed and jailed, and they have been courted, coddled and paid state salaries along with just about everything in between ...' (Logan 2008). The state might alternatively abdicate its role completely (Mkutu 2008; Wunder and Mkutu, upcoming) and fail to intervene in a timely fashion when conflict is severe, following which, it may use heavy-handed methods to control insecurity (this has been observed countless times in the Ateker cluster, by both colonial and post-colonial states) (Mkutu 2008).

Augsburger (1992) notes these 'pathways in the ethnic wisdom' for managing conflicts may be lost due to the influence of westernisation. This change, which is currently impacting many African societies may encompass the various components of modernisation, technological advancement, democratisation and the influence of Christianity. These may challenge traditionally patriarchal systems with concepts of human rights and gender rights, while the market economy brings new choices, opportunities and attractions for young people which may lead them to discard traditional systems and values which do not seem relevant, useful or desirable in the new context. Duffield (1997) notes that the elders' authority has been undermined by the introduction of a market economy and the increased polarisation of rich and poor that resulted in labour migration.

Advances in technology, namely, modern weapons have transformed crime and warfare and changed the balance of power within the societies in pastoral areas. As described, the gun has increased the ease with which life can be taken and conflict can be waged. Localised arms races and shady rackets for dealing in arms and cattle have emerged, often with prominent local businessmen and politicians at the fore (Mirzeler and Young 2000; Mkutu 2008). Guns have changed the balance of power, favouring youths and the 'warlords' in charge of them, while the power of the elders has been eroded by runaway lawlessness caused by the gun (Mkutu 2008), leading to youths organising their own raiding parties, as a youth and a pastor both related.

3.3. The New Context, Conflict and Peace

The following sections describe the recent dynamics of conflict, and in some cases, peace in the new context of devolution and the changes brought by the extractive industry. Where possible, the impact on local conflict resolution processes and the potential for these processes within the new context has been considered.

3.3.1. Devolution

In 2013 Kenya enacted a devolved system of government according to the new 2010 Constitution of Kenya, bringing many administrative functions and services, and 15 per cent of the budget under the 47 county governments in a move intended to rectify current inequalities and marginalisation of peripheral parts of Kenya. Counties have indirect roles in security functions through oversight of County Security Committees in which they work with the national government administration and the police, as well as through a body known as the County Policing Authority. Devolution also offers an important opportunity to address the drivers of crime and violence such as marginalisation, underdevelopment and unemployment. A study on the early impacts of devolution on security did however reveal an increase in power struggles and ethnic tensions at the local level, as well as internal border conflicts (Mkutu et al. 2014).

Pre-devolution, elders have been connected with political processes mainly via chiefs who involve them in issues of land and conflict, and this is likely to continue. Peace Committees operating under the national government in several districts since 2001 have also harnessed local mechanisms for conflict resolution, arranging cross-border peace meetings with neighbouring ethnic groups. Since devolution however, their ongoing role is uncertain, and direct funding has been cut, requiring them to apply to the county for funding; in some parts of Kenya they are no longer operating.[6] According to Kenya's 2010 Constitution, peace building is a shared mandate between National Government, and County Government. Civil society and faith-based organisations have also often facilitated and funded local peace-building efforts.

In terms of local mechanisms for negotiation and conflict resolution, devolution has the potential to work with these in a number of ways. County Policing Authorities are forums for public participation and are also tasked to oversee community policing activities. A Peace Ambassador, who is an elder, has been appointed to work with the County Government, and a County Peace Directorate has been created to map and coordinate the peace stakeholders in the county and their activities (Turkana is one of 26 counties which have this structure). The Directorate also places monitors at the kraal level, while the county funds and attends cross-border intergovernmental engagements for peace, and trade links, celebration and commemoration of peace events such as the Lokiriama Peace Accord and Moru Atanayeche amongst others. Lastly, the National Land Commission boards at the local level are compelled to involve elders in land matters, and the boards are chaired by elders.

New Turkana elites (politicians and administrators) are emerging along with devolution and currently seem to be valuing the legitimacy of the elders and local level processes. A county administrator said that devolution is 'bringing the elites home' and also 'bringing back the elder', because the former relies upon the latter in terms of votes or support. The Turkana Professionals Association is an example of this, in the funding of various development projects.

3.3.2. Cultural Change
Turkana society is socially organised around temporary fenced settlements known as cattle kraals with elders making most of the key decisions using a customary code. Decisions of the elders are collectively binding both on all members of the kraal, which is also

the social unit for pursuing traditional mechanisms of conflict resolution. When the kraal structure is weakened by factors such as erosion of herd sizes and composition, urbanisation or general modernisation, the elders' authority too becomes eroded and, as a result, they lose control over the affairs of the kraal leading to a threat to security, unless a quick re-organisation occurs to fill the power vacuum (Mkutu and Wandera 2014). The proliferation of arms in the Ateker cluster has already been shown to challenge the authority of elders as noted (Mkutu 2008). Oil opportunities have led to the diversion of some community security personnel (National Police Reservists (NPRs), volunteers armed by the state to protect their communities), leaders from kraals (some are both NPRs and leaders) and youths. This and the development of Turkana in which the oil and devolution are factors may challenge traditional dispute mechanisms in years to come.

A subcontractor for CEPSA mentioned that in a report by one of the oil companies, some people in the northwest said that they were afraid that oil would bring a 'mini town' and cars to their land, which they did not want as it would disrupt their way of life. People also feared that the influx of outsiders was bringing HIV, prostitution and other harmful lifestyle changes, which was evident in Lokichar, south Turkana. Another cultural issue described by a civil society worker was the disruption of traditional gender roles and marriages as women managed to find work in and around oil installations (usually running small kiosks and cooking meals and snacks) which kept them away from home for several weeks at a time. These social changes are important because they have the potential to lead to social fragmentation and thereby impair traditional mechanisms for peace.

3.3.3. Border Disputes

(a) Turkana–Pokot

County border disputes have become a hot issue since devolution, involving almost half of Kenya's counties, as ethnic communities fight for resources and key installations (Kiplangat 2015). A border conflict between Nandi and Kisumu recently led to seven deaths, and several injuries and displacements (Odhiambo

2016) with nearly 5,000 pupils out of school due to the conflict (Matoke 2016). One administrator called the issue, 'the next big insecurity threat after Al Shabaab' (Musau 2015).

Destructive raiding between Pokot and Turkana has been a relapsing problem for many decades, exacerbated by the influx of arms (Bollig 1990). Conflict resolution mechanisms have included the meeting of elders from the warring groups with ritual sacrifices of animals and cattle recovery or compensation, and hybrid approaches involving elders, civil society and district administrators, as well as disarmament by the Kenya government. Conflict became particularly severe during 2014 with almost daily raiding and road banditry, besieging and burning of villages (which are uncommon forms of intercommunal conflict). A civil society worker documented deaths averaging 12 per month in the first quarter of 2015. Particular incidences include a series of sieges on villages in Turkana, the killings of 21 police officers by bandits in Kapedo in November 2014 and a revenge attack by the Turkana on the Pokot in May 2015 in which 92 people died (Ndanyi 2015). A peace worker and others stated that politicians were inciting and financing aggression, while others commented on the organisation of the Pokot force, suggesting outside assistance. The County Commissioner for Baringo which borders the area commented that recruitment of teenaged boys was being funded by politicians and elites (Koeach 2015). The frequent and consistent pattern of raids and violence was, according to a local administrator, intended to cause forced displacements of Turkana kraals to pave way for the occupation by the Pokot. In one area, a Turkana administrator said that Turkana were successfully forced out, a Pokot chief installed, the place renamed to Akulo, and signs on Turkana Community Development Fund (CDF) projects such as schools were repainted to say that they were funded by West Pokot County Government. As well as devolution, newly harnessed resources, especially oil and gas, are important drivers of this conflict, as numerous respondents from administrators to peace workers and religious leaders noted. A civil society worker reported, 'Pokot are saying "You cannot take the oil alone"'.

The conflict was finally mitigated in 2015 by an inclusive peace process involving politicians directed by national government, kraal leaders, elders and active and reformed warriors from both sides in Turkwel and Lorogon. The Peace Caravan, which started in May 2015, led by 15 political leaders, travelled through the area hosting peace meetings. A researcher described the importance of both politicians and local elders in its success.

The Peace Caravan is currently working since May 2015 … because there is [now] political will. But what is making it strong is the participation of both Pokot and Turkana elders in following up the raided animals and making sure they are returned to the rightful owners. A prominent name here is Loriono from Pokot side and Naperit from the Turkana side. They are ever moving together to maintain peace![7]

During Christmas 2015, a local representative of the media reported,

> For the first time in over 50 years, the warring communities of Pokot and Turkana ate together at the Lorogon border as they celebrated Christmas together. Members of both communities who attended the meeting in their hundreds sang and danced together as elders from both sides assured each other of cooperation to end conflict that has defined the relationship between Turkana and Pokot for decades (Shaanzu 2015b).

A Turkana county government official noted that both Turkana and West Pokot counties have also been collaborating towards peace and recovery of animals, and have trained sub-county and ward administrators in peace building. As of December 2016 however, conflict has flared again, illustrating the volatility of the situation.

(b) The North

The Kenya-South Sudan international boundary is around 320 km long and is often inhabited by nomadic pastoralists from all three countries: Turkana, Toposa of South Sudan and Nyangatom of South Sudan and Ethiopia all use the area, particularly during dry times, which results in cyclical conflict and raids. From January to

December 2015, a peace worker documented the raids by the Toposa against the Turkana at around two per month, with four deaths. Injuries and rapes are not uncommon and up to 600 cattle may be raided at any time. Banditry along the Kenya-South Sudan highway is also rife and related to livelihood needs.[8] The border is reportedly saturated in arms by all accounts. The Toposa have received modern arms from the Sudan Peoples Liberation Army (SPLA) and South Sudan government both pre- and post-secession respectively (Eulenberger 2014). Allegedly many Toposa kraals belong to close relatives in government and the provision of arms to these has been a priority.[9] Eulenberger (2014) concurs on this. Other sources of arms mentioned by civil society workers and chiefs are the Central African Republic, sales by the military to boost their income, refugee flows and Dinka traders. In a stakeholders' meeting it was revealed that a peace agreement between Turkana and Toposa lasted a year from June 2013 and collapsed in May 2014, punctuated by the killings of two Turkana. In a peace meeting arranged by civil society and attended by Turkana and Toposa delegates as well as local administrators, barriers to peace noted included insufficient collaboration between communities in planning and negotiating land access, for reasons which were unclear and that resolutions made in peace meetings are often not followed by communities, suggesting a lack of local ownership. Livestock recovery, which is essential in conflict resolution was mentioned and there was a call for assistance by governments and official security in this and in the apprehension of offenders. Kraal leaders links with politicians were also mentioned (LOKADO 2015).

Border disputes are exacerbated by new mineral and oil finds, which links with political incitement in eastern equatorial state (of South Sudan) (Moro et al. 2011), especially as elections loom closer in 2017. This includes community leaders (of cattle kraals) as a civil society worker noted. That South Sudan administrators are politicians (as opposed to Kenyan administrators who are career civil servants) complicates the situation further, as civil society workers noted that local leaders are tribally affiliated and may own kraals. Similarly the disputed Ilemi triangle seems to have become a hotter issue in the recent past, possibly as a result of oil; in 2012, Kenyan press reports stated that South Sudan had renewed its claims to the Triangle, although the government in Juba denied this (Olick 2012). As noted, tensions at the national and international level do impact upon the local conflict dynamics and could threaten local peace processes.

At the local level, Toposa are attempting to lay claim to parts of Northern Turkana, which were not previously disputed, resulting in increased raids. This may be related to the extractive industry, as noted, 'Toposa allege that the oil and gas is in their area in South Sudan… most of the South Sudan leaders are arguing that the oil fields are in South Sudan'.[10] Other tensions mentioned by a peace worker surrounded the marking of the border by Kenya and the planning of roads. Gas exploration in Lotikipi, oil in Lowerengak and the proposed creation of a wildlife conservancy around the Lotikipi swamp threaten to squeeze pastoralists further and heighten existing demands for land.

Negotiations between Turkana and Toposa for access to pasture and water was, around 10 years ago, an inter-communal affair but now it increasingly takes place at a state and inter-state level. Governors of Turkana county and Eastern Equatorial State of South Sudan have met together on several occasions since 2015, as have national government leaders, to discuss the escalating insecurity on the border (Menas 2015). However these meetings do take place in local settings and are attended by local community members and supported by civil society and faith-based organisations. Local traditions are usually observed (and are similar across the border) such as the ritual slaughter of bulls both for peace and to feed the participants.

(c) Northeast Turkana–Ethiopia border

The Turkana–Ethiopia border is approximately 50 km in length, including its passage through Lake Turkana. The lower Omo valley and delta (around Kibish) and the north of Lake Turkana are home to the Dassenech, Nyangatom (who are also found in South Sudan and in the lower Omo valley) and Turkana. There is conflict between Turkana with both groups, especially the Dassenech. Lethal conflicts between Turkana and Dassenech reached the headlines in 2011 after the Todonyang massacre, in which over 40 Turkana pastoralists were shot as they entered Ethiopia to trade (Ng'asike 2012). The attack was followed by at least 10 other similar killings in the same year, leaving many orphans and internally displaced families, as related by a chief and also a nursing sister. A Catholic father noted,

> There are raids and revenge raids and guns. Revenge is a generational issue; even those who are not affected want to revenge. There is no friendly interaction across the border, no freedom and no exchange programmes. Before the Todonyang massacre there was trade in millet from Ethiopia, and some [Dassenech] students were studying in Lowerengak, but it completely ended.[11]

On Lake Turkana, fishermen and local leaders described conflicts between Turkana and Dassenech which are also frequent and severe, leading fishermen to go with their guns or with NPRs on the lake. Arms are present in great number in the area; a security officer noted that in Ethiopia, the state has armed communities for protection of their livelihoods.

Importantly, the cultures of Dassenech and Turkana are very different, leading to mutual suspicion and hatred. Chiefs complained that the Dassenech must prove manhood by killing an enemy, targeting the Turkana frequently. Peacebuilding activities organised by civil society have been helpful at times, bringing peace between Dassenech and Turkana from 2005–2008, as a civil society worker noted.

An important new challenge for inter-communal relations is the severe pressure faced by the Dassenech from large-scale agricultural and hydroelectric schemes in the Omo valley, forcing them into Turkana (Little 2014). The conflict is further exacerbated by the diversion of the Omo River's flow to Ethiopia's upstream dams (including Gilgel Gibe III), considered the largest hydro-power project south of the Sahara, opened in December 2016 and was funded by the African Development Bank among others. Some hydrologists argue that the agricultural developments resulting from the Gibe III dam allows could reduce flow to Lake Turkana by up to 70 per cent. This would kill ecosystems and greatly reduce the water level of the lake resulting in severe competition for resources for communities downstream in Turkana (Videl 2015).

(d) West Turkana–Uganda border

Turkana's border with Uganda is approximately 250 km long. Groups residing in this area include the Karimojong and their relatives (noted above), the Ik, and the Dodoth (who also move in and out of South Sudan). Civil society groups related that the Turkana have had peace with several groups on this border (Karimojong related groups and Jie of Uganda), for around five years, owing to close family ties and also to peace agreements, especially the 1973 Lokiriama Accord which is the most honoured agreement between many ethnic groups in Karamoja (though not universally honoured). The two governments (Kenya–Uganda) and civil society support these activities.

State and local mechanisms for peace (supported by civil society) can both be observed. Forceful disarmament has taken place on the Uganda side of the border, (Mkutu 2008) and the Ugandan military (UPDF) is stationed on the international border area, prohibiting the Turkana to carry their arms if they move into Uganda and to curb cattle rustling. A civil society worker noted, 'Karamoja was once ungovernable ... but now we have police, prisons and magistrates. ... For the first time police are being distributed to sub-counties. Due to disarmament, police are now able to arrest criminals'. A Father from Torit in Sudan noted that commissioners of the different states are cooperating for conflict management and cattle recovery. At the same time, elders may enforce livestock tracking, recovery and compensation, while civil society groups said that they aim to educate young people against raiding, and faith leaders described the dissolving of barriers between cross-border communities.

A civil society leader was concerned that the large number of nomadic Turkana in Uganda and their 63–70,000 cattle would soon be unsustainable. As in other areas the issue became politicised prior to the 2016 election in Uganda. Politics is also leading to tensions amongst Turkana kraals in Uganda and is derailing peace processes in the cross-border area, as a county administrator noted. He also noted that the county recognises the problem of the swelling Turkana kraals in Uganda and works with communities to promote peace.

Dodoth and Turkana grazing patterns frequently result in conflict, especially during droughts. Civil society workers revealed that some Dodoth managed to hide and escape the disarmament process and use their arms against the Turkana. Stock depletion due to tsetse fly is another trigger for raiding. Peace meetings and agreements over compensation and recovery have apparently assisted in reducing raids between Dodoth and Turkana. Governments of the three countries also met together and attempted to resolve this problem as was noted by civil society workers (LOKADO 2014a).

Near the border lies the refugee camp at Kakuma, established during Sudan's years of internal conflict. Since December 2013 when civil war broke out in the new nation of South Sudan, around 43,000 more refugees have arrived in the camp;[12] the camp has grown to around 150,000 people and is unable to accommodate any more. Thus according to the chief of Kakuma, the United Nations High Commission for Refugees UNHCR is seeking to secure more land at Kalobeyi, around 20 kms from Kakuma. The proposal is opposed by locals, however, who fear, amongst other things, being sucked into the South Sudan civil war, i.e. warriors could regroup on Turkana soil, especially given that South Sudan has territorial claim to Turkana land.

These findings demonstrate how resource and investment, supposed to benefit the region, have brought tension due to inequalities across borders, and increased competition for local resources such as pasture and water to meet livelihood needs, which puts strain on local negotiations for resource sharing. There is a common theme of the role of politicians in both exacerbating conflict and in peace building in collaboration with local communities. The most effective mechanism for peace on the Kenya–Uganda border has been security provision for communities by the Ugandan state, although the locally negotiated Lokiriama Accord also has had an important role.

3.3.4. Local Conflict Resolution and Powerful Players

(a) Investor–Community Tension and Negotiation

There have been considerable tensions between communities and investors, which have focused mainly around land and resources, and jobs and benefits, and raise important issues of participation and conflict resolution. In a large stakeholder meeting in July 2012 in the main town in Turkana (Lodwar), community leaders accused local officials of illegally acquiring title deeds, misappropriating community-owned land and using intimidation and violence to displace communities within the region's oil-rich Ngamia 1 and Twiga South-1 localities. The investor, Tullow Oil, was accused of failing to publicise environmental impact assessment (EIA) reports, paying insufficient compensation to communities, bribing local councillors and leaders as a means of securing control of resource-rich land and outsourcing basic services and expertise, denying jobs to local people (Cummings 2013).

Most of Turkana's land is designated as community land and is held in trust by the county for pastoralist communities, but much of it has now been allocated as oil blocs in agreements with investors. While a relatively small proportion of the allocation is actually explored or drilled, around 13 acres of land is fenced for each well which has at times disrupted seasonal grazing grounds and migration routes, and caused land degradation when acacia trees are cleared. This may result in real livelihood difficulties, high levels of anxiety and added pressure on agreements to share access to land. Water sources may be another problem, although six boreholes have been provided to communities in various parts of the county. Water tanks have also been provided in south Turkana, but an administrator noted that these may disrupt the more established and sustainable grazing patterns by causing people to cluster around them.

According to Tullow Oil, in south Turkana, around half of employees (comprising all the unskilled posts and some semi-skilled posts) are sourced from Turkana communities, along with tenders for driving and supplies of some construction materials and other resources. However, community members still perceive that outsiders are getting preferential treatment. Moreover, as the companies move into new phases of exploration, or withdraw from unprofitable sites, workers may be laid off; inadequate communication with communities and participation processes then lead to increased tension. Once again, the involvement of political elites can make matters worse, as they influence who benefits from opportunities. In south Turkana, Tullow and Toyota Kenya agreed on a scheme of leasing 36 vehicles which would be driven by local drivers for Tullow and eventually would become the property of those drivers, thereby benefitting the local people. However, protestors in a public meeting in February 2015 complained that those who benefitted were the politically linked and that 'the new scheme in Tullow only benefitted the big fish.'[13]

As a result of these tensions, frequent demonstrations, road blocks and attacks have been witnessed around oil sites. In October 2013 violent attacks on the company's site forced them to suspend operations for three weeks and evacuate their non-local staff. An interesting view on the local perception of this event was explained to the author by a county official. In Turkana, foreigners are referred to as either *'emoit'* of the razor, a stranger with whom friendly relations can be maintained, and who is welcome to come and contribute to Turkana, and the *'emoit'* of the spear, who are enemies to be fought. A security officer added that the *'emoit'* in this case is 'not taking goats but is taking opportunities'.[14] When the community demonstrated and invaded workers' camps with pangas and spears, it was noted by a politician that '54 aeroplanes came to ferry the *emoit* away'. These were both non-Kenyans and Kenyans from outside Turkana as a Tullow worker confirmed.

Conflict resolution attempts between the communities and the company have had variable success. Quarterly meetings between Turkana Leadership Forum (representing the community), Tullow Oil and Turkana County Government (*Daily Nation* 2014) were said to be dominated by political figures. District Advisory Committees (DACs) were also criticised for being unrepresentative and being unhelpful because people were dispersed widely and could not attend. *Barazas* (public meetings) organised by the oil company's community liaison officers were said to be rather one-sided, and as a district peace monitor said of the officers, '[They] turn their faces to the company', while community or kraal leaders employed by oil companies as liaison officers may also be compromised by their wage, and fail to represent their communities.

Turkana communities and their leaders in the north of the county, seeing the problems in the south, were able to create a more representative and convenient structure proposed by local community leaders in northeast Turkana. The Local Advisory Committee (LAC) in the northeast includes youth representatives and people from various faith-based organisations (Salvation Army, Catholic and Pentecostal church and Moslem youths) as well as chiefs. A member said that it was able to oversee the distribution of jobs and tenders and hold subcontractors to account for payment of services rendered. Similarly, in the northwest a Community Liaison Committee (CLC) was created to represent all wards to CEPSA. The Chair described how the members had visited the south of the county to understand the successes and failures in the community–investor relations, resulting in the decision that politicians would not be allowed to be representatives. The CLC was instrumental in agreeing favourable terms of engagement with the oil company in which six boreholes would be provided to the community, as one of the subcontractors noted. In its own terms, 'CLC engages, negotiates, mediates, protects the community, protects against environmental degradation, ensures equity in job opportunities and identifies corporate social responsibility projects in consultation with the community and its leadership'.[15] These structures are an example of the capacity amongst communities to create structures for negotiation/conflict resolution that are responsive to the new context.

(b) Inter-clan Conflict

According to various interviews with communities and civil society, the new dynamics brought by the extractive industry in Turkana have also brought conflict between the different Turkana clans, south and north claiming the resources belong to them. In the south in Lokichar basin, a peace worker said that 'Jobs are leading to clanism, because they are often reserved for people from that area'.[16] In the northeast, a Catholic Father noted,

> The oil has split people into clans, saying 'We are the ones supposed to get the jobs'. Last month (February 2015) people in

Lowerengak did not accommodate Kalkol, Lokitaung, Kataboi, …
They claimed that oil is in their place and they should produce the
workers, causing a lot of differences.[17]

According to another Catholic Father,

Last year there were interviews for drivers for Tullow in Lokitaung.
People came from other parts of Turkana, and local youths wanted to
stone them. The chief calmed them down. The chief of Lowerengak
was beaten in the first week of March 2015, and is in hospital, because
of differences in the community. He was protecting his people and
trying to stop people from outside Lowerengak from benefiting.
Outsiders came together with some insiders and beat him.[18]

Youths in Lokitaung also confirmed that the jobs have created
new conflicts amongst the Turkana communities. 'Beneficiaries are
the people living near. When we go, we are chased. That is creating
riots. Local communities do not want people from far'. A senior
administrator noted that the situation is complicated by elite interests,
which influence who is employed and from which ethnic group. A
peace worker concurred, 'Leaders want their own clan or relatives to
get the jobs'. There is a risk that this conflict may escalate as the 2017
election approaches, in which oil and land will almost certainly be
campaign issues. The compensation of certain displaced clans by
Tullow has also led to demands by other clans and inter-clan conflict.
In Lochwaa location near the Etom 1 well in South Turkana, one
clan of Ng'ipong'a enjoyed compensation from Tullow while others
did not.

The Community Liaison Committee previously described in
northwest Turkana was responsible for transparent and equitable
distribution of job opportunities among the seven wards in Turkana
West sub-county; thus employment issues were largely peaceful,
according to a subcontractor. He described how CLCs were
apparently involved in working with chiefs and ward administrators
to recommend suitable personnel for non-skilled jobs, while skilled
personnel were recruited according to their experience. This was said
to be non-discriminatory, since even a person from the Somali clan,

born in Turkana was given a driving job. This demonstrates the value of local mechanisms in maintaining a united Turkana, in the face of potentially divisive forces, allowing benefits to be shared. As the colloquial saying goes in Kenya, 'You cannot eat alone'. This is one of the laudable qualities of African mechanisms for negotiation and conflict resolution, echoed in the term 'African socialism' coined by Nyerere, the first president of Tanzania.

3.3.5. Conservancies, a New Model for Land Sharing and Leadership?

Conservancies are a fairly new development in Kenya over the two decades, created initially in North Rift counties of Laikipia, Samburu and Isiolo. Conservancies may be privately owned, community owned or government owned, and are intended as wildlife havens, enabling protection from poachers by teams of scouts/rangers. These are drawn to a large extent from among the National Police Reserve (NPR) because these personnel are allowed to carry arms (Mkutu and Wandera 2013). An important impetus for the creation of privately owned conservancies was the then soon to expire 100 year leases upon privately owned ranches, such that renewal would be assisted by the demonstration of conservation activities, valuable for Kenya and its tourism industry. Community owned conservancies are registered as not-for-profit companies, trusts or community-based organisations and many of these fall under the umbrella of the National Rangelands Trust (NRT). The NRT was established by a private conservancy in order to extend its expertise and support communities in conservation, security provision and management of conservancies. The trust has the strong support of several donor agencies and civil society organisations, the Kenya government and its parastatals (including Kenya Wildlife Service) and some county governments.

In January 2014, a group of 26 elders from Turkana were hosted by NRT to view conservancies in Isiolo and Samburu and discuss how they might extend this model to Turkana for better grasslands management and cooperation between the various ethnic groups using the same areas. In October 2015 an agreement was reached between NRT and Tullow Oil in which the latter would provide a grant to the former to establish six community conservancies in south Turkana–West Pokot areas in and around the southern and southwestern oil blocks. NRT's CEO noted that this would 'promote peace, manage the rangelands, explore alternative markets for livestock and promote diversification of livelihood activities [which] will help improve lives'. Tullow Oil's country manager noted that it was part of the company's commitment 'aimed at ensuring that the oil and gas sector brings real and long lasting benefits to host communities where we operate and that the impacts of oil development are adequately managed'. According to plans, the conservancies would employ around 180 community members as conservancy management staff and rangers.

The plan was supported by the governor of Turkana as well as other politicians. Initially at the time of writing, however, the county governor had suspended the process due to several concerns raised by stakeholders and members of the county government. A point of contention is that zones traverse disputed Turkana–Pokot boundaries which residents view as a plan to take their land, and also that there has been inadequate participation in planning, since crucial parties such as kraal leaders, kraal commanders and warriors have not been involved.

Conservancies raise important questions about land management, since they propose an entirely new structure for this, in which communities must also negotiate with other stakeholders. Little (2014, p. 66), discussing community, private and government partnerships in conservancies in Kenya (particularly Laikipia) notes,

> While local partnerships may be a worthy goal, they usually reflect very unequal power relations, with the local community often having little clout to negotiate the terms of the partnership. Hence, rather than partnership many of these become patron–client arrangements with the powerful patron company or INGO dictating the terms for the arrangement and monopolizing most of the critical information.

Other criticisms raised by Little (p. 68) include the sometimes exorbitant profits for private business while communities benefited little. Further he argues that the increasing land under conservation represents significant losses of communal pastoral grazing areas and alternative livelihood activities such as dryland farming (p. 75). Mburu et al. (2003, pp. 66–67) show that Kimana Group Ranch members (belonging to a community-based conservancy in Amboseli National Park) who have given some of their best grazing lands to wildlife, still earn considerably more revenue per hectare from pastoralism and agro-pastoralism than they do from wildlife conservation/eco-tourism, because the latter is volatile and not self-sustainable (it depends on outside funding). Moreover, they have little say in the management of the conservancy and the revenues are not equally distributed.

Campbell et al. (2009) note several conflict dynamics that arise from conservancies. First is the attempt to establish a conservancy as a legal entity, which appears to secure tenure for pastoralists to valuable land. However it has been seen to 'exacerbate natural resource conflict dynamics' especially where pasture and water are not evenly distributed. Where access is required by multiple groups from different areas, establishment of a conservancy can also be seen as a 'land grab', which limits access for non-conservancy members. Where a conservancy is formed (commonly) by members of one ethnic group it may polarise and deepen ethnic divides. The same authors refer to Sera conservancy in Laikipia, which was originally a grazing area where communities from neighbouring regions (Rendile, Borana and Samburu) converged during the dry season. The creation of the conservancy has enabled the Samburu to strengthen their security through the use of armed scouts backed up by the NRT, heightening disputes with the other communities who previously shared the area. As they state, 'The formation of conservancies sought to legally define and clarify land ownership, which previously had been shared and arguably ambiguous'. (p. 24). Conservancies, by nurturing wildlife, may also exacerbate human–wildlife conflict, and even attract poachers and fuel arms proliferation (Bond 2014).

Decision-making processes are also altered through conservancies (Campbell et al. 2009). Although effective, concerns exist about management capacity and vested interests in decision-making processes, creating tensions between communities. Importantly *morans* (Samburu or Maasai young male warriors) have not been included despite being the main actors in conflict and the main perpetrators of violence, for whom there is a cultural expectation to war. Decision making at the higher level is said to be largely independent of local government structures, and has few links between the local peace mechanisms and those of conservancy. The failure to connect with and receive support from the government makes the conservancy community conflict-resolution mechanism less sustainable (p. 24).

Therefore, conservancies change the existing dynamics of negotiation between land users (pastoralist communities) and bring in new and powerful stakeholders. They also interrupt existing local arrangements for land management; by pastoralists committing to community ownership of a conservancy this implies limited rights to another. It is not clear how mobility will be negotiated and how this will impact pastoralist livelihoods, conflict and conflict-resolution processes although NRT claim that conservancies assist conflict resolution and shared access. Conservancies also raise security concerns since they create new armed forces with new loyalties, and complicate security governance.

A related issue is the Community Land Act of 2016 which allows communities to register as joint owners of community land. This is an interesting prospect because, again, it requires communities to demarcate the land they need to protect for their livelihood, even though different communities are likely to have overlapping territories and movements are currently subject to constant and ongoing negotiation processes dependent upon the climate amongst other variables. A 'once for all' arrangement may be difficult for communities to decide. Moreover barriers to registration such as illiteracy and lack of knowledge of the law may create a situation where elites can take over the process. The necessary detail on what constitutes 'the community' is missing from the Bill.

3.4. Discussion and Conclusion

The work has examined the traditional pastoral local and cross-border international conflicts in Turkana which have been managed through a collaborative approach (local and national government) continuing amidst new challenges of oil and devolution. Inter-communal relationships are dynamic and move in and out of conflict and peace, dependent upon many drivers and capacities, both internal and external. Survival needs and cultural practices may work in either direction, and while peace might seem desirable to the outsider, war might seem necessary to community members either individually or collectively, in order to re-stock depleted livestock, claim access to land, demonstrate bravery and strength, acquire cattle to marry or to meet the desire or perceived need for a 'righteous' act of revenge. As one pastoralist elder remarked fatalistically on the subject of raiding for bridewealth, 'We found it like this, what should we do?'[19] Likewise there may also come a time when peace seems favourable, or there is a feeling that 'enough' blood has been shed, and community capacities for making peace come into play. This is reminiscent of Novelli's (1999, p. 330) comment about the Karimojong 'Karimojong pragmatism is always ready to re-consider his list of friends and foes, according to the interests of their life'.

External factors such as environmental fluctuations, disease, land alienation by governments and small arms may push the relationship in the conflict direction, while other external influences may do the opposite. New challenges in this context both increase the tensions and risks of conflict, and may interfere with local negotiations and peace processes. Where pastoralist resources are depleted due to displacement by oil or agricultural projects, this puts resource-sharing agreements under unbearable strain. Where resources bring benefits, local people, or more often, elites may dispute about which communities should benefit, and to complicate this, politicians may bring their own dominant agendas and incite conflict directly, or disrupt peaceful arrangements for sharing. The arming of kraals by the South-Sudan government, the border disputes heightened by oil issues, displacement of pastoralists by investors and the investor/civil society agenda of conservancies all have been shown to complicate existing arrangements for sharing of pastoral resources.

Turkana is one of the most marginalised and least developed areas in Kenya, saving the technology of the gun with which many pastoralists are armed. With devolution and investment, economic and social change has been described which could threaten indigenous mechanisms for negotiation and conflict mitigation unless the latter can adapt (with support). Just how this would happen is a question for the county government and its peace ambassador. The opportunity also exists to support local mechanisms for peace. The work also demonstrates a role for local mechanisms in bringing people together to represent their interests to the state and the investor, and to prevent inter-clan conflict where distribution of jobs and benefits of the oil industry is such a divisive issue.

Across county and international borders, the new changes have brought tension, inequality and increased competition for resources such as pasture and water to meet livelihood needs, which has always been an important root cause of pastoral conflict. Under such circumstances, peace is further challenged. The work shows the role of politicians (and the national government) in conflict and then in peace building through the Peace Caravan in consultation with the local communities and other peace activities. The role of the state is also vital in providing security to its citizens as the Ugandan government has done, although local agreements were also a valuable part of this, because an armed cross-border community can potentially fight the UPDF and has done on occasion. Likewise, the issue of commercialised raiding illustrates this simple point about security provision. Without police assistance in quick recovery of livestock, cattle are sold and cannot be recovered, therefore peace will be much more difficult to broker, and the wrong people may be targeted, leading to more cycles of revenge. Therefore a combined effort is needed.

The hottest issue at present in Turkana is the issue of conservancies, which could change the current existing resource-sharing negotiations between land users (pastoralist communities), replacing them with more legally defined areas for groups which may limit mobility and exacerbate divisions. Local leadership may also be weakened and new powerful interested parties may be able to dominate on questions of land use. The same concerns apply to the Community Land Act which plans to issue formal titles to self-defined community groups of land users.

In conclusion, politics, resources, geo-politics, regional conflicts, crime syndicates, non-state security actors such as militias and refugees are just some of the factors complicating local conflict dynamics and increasing the number of players, and dwarfing the authority of traditional systems. While the latter may still have a role in peace processes, they may lack sufficient influence outside of their own localities, and few mechanisms exist to incorporate them into higher level discussions.

So what can we say about the hybridisation or adaptation of traditional governance institutions? Boege (2006) argues, 'We should think of hybrid political orders in which pre-modern, modern and post-modern elements mix and overlap'. Outside funding from western donor agencies has certainly led to an increase in hybridisation efforts, and this work acknowledges that for the most part we are not looking for 'pure' African mechanisms, rather for locally and currently relevant efforts in which people are engaged to secure peace. This work has repeatedly referred to a broader context of peace, as not simply peace-making negotiations to mitigate conflict but, rather, the concept of local conflict resolution mechanisms as providing a structure for equitable distribution of benefits, and in doing so, preventing conflicts. It is important to note that Turkana is being taken down a capitalist path and could lose some of these benefits unless the important elements are maintained. This is in line with the 2010 Constitution of Kenya which states that courts and tribunals should be guided in part by principles of traditional dispute resolution (Cap 10: Section 159). As the stakes rise in Turkana it is important that local people are assisted to understand and participate in the bigger picture so that they can add their perspective and their expertise into negotiations. Where inter-communal conflict exists, there should be hope that local mechanisms, which themselves are not static, but which may evolve to the changing context, may still provide ways to inform and assist conflict resolution. Therefore these may still have value in stabilising Turkana and the cross-border regions.

Notes

[1] This work was made possible by funding from Open Society Initiative East Africa (OSIEA) and Pax for Peace, Netherlands. My thanks go to them to the county and national government administrators and people from civil society and faith-based organizations who have been very supportive. Lastly, thanks go to the reviewers and to Tessa Mkutu for editing the paper.

[2] This definition of poverty is contestable, referring as it does to a cash economy, while Turkana wealth is measured in cattle.

[3] Taken from Mkutu and Wandera (2014)

[4] See http://northriftnews.com/turkana-governor-josephat-nanok-delivers-3rd-state-of-the-county-address

[5] See LOKADO 2014a, b, 2015.

[6] See http://www.nscpeace.go.ke/nsc/

[7] E-mail correspondence with Dr Darlington Akibwai, 16 January 2016.

[8] A participant of the Pax for Peace partners meeting, a Catholic father from Torit in Southern Sudan was apprehended by bandits on his journey in a private car. Thankfully he was unharmed, although shaken.

[9] Interview, Professor with extensive research in the area, name withheld. He also commented that population growth in both animals and human beings could explain why the Toposa have become aggressive and demanding Nadapal. It is difficult to explain the increase in population but this could be partly due to the end of the war with the north hence IDPs returning home.

[10] Interview with representative from LOKADO, Lokichoggio, 23 February 2015

[11] Interview, Catholic Father, Lokitaung, 12 March 2015

[12] The camp has refugees from Somalia, Ethiopia, Burundi, Democratic Republic of Congo, Eritrea, Uganda and Rwanda

[13] Comment made in a *baraza* between.

Tullow/Community/Government public meeting, 13 February 2015

[14] Interview, former security officer, 23 February 2014

[15] Terms of engagement between CEPSA and the CLC, provided by Chair of CLC for Turkana West.

[16] Comments from a peace worker, Diocese of Lodwar, Lokichoggio, Pax for Peace partners' meeting.

[17] Interview, Catholic Father, Lowerengak, 10 April 2015.

[18] Interview, Catholic Father, Lokitaung, 12 March, 2015.

[19] A Karimojong elder in Nakapiripirit in 2001.

References

Assefa, H. (2005) 'Reconciliation, challenges, responses and the role of civil society', in P. van Tongeren, M. Brenk, M. Hellema and J. Verhoeven (eds.) *People Building Peace 2, Successful Stories of Civil Society*, London: Lynne Rienner, pp. 637–45.

Augsburger, D. (1992) *Conflict Mediation across Cultures: Pathways and Patterns*, Westminster: John Knox Press.

Bond, J. (2014) 'Conflict, development and security at the agro-pastoral, wildlife nexus: A case of Laikipia County, Kenya', *Journal of Development Studies*, Vol. 50, No. 7, pp. 991–1008.

Boege, V. (2006) 'Traditional approaches to conflict transformation: Potentials and limits', in *Berghof Handbook for Conflict Transformation*, Berghof Research Center for Constructive Conflict Management, Berlin, http://www.berghofhandbook.net/documents/publications/boege_handbookII.pdf (Accessed 12 February 2016).

Bollig, M. (1990) 'Ethnic conflicts in north-west Kenya: Pokot–Turkana raiding', *Zeitshrift für Ethnologie*, No. 115, pp. 73–90.

Campbell, I., Dalrymple, S., Craig, R. and Crawford, A. (2009) *Climate Change and Conflict: Lessons from Community Conservancies in Northern Kenya*, Conservation Development Centre, International Institute for Sustainable Development, Saferworld.

Cummings, R. (2013) 'Kenya: Predicting Africa's next oil insurgency – the precarious case of Kenya's Turkana County', *Think Africa Press*, 13 September 2013.

Daily Nation (Nairobi) (2014) 'Tullow, county agree on how to end dispute', 2 May 2014.

Duffield, M. (1997) 'Ethnic war and international humanitarian intervention: A broad perspective', in D. Turton (ed.), *War and Ethnicity: Global Connections and Local Violence*, Rochester, NY:

University of Rochester Press.

Egesa, J. and Mkutu, K. (2000) *The Proliferation of Small Arms Control and Management through Indigenous Approaches: The Case of the Sungu Sungu Experiences*, African Peace Forum (APFO) and International Resource Group (IRG).

Eulenberger, I. (2014) 'Gifts, guns and governance: South Sudan and its southeast', in S. Calkins, E. Ille and R. Rottenburg (eds.), *Emerging Orders in the Sudans*, Bamenda: Langaa RPCIG, pp. 153–96.

Heald, S. (2006) 'State, law and vigilantism in northern Tanzania,' *African Affairs*, Vol. 105, No. 419, pp. 265–83.

Government of Kenya (2011) *National Policy for the Sustainable Development of Northern Kenya and Other Arid Lands*, Nairobi: Government Printers.

Kiplang'at, J. (2015) 'Senate proposes tough law to end boundary disputes that threaten to derail devolution', *Daily Nation*, 10 September 2015.

Koeach, F. (2015) 'Child warriors initiated into banditry', *Daily Nation* (Nairobi), 21 June 2015.

Lamphear, J. (1992) *The Scattering Time: Turkana Responses to the Imposition of Colonial Rule*, Oxford: Oxford University Press.

Little, P. (2014) *Economic and Political Reform in Africa: Anthropological Perspectives*, Indiana: Indiana University Press.

Logan, C. (2008) 'Traditional leaders in modern Africa: Can democracy and the chief co-exist?', Working Paper No. 93, *Afrobarometer*, Ann Arbor, MI: University of Michigan.

LOKADO (2014a) *Proceedings of the Cross Border Intergovernmental Consultative Meeting*, held at Kaabong District Hall on 20-24 February 2014.

----------(2014b) *Proceedings of the Moru Anayeche Peace Commemoration*, held at Nakapelimoru in Kotido on 21 December 2014.

----------(2015) *Proceedings of the Cross Border Peace Dialogue Meeting between Toposa and Turkana*, held in Lokichoggio on 31 December 2014.

Matoke, T. (2016) '5,000 pupils out of school following clashes in Nandi, Kisumu counties', *Daily Nation* (Nairobi), 12 January 2016.

Mburu, J., Birner, R. and Zier, M. (2003) 'Relative importance and determinants of landowners transaction costs in collaborative wildlife management in Kenya: An empirical analysis', *Ecological Economics*, Vol. 45, No. 91, pp. 59–73.

Menas Associates (2015) 'The fight for Turkana's resources continues', *Menas News*, 1 April 2015, https://www.menas.co.uk/the-fight-for-turkanas-resources-continues/.

Menkhaus, K. (2007) 'Kenya Somalia border conflict analysis', Development Alternatives Inc., http://www.somali-jna.org/downloads/Kenya-Somalia%20Menkhaus%20(2).pdf.

Mirzeler, M. and Young, C. (2000) 'Pastoral politics in the northeast periphery in Uganda: AK-47 as change agent', *Journal of Modern African Studies*, Vol. 38, No. 3, pp. 407–29.

Mkutu, K. (2008) 'Disarmament in Karamoja, northern Uganda: Is this a solution for localized violent inter and intra-communal conflict?', *The Round Table: The Commonwealth Journal of International Affairs*, Vol. 97, No. 394, pp. 99–120.

----------(2010) 'Complexities of livestock raiding in Karamoja', *Nomadic Peoples*, Vol. 14, No. 2, pp. 87–105.

Mkutu, K. and Wandera, G. (2013) *Policing the Periphery: Opportunities and Challenges for Kenya Police Reserves*, Report, Geneva: Small Arms Survey.

---------(2014) 'Crime and violence amongst the Turkana of northwest Kenya', in *Studies in Crime and Violence Prevention in Kenya: A Tool for Training,* Kenya School of Governance, United States International University, and Open Society Initiative East Africa, Nairobi, pp. 66–85.

----------(2015) *Conflict, Security and the Extractive Industries in Turkana Kenya: Emerging Issues*, Report, USIU-Africa and KSG and DDG.

Mkutu, K., Marani, M. and Ruteere, M. (2014) *Securing the Counties: Options for Kenya after Devolution*, Nairobi: Centre for Human Rights and Policy Studies.

Moro, L., Akec, J. and Mekalilie, B. (2011) 'Scrutiny of South Sudan's oil industry: Community relations, labour practices and impact on land use patterns', Utrecht: Pax for Peace and European Coalition on Oil in Sudan, p. 17.

Musau, N. (2015) ''Declare border rows a national disaster' leaders say', *Standard* (Nairobi), 24 April 2015.

Ndanyi, M. (2015) 'Kenya: 92 feared dead in Turkana, Pokot fighting in Baringo', *Star* (Nairobi), 6 May 2015.

Ng'asike, L. (2012) 'Insecurity: High number of orphans is the order of the day in Todonyang', *Standard* (Nairobi), 22 October 2012.

Novelli, B. (1999) *Karimojong Traditional Religion: A Contribution*, Kampala: Comboni Missionaries.

Odhiambo, M. (2016) 'Death toll rises in Nandi Kisumu border clashes', *Daily Nation* (Nairobi), 10 January 2016.

Olick, F. (2012) 'South Sudan denies claims on Ilemi triangle take over', *Standard* (Nairobi), 23 August 2016.

Osman, A.A. (2010) 'Order out of chaos: Somali customary law in Puntland and Somaliland', *Accord*, Issue 21.

Omari, E. (2011) 'Named: Kenya's richest and poorest counties', *Daily Nation* (Nairobi), 17 December 2011.

Shanzuu, I. (2015a) 'Leaders trade accusations during Turkwel peace caravan visit', *Standard* (Nairobi), 26 May 2015.

----------(2015b) 'Pokots, Turkanas mark first peaceful fete in decades' *Standard* (Nairobi), 28 December 2015.

Videl, J. (2015) 'Ethiopia dam will turn Lake Turkana into "endless battlefield", locals warn', *Guardian* (Nairobi), 13 January 2015.

Wunder, L.C., and Mkutu, K. (upcoming). 'Policing where the state is distant: Community policing in Kuron, South Sudan', in K. Mkutu (ed.), *Security Governance in East Africa: Local Perspectives*. Lanham, Maryland: Lexington Books.

Zartman, I.W. (2000) 'Introduction: African traditional conflict "medicine"', in I.W. Zartman (ed.), *Traditional Cures for Modern Conflicts. African Conflict 'Medicine'*, Boulder, Colarado: Lynne Rienner, pp. 1–11.

Other Documentary Evidence

Letter from Chief of Loima to OCPD for Loima, ref LOI/L&O/Vol 1/12 dated 30 July 2012.

Chapter 4

Negotiating Statehood:
Handling the Crisis of South Sudan

Samson S. Wassara and Eisei Kurimoto

4.1. Introduction

South Sudan had barely matured when the country drifted into rebellions marked by the emergence of various armed groups. The political environment of violence distracted leaders of the country from state building and nation building to negotiating survival of the state with the main rebel movement and a host of other armed groups. Potentials of South Sudan to create a peaceful environment for development were consumed by negotiations and the search for political and social stability, which are a crucial for a viable state thriving in peace with itself and its neighbours. The relevance of this paper lies in its attempt to explain why and how South Sudan's negotiating efforts are overwhelmed by recurrent violence in communities.

Consequently, the government has simultaneously been negotiating with the main rebel group and with other armed groups inside the country. They have created unfavourable socio-political environments in different parts of the country; thus engaging the government in negotiations of their local grievances. This situation leaves researchers to grapple with answers to questions about the political and social situation of a country, which is yet to exercise its full sovereign authority after independence from Sudan. Why and how did the country get engulfed in political disorder to the extent of threatening statehood? What kind of national and local grievances are subject to negotiation of statehood in South Sudan? To what extent could confidence be built between political leaders to ensure conflict prevention? Most importantly, who are the actors involved in negotiating statehood of South Sudan?

The purpose of this study is to examine those essential elements of statehood of South Sudan that are threatened by multiple on-going crises. South Sudan is already a state by virtue of the Montevideo Convention of 1933 (Wassara 2015, pp. 637–39), although some ingredients of sovereignty and effective territorial control remain questionable. Negotiating the country's statehood centres on two of the four elements of a state: the government and sovereignty. Other associated elements such as power, identity, ethnicity and wealth are explored further to find out how they relate to violent politics. This is where the relevance of negotiating statehood needs to be anchored in the elite class and in grassroots communities.

This study focuses also on the on-going conflicts, which threaten not only the state, but also human security and livelihoods in South Sudan. The intensity of conflicts is felt both in the government and in the rural or urban communities. The methods used for examining conflicts that threaten statehood of South Sudan are threefold. The first method used in this research is the event data research. This tool of analysis is event data analysis. The latter involves identification of conflict locations and then tracking conflict events, which may include fatalities and other associated consequences of conflict (Daoust 2015, pp. 1–4). Secondly, the method of observation is applied. The authors of this paper have observed South Sudan's conflicts, processes of negotiations and reactions of a variety of stakeholders over a period of time and at the two levels: the macro-politics of the state and grassroots communities in the country. Finally, conflict analysis constitutes an important tool for understanding of dynamic relations between the government and communities at the sub-national level. While Sudan People's Liberation Movement/Army (SPLM/A) factional conflicts are negotiated under the auspices of the Intergovernmental Authority for Development (IGAD) with occasional involvement of the African Union (AU), many grassroots communities have engaged in negotiating inter-communal local grievances at the level of sub-national government authorities.

This study finds that those negotiations under the IGAD mediation were sluggish and not yielding expected outcomes because some member states of the organisation were directly or indirectly part of the problem of South Sudan. Negotiations dragged on for years because of deep mistrust among factions of the SPLM/A. Another finding is that the government of South Sudan neglects its role of maintaining law and order at national and sub-national levels. Little attention is paid to grassroots conflict resolution, inter-communal reconciliation and social healing. Potentials of the state and the people to address conflicts threatening the very existence of internal sovereignty are constrained by attitudes and actions of the political elites. Moreover, the government leaves narrow space for domestic actors to creatively reconstruct credible governance systems and institutions at both the national and sub-national levels so that social relationships are in-built for the survival of the state to exercise its authority (Kurimoto 2012; 2014).

Our study concludes that independence was achieved under the leadership of the SPLM/A without intra-party harmony or substantial social healing in communities, thus plunging South Sudan's statehood into serious doubts about its viability and sustainability. The unity witnessed during the referendum conducted in January 2011 evaporated soon after independence of the country as factional politics came into play over power and control of resources. Therefore, enhancing South Sudan's potentials to overcome political and social instability requires more work on behaviour change in communities to embrace sustainable confidence-building, reconciliation and peaceful coexistence.

4.2. The Concept of African Potentials with Relevance to South Sudan

Discourses on social and political disorder in Sudan and the Horn of Africa have been familiar in scholarship over decades, long before the independence of South Sudan. Past civil wars in the region spilled over into neighbouring countries leading to different levels of negotiations. Particular emphasis is put on Sudanese civil wars that had been negotiated in capitals of countries of the region such as Ethiopia and Kenya, which mobilised their potentials to pursue decades of mediation of Sudanese conflict (Abraham 2006, pp. 158–60). This paper avoids, however, dwelling much on negotiation processes of the past civil war, but concentrates on negotiating the post-independence crises that unleash a host of challenges to the statehood of South Sudan.

Conflicts that challenge the statehood of the country are mostly internal and structural but with serious consequences for neighbours and the international community. Destabilisation of the country's statehood has its immediate origins in the government and party structures with unclear delineation power limits, procedures and hierarchies in the political system. But earlier than that, conflicts were also traced back to the persecution of the war of liberation by the SPLM/A characterised by the division of the movement into the Nasir faction and the Torit faction in 1991.[1] The interim period of the Comprehensive Peace Agreement (CPA) saw ideological contradictions, individual and group animosities, and competitive factional leadership in SPLM/A. These relationships played an adverse role in the formation of South Sudan as a state. People of the then Southern Sudan united to vote for independence in the referendum of January 2011. They got the independence but their aspirations were soon betrayed by an aggressive competition for leadership and power in less than three years.

The question we pose here is how was the idea of African potentials relevant to South Sudan's political development after independence? African potentials, as a research tool for analysis of peaceful coexistence, reconciliation and social healing emerged to address many conflicts in different parts of Africa. The launch of the African Forum in Nairobi in 2011 came about when South Sudan was experiencing different forms of conflict. The nature of conflicts was related to the struggle of militia groups left behind by the Juba Declaration of January 2006 (Young 2006), which enabled Southern Sudan Defence Forces to integrate into the SPLA. According to the Armed Conflict Location in Africa Database (ACLED) data, conflict events were already escalating during the period 2010–2011 and intensified in 2013 (Daoust 2015, p. 1). The reason for conflict escalation was associated with the absence of reconciliation forums, insensitivity of the government to intra-community tensions and lack of protection of citizens from external threats like the Lord's Resistance Army (LRA). The Nairobi African Forum of 2011 provided an opportunity for researchers and policy makers to begin thinking seriously about how to relate tools of African potentials to issues of statehood of the newly independent South Sudan.

Realities of African potentials as a research tool and a method of analysis became more relevant to the situation of South Sudan and the neighbouring countries during the 3rd African Forum, organised by Eisei Kurimoto, that took place in Juba on 6 –8 December 2013 in Juba. The Forum addressed the escalation of violence at different levels of society. Despite the independence of South Sudan, armed conflicts continued to ravage the countryside while peaceful coexistence was absent in most communities of South Sudan. The Juba Forum paved the way for discourses of peace from perspectives of scholars and policy makers. It is against this background that organisers of the Forum invited African, Japanese and South Sudanese scholars to reflect together on different dimensions of the problem. Participants in the Forum were not only academics and scholars, but many policy makers, legislators and leaders of faith-based organisations contributed effectively to discourses on South Sudan and cross-border experiences. South Sudanese and Japanese researchers expounded their findings on internal and external dynamics of armed conflicts, peace building, reconciliation, case studies and views across national borders. Most presentations made by South Sudanese during the Juba meeting sharpened the understanding of the problems of South Sudan at independence in July 2011.[2] The Juba meeting was timely and conflict did not take long to explode into a deadly violence on 13 December 2013.

4.3. Overarching Contextualisation of Situation

The Horn of Africa was characterised by political and social disorder of which the Sudan was one of the contributors before South Sudan became independent. Scholars (Abraham 2006, pp. 13–20; Woodward 2013, pp. 18-50; Johnson 2003) analysed the nature and evolution of the disorder dating back to many decades. Their studies postulated that conflicts in the region have spill-over effects across national boundaries that invite discord among countries of the region. This situation continued during the long civil war of the

111

Sudan waged by the SPLM/A. The war used to inflame acrimonious relations between Sudan and Ethiopia as well as between Sudan and Uganda during different stages of political developments in the region. Countries of the region used their potentials to engage in the decade-long mediation of the Sudanese conflict under the auspices of the IGAD that culminated in the CPA signed in Nairobi in 2005. The conclusion of the CPA marked the new beginning of the internal negotiation of state sovereignty of South Sudan, especially after this country achieved independence on 9 July 2011.

South Sudan was born into a situation of politically fragmented society caused by protracted civil wars. The CPA interim period was marked by the phenomenon of militia groups that were either 'integrated' into the SPLA or stood out to later claim inclusion into the army on the basis of patronages after South Sudan was already independent (Wassara 2010, pp. 275–277). Those who did join the SPLA under the terms of Juba Declaration of January 2006 enjoyed privileges such as high ranks in the SPLA and others saw themselves in high ranking political and civil service positions. Most significant among militia groups was the South Sudan Defence Force (SSDF) under the leadership of Paulino Matip Nhial, which was formerly sponsored by the Khartoum government to fight the SPLA during the civil war in the then Southern Sudan.

The process of absorption of the SSDF into the SPLA brought about not only new problems in the territorial and command structures, but also created fear of infiltration of militia groups loyal to military intelligence of the Sudan Armed Forces. State boundaries did not limit SPLA formations and the army is very much centrally controlled at its headquarters in Juba. Military formations were spread throughout South Sudan creating communication and logistical challenges. The need to absorb and integrate 17 major generals of the SSDF within the framework of the Juba Declaration of 2006 resulted in a split in the ranks of the SPLA senior commanding officers. They wanted to differentiate themselves from the absorbed officers. This prompted promotions into higher ranks in the SPLA, which corresponded to the creation of new structures. The senior core officers of the SPLA were promoted to the status of lieutenant- generals in 2009. The massive integration of other armed groups besides the SSDF into the ranks of the SPLA diluted its initial capabilities and capacities at the time of signing the CPA (Rands 2010, pp. 9–12). The inclusion of militia groups into the SPLA increased illiteracy in the military, a factor, which eventually contributed adversely to negotiation of statehood during political crises.

Despite opportunities the Juba Declaration of January 2006 provided for the inclusion of militia groups into the SPLA, a significant number of militia groups held out while continuing to pay their allegiance to the Sudan Armed Forces.[3] When South Sudan gained independence militia groups became isolated, but devised a method of comeback by launching political and armed movements against the government of Juba. An example was the South Sudan Democratic Movement and its armed wing, the South Sudan Democratic Army (SSDM/A).[4] For the sake of unity of South Sudan, the government entered into negotiations that culminated in a series of amnesties and inclusion of a variety of militia groups especially from the Upper Nile region into the organised forces.[5] Scholars (Jok 2015, pp. 6–8) argue that this policy encouraged the 'big tent' approach that involved political and military patronages such as inclusion into the state apparatus. This policy is identified as the source of future violent conflicts after independence of South Sudan. The militia groups thus absorbed changed the political structure of the SPLM/A in later events. They were the core stakeholders in negotiating statehood after the event of December 2013 in Juba. As do critiques of many scholars flow, Jok Madut articulates the shortcoming of the 'big tent' approach to absorption inter alia:

> This was a peace buying approach, prioritizing compromise over the state monopoly on the use of force on armed non-state actors. After all, these actors had been part to the conflict, excluded from the peace negotiation with Khartoum and were expected to be accommodated in the final political settlement, or they become spoilers. This approach was commended and praised by many citizens and peace advisors who wanted the chapter of military rivalries to close and once for all, now that the country was working towards its independence and consolidation of its sovereign existence. However,

this policy backfired in so many ways. It contributed to the creation of a monstrous and unwieldy army, too undisciplined to maintain a coherent chain of command and unwilling and incapable of reform (Jok 2015, p. 1).

Martial attitudes and actions in the wake of independence represented an aggressive search for inclusion into the political system and institution. As mentioned earlier, militia groups were proving to be spoilers of a stable and peaceful South Sudan. In the light of mini-rebellions by disgruntled non-state actors, the government under the leadership of President Salva Kiir reverted to the African value of forgiveness and accommodation. This potential of conflict resolution worked for the short-term, but became later the trigger of violence. Astill-Brown (2014, pp. 8–11) provides a similar critique like Jok Madut, but adds another dimension. He argues that:

> Following the CPA, Salva Kiir pursued a policy of offering armed militias amnesty and integration into the SPLA. While ending some insurgencies, this strategy also undermined the professionalism of the army by giving senior ranks to the leaders of disloyal units without establishing command and control through proper integration and training. The national army swelled along distinct ethnic lines, which contributed to its fracture when the conflict erupted in December 2013 (Astill-Brown 2014, p. 8).

Issues in negotiating statehood are both external and internal. The former came into the picture when South Sudan claimed sovereignty over its natural resources – mainly the oil. The linkage of the border between the Sudan and South Sudan was juxtaposed to natural resources such as water and pastures in the contested border regions. Claims and counter-claims of oil theft by the Sudan and the ownership of the Heglig oilfield led to border skirmishes between the two countries in April 2012 (Silva 2014, pp. 73–5). The situation was seen in South Sudan as an attempt to undermine its national sovereignty by Sudan. Negotiations ensued under the auspices of the AU, which resulted in the Cooperation Agreement between Sudan and South Sudan signed on 27 September 2012 in Addis Ababa

(Conflict Risk Network 2012, pp. 2–9). Most provisions of this agreement did not materialise, but remain to be a talking point in diplomatic relations between Sudan and South Sudan. The inertia in resolving border issues and natural resources conflict is much more influenced by the ambiguous status of the SPLM/A forces in Blue Nile and the Nuba Mountains regions of the Sudan. The same applies also to the movements of Darfur rebels like the Justice and Equality Movement (JEM), the Sudan Liberation Movement/Army (SLM/A) and the Sudan Revolutionary Front (SRF) in the border regions to the west of both countries (Wassara 2015, 640–642; Daoust 2015, p. 6). Although the post-secession conflict with Sudan affects the sovereignty of South Sudan, the main focus of this study is about the internal political dynamics of South Sudan before and after the flare-up of violence on 15 December 2013, which resulted in carnage around Juba, Bor, Bentiu and Malakal. These events and the subsequent violence tested African potentials to mediate and promote dialogue between factions of the SPLM/A In Opposition (IO), the Former Detainees (FD) on the one hand and the SPLM/A in Government (IG) on the other.

The rise of factionalism within South Sudan is also of far-reaching consequence. It results from the very nature of a highly decentralised and tribal society, the prevalence of martial values, a culture of cattle raiding, the widespread illiteracy, and enduring conflict between pastoralists and peasants. Moreover, in the absence of a strong commitment to ideology, or leadership by a class, ethnicity and regionalism has been the mainstay of political organisations such as the SPLM, and the emerging political parties. Throughout the interim period and since the independence of South Sudan, a number of studies (Hutton 2014, pp. 13–15; Astill-Brown 2014, pp. 3–6; Radon and Logan 2014, pp. 147–167; LeRiche and Arnold 2012; Thomas 2015) indicate that regionalism, ethnicity, tribalism and factionalism far outweigh institutional mechanisms for employment, access to power and other opportunities within South Sudan. Even private enterprises are not immune to family and tribal connections that dictate hiring and firing practices of most businesses. Thus, internal conflict drives aggressive competition resulting in erosion of sovereign authority of South Sudan more than external conflicts with Sudan. One scholar described the role of tribalism in fomenting internal conflict as follows:

> No less critical than its external conflict with Sudan is South Sudan's myriad of domestic challenges. The basic problem stems from the disparate tribal societies that constitute South Sudan's population. It is estimated that the country is comprised of more than sixty distinct cultural and linguistic groups, each of which have strong tribal loyalties (Silva 2014, p. 78).

The signing of the CPA ushered in a new era, one that envisioned a democratic multi-party system. However, after two decades of civil war a yet uncertain political landscape was emerging for political participation and competition. The SPLM/A, by virtue of being the signatory to the CPA, dominated the political arena. Also, a host of new political parties entered the political stage in order to participate in the government and the legislature.[6] However, scepticism reigns over whether these parties could rise to the democratic challenge of representation or whether they only represent an elite fractionalisation in pursuit of control over public sector resources and wealth. While political competition in South Sudan has largely been defined by ethnic politics, it is also motivated by systemic patronages. Ethnicity and regionalism contribute to the proliferation of political parties based on unsustainable political ideologies that allow political parties to organise around personalities instead of programmes. Some principles of the CPA were not in conformity with democracy building, but upheld beliefs of the principal signatories of the agreement, which were the NCP and the SPLM. So, to date ordinary people, including the parliamentarians, are still unable to exercise significant influence over political elites in the executive branch of the government. Besides the SPLM, groups of individuals have constituted themselves into political parties without proven mandates of an electorate. Instead community councils, tribal associations and region groupings of South Sudan are substituting political parties to influence governance.[7] The competition for power under the current political system is based on institutionalised elitism, ethnicity, participation in underground movements and the military.

These same characteristics have also been important criteria in the selection of people for government positions.

South Sudan has become famous for protracted civil wars. Many thinkers believe that leaders of the country and their unconscious followers are to blame for the brutality of senseless wars and mishandling civilians who are victims of societal moral decay and psychological weaknesses. They care more about grabbing power at any cost than caring about citizens (Kussala 2015, pp. 20–1). The very fact that many non-state armed groups in the post-independence era were fighting for power or patronages meant harmony was a distant principle of peaceful coexistence and reconciliation. The split of the SPLM/A into hostile camps invited serious mistrust among leaders of the movement despite those reconciliation efforts that brought back Riek Machar and Lam Akol into the SPLM/A in 2002 and 2003, respectively. The persistence of armed conflict in South Sudan after independence is explained by the drive of politico-armed factions to control power as the means of controlling economic resources (CIGI 2010, p. 5). This is the point where the issues of exclusion and inclusion met to inflame factional competition in the class of political and military elites over leadership of South Sudan. The potentials of the ruling party, the SPLM, to create an environment of peace, coexistence and reconciliation were hampered by multiple crises at the national level (Jok 2015, pp. 8–9).

4.4. Handling Statehood under Threat of Rebellion

South Sudan's slide into civil war soon after independence was the result of multiple crises resulting from indifference of the society to simmering problems of leadership and legitimacy. Many crises cropped up in 2013, which were left to evolve without interruption. There was a total absence of national civil society organisations, other national political parties and regional actors to initiate potentials for trust building, reconciliation and healing in the hierarchy of the ruling party before and after independence. IGAD mediators forgot about the fate of South Sudan once the CPA was signed and more when South Sudan got independence. It was only when the violence erupted that a team of envoys or mediators, consisting of Kenyan and Sudanese nationals under the chairmanship the Ethiopian foreign minister, was constituted.

For example, the power struggles and conflict within the leadership of the SPLM/A were left to escalate uninterrupted. The SPLM publicised its plans to hold a National Convention in May 2013. The Deputy Chairman of SPLM, Riek Machar, declared his intention to run for leadership of the party. This did not augur well for party Chairman, Salva Kiir. He suspended the holding of the Convention. Disputes among members of the SPLM's senior executives infiltrated the government and the army. The situation could no longer be tolerated by Salva Kiir who doubled as the party Chairman and the Head of State. He suspended Pagan Amum, the Secretary General of the SPLM. Disputes intensified and paralysed functions of the party resulting in subsequent dissolution of the entire government in July 2013 (Hemmer and Grinstead 2015, pp. 1–4). The army, which had thin boundaries between it and the SPLM, began to crack along regional and ethnic lines.

National, regional and international actors were nowhere near in containing the growing crisis until it exploded into a fierce armed violence when the SPLM National Liberation Council meeting was in full session on 14-15 December 2013. National and regional potentials of preventive diplomacy missed out completely. The divided presidential guards triggered armed clashes at night on 15 December 2013, which lasted for days. The government cried foul, alleging Riek Machar and his group staged a coup d'état. Nuer individuals and families were victims in and around Juba. The cause of the crisis was not ethnic but a crude struggle for power within the SPLM/A as proved by research. This can be seen in the ethnic composition of the eleven individuals who were detained in the aftermath of the alleged coup. Two scholars (Radon and Logan 2014, p. 150) made the following observation: 'Of the eleven politicians arrested by the government in connection with the alleged coup, six of them were Dinkas, two were Nuers, and the other three were from different ethnic groups, thus seemingly negating possible ethnic motivations.'

The crisis escalated very fast and developed into an active rebellion. The states of Jonglei, Upper Nile and Unity were engulfed in a civil war that metamorphosed into ethnic conflict along tribal origins of the SPLM leaders: President Salva Kiir and the former Vice President Riek Machar. With exception of the Church, political parties and civil society organisations that should have intervened to mediate the conflict when it was escalating did little to mount pressure on the fractionised SPLM. The Church attempted in vain to persuade the SPLM to postpone the National Liberation Council meeting. Regional and international actors thought of addressing the crisis only when considerable damage was done to people and their properties. The anticipated potentials of the actors to fix the problem were there only to put out flames of violence when ordinary citizens had already fallen victim to the insane violence. Although it is not the aim of this paper to describe the extent of the damage incurred on the civilian population, the conflict created a new environment of human insecurity. South Sudanese civilians sought protection en masse at United Nations Mission in South Sudan (UNMISS) bases in South Sudan while others fled the country to take refuge in the neighbouring countries. Therefore, handling of the December 2015 crisis and the civil war that ensued can be described as a fire brigade exercise. Both the IGAD and its partners, the national civil society organisations, the AU and the United Nations did not use their potentials to silence the guns.

The split of the SPLM/A after the December 2013 undermined the African potentials to deal with the conflict in order to restore peaceful coexistence and healing both at national and regional levels. Just like the conflict fractured political players in South Sudan, it also fractured peace makers in their attempts to mediate the conflict. The crisis of December 2013 fractured the SPLM/A into three distinctive factional groups. The first group is the SPLM/A in government (IG); the second group in the SPLM/A in opposition (IO) referred to by the government as rebels and the third group is the SPLM former detainees (FD). These identities were confirmed by the IGAD mediators in documentation concerning the crisis. The new landscape of the South Sudan political crisis presented a serious challenge to mediation efforts of the IGAD and its partners. The fragmentation of the SPLM/A influenced attitudes, representation and demands of civil society organisations that participated in negotiations in Addis Ababa. Thus, the potentials to mediate the conflict were always fragmented as will be seen later.

For this reason, those cessations of hostility agreements concluded had no effect on the ground. Such agreements were considered as elites' exercise to buy time for more military confrontations. The agreements seemed to have never trickled down to field commanders. It was observed that the conflict escalated further whenever such agreements were underscored by the negotiating parties in Addis Ababa. On their part, members of the SPLM-FD were busy articulating conflicting points of view on social media and other forums as a result of their exclusion from the negotiating table. Processes of reconciling the three factions became tricky and complex for the IGAD and other regional actors.

Mediators in the IGAD region and beyond found themselves embroiled in the messy negotiations of the South Sudanese crisis. Conflicts of interest crept relatively faster into relations among IGAD mediators as a consequence of the military intervention of Uganda to fight on the side of the South Sudan government. It is believed that Sudan reacted to the Ugandan intervention by covertly supplying military bases, logistics and hardware to the SPLM/A (IO) for operations in Upper Nile (Wassara 2015, pp. 636–7). Sudan and Uganda were the member states of the IGAD that were expected to handle the crisis in South Sudan with neutrality. That did not happen, thus undermining potentials of the regional organisation to provide an African solution to an African problem in the country. This situation impaired the capacity of IGAD summits to thrash out the violence in South Sudan.

As the IGAD-led negotiations stagnated, it was thought that the fragmentation of the SPLM/A into three factions was the real handicap to progress of any peace initiative. So, other African leaders of political parties took the initiative of unifying the SPLM as a prerequisite for finding a way forward for the crisis of South Sudan. African Ruling parties like the Chama Chama Mapinduzi of Tanzania and the African National Congress of South Africa convened in Arusha to reconcile the fractured SPLM. Unity of the party was prioritised as a way forward to end the devastating civil war that raged in South Sudan. All factions of the SPLM/A concluded a deal, which underscored the need to implement the Cessation of Hostilities Agreement signed by parties to the conflict (UN Doc S/2015/118). Proponents of the initiative underrated the degree of mistrust in the SPLM. The Arusha initiative culminated in an Agreement signed on 21 January 2015. The agreement did not change the attitude of the warring parties on the ground. Many people and interested observers considered the Arusha Forum as a diversion from the mainstream negotiations that were taking place in Addis Ababa under the IGAD auspices. Others thought it was a process of forum shopping to evade immediate solution of the crisis.

4.5. From an Agreement on Paper to a Bloody Peace

South Sudanese conflict divided the IGAD peace makers like it divided national communities. Relations soured among the mediators of the conflict in South Sudan in the days leading to the compromised Agreement on the Resolution of the Conflict in South Sudan (ARCISS). Uganda's support to the government of South Sudan was considered a stumbling block to the progress of negotiations. Ethiopia felt that Uganda was undermining the Ethiopian-led IGAD peace process. The situation was aggravated when Uganda, a week before signing the peace agreement, called for a mini summit comprised of Ethiopia, Kenya, Sudan and Uganda. The purpose of the mini summit was to assure the President of South Sudan that those provisions he disagreed with would be dropped from the text of the agreement. The provisions of the agreement objected to by the government of South Sudan were, among others, the demilitarisation of Juba, withdrawal of foreign troops from South Sudan, the monitoring and verification mechanism, cantonment of forces, accountability for war crimes, separate armies and the like (Africa Confidential 2016, p. 5). Tensions among mediators persisted until the deal dubbed Agreement on the Resolution of the Conflict in South Sudan (ARCISS) was signed on 17 August 2015. Ethiopian and Ugandan presidents ran into a verbal encounter resulting in early departure of Yoweri Museveni before signature of the agreement. It was only signed by the leaders of the SPLM/A (IO) and the representative of the SPLM/A (FD) and other stakeholders. The

President of South Sudan declined to append his signature to the agreement on 17 August 2015. He later signed the agreement on 26 August in Juba after registering sixteen reservations.[8] The rivalries among mediators of the crisis are summed up by Africa Confidential inter alia:

> Ugandan President Yoweri Museveni had a sharp exchange of words with IGAD Chairman Hailemariam Desaleign after the Ethiopian Prime Minister complained that Kampala's backing of Juba was complicating regional efforts to persuade Salva Kiir to sign the deal. That appears the main reason for Museveni's abrupt departure from the meeting in Addis Ababa before the rebel Commander Riek Machar Teny Dhurgon and the Sudan People's Liberation Movement Secretary General, Pa'gan Amum Okiech, had signed on 17 August (Africa Confidential 2015, p. 4).

The AU propped up the IGAD peace process in many ways. It supported the peace process that the IGAD and the Team of IGAD Special Envoys were mediating in Ethiopia. But the launching the Commission of Inquiry on the Situation in South Sudan led by Obasanjo, the former President of Nigeria, was a significant boost for the IGAD peace process. The Commission's report detailed the situation of the civilians trapped between the warring parties. More important was the report's Chapter IV on issues on healing and reconciliation. The report proposed mechanisms for mending relationships between communities such as reparation and reconciliation, institutional reforms and reconciliation, truth and reconciliation (African Union 2014, p. 233–73). The contribution of the AU in this respect is an important aspect of African potentials for conflict resolution and healing.

However, the acrimonies demonstrated during negotiations and the signature of the ARCISS continued to haunt its implementation. Delays in the process of return of the opposition leaders into the country and hostile rhetoric between the two main signatories of the ARCISS signalled possibilities of post-agreement violence. Undoubtedly, the shaky relationships between the SPLM-IG and the SPLM-IO generated indifference in the society to the extent that people doubted the future effectiveness of the Transitional Government of National Unity (TGoNU) formed on 29 April 2016. Citizens followed statements of members of the new government in the media and reports on meetings of the Council of Ministers and of the Joint Monitoring and Evaluation Commission (JMEC). These were political indicators of troubled relationships among partners of ARCISS. The TGoNU was formed and that the legal framework was not enshrined in the Constitution remained problematic. It was obvious that there were articles of the peace agreement which were in stark contradiction with dispositions of the Constitution[9] (Wassara 2016). People expected the harmonisation of the interim Constitution of South Sudan with the ARCISS, which did happen until violence engulfed the country on 8 July 2016.

The latent conflict exploded in July 2016 and escalated faster than expected to reach the point of extreme violence in Juba. On 2 July, a senior SPLA (IO) officer was gunned down in a dubious circumstance. The SPLA (IO) forces killed five government soldiers in retaliation at a checkpoint in Juba. The period 7–11 July witnessed deadly clashes in Juba between the SPLA (IG) and SPLA (IO) in which over 300 people perished, including two Chinese peacekeepers. At the same time, approximately 36,000 people sought protection at UNMISS facilities in the capital city. Riek Machar and some of his soldiers escaped to the bushes of Equatoria. Government forces, the SPLA (IG), pursued Riek Machar with his forces until they entered the Democratic Republic of the Congo where Mission de l'Organisation des Nations Unies pour la stabilisation en RD Congo (MONUSCO) received them in Garamba National Park. The Juba violence distorted provisions of the ARCISS, which has led to revised implementation of the power-sharing and security arrangements. This development prompted the IGAD Plus and AU Peace and Security Council to issue communiques endorsing deployment of the Regional Protection Force (UNSC 2016a, p. 1). Following the deteriorating security and humanitarian situation in South Sudan, the UN Security Council adopted resolution 2304 on 12 August 2016 (UN: 2016), which extended and detailed the new mandate of UNMISS. The resolution raised the number of its troops to 17,000 including the authorisation of 4,000 troops. The latter is mandated to protect key facilities in Juba including the airport (UNSC 2016b, p. 1–2).

The most worrying development is that violence spread to other towns like Yei in Equatoria. The manner in which the SPLA (IG) treated civilians during the pursuit of Riek Machar and remnants of his forces might have sparked hostile attitudes among the youth in Yei River State counties. There is rebellion in the area and across the Nile in the east. These military operations have forced an exodus of the civilian population to neighbouring countries. South Sudanese refugees have flooded Uganda with roughly 175,000 people who have filled refugee camps (MSF 2016). The immediate problem is that new rebel groups have sprung up in formerly peaceful areas. Some of these groups claim to pay allegiance to the SPLA (IO), while others do not. This new development complicates the security and power-sharing arrangements stipulated in the ARCISS of August 2015. So, the government is seeking other means of addressing the political disorder in South Sudan after the violence of July 2016 and subsequent spread of rebellions to Equatoria. It is against this background that the President of the Republic of South Sudan opted for the National Dialogue in South Sudan declared on 14 December 2016 in his address of the joint session of the National Legislative Assembly and the Council of State.

4.6. Negotiating Statehood with Other Non-state Armed Groups

The phenomenon of non-state actors is not limited to South Sudan alone; it exists in many parts of the world where extreme poverty affects the population and where conflicts rage. Non-state armed groups emerge in circumstances where contradictions creep into politics, the economy and the society. Militias and similar armed groups have attracted the attention of researchers in many parts of Africa. Researchers (Okumu and Ikelegbe 2010) produced studies, which investigated different types of non-state armed groups in the African continent. The result of all the studies suggested that state crises and human insecurity prevail in all parts of Africa. Other studies (Zech 2015) attributed the existence of militias and self-

124

defence groups to the growing third parties in civil wars. Accordingly, armed groups are either the creation of warring parties or they emerge spontaneously to defend their communities where threats to their livelihoods are either perpetrated by the warring parties or other armed groups, or where governments are incapable of protecting citizens and their properties from such predators. Scholars have shed more light on conceptualisation of different ideal types of community-based armed groups according to their roles in society. Results of studies still point to the fact that militias, community-defence groups, 'tend to turn bad' in the words of Schuberth. In the end they do harm to the very communities that participated in establishing them. In his research in Haiti and Kenya, Schuberth revealed that adverse behaviour of contemporary community-based armed groups is related to material factors and lack of control-mechanisms like a legal framework, and external oversight and accountability measures (Schuberth 2015).

These circumstances create breeding grounds for the emergence of private security protection, crime groups, militias, vigilantes and gangs among others. Our analysis focuses more on militias and community-defence groups because they are the best known destabilising groups in South Sudan. These two types of non-state armed groups shaped the security sector and the persecution of civil war in Sudan for decades. They have been instrumental in influencing dynamics and trends of civil wars in Sudan and South Sudan. It is important at this juncture to provide a description of militias and similar armed groups. Literature describes them as:

> ... a form of self-help to escape particular circumstances [that have] (sic) flourished where inaccessibility and administrative insufficiency and complication [are] the rule. Where protection from violence is absent and where communities lack resources to purchase private security, they are left with no option but to resort to justice 'through rudimentary vigilance and legal self-help'. Militias are a product of extreme insecurity, of situations in which insecure reservations of communities come to see no alternative to lynching, [grabbing] and vigilante justice (DCAF 2015, pp. 15–21).

There are consequences of militia and other armed groups for the state in which they have presence. One of such consequences is the challenge to the authority of the state over certain parts of its territory. This situation leads the state to make choices of action. It may use its legitimate coercive powers to suppress militias and community self-defence groups or it may be obliged to negotiate its legitimate authority with them in return for patronages. Either way the state may restore its authority in that particular area and exercise its sovereignty. In this respect, statehood depends on the ability of a state to exercise its powers and provide security to citizens, and re-establish its sovereignty. Then we move from the world of conceptualisation to realities of militias and community self-defence groups in South Sudan.

South Sudan witnessed a variety of non-state armed groups whose origins could be traced back to decades of the civil war in Sudan. Theoretical considerations concerning non-state armed groups have, in general, been treated to pave the way for understanding issues that confront South Sudan in its attempts to own sovereign authority as a factor of statehood. The country inherited many non-state armed actors (CIGI 2010, pp. 5–6) while others were created by the government or the opposition since the eruption of the crisis in December 2013. Hence, the list of militias and community self-defence groups keeps on growing. Also, some pre-independence armed groups metamorphosed into fighting forces for the government or for the opposition. Besides the rebel army of the SPLM/A (IO), other groups like the White Army, SSDM/A, Agwelek, Arrow Boys, Gelweng, Titweng, Mathiang Anyoor and Maban Defence Force re-emerged during or after the December 2013 crisis. The question to ask is how and when do the non-state armed groups force negotiations with the government? This is a question, which is mind-boggling as far as authority and sovereignty of South Sudan are concerned.

The government's handling of militias and other armed groups was a complex process before and after independence. At one extreme, the government used force trying to impose its authority in areas controlled by militias and community self-defence groups. These groups are so many in the country that we cannot treat all of them at the same time. Only a few cases of non-state actors are examined as examples among many. Three cases are examined here to demonstrate how and when the government, militias and community self-defence groups are involved in handling statehood crises.

The first case is the tendency of the government to use force against militias and then reversal of such a policy for offering amnesties to enhance integration into the army. During the CPA period the government launched forced disarmament programmes in the former Greater Upper Nile region in the Murle, Nuer and Shilluk homelands (CIGI 2010, pp. 6–10). Among the Nuer, the White Army felt this was an assault or revenge over their support to the Nasir faction in 1991.[10] Similarly, the SPLA disarmament of militias in the Shilluk kingdom was so brutal that many villages were razed to the ground. This was seen by the Shilluk community as attempts to depopulate parts of the kingdom to enable the Dinka to occupy those areas. The heavy-handed approach by the army increased the intensity of the conflict in South Sudan. For this reason, prospects for peaceful coexistence and reconciliation were unthinkable. The overt resistance of militias and community self-defence forces in Upper Nile region led the government to reconsider its approach to extending its authority is areas where militia forces held out. It adopted the policy of amnesty for all armed groups that laid down their arms to be integrated into the army and civil service.

It was under the new policy that a number of militia groups integrated into the SPLM/A. The contending issues are whether those militias had confidence in the local peace process or whether the government consolidated its authority in areas that were formerly under the militia commanders. The outbreak of the civil war in December 2013 exposed attitudes of some militia groups vis-à-vis the government. The case of the SSDM/A illustrates the shortcoming of the government policy of enforcing its authority over territories, which were once controlled by militia leaders integrated into the SPLM/A. For example, Johnson Olony and his SSDM/A were given an amnesty in April 2013. His forces were part of the SPLA. Olony's forces were part of government offensives against the SPLM/A (IO). However, things changed abruptly when simmering conflict began to surface between the Shilluk community of Fashoda and the Padang Dinka of Akoka. The situation got out of hand when Olony's deputy, James Bwongo, was killed by Dinka fighters between Malakal Town and Akoka village in Upper Nile. He shifted side and fought government forces. Olony created a militia group under the name of Agwelek, which signed an agreement with the SPLM/A (IO) to jointly fight government forces (Human Security Baseline Survey 2015, pp. 8–9). The government lost full control of larger areas of Upper Nile.

The second case is about the government's search for dialogue with militia groups during the civil war against the SPLM/A (IO). While the civil war was intensifying in Upper Nile, Pibor was another area where the government had the intention of enforcing its authority in contested areas through its military might. A section of the SSDM/A under David Yau Yau known as the Cobra Faction had been fighting government in Pibor county before the 15 December crisis. The government deployed General Peter Gadet to subdue the Murle before he defected to join Riek Machar's SPLM/A (IO). Reports indicate that the SPLA brutality in Pibor County against the Murle people galvanised the rebel ranks by the middle of 2013. SPLA's conduct of disarmament and methods of handling David Yau Yau's rebellion led to the exodus of the Murle population from the towns of Lekwangole and Pibor to rebel-held areas in Boma Plateau (Tadisco 2015, pp. 17–31). The Cobra Faction of the SSDM/A began to gain momentum and the government found it hard to sustain war on multiple fronts. It showed willingness to consider Yau Yau's demands. The government tried in vain to reach Yau Yau through Murle political leaders in Juba. The Sudan Council of Churches attempted to mediate the conflict through the leadership of Archbishop Daniel Deng, but Yau Yau's Cobra Faction rejected the initiative.

National potentials to deal with the Murle rebellion became a reality only when a new initiative dubbed 'Church Leaders Mediation Initiative (CLMI)' was unveiled by bishops and clergy under the leadership of Bishop Paride Taban in May 2013. The actual negotiations started in August 2013 with the blessing of the government. The eruption of December 2013 took place while negotiations with the Cobra Faction were in progress. Government representatives of the Council of State joined together with the CLMI members to wage the peace. They met the representatives of the Cobra Faction in Addis Ababa on 23 January 2014 while the government was also negotiating with the SPLM/A (IO) in the same city. The two parties (Government and Cobra Faction) signed a ceasefire agreement, which they ratified on 30 January 2014. Representatives of the government and the Cobra Faction signed the final agreement on 9 May 2014. CLMI leaders witnessed the agreement (Tadisco 2015, pp. 34–42). The Agreement gave birth to Greater Pibor Administrative Area under the leadership of David Yau Yau. This case demonstrates that the Murle militia assumed the role of defending rights of the people through armed struggle and negotiations. The case is a demonstration of the effectiveness of African potentials for conflict resolution spearheaded by faith-based institutions. It is through negotiation with Murle militia that the state was able to exercise its authority over a formerly rebellious territory.

The third case is about the spontaneous emergence of a community self-defence group in 2008 known as the Arrow Boys in Western Equatoria. It was a community vigilante group whose primary function was to protect its community from abuses of a foreign rebel movement, the Lord's Resistance Army (LRA) (Koos 2014; Willems and Van der Borgh 2016).

This was a Ugandan rebel group fighting the government since taking power in Kampala in 1986. As the Sudanese and Ugandan civil wars dragged on, some kind of alliances of opposite directions were forming. The SPLM/A allied with Uganda during the civil war with Sudan while LRA found an accommodation with the Sudanese government. It is these complicated relations that brought the LRA to operate on Sudanese soil with the complicity of the Sudan Armed Forces. The signature of the CPA changed the political configuration. Juba became the seat of the Government of South Sudan with the SPLA as its army. An agreement was reached between Sudan and Uganda to relocate the LRA from the Uganda border to a new location at Li-Kwanga on the Democratic Republic of the Congo (DRC) border with Southern Sudan in the then Western Equatoria State. In later events the agreement collapsed after the failure of the

Ugandan Operation Lightening Thunder failed to destroy Kony and his LRA rebels in the region in December 2010 (ICG 2011, p. 3). The LRA broke into bands that established several bases all along the border regions in the DRC, the Central Africa Republic (CAR) and South Sudan.

Dispersed LRA bands occupied the forests of the DRC and Central African Republic (CAR), began to kill civilians, abduct children, and mutilate people, rape women and loot properties. Statistics of casualties related to LRA operations kept increasing (ICG 2011, p. 1). The unfortunate thing was that the neither the Government of South Sudan nor the SPLA cared about protecting civilians from the scourge of the LRA. Civilians in Western Equatoria found themselves in confusion and total helplessness. This situation led to the spontaneous formation of the community self-defence groups in most of the counties of Western Equatoria State under the name Arrow Boys. The Arrow Boys did their work faithfully without turning on their communities for extortion or any other crimes. By the end of 2011 the Arrow boys had thrown out the LRA from South Sudan (ICG 2011, pp. 8–10). They were useful for intelligence sharing with the SPLA, the UPDF and the AU Task Force tracking the LRA with their base in Yambio and Nzara. These vigilante groups were accountable to traditional chiefs and higher level local authorities without any military ranks.

When did the Arrow Boys start to go bad? Many factors contributed to the Arrow Boys' discontent with the government. The first and foremost factor was the idleness of the self-defence groups after driving out the LRA from Western Equatoria. Secondly, they expected a kind of reward for the job well done. In 2010, during the reconciliation conference on post-elections healing in Yambio, the Speaker of the National Legislative Assembly, Wani Igga, promised five million Sudanese pounds to support activities of the Arrow Boys. It was a promised contribution from the government to encourage their fight against the LRA and protection of their communities. The Arrow Boys were renamed the Home Guards during the conference.[11] But years came and passed without the promise materialising. Thirdly, in later events, cattle crises began to develop, which soured relations between community self-defence groups and pastoralists in the eastern counties of Western Equatoria. Pastoralists from the Lakes State invaded the counties destroying crops of communities. By comparison, people equated activities of pastoralists such as destruction of crops with those of the LRA who used to plunder harvests of communities. Several conferences were held about cattle crises without tangible results. Local communities and Arrow Boys turned their anger on soldiers who were accused of accommodating cattle herders who were intruding their farms and destroying crops. This brought about skirmishes between local self-defence groups and pastoralists and SPLA soldiers in Mundri and Maridi counties.[12] Thereafter, the conflict between communities with pastoralists began to take political dimensions and armed confrontations. The intervention of the SPLA in such confrontations led to mini rebellions in many counties of Western Equatoria State.

4.7. Concluding Remarks

It is fair to conclude that South Sudan achieved independence without sustainable intra-party harmony or substantial social healing in communities. This situation dragged South Sudan's statehood into fragility. Based on history, South Sudan is an ethnically divided society owing to its distant and present past. The statehood of the country has remained fragile because of so many unresolved issues ranging from fighting rebel movements to resistance of non-state armed groups. Communal violence in South Sudan is linked to tensions within the ruling political party over leadership, militarisation of communities and apparent neglect of timely intervention to protect civilian populations. Political leaders of South Sudan have the tendency to mobilise communities and their self-defence groups to take sides in armed conflicts. There are connections between local violence, governance and resource control. It is safe to assume that conflicts buried in the past were unearthed by emerging new conflicts. For instance, past relationships between actors of the split of the SPLM/A in 1991 were easily exploited by the events of the December 2013 crisis. The aftermath of the crisis revealed the degree of mistrust that constrained confidence-building despite assurances of peaceful coexistence given by successive agreements since signature of the CPA in 2005.

Further, South Sudan was in continual negotiations about its authority and sovereignty with disparate rebel groups, militias and community self-defence groups since its independence from Sudan. Our treatment of statehood of the country focuses on macro- and micro-analysis of dialogue with a host of fragmented militias and community-based armed groups. Among them are the SSDM/A (Olony's faction, later Agwelek), SSDM/A-Cobra Faction and the Arrow Boys which we selected as cases where elements of lower-level applications of African potentials of conflict resolution were put into action.

Our study reveals also that there was a failure of the leadership of South Sudan to prevent simmering conflicts in the ruling party, the SPLM. This party won national admiration, confidence and pride, especially after independence of the country in July 2011. Its weakness, however, became apparent when it was left powerless to stop intra-party bickering. This was the case when Riek Machar announced his intention to run for leadership of the party at the beginning of 2013. The division within the party revealed the lack of mechanisms for dealing with internal conflicts. The party should have intervened to prevent the political problem that was progressively engulfing the state. This raises the question of loyalty of the army where absorbed militia groups were left free to stay in or go out of the SPLA at will. This kind of behaviour undermined the ability and capacity of the SPLA to stop indiscipline and political demands based on narrow ethnic aspirations.

The methods of disarmament of self-defence groups were so cruel to the extent of inviting communities' sympathies for their youth. Communities were even in solidarity with their self-defence groups when such groups acquired new identities that contradicted the initial goals and objectives for which they were created in the first place. This situation was witnessed in Western Equatoria during confrontations between armed youth, pastoralists and the SPLA. Chiefs and traditional leaders organised the youth into self-defence groups to protect them from the LRA. After the successes of the Arrow Boys in driving out the LRA from Western Equatoria and as time passed, self-defence forces began vying for influence and political power. This assumption explains how elements of the Arrow Boys re-organised themselves into military-like formations. Then they gave themselves political identities like South Sudan National Liberation Movement/Army and Arrow Boys in Opposition imitating what was already happening on the political arena of South Sudan.[13]

However, potentials for conflict resolution have not been absent from the crises of South Sudan. National and regional stakeholders engaged in mediations and negotiations at varying degrees of conflict escalation. This could be seen in the participation of non-state actors, civil society organisations and faith-based organisations in the IGAD-led peace process. They influenced trends of negotiations, attitudes of the warring parties and discussed proposals of mediators in Addis Ababa. Elements of African potentials have worked at different levels and speeds in South Sudan.

At the domestic level, we have seen the difficulties of the government to initiate dialogue with non-state armed actors. This is attributable to the lack of confidence or trust of self-defence groups in government initiatives. On the contrary, communities, armed groups and self-defence groups respond readily to initiatives of faith-based institutions. That was the case of the CLMI and the Cobra Faction of David Yau Yau of the Murle community in Pibor County. The CLMI paved the way for the government to negotiate with the Cobra Faction. This culminated in the agreement of May 2014 creating the Greater Pibor Administrative Area. The issue of honouring the agreement splits parties into factions. That is why a faction of the Cobra Faction is seen to be breaking away from the mainstream group owing to political dynamics in South Sudan in 2016.

A similar pattern was recently followed in Western Equatoria, but is rather different because the issue of the LRA was a regional phenomenon. Activities of the rebel group affected four countries: Uganda, DRC, CAR and South Sudan. Civil society stakeholders sought a coalition in order to deal with the atrocities of the LRA. Community leaders in the four countries and faith-based organisations formed the Regional Civil Society Task Force. They formed the task force to enable discussion of common challenges and adoption of common strategies to deal with the common problem. An organisation known as Conciliation Resource coordinated activities for community leaders, civil society organisations and faith-based organisations to tackle the regional rebel movement.[14] This initiative was an example of pooling together potentials for resolving a common problem. It empowered faith-based institutions, civil society and community leaders to initiate dialogue between the government and the SSNLM/A. The initiative ended up in the agreement on cessation of hostilities signed on 2 April 2016 in Yambio (GRRS 2016).

Finally, advanced levels of dialogue and peace initiatives, like the IGAD Peace Process, are what we consider as African potentials for conflict resolution. The protracted civil war in South Sudan raised concerns in the Horn of Africa region and beyond. The IGAD peace process was led by a team of mediators from Ethiopia, Kenya, Sudan and Uganda until an agreement was signed on 17 August 2015. Also, the AU played its role in guiding the process through its Security Council despite the reluctance of the SPLM/A (IG) and SPLM/A (OI) to implement the peace deal. Despite the August 2015 agreement, violence continues to spread across South Sudan. Active conflict zones and the number of armed groups continue to grow while operating in different parts of the country. Studies reveal that it is fair to conclude the discourse with a relevant finding (ACLED 2016, pp. 1-5) stating that, 'There are several active conflicts throughout the state, which are linked through strategic relationships, but are loosely integrated into the dominant competition between the SPLA and the SPLA (IO)'. Given the July 2016 crisis in Juba that is engulfing other areas in South Sudan, the ARCISS has obviously little effect on fighting patterns throughout the country. Therefore, it remains to be seen how South Sudan's potentials will overcome political and social instability and trigger behaviour change in elites, leadership and communities to embrace sustainable peaceful coexistence, confidence-building, reconciliation and national healing.

Notes

[1] Historical grievances tend to influence the civil war in independent South Sudan. Many sources, including UN reports, point to the ferocity and mistrust of the warring factions of SPLM/A. Refer to UN Document S/AC.57/2016/PE/OC.07 dated 22 January 2016, paragraph 16, pp. 8–9. It is the Final Report of the Panel of Experts on South Sudan established by the Security Council Resolution 2206 (2015).

[2] See the Forum Outline at Http://www.africanpotential.kyoto-u.ac:jp/en/research_activities-en/internationalsympos...1/4/2016.

[3] The list of militia groups during the time of the Juba Declaration is long as compiled in John Young's publication. See John Young (2006) *South Sudan Defence Forces in the Wake of the Juba Declaration*, Geneva: Small Arms Survey, Graduate Institute of International and Development Studies.

[5] The SSDM/A was spearheaded by the Shilluk whose villages were destroyed during the SPLA disarmament campaign in 2010 headed by Johnson Olonyi. The SSDM/A joining the SPLA was just a strategy to advance the Shilluk cause for carving out a zone of influence in Upper Nile. See Human Security Baseline Assessment (HSBA) (2015) *The Conflict in Upper Nile*, Geneva: Small Arms Survey, p. 9. Can be accessed at www.smallarmssurveysudan.org.

[6] The Registrar of political parties recorded 18 political parties, some of which are splinter or breakaway groups from the main political parties.

[7] This argument is substantiated by the existence and interventions of regional Councils, tribal Elders, Council of Elders, and Community Associations.

[8] See the document GRSS (2015), *Reservations of the Government of the Republic of South Sudan, on the Compromise Agreement on the Resolution of the Conflict in South Sudan, Juba 26th August 2015*. The few reservations are extracted from a list of 16 reservations in a matrix duly initialled by the President Salva Kiir on that date.

[9] See details in Samson S. Wassara (2016) *Peace without Euphoria in South Sudan*. Can be accessed at https://zambakariadvisory.wordpress.com/2016/06/03/peace-without-euphoria-in-south-sudan 3 June.

[10] This approach was criticised by UN agencies and human rights groups. Details appeared on the UN website in 2008. See IRIN (2008)

Sudan: Civilian Disarmament Remains Elusive as Government Rethinks, 3 December.

[11] The author (Wassara) was present when the donation was announced, and was in the team for drafting the communiqué and resolutions of the conference.

[12] Chairman of Maridi Community Association in Juba issued a press statement on 11 June 2015 condemning violence by cattle keepers in Maridi.

[13] A section of the Arrow Boys decided to transform their community self-defence status to a political organisation under the identity of South Sudan National Liberation Movement/Army when an agreement between the SPLM/A (IG) and SPLM/A (IO) already signed the Agreement of 17 August 2015.

[14.] Details can be found at the website http://www.c-r.org/news-and-views/comment/south-sudan-new-opportunities-ongoing-challenges.

References

Abraham, K. (2006) *The Horn of Africa: Conflicts and Conflict Mediation in the Greater Horn of Africa*, Addis Ababa: Ethiopian International Institute for Peace and Development.

ACLED (2016) *Country Report: South Sudan Update*, http://www.acleddata.com/wp-content/uploads/2016/ACLED_Africa_Country-Reports_South-Sudan_July 2016 (Accessed July 2016).

Africa Confidential (2016) Vol. 58, No. 17, 28 August 2016.

African Union (2014) *Final Report of the African Union Commission of Inquiry on South Sudan*, Addis Ababa, http://www.au.int/en/auciss (Accessed 15 October 2014).

Astill-Brown, J. (2014) *South Sudan's Slide into Conflict: Revisiting the Past and Reassessing Partnerships*, London: Chatham House.

CIGI (2010) *Security Sector Reform Monitor: Southern Sudan, No. 2*, Waterloo: The Centre for International Governance Innovation, http://www.cigionline.org (Accessed April 2010).

Conflict Risk Network (2012) *The Sudan-South Sudan Agreements: A Long Way to Go*, Washington: United to End Genocide.

Daoust, G. (2015) *Country Report: Sudan and South Sudan*, ACLED Project, http://www.acleddata.com/wp-content/uploads/2015/01/ACLED-Counrty-Report-Sudan-and-South-Sudan.pdf (Accessed October 2015).

DCAF and Geneva Call (2015) *Armed Non-State Actors: Current Trends and Future Challenges* (Working Paper No. 5), Geneva: The Geneva Centre for Democratic Control of Armed Forces.

GRSS (2015) *Reservations of the Government of the Republic of South Sudan, on the Compromise Agreement on the Resolution of the Conflict in South Sudan*, Juba, 26 August 2015.

---------- (2016) *Agreement on Cessation of Hostilities between Government of the Republic of South Sudan (RSS) and the South Sudan National Liberation Movement/Army*, 2 April 2016.

Hemmer, J. and Grinstead, N. (2015) *When Peace is an Exception: Shifting the Donor Narrative in South Sudan* (CRU Policy Brief), Clingendael: Netherlands Institute of International Relations.

Human Security Baseline Assessment (HSBA) (2015) *The Conflict in Upper Nile State*, Geneva: Small Arms Survey, http://www.smallarmssurveysudan.org/facts-figures/south-sudan/conflict-of-2013-14/the-conflict-in-upper-nile.html.

Hutton, L. (2014) *South Sudan: From Fragility at Independence to a Crisis of Sovereignty* (CRU Report), Clingendael: Netherlands Institute of International Relations.

ICG (2011) 'The Lord's Resistance Army: End game?' *Africa Report*, No. 182, Brussels: International Crisis Group.

IRIN (2008) *Sudan: Civilian Disarmament Remains Elusive as Government Rethinks*, 3 December 2008.

Jok, M.J. (2015) 'Negotiating an end to the current civil war in South Sudan: What lessons can Sudan's comprehensive peace agreement offer?', *Inclusive Political Settlements Papers*, Berlin: Berghof Foundation.

Johnson, D. H. (2003) *The Root Causes of Sudan's Civil Wars*, Oxford: James Currey.

Koost, C. (2014) 'Why and how civil defense militias emerge: The case of the Arrow Boys in South Sudan', *Studies in Conflict and Terrorism*, Vol. 37, No. 12, pp. 1039–57.

Kurimoto, E. (2012) 'New state-building and conflict: The prospect of the Republic of South Sudan', in I. Tomiyama and S. Tanuma (eds.), *Conflict kara Tou*: Osaka University Press, pp. 35–69 (in Japanese).

----------(2014) 'Limits and possibilities of grassroots peacebuilding in the Southern Sudan', in H. Oda and Y. Seki (eds.), *Heiwa no Jinruigaku*, Tokyo: Horitsubunkasha, pp. 27–48 (in Japanese).

Kussala, Barani E. Hiboro (2015) *Reconciliation, Healing and Peace in South Sudan: Reflections on the Way Forward*, Nairobi: Paulines Publication Africa.

LeRiche, M. and Arnold, M. (2012) *South Sudan: From Revolution to Independence*, London: Hurst.

MSF (2016), *Uganda: Country Overwhelmed as Tens of Thousands Flee Violence in South Sudan*, htpp://www.msf.org/en/article/uganda-country-overwhelmed-tens-thousands-flee-violence (Accessed 13 December 2016).

Okumu, W. and Ikelegbe, A. (eds.) (2010). *Militias, Rebels and Islamist Militants: Human Insecurity and State Crises in Africa*, Pretoria: Institute for Security Studies.

Radon, J. and Logan, S. (2014) 'South Sudan: Governance arrangements, war, and peace', *Journal of International Affairs*, Fall/Winter Vol. 68, No.1, pp. 147–67.

Rands, R. (2010) *In Need for Review: SPLA Transformation in 2006–10 and Beyond*, Geneva: Small Arms Survey, Graduate Institute of International and Development Studies.

Schuberth, M. (2015) *When Self-Defense Forces "Go Bad": Evidence from Kenya and Haiti*, http://politicalviolenceatglance.org (Accessed 27 October 2015).

Silva, M. (2014) 'After partition: The perils of South Sudan', *University of Baltimore Journal of International Law*, Vol. 3, No.1.

Tadisco, C. (2015) *Real but Fragile: The Greater Pibor Administrative Area*, Geneva: Small Arms Survey, Graduate Institute of International and Development Studies.

Thomas, E. (2015) *South Sudan: A Slow Liberation*. London: Zed Books.

UN (2015) Document S/2015/118, *Report of the Secretary-General on South Sudan*, New York: Security Council, 17 February.

----------(2016) Document S/AC.57/2016/PE/OC.07, *Final Report of the Panel of Experts on South Sudan Established Pursuant to the Security*

Council Resolution 2206 (2015), New York: Security Council, 22 January.

----------(2016) Document S/RES/2304 (2016), Adopted by the Security Council at its 7754th meeting, New York: Security Council, 12 August.

UNSC (2016a) *September 2016 Monthly Forecast: Security Council Report*, http://www.securitycouncilreport.org/monthly-forecast/2016-09/south_sudan_22.php.

----------(2016b) *South Sudan Chronology of Events: Security Council Report*, http://www.securityccouncilreport.org/chronology/south-sudan-.php.

Wassara, S. S. (2016) *Peace without Euphoria in South Sudan*, https://zambakariadvisory.wordpress.com/2016/06/03/peace-without-euphoria-in-south-sudan (Accessed 3 June 2016).

---------- (2015) 'South Sudan: Sovereignty challenged at infancy', *Journal of Eastern African Studies*, Vol. 9, No. 4.

----------(2010) 'Rebels, militias and governance in Sudan', in W. Okumu and A. Ikelegbe (eds.), *Militias, Rebels and Islamist Militants: Human Insecurity and State Crises in Africa*, Pretoria: Institute of Security Studies.

Willems, R. and Van der Borgh, C. (2016) 'Negotiating security provisioning in a hybrid political order: The case of the Arrow Boys in Western Equatoria, South Sudan', *Conflict, Security & Development*, Vol.16, No. 4, pp. 347–64.

Woodward, P. (2013) *Crisis in the Horn of Africa: Politics, Piracy and the Threat of Terror*, London: I. B. Tauris.

Young, J. (2006) *South Sudan Defense Forces in the Wake of the Juba Declaration*, Geneva: Small Arms Survey, Graduate Institute of International and Development Studies.

Zech, S.T. (2015) *From Protection to Predation, Part I: When Self-Defense Forces Go Bad*, https://politicalviolenceataglance.org/2015/10/27/from-protection-to-predation-part-i-when-self-defense-forces-go-bad/.org/ (Accessed 27 October 2015).

Part Two

Lived Experiences of

Overcoming Challenges

Chapter 5

The *Fambul Tok* ('Family Talk') Project: A Hybrid Attempt for Local Transitional Justice in Sierra Leone

Kyoko Cross

5.1. Post-conflict Sierra Leone: A Testing Ground for Liberal State-building

The infamously brutal civil war in Sierra Leone that began in 1991 and lasted until 2001 can be described as a typical example of internal conflicts that conform to characteristics of state collapse following the end of the Cold War. As has also been seen throughout Africa, Sierra Leone's independence at the end of the colonial era was followed by an extended period of rule under a single-party dictatorship. However, as the centralised rule began to weaken due to the economic crises in the 1980s, coupled with a shift in post-Cold War aid policies, frequent military coups and disruptions gradually eroded the state's capability to govern its own territory. This situation invited an armed uprising by the Revolutionary United Front (RUF), led by Foday Sankoh with the backing of Charles Taylor (later the President of Liberia), which resulted in the outbreak of the devastating eleven-year civil war.

The post-Cold War internal conflicts, including the Sierra Leone Civil War, are frequently referred to as 'new wars' (Kaldor 1999), which are grounded in a globalised war economy, as exemplified in the use of diamonds and other natural resources as sources of revenue to fund the procurement of foreign arms. Unlike conventional 'old wars' fought among sovereign states on the basis of geopolitics and ideology, the new wars of the post-Cold War era are fought in the name of identity. In addition to the difficulty to deter violence in a rational manner, these conflicts are also characterised by the variety of actors who participate in them, which blurs the boundary between combatants and non-combatants and thus leads to acts of gruesome violence directed against civilians. In Sierra Leone, grisly forms of violence against civilians targeted by the RUF and militias swept across the entire country, including amputation, indiscriminate slaughter, rape, sexual slavery, and the forced recruitment of child soldiers. The perpetration of such atrocities, moreover, was not limited to anti-government insurgents. In fact, violations of international humanitarian laws were reported on the part of the government's forces, the Economic Community of West African States (ECOWAS) Monitoring Group (ECOMOG) largely comprised of the Nigerian Armed Forces, and other regular armies (SLTRC 2004, Vol. 2). It is estimated that between 50,000 and 75,000 people lost their lives and approximately two million people, which culminated in two-thirds of the national population then, were displaced internally or across the borders during the civil war (Keen 2005).

In response to the serious human rights violations that took place during the conflict, the government of Sierra Leone implemented formal transitional justice processes with the support of the international community. Specifically, the Special Court for Sierra Leone (SCSL) was established for prosecuting those individuals who bear the greatest degree of responsibility, and the Sierra Leone Truth and Reconciliation Commission (TRC) was also created to investigate the root causes and identify the perpetrators and victims in order to confront the past and promote national reconciliation. In addition, Security Sector Reforms (SSRs) were carried out with the goal of preventing the reoccurrence of violence in the future. Moreover, in response to recommendations made by the Sierra Leone TRC, victims of the conflict have been provided with small amounts of financial compensation and medical services with assistance from the UN Peacebuilding Fund and International Organization for Migration (IOM).[1]

Sierra Leone is often regarded as a kind of testing ground for post-conflict liberal state-building, with a variety of external actors, including the UN, regional organisations, donor countries and NGOs, involved in the peacekeeping and peacebuilding processes undertaken since the end of the conflict (Harris 2013). In light of the failure of liberal peacebuilding that had relied on support for democratisation and the introduction of economic liberalism in the 1990s, the early 2000s became a turning point that reoriented peacebuilding toward the (re)construction of state functions and institutions that could ensure the rule of law and good governance – that is, towards support for state (re)construction itself (Paris and Sisk 2009). In terms of post-conflict transitional justice in the framework of state-building, a comprehensive approach was taken in Sierra Leone that employed multiple diverse methods in the form of future-oriented institutional reforms that respect the culture of human rights and the rule of law, in addition to the pursuit of accountability, reconciliation, revealing truth and provision of compensation to victims of past serious human rights violations, as has already been mentioned.

Despite the development of the concept and practices of transitional justice, the adoption of 'one-size-fits-all' approaches that come packaged through international involvement have been questioned regarding whose and what kind of justice it seeks to achieve (Nagy 2008). Indeed, there is growing criticism that whereas the improvement of fair and just forms of governance and the establishment of political stability that do not permit corruption or human rights violations are seen to be prerequisites such as for development intended to reduce poverty as a root cause of conflict, the methods of transitional justice, which lay their emphasis on building the state-level institutions centring on criminal justice and security sectors, have lost touch with the real needs of people in the wake of the conflict (Cubitt 2012). As discussed below, some commentators argue that even the institutional design of the Sierra Leone TRC, which was set up with the aim of encouraging reconciliation and the recovery of victims' dignity, did not give adequate consideration to local culture and norms, thereby hampering its ability to serve in the role that it was originally expected to play (Shaw 2010).

In this context, a notable point with regard to Sierra Leone is that, in order to bridge the gap between the formal transitional justice brought in at the state level and the kinds of justice demanded in the local context of post-conflict society, informal methods of restorative transitional justice under the initiative of its residents have

145

been implemented throughout the country (Park 2010). That is, reconciliation processes based on traditional 'cleansing' rituals have been conducted at the village level with assistance from NGOs and other external actors, aiming to further the reintegration of former combatants and child soldiers as well as girls who acted together with the armed forces as sex slaves or 'wives' back into their home communities. Having ascertained the effectiveness of such customary methods of conflict resolutions, 'reconciliation ceremonies' involving local chiefs and traditional religious leaders have come to be incorporated into the public hearings conducted through the TRC as a formal institution for transitional justice. The limited financial resources and duration of the TRC, however, exposed the limits on the state's promotion of reconciliation at the community level. Thus, a local NGO launched a project called 'Fambul Tok' (the Krio language term for 'family talk') to carry on with the promotion of local-level reconciliation that the TRC had been unable to complete. Fambul Tok is a people-centred reconciliation process that is rooted in traditional rituals and customs. Its purpose is to forgive perpetrators and reintegrate them into society by having victims and affected communities accept perpetrators' confessions and apologies for their crimes. The emphasis here was on local residents' ownership of the reconciliation process. The ultimate aim was to defuse remaining flashpoints of local conflicts and rebuild sustainable communities that would foster development and lasting peace by bringing conflicts around the country to an end through locally unique reconciliation ceremonies and rituals.

This chapter focuses on the fact that the local restorative transitional justice in Sierra Leone was not restructured merely by reproduction or reclamation of traditional, local conflict resolutions that had been disrupted by the conflict, but rather it was created under the influence of the concept and methods of global transitional justice. This can be understood as a new approach to transitional justice that is neither global nor local, what critics of liberal peacebuilding described as a 'hybridity' that combines local norms and institutions with their global counterparts as 'post-liberal peacebuilding' (Sharp 2015). This initiative indicates an attempt to overcome the challenge to transitional justice in Africa – the dissonances between the international, national and local measures by which justice is defined. This chapter has two purposes. Firstly, it will explore the context in which *Fambul Tok* came to be established as an organisation for promoting reconciliation at the village level and analyse how a hybrid reconciliation model consisting of global and local elements has come to be institutionalised. Secondly, it will examine what kind of role this new, locally rooted approach to transitional justice has played in Sierra Leonean society, where coexistence with so-called 'intimate enemies' remains a challenge even after the conflict.

The chapter is organised as follows. Firstly, it will look over the political turmoil after the signing of the 1999 Lomé Peace Accord, before offering a detailed account of the establishment and activities of the SCSL. Then, in addition to detailing the activities of the TRC, it will consider the factors behind why, despite the attempt at an institutional design that conformed to the conflict and regional characteristics, it had only limited impact on Sierra Leone's local communities. Lastly, after analysing the background that led to the conceptualisation of *Fambul Tok* and its activities, it will examine how global and local transitional justice elements were hybridised and reconfigured into a new approach to reconciliation. In conclusion, it will consider the roles that the local forms of restorative transitional justice play in the context of post-conflict peacebuilding as 'African potential' in Sierra Leone.

5.2. Political Turmoil and the Establishment of Special Courts after the Peace Agreement

After the outbreak of civil war in Sierra Leone in 1991, the armed struggle with anti-government insurgents was compounded by successive military coups that served to further weaken the government's political base. Consequently, foreign military forces, including those of Guinea, the UK and ECOMOG led by the Nigerian Armed Forces began to actively intervene in the civil war at the request of the Sierra Leonean government. Even so, the struggle against the RUF, which was receiving military support from Liberia in exchange for abundant mineral resources, proved extremely difficult, and the civil war continued to escalate. Following the coup by the Armed Forces Revolutionary Council (AFRC) that took place in 1997, the RUF established a military coalition government together with the AFRC. This caused a large military reinforcement by the international community, with the result that the capital was retaken by ECOMOG in the following year, reinstating the government of President Ahmad Tejan Kabbah, who had until then been in exile in Guinea. Sankoh and other leaders of the anti-government forces were captured, 24 of whom were executed, while Sankoh was sentenced to death for the crime of treason (Keen 2005).

Despite this military victory on the part of the government forces, the RUF and AFRC that had been driven from the capital soon recovered the offensive, and tensions over their recapture of the capital rose in early 1999. In response to this situation, international sentiment for peace moves began to increase, Sankoh was released from his imprisonment, and in May 1999 peace talks were opened in Lomé, the capital of Togo.

These peace talks, which began with the RUF occupying high ground, resulted in a peace agreement with significant concessions by the Sierra Leonean government, incorporating many conditions that benefited the RUF, including Sankoh's being installed as vice president and acquiring a key post in the management of diamonds and other national resources. Amongst the most problematic of these conditions was the provision of a blanket amnesty for all the warring parties that had been involved in the conflict, including Sankoh himself. Against this promise of impunity for the RUF leadership, who were known to have committed atrocities against civilians, representatives of the UN and other observing citizen's groups participating in the Lomé talks expressed their strong opposition.[2] Nevertheless, the concessions to the RUF of a blanket amnesty and a power sharing were essential to the ceasefire agreement. Thus, a new provision was inserted in the Lomé Peace Accord to create the TRC as a mechanism to achieve accountability for serious human rights violations instead of criminal trials.

However, while the Lomé Peace Accord had negotiated the disarmament of the RUF under UN monitoring, the RUF ultimately never complied with this condition. Meanwhile, in May 2000, an incident took place in which RUF soldiers who had been dissatisfied with the disarmament condition detained approximately 500 members of the United Nations Mission in Sierra Leone (UNAMSIL) and the UN Peacekeeping Operation (UNPKO) forces stationed in Sierra Leone, and confiscated weapons and vehicles from the UNAMSIL. Moreover, the RUF soldiers who had taken these weapons went on to commit atrocities, including raiding villages and forcibly recruiting children, and then advance on Freetown, the capital of Sierra Leone (Keen 2005, p. 263). These violations of the Lomé Peace Accord by the RUF led to an expanded mandate for the British military intervention and the strengthening of UNAMSIL, which signalled a turning point for ending the conflict, followed by the subsequent arrest of Sankoh and other RUF leaders, a renewed ceasefire agreement between the government and the RUF, and the declaration by President Kabbah in March 2002 that the civil war had officially ended. Amidst these series of moves, Kabbah submitted a request to the UN Security Council regarding the establishment of an international tribunal, which resulted in the January 2002 agreement between the UN and Sierra Leonean government to establish the SCSL.[3] Much like the Special Panels of the Dili District Court in East Timor, the SCSL was established as a hybrid court that employed the laws and legal professionals of both Sierra Leone and the international community.

The court was convened 'to prosecute persons who bear the greatest responsibility for serious violations of international humanitarian law[4] and Sierra Leonean domestic law committed in the territory of Sierra Leone since 30 November 1996', and imposed some limitations on the application of the amnesty provisions that had been a part of the Lomé Peace Accord.[5] By dating the court's temporal jurisdiction not from the outset of the civil war in 1991 but from the date of the Abidjan Peace Accord in 1996,[6] and establishing its personal jurisdiction over 'persons who bear the greatest responsibility' rather than those who were 'the most responsible', the kind of individuals who were subject to the court's prosecution were extremely limited (Park 2010). After commencing activities in July 2002, the SCSL prosecuted thirteen individuals, most of whom had been leaders in the RUF, AFRC, and other militias.[7] While the SCSL was physically located in Freetown, the trial of Charles Taylor, the past president of Liberia arrested in 2003, was transferred to The Hague in the Netherlands because of the security concerns of having trial proceedings in the capital.

On the one hand, in addition to the fact that the SCSL was the first international criminal court to prosecute and convict a former head of state since the Nuremberg trials, its prosecuting of cases of forced marriage and the conscription of child soldiers as crimes under international humanitarian law is recognised as having contributed significantly to the development of international criminal justice. On the other hand, having been established by an agreement between the Sierra Leonean government and the UN rather than as an enforcement measure under Chapter VII of the UN Charter, the SCSL had no powers with which to compel the extradition of inductees against the UN member states. Furthermore, the court was always plagued by lack of financial resources due to the fact that it had to rely on voluntary contributions from the UN member states for funding (Park 2010, pp.97–98).

As regards the impact on the population, there was general dissatisfaction with regard to the fact that the extremely limited target of prosecution meant that, in fact, many perpetrators were left unpunished. Moreover, as discussed in the next section, the fact that some perpetrators would refrain from giving testimony to the TRC for fear of prosecution at the SCSL on the basis of such testimonies, is seen to have had a negative impact on the TRC's activities (Kelsall 2009). These problems, however, were caused by the blanket amnesty that was introduced in the peace agreement in order to prioritise peace, and also a result of the fact that the differences and relationship between the two institutions was not sufficiently understood among the people. Indeed, despite the physical and psychological distance between the residents in the capital where the trial proceedings were held and those in rural communities, it appears that people in general supported the activities of the SCSL in prosecuting those who bore the greatest responsibility for the serious human rights violations that had taken place during the conflict (Sawyer and Kelsall 2007).

5.3. Reconciliation through the Truth and Reconciliation Commission: Global and Local Hybridity in Formal Institutions

5.3.1. The Truth and Reconciliation Commission's Search for Local-level Reconciliation

In contrast to the SCSL, whose establishment had been unscheduled, the creation of the TRC was incorporated into the Lomé Peace Accord in place of criminal trials with the goal of seeking accountability for criminal acts committed during the civil war and building a shared history based in the actual experience of its ravages. The creation of a Truth Commission had been proposed by domestic NGOs, the UN Office of the High Commissioner for Human Rights (OHCHR) and other groups since even prior to the end of the civil war (O'Flaherty 2004). Because of the concerns over the blanket amnesty that might be granted to the anti-governmental rebel groups during the peace negotiations, the establishment of a Truth and Reconciliation Commission based on the South African model was envisioned, having the authority to grant 'amnesty for truth' that left room to pursue accountability for serious human rights violations.[8] However, because the blanket amnesty had been introduced in the Lomé Peace Accord, the TRC had not been given the authority to grant amnesty. Thus, the questions of how to elicit statements and how to encourage reconciliation in the community presented challenges from the very beginning of the institutional design since there was no benefit to perpetrators in terms of the conferral of amnesty as the price of their testimony.

The institution of the TRC was designed and created with the full support of the OHCHR. During the planning period, it provided opportunities for advance consultation with civil society and government officials in meetings lasting from July to December 1999 in order to reflect diverse regional needs and the realities of post-conflict society (SLTRC 2004 Vol.1). One of the challenges identified in the course of these advance consultations was the need for methods of conflict resolution aside from that of criminal trials. In other words, reconciliation was necessary in order to reintegrate former combatants and other conflict perpetrators into their communities. In closely knit local communities where people had to rely on each other in the course of their daily lives, not being reintegrated into their communities after the end of the conflict was a matter of life and death for perpetrators, while the continued coexistence of victims and communities with perpetrators entailed the necessity of restoring these damaged relationships. The fact that many of the abducted combatants in the Sierra Leone Civil War had been forced to commit atrocities against their families and communities to sever bonds with their communities had left a lingering aftertaste, and forgiveness by traditional local authorities and reconciliation through cleansing rituals were strongly requested as a means of reintegration into their communities.

Therefore, as one of the preparation activities prior to the establishment of the TRC, the OHCHR commissioned the NGO, called Manifesto 99, to investigate how traditional methods of conflict resolution throughout Sierra Leone could deal with problems such as murder, robbery, arson, land issues, marriage, violence and assault. It was found that most ethnic groups in Sierra Leone had mechanisms for promoting reconciliation and telling the truth that were based in traditional animist beliefs (SLTRC 2004 Vol. 3B). Hence, perpetrators who confessed the truth of their criminal actions were found to be reintegrated into society by being subjected to cleansing rituals or else obtaining forgiveness from their communities directly. Moreover, it was found that many of the violent actions that had taken place during the civil war could be dealt with by traditional methods of conflict resolution by any tribe, and given that the blanket amnesty had been granted by the Lomé Peace Accord, it was proposed that, on the condition of the reintegration of former combatants, traditional methods could be adjusted and restructured so as to handle serious crimes that included amputation, abduction, murder and arson (SLTRC 2004 Vol. 3B). In the end, it reported that rituals to reintegrate former combatants into society were actually being carried out across the country, as with cleansing rituals for child soldiers.

In this way, in order to secure the accountability of serious crimes as well as social reintegration of the perpetrators who had been given amnesty under the Lomé Peace Accord, civil society strongly wished to achieve reconciliation based on existing local methods of conflict resolution, and it was confirmed that there were already some examples where these were being performed by local residents. Responding to these findings, in the provision of Article 7(2) of the Truth and Reconciliation Commission Act, it was stipulated that 'the Commission may seek assistance from traditional and religious leaders to facilitate its public sessions and in resolving local conflicts arising from past violations or abuses or in support of healing and reconciliation',[9] and traditional religious leaders were encouraged to participate in the TRC process. Hence it was determined to introduce local methods of conflict resolution in order for chiefs and traditional religious leaders to carry out reconciliation ceremonies to round out the hearings of the TRC. In terms of implementation, cooperation was called by to the National Commission for Disarmament, Demobilisation and Reintegration (NCDDR) and local NGOs, which had already had experiences of supporting similar initiatives as a part of DDR activities, and resulted in joint implementations (SLTRC 2004 Vol. 3B).

5.3.2. The Truth and Reconciliation Commission's Institutionalisation of Local Reconciliation

While the forms of reconciliation that represent the objective of transitional justice can include a variety of approaches, including reconciliation between citizens, between communities or between individuals, as with between victims and perpetrators, the TRC focused its efforts on promoting reconciliation between victims and perpetrators on the one hand and between perpetrators and communities on the other (SCTRC 2004 Vol. 3B). Reconciliation ceremonies that were conducted in the context of the TRC were carried out according to the following procedure. First of all, in the first stage of activities that focused on the collecting of testimonies, the TRC, in addition to exploring the need for reconciliation through repeated consultations with local chiefs, community representatives and other local authorities across the country, strove to understand the relevant complicating factors. Local chiefs and community members were then enlisted to encourage the perpetrators in question to attend the collecting of testimonies and public hearings.

In the later stage of activities that began in April of 2003, when public hearings were held across the country, the TRC visited the capital and twelve districts, and hosted public hearings over the course of approximately one week in each location. The TRC not only asked perpetrators to testify voluntarily at the hearings, but in the event that a specific perpetrator's name came up in a hearing a victim was attending, the perpetrator in question would be urged to come forward to offer a response to the allegation in the remaining hearing. If a community and victims agreed to forgive and accept perpetrators' acknowledgement of their crimes and their apologies, local chiefs and other traditional authorities would perform reconciliation ceremonies to proclaim forgiveness. While the reconciliation ceremonies carried out by the TRC were never given any formal legal status, they may nevertheless be seen to have played the role of granting 'amnesty' for past crimes by virtue of an authority that carried cultural and traditional legitimacy.

By August of 2003, the TRC had heard testimonies from 7,706 individuals, while more than 450 had testified at public hearings. These hearings were also broadcast over radio and television networks. However, it was said that the hearings had not been able to obtain enough testimonies from perpetrators. One reason for this is that perpetrators had become reluctant to testify for fear of being prosecuted by the SCSL. Even though the fact that the SCSL was established to prosecute those who bore the greatest responsibility meant that the majority of former combatants fell outside its jurisdiction, for the general populace these two institutions were indistinguishable, which led perpetrators to refrain from testifying out of the concern that their testimony at the TRC would be adopted for use as evidence for future criminal prosecution (Kelsall 2009). In fact, because no arrangements concerning the relationship between the SCSL and the TRC were ever clearly made, some disputes also arose between the two institutions over the hearing of testimonies and treatment of those suspected of serious crimes (Schabas 2004). In this way, even though the SCSL's criminal prosecution of those responsible for serious crimes in violation of international humanitarian law was implemented by partially overturning the earlier provision of amnesty, the testimonies to cooperate with the

TRC could not be sufficiently obtained from the former soldiers who benefited from that amnesty, which consequently made the TRC process end without having achieved the adequate truth and accountability that had been anticipated.

5.3.3. Friction between Global and Local: The Limits of the Pursuit of Reconciliation by the Truth and Reconciliation Commission

As already mentioned, the reconciliation ceremonies of the TRC were transplanted from the local methods of conflict resolution that had been carried out at the grassroots level in an effort to rebuild relations of mutual trust through the establishment of moral obligations created though apologies and confessions for crimes. However, the TRC incorporated international human rights concepts and procedures such as gender equality, the protection of the rights of children and consideration for the victims of sexual abuse into these traditional mechanisms. Moreover, bodily harm was not accepted as a punishment consistent with the culture of human rights, even where physical punishment had some basis in local traditions or culture (Kelsall 2009). Therefore, the TRC's reconciliation ceremonies could be understood as a form of global and local hybridity that combined international notions of human rights with the base of local methods of conflict resolution.

Among these hybrid global and local elements, however, some were included that did not necessarily conform to local norms or culture in Sierra Leone. While the TRC emphasised the claim that the speaking of truth in public would lead to healing, this understanding is based on Western Christianity, especially Catholicism, and may, as some have argued, in fact, run counter to cultural norms in Sierra Leone (Shaw 2005). At a glance, this seems to contradict the traditional customary practice in Sierra Leone that was described as reconciliation through truthful confession in the report of Manifesto 99. However, in Sierra Leone, the confession of truth was not rendered up voluntarily, but rather 'truth' was understood as something to be elicited forcibly through curses and religious rituals, and thereby held to be effective in conflict resolution (Kelsall 2009). Therefore, those testimonies at the hearings of the TRC had no credibility since they had no basis in local traditional and cultural norms and institutions, thus perpetrators' confessions of crimes were regarded as lacking the power to move people's hearts (Shaw 2005).

The fact that the local traditional methods represented by curses and other religious rituals were not fully utilised for the TRC did not simply arise out of some lack of understanding of local moral and religious practices on the part of the international staff working for the TRC. Rather, it derived in large part from a sense of aversion to local chiefs whose cooperation was indispensable to the process, and yet who in many cases were believed to have been directly involved in the conflict. In addition, it is also believed that utilising traditional systems caused feelings of resistance among the international staff toward conferring legitimacy on the repressive structures by which chiefs and elders exploited younger generations, a phenomenon believed to have been one of the root causes of the civil war. In its final report, the TRC acknowledged that the Commission had 'not felt entirely comfortable relying on traditional structures' (SLTRC 2004 Vol. 3B: 438). In fact, many of the former combatants welcomed back to traditional reconciliation ceremonies were youths who had opposed the unduly heavy sanctions, fines and labour levied on them by chiefs and elders in the rural areas where they had once lived, leading them to become adherents of the revolution advocated by the anti-government faction (Richards 2005). For these people as well, supplicating their chiefs and communities for forgiveness and reintegration implied rebuilding the very social structures they had fought against. Although reconciliation between the former combatants, as both victims and perpetrators, and their communities was essential for the stability of the social order, the TRC had been unable to make any forward progress with regard to the above issue of the non-democratic structures of governance that were regarded to have been a root cause of the conflict.

Conversely, the various rituals of the reconciliation ceremonies employed by the TRC were described as having had the effect of justifying community reintegration of perpetrators, as well as assuaging painful memories of the past for both victims and local communities, and at last bringing an end to the conflict (Kelsall 2009). While certainly not many, the fact that there were those perpetrators who dared to come forward to testify before the Commission even in the absence of legal guarantees of amnesty for their testimony demonstrated that the TRC was understood to be a forum for social reintegration of perpetrators and its necessity recognised by many Sierra Leoneans (Park 2010). In this way, reconciliation ceremonies of the TRC may be seen to have played a certain role in promoting the social reintegration of former combatants, even as the exploitative structure of these ceremonies remains problematic. However, constrained in terms of both time and finances, the TRC was also unable to push its activities throughout the country at the local village level.

5.4. Leveraging Local 'Potentials': The *Fambul Tok* Experiment

5.4.1. Lessons Learnt from the TRC

As already mentioned, the TRC was established with the support from many local civil society groups. However, their different motivations behind the promotion of the TRC showed apparently that the human rights community in Sierra Leone was far from monolithic. In fact, at the time of the Lomé peace negotiations, whereas international human rights NGOs such as Amnesty International ultimately grasped the TRC as an alternative to criminal justice out of their steadfast opposition to any amnesty for serious violations of international law, some domestic human rights NGOs worked actively to promote the adoption of the South African TRC model, which advocated 'amnesty for truth'. The human rights NGO Forum of Conscience (FOC) is an example of the latter. Its director, John Caulker, advocated a TRC approach, which is neither a court that could inhibit the creation of peace nor the implementation of blanket amnesty, but rather offers amnesty in exchange for the confession of truth (Hoffman et al. 2011).

Although this idea was dismissed in favour of the blanket amnesty adopted into the Lomé Peace Accord during the preparatory phase of the TRC, the FOC came up with the idea of establishing 'mini TRCs' inside the framework of the TRC, to be practised at an even more grassroots level than the South African TRC model. In order to have people speak the truth and achieve real reconciliation, the FOC considered it necessary for hearings to be held in line with local customs – in communities where residents would be able to take part, rather than in the large halls of distant towns. The FOC then called for these 'mini TRCs,' which would emphasise dialogue among local residents and their ownership, to be established at the local village level around the country. However, according to Caulker, the idea ultimately failed to come to fruition after being 'dismissed by international community officials due to lack of precedent'.[10] The FOC later became a key player in the Truth and Reconciliation Commission Working Group (TRC-WG; later renamed TR-WG), an umbrella organisation made up of approximately 60 NGOs. From the preparations to set up the TRC until its activities were concluded, it provided monitoring and other support for the Commission's activities.

Reflecting on the activities of the TRC over eighteen months, Caulker, who was appointed as a chair of the TR-WG, while highly appreciative of the principles behind the Commission's activities and its reports, also voiced the following criticism: 'The people of Sierra Leone had no ownership over the process of the Truth and Reconciliation Commission. The hearings were only held for a week, and weren't held in the villages and chiefdoms where reconciliation was truly necessary. The residents in remote communities were still told make their way to the district cities if they wanted to attend a hearing despite the fact that the villagers had no means of transportation.'[11] This critique was also raised in a follow-up survey carried out by the TR-WG that interviewed foreign and domestic TRC officials after the conclusion of the TRC's activities. This study brought the following view expressed by Joe Rahall, Executive Director of Green Scenery (NGO) to light: 'The TRC has not achieved any true reconciliation. The "shaking hands" approach does not work here. Perpetrators tended to play a "role" in hearings. Victims are still waiting for revenge. It needed a cultural dimension and sustainability for at least three years.' (TR-WG 2006, p. 9).

On the basis of the findings of this study, in 2007 the TR-WG embarked on a project that would undertake the community level reconciliation that had not been achieved by the TRC (Park 2010). This project, which had earlier been conceived as 'mini-TRCs,' was intended to establish a reconciliation committee in each chiefdom across the country – five-member panels made up of a community leader, a religious leader, a women's representative, a youth representative and a community representative. These committees would not pursue reconciliations as one-off events as had the TRC, but were envisioned as a long-term process that would foster reconciliation between victims and perpetrators as well as among community members. At this point, however, TR-WG was unable to secure adequate funding and thus was never put into actual practice. This concept needed to wait for its realisation as the *Fambul Tok* Project.

5.4.2. The Launch of 'Family Talk'

Almost a year after the derailment of the TR-WG's mini-TRC initiative, *Fambul Tok* launched its activities in December 2007 after the FOC gained financial support from the American NGO Catalyst International.[12] The initial preparation phase for the project's activities were devoted to summarising hopes and needs vis-à-vis reconciliation from a broad spectrum of citizens throughout Sierra Leone. This was followed by the implementation of a first pilot programme in Kailahun District in the country's Eastern Province in March 2008. For the next two and a half years, more than 75 reconciliation ceremonies were carried out as the project's activities spread across the country. Although originally envisioned as a programme of mini-TRCs at the chiefdom level, consultations with local residents led to *Fambul Tok*'s institutional design eventually coming to be implemented at the even more local scale of small 'sections' made up of multiple villages.[13]

Fambul Tok was inspired by the fact that before the conflict community problems had been traditionally resolved through dialogues in a family-like environment where local community members could feel at ease. It aims at sharing the unsolved problems of the civil war period among the entire community based not on the punitive Western concepts of crime and punishment, but on a spirit of African community. *Fambul Tok* aimed at their solution in that same spirit. This programme was broadly divided up into the following four phases: (1) consultations regarding the need for reconciliation; (2) approaching communities and stakeholders toward reconciliation; (3) truth-telling around a bonfire and cleansing ceremonies; and (4) follow-up reconciliation initiatives (Hoffman et al. 2011). In all of these phases, the beliefs underlying activities are imbued with a conscious awareness of sustainability as well as residents' participation and ownership.

Phase (1) begins with a national coordinator entering into consultations with chiefdom officials in each district. After a careful review of residents' wishes and needs with respect to reconciliation in the community over the course of several months, a five-member reconciliation committee (similar to what had been envisioned for the mini-TRC concept) is then elected from the community, as well as a two-person outreach committee consisting of a youth representative and a community representative. The outreach committee is tasked with informing residents about the *Fambul Tok* process and convincing everyone involved of the necessity of reconciliation. Members from both committees take courses that provide instruction on *Fambul Tok*'s core beliefs and processes, as well as training with regard to arbitration techniques and trauma treatment. Then, in Phase (2), outreach activities are carried out to generate momentum for reconciliation in the community, while the reconciliation committees provide arbitration in relation to any issues arising in this period as well as psychological support to victims and perpetrators. Phase (3) involves the actual reconciliation ceremonies. Firstly, seated around a bonfire under the evening sky, victims and perpetrators each relate their own conflict experiences and thoughts aloud in a community forum. When perpetrators apologise and beg for forgiveness, they are usually forgiven by victims. In cases where victims are unwilling to follow the path of reconciliation, the reconciliation committee begins arbitration. Then, on the day after the bonfire, cleansing ceremonies are performed based on local tradition and religion to symbolically reintegrate the perpetrators into the community, which is followed by a celebratory feast. Finally, in Phase (4), in order to further solidify the achieved reconciliation into something sustainable, various joint activities are planned and put into practice. In one activity, called the 'Peace Tree,' a bench is placed beneath a symbolic tree to establish a site where conflict resolutions can take place in the community. Other examples include a 'radio listening club' in which conflict experiences and reconciliation initiatives are shared throughout the country by radio broadcast, 'peace farms' worked as joint agricultural projects and soccer matches for promoting reconciliation. These reconciliation projects, which are open to the entire community, are planned and put into practice by local residents themselves.

5.4.3. Local/Global Hybridity in Informal Approaches to Transitional Justice

One of the notable points about *Fambul Tok*'s activities is that the project has revived local traditional norms and customs, using social sanctions to achieve the social reintegration of perpetrators, thereby putting reconciliation into practice at the local level. Also important is that the initiative has prompted residents' rediscovery of the effectiveness of restorative transitional justice. Truth-telling in front of a bonfire and the subsequent cleansing ceremonies are carried out in the context of perceived dialogues with ancestral spirits in a variety of techniques unique to their respective communities. Since such customs were in many cases lost during the civil war, the project has become an opportunity for residents to reclaim these traditions (Park 2010). In addition, as also became evident in the TRC, while injustices and repression by the traditional authorities that carry out these rituals remain problematic, here too there has been a rediscovery of the power of ritual roles in ending conflicts and restoring order to the community.

Furthermore, in several senses, *Fambul Tok* could also be understood as an attempt to transform structural problems imbedded in Sierra Leone's rural areas, which have been seen as one of the root causes of the conflict. Firstly, we can observe its effect from the way that the residents participated in the process and democratic methods of collecting opinions were respected. For instance, although *Fambul Tok*'s reconciliation ceremonies comprised two elements, bonfires and cleansing rituals, the way they are conducted are flexible enough to accommodate residents' opinions expressed at the consultation meetings in each community. In addition, it could be described as an attempt to respect the human

161

rights and other relevant rights of both parties that in the process of institution design, views of victims and perpetrators, between whom reconciliation is most essential, are asked for. Secondly, *Fambul Tok* makes a conscious effort to enhance the roles of those who have traditionally been relegated to the periphery of rural society, such as women and the youth. In addition to the election of representatives from these groups to the outreach and reconciliation committees, programmes that could accommodate the needs of women in the post-conflict context are introduced with an intention to encourage their recovery from emotional and physical damage. Moreover, *Fambul Tok* seeks to enhance human resources who will actively contribute to the maintenance of the order and social development in the communities. One such example is the 'Peace Mother' initiative launched in 2010 as a reconciliation follow-up project and which is a collaborative activity carried out by and for women in the villages. This project expanded the scope of pro-women activities from just providing traditional birthing assistance and farm management, to assisting women with small enterprises and so forth. Thirdly, *Fambul Tok* has facilitated the institutionalisation of conflict resolution methods that are not reliant on traditional authorities. While local chiefs and elders in rural areas were traditionally responsible for resolving conflicts on the basis of customary law, the arbitrary exploitation of the youth, through such punishment as the imposition of unduly heavy fines and labour, generated grievances, which have been seen as a remote cause of the civil war in Sierra Leone (Richards 2005). Despite this deficit, most people still had to rely on customary law as the development of public judicial institutions has made little progress even after the conflict, and meanwhile traditional methods were nevertheless considered to be expensive, opaque and frequently corrupt (Archibald and Richards 2011). In contrast, the reconciliation committees set up by *Fambul Tok* continue their mediation activities to work on community issues at no charge under the 'peace trees' even after they finished conducting reconciliation ceremonies. The reconciliation committees, while maintaining the existing forms of customary methods of conflict resolution, seem also to be working deftly to block the revival of exploitative structures by preventing the centralisation of authority (Hoffman et al. 2011).

Fambul Tok can thus be understood as a hybrid programme that, while relying on existing restorative methods of conflict resolution, simultaneously subsumes liberal value concepts such as democratic decision making and the rectification of social inequality. Its major difference from the TRC, which incorporated similar hybrid reconciliation ceremonies, lies in the fact that *Fambul Tok* is an informal approach to transitional justice created by locally based NGOs. Therefore, *Fambul Tok* has been successful in adapting to local needs without getting overly caught up in global norms and institutions. In addition, taking a long-term perspective with the added goal of social transformation has enabled the programme to work from within on the problems of structural violence which, although held to have been one of the root causes of conflict, had nevertheless been beyond the reach of formal transitional justice.

5.5. Beyond the Local and Global Dichotomy

In Sierra Leone, a dichotomous and undemocratic structure of governance, in which political power and economic resources at the centre were monopolised by a small elite while arbitrary rule was distributed among hereditary chiefs in the rural areas, has been regarded as a major factor of the outbreak and prolongation of the civil war through the 1990s (Richards 2005). In order to respond to these root causes, formal transitional justice has been introduced in the framework of peacebuilding activities aiming at preventing the recurrence of conflict. While this effort was made to engage with the structural problems of the former through institutional reforms of the security sector as well as the punishment of those bearing the greatest responsibility for serious human rights violations, it ultimately failed sufficiently to address the latter problems embedded in the local context. In fact, the problem of the social reintegration of perpetrators into rural agricultural villages is in many cases at the same time directly linked to issues of justice that face women and the youth as vulnerable social actors. For example, whereas former combatants received small benefits payments and vocational training through DDR initiatives, many women who had been victimised during the conflict were forced to live alongside the perpetrators of their abuse while continuing to suffer distress and deep poverty even after the end of the conflict. In addition, the fact that reintegration into the community by means of reconciliation ceremonies such as cleansing rituals has signalled an implicit promise by former combatants to obey existing value systems also raises the problem of such practices being predicated on the assumed ideal of a return to pre-conflict society (Stovel 2008).

Fambul Tok was established in order to engage with these local-level challenges to transitional justice. This programme, which was institutionalised by local NGOs in light of the limits of state-level approaches to formal transitional justice that became apparent in support for the Sierra Leone Truth and Reconciliation Commission, went with the tide of global transitional justice to transplant liberal value concepts while simultaneously relying on existing cultural and traditional norms and institutions. While South Africa's TRC model was established to reflect national particularities after a critical examination of similar experiments in other countries (Boraine 2001), this chapter has shown how the critical examination of formal transitional justice resulted in the model's further localisation, leading ultimately to the construction of informal institutions more suited to local conditions.

What became apparent in the process leading from the design of formal and informal transitional justice institutions in Sierra Leone to the implementation of their activities is the necessity of citizens' ownership of and participation in the conflict resolution process. Preventing the recurrence of conflict requires not only the punishment of those responsible for serious offences, but also the reconstruction and strengthening of sustainable communities. The capability of people to support these ends must be strengthened. The introduction of transitional justice through international involvement might have presented an opportunity to draw attention to these 'potentials' in the creation of hybrid mechanism held by the people of Sierra Leone.

Fambul Tok's activities have also begun to attract interest in other African countries, including Liberia, Guinea, Uganda, Kenya and Zimbabwe.[14] This chapter has focused on *Fambul Tok*'s institution-building processes rather than seeking to evaluate the outcomes of its activities. Further study will be needed regarding the merits or otherwise of introducing similar processes elsewhere. However, in thinking about the unique challenges that Africa faces in terms of the coexistence of traditional orders with modern states, the fragile states and conservative elites that accompany the legacy of colonial rule, and urban and rural disparities, the *Fambul Tok* initiative may offer an approach with the potential to overcome the dichotomy of local and global justice.

Notes

[1] Victims' applications for compensation were started in 2008, with approximately 30,000 people registered as target recipients. In 2009, 100 US dollars were paid out to approximately 19,000 of those who had been recognised as victims of dismemberment, injury or sex crimes during the conflict. In 2012, 80 US dollars were paid out in supplementary support to victims who had not yet received compensation.

[2] A UN representative who took part in the negotiations added the following disclaimer with regard to the amnesty in a handwritten annotation to the peace agreement document inserted next to the UN signature: 'The United Nations holds the understanding that the amnesty and pardon in Article IX of the agreement shall not apply to international crimes of genocide, crimes against humanity, war crimes and other serious violations of international humanitarian law' (Hayner 2007: 5).

[3] Lomé Peace Accord, Peace Agreement between the Government of Sierra Leone and the Revolutionary United Front of Sierra Leone. Signed on 18 May 1999. Available at http://peacemaker.un.org/sites/peacemaker.un.org/files/SL_990707_Lo mePeaceAgreement.pdf.

[4] The serious crimes here include crimes against humanity, war crimes and other serious violations of international humanitarian law.

[5] The UN resolved that there had originally been no application of 'amnesty' for the major violations of international law, deeming that the government's amnesty had been applied only to crimes as defined by domestic laws.

[6] The Abidjan Peace Accord, although signed by President Kabbah and Foday Sankoh in November 1996, was never implemented.

[7] Of these, ten were put on trial, and nine were convicted (another defendant died during the trial). Of the remaining three, Sankoh and one other died before the prosecution proceedings began, while the other escaped and fled before prosecution began. Later, additional charges of contempt of court were brought against a further eight people. See for more details at Special Court for Sierra Leone and the Residential Court for Sierra Leone, http://www.rscsl.org/.

[8] For a detailed account of the 'amnesty for truth' of the South African TRC model, see Tutu (1999) and Audrey R. Chapman and Hugo van der Merwe, eds., (2008).

[9] The Truth and Reconciliation Act 2000, 22 February 2000, Article 7(2).

[10] Interview with J. Caulker, a former director of Forum of Conscience and the TR-WG, on 10 August 2012 in Freetown.

[11] Interview with J. Caulker, *ibid.*

[12] Forum of Conscience merged with Catalyst International in 2009 to become *Fambul Tok* International. For further details, see the organisation's website at http://www.fambultok.org/.

[13] Sierra Leone is made up of a Western Area and three provinces, and the provinces consisting of 12 districts containing 148 chiefdoms. Chiefdoms are further subdivided into sections, extended villages and villages.

[14] For example, while conducting fieldwork in Liberia in 2014, the author was told by an official of the Independent National Commission on Human Rights of Liberia that there were plans to visit Sierra Leone and examine the *Fambul Tok* model.

References

Archibald, S. and Richards, P. (2011) 'Converts to human rights? Popular debate about war and justice in rural Central Sierra Leone', *Africa*, Vol. 72, No. 3, pp. 339–67.

Boraine, A. (2001) *A Country Unmasked: Inside South Africa's Truth and Reconciliation Commission*, Oxford: Oxford University Press.

Chapman, A.R., and Van der Merwe, H. (eds.) (2008) *Truth and Reconciliation in South Africa: Did the TRC Deliver?*, Philadelphia: University of Pennsylvania Press.

Cubitt, C. (2012) *Local and Global Dynamics of Peacebuilding: Post-Conflict Reconstruction in Sierra Leone*, London: Routledge.

Harris, D. (2013) *Sierra Leone: A Political History*, London: Hurst & Company.

Hayner, P. (2007) *Negotiating Peace in Sierra Leone: Confronting the Justice Challenge*, Geneva: Centre for Humanitarian Dialogue/The International Center for Transitional Justice.

Hoffman, L. et al. (2011) *Fambul Tok*, New York: Umbrage Editions.

Kaldor, M. (1999) *New and Old Wars: Organized Violence in a Global Era*, Stanford: Stanford University Press.

Keen, D. (2005) *Conflict and Collusion in Sierra Leone*, New York: Palgrave.

Kelsall, T. (2009) *Culture under Cross-Examination: International Justice and the Special Court for Sierra Leone*, Cambridge, UK: Cambridge University Press.

Millar, G. (2010) 'Assessing local experiences of truth-telling in Sierra Leone: Getting to "why" through a qualitative case study analysis', *The International Journal of Transitional Justice*, Vol. 4, No. 3, pp. 477–96.

Nagy, R. (2008) 'Transitional justice as global project: Critical reflections', *Third World Quarterly*, Vol. 29, No. 2, pp. 275–89.

O'Flaherty, M.L. (2004) 'Sierra Leone's peace process: The role of the human rights community', *Human Rights Quarterly*, Vol. 26, No. 1, pp. 29–62.

Paris, R. and Sisk, T.D. (2009) *The Dilemmas of Statebuilding: Confronting the Contradictions of Postwar Peace Operations*, London: Routledge.

Park, A.S.J. (2010) 'Community-based restorative transitional justice in Sierra Leone', *Contemporary Justice Review*, Vol. 13, No. 1, pp. 95–119.

Richards, P. (2005) 'To fight or to farm? Agrarian dimensions of the Mano River conflicts', *African Affairs*, Vol. 104, No. 417, pp 571–90.

Sawyer, E. and Kelsall, T. (2007) 'Truth vs. justice? Popular views on the truth and reconciliation and the special court for Sierra Leone', *Online Journal of Peace and Conflict Resolution*, Vol. 7, No.

1, http://www.trinstitute.org/ojpcr/7_1SawKel.pdf.

Schabas, W. (2004) 'A synergistic relationship: The Sierra Leone truth and reconciliation commission and the special court for Sierra Leone', in W. Schabas and S. Darcy (eds.), *Truth Commissions and Courts: The Tension Between Criminal Justice and the Search for Truth*, Dordrecht, The Netherlands: Kluwer Academic Publishers, pp. 3–54.

Sharp, D.N. (2015) 'Emancipating transitional justice from the bonds of the paradigmatic transition', *The International Journal of Transitional Justice*, Vol. 9, No.1, pp.150–69.

Shaw, R. (2005) *Rethinking Truth and Reconciliation Commissions: Lessons from Sierra Leone*, Washington, DC: United States Institute of Peace Press.

Shaw, R. (2010) 'Linking justice with reintegration? Ex-combatants and the Sierra Leone experiment', in R. Shaw and L. Waldorf (eds.), *Localizing Transitional Justice: Interventions and Priorities after Mass Violence*, Stanford: Stanford University Press, pp.111–34.

SLTRC (Sierra Leone Truth and Reconciliation Commission) (2004) *Witness to Truth: Final Report to the TRC*, SLTRC: Freetown, http://www.sierraleonetrc.org/.

Stovel, L. (2008) '"There's no bad bush to throw away a bad child": "Tradition"-inspired reintegration in post-war Sierra Leone', *The Journal of Modern African Studies*, Vol. 46, No. 2, pp. 305–24.

TR-WG (The Sierra Leone working group on Truth and Reconciliation) (2006) *Searching for Truth and Reconciliation in Sierra Leone: An Initial Study of the Performance and Impact of the Truth and Reconciliation Commission* (unpublished).

Tutu, D. (1999) *No Future without Forgiveness*, New York: Doubleday.

Chapter 6

National Integration, Political Violence and People's Livelihoods: Conflicts and Coexistence in Rural Kenya

Motoki Takahashi and Masashi Hasegawa

6.1. Introduction: Nation-building as an Impossible Dream?

African countries, in most of cases, were shaped exogenously, their divisions determined through the scramble for Africa during a period of colonisation resulting in nations being formed including multiple ethnic groups. Now, almost a half-century after gaining independence, it seems pertinent to ask what progress has been made in their post-independence aspirations toward national integration that overcomes ethnic differences. Have they been able to ensure equitable access to public services and a unified market system? In this context, how do ordinary citizens of contemporary Africa perceive the present situation and do they think the nation and ethnic relations in the nation are politically and economically fair? Finally, can we discover possibilities for Africa – or African potentials – through exploration of ordinary people's perceptions and thoughts about coexistence among different groups within countries? To a significant degree, in the context of Africa, Kenya is one example where inter-ethnic relations have emerged as a major factor driving the political economy (one may call this kind of situation as 'tribalism' if we can use a colloquial expression). It is said that the country was brought to the brink of collapse as a result of inter-ethnic conflict manifested in the post-election violence (PEV) that broke out at the end of 2007 and continued the following year. While Kenya's former Rift Valley Province[1] was a principal epicentre of this conflict, some of the most horrific violence was in fact perpetrated near the city of Eldoret, in the Uasin Gishu District (now County).

In the former Rift Valley and Uasin Gishu, members of the Kikuyu people settled in mainly after independence and lived

169

alongside other groups such as the Kalenjin people, long-time residents even before colonisation. Of the Kalenjin, the Nandi, a sub-group, was the most populous. It is suspected that some among the Nandi engaged in brutal assaults on the Kikuyu and other peoples. Because of this background, this region seems to be a good example to explore the ordinary people's perceptions and thoughts of what it means to be a nation, as outlined earlier. This study seeks answers to questions of nationhood on the basis of data and findings of our field study conducted in villages inhabited by both the victims and perpetrators (suspected) of the assaults.

In this chapter, Section 2 starts with a brief overview of the political process leading up to the outbreak of the PEV in Kenya. Then, drawing on the results of an interview-based field study conducted among households in two neighbouring villages in Uasin Gishu District, Section 3 undertakes a comparative analysis that considers the political awareness and land rights in the villages of both the victims and the suspected perpetrators. Based on the results of this analysis, Section 4 discusses the villagers' concepts of their nation and respective ethnic groups, and, in light of this, what it says about the progress of nation-building in Africa, and people's perceptions thereof. The chapter concludes with the authors' views on the remaining possibilities and challenges of coexistence among the people of Kenya.

6.2. The Political Process in Kenya in the Lead-up to the PEV

6.2.1. Conflict since the Introduction of a Multi-Party System

By the start of the 1990s, the tidal shift towards multiparty democracy that had been sweeping across African countries also reached Kenya. The nation's second President, Daniel arap Moi – severely criticised by the international community and some of his compatriots for authoritarian rule, ethnically-biased public resource distribution, alleged corruption – finally acceded to the abolishment of the one-party system, no longer able to maintain his resistance against internal and external pressures. Moi belonged to the Tugen, a sub-group of the Kalenjin people, and Moi and his henchmen depended on political support from other such small sub-groups.

Since the population of Kalenjin as a whole was smaller than Kikuyu and other major ethnic groups, this devolvement into multiparties also implied a risk to state power itself and thus access to public resources.

With this sense of crisis as a backdrop, Kalenjin politicians and others in the government resurrected the principle of 'Majimboism.' Majimboism was the concept, claimed by politicians representing Kalenjin people and other minority people in the process leading up to Kenyan independence, of adopting a federal system in which the administration, such as land system management including surveying and registration and distribution of properties seized by Europeans in the colonial period, would be carried out autonomously in each region.[2] Specifically, this meant that after independence, Kikuyu people living in the Rift Valley Province, which Kalenjin people regarded as their own territory, would be deprived of a prerequisite for land ownership and the Kikuyu would be excluded from politics in the province. However, after independence in 1963, along with the establishment of a Kikuyu-led political regime under Kenya's first president, Jomo Kenyatta, Majimboism was politically shelved, and not seen again until the beginning of the 1990s.

It is important to note that collective self-identity of Africa's indigenous ethnic groups was in some aspects reinforced under colonial rule. For example, the Kalenjin were formed as a distinct people sometime around the 1950s when smaller groups such as the Nandi and Tugen, who shared a mutual relatedness as well as other common characteristics such as language, culture and residential areas, began to take on a singular identity (Huntingford 1953, p. 1). It is believed that, in the latter half of the colonial period, this process of Kalenjin ethnogenesis was strongly influenced by their relationship with more 'advanced' ethnic groups such as the Kikuyu. The Kikuyu exerted a powerful presence through their economic activities and resistance to colonial rule. In addition to this a considerable number of those who had been left as landless farmers, in large part due to land seizures by the Europeans, had migrated into the Rift Valley Province from the former Central Province, the so-called Kikuyu homeland. As a result of this, Gabrielle Lynch has argued, a consciousness of marginalisation and sense of shared misfortune appeared to deepen among the different Kalenjin groups, providing incentive for the formation of a common identity (Lynch 2011). Yet, while they regarded themselves as Kalenjin, many of these people continued to maintain their separate identities as members of sub-groups such as the Nandi and Tugen.

Now, while the concept that the rights to land in the Rift Valley Province belonged to members of ethnic groups originally inhabiting the region is fundamental to Majimboism, from the 1990s, this idea was frequently advanced by political elites associated with the Moi regime in order to incite conflict among the people. There were calls that the Kikuyu and other newcomers to the Rift Valley should be expelled (HRW/AW 1993, p. 31; CIPEV 2008, p. 50).

Then, starting around 1991, the year before the first election after the abolition of the single party system, conflict in the province began to occur more frequently. In many cases, incidents unfolded as attacks by groups of the majority Kalenjin, sometimes thousands strong, against immigrant groups such as the Kikuyu and Luo, followed by counterattacks. One of the principal settings for such violence was in Nandi-inhabited districts such as Uasin Gishu.

It seems likely that a rekindled Majimboism to some extent justified and encouraged the Kalenjin attacks on the Kikuyu and others. Indeed, it cannot be denied that a series of conflicts was organised 'from above' by politicians at the heart of the Moi regime to interfere with voting by opposition supporters and secure victory in the election campaign (Lynch 2011, p. 200). In a series of conflicts, the 'Majimboists' advanced their claim that the lands of the Rift Valley Province that had been grabbed by Europeans during the colonial period should belong to the Kalenjin, and that the Kikuyu and others, who had come to settle the region as 'newcomers' with the backing of the regime of Jomo Kenyatta, the first president and a Kikuyu leader after independence, were not the rightful owners. Radical Majimboists advocated that these 'newcomers' should be driven out of the settled and inhabited areas as 'spots' (*madoadoa* in Kiswahili), and that the lands in question should be taken back by the Kalenjin. It is certain that the historical injustice of the land grab by Europeans produced large numbers of 'unlawful' Kalenjin 'squatters' for whom a variety of problems remain unresolved even today. The view that settlement on former European farms in the Rift Valley by the Kikuyu had to some extent carried on this injustice is believed to have provided a basis for acquiring the support from among at least a part of the Kalenjin people.

However, this did not mean that radical Majimboism, that called for the violent expulsion of Kikuyu and others seen as outsiders without any rights to land in the former Rift Valley Province, was shared by all Kalenjin. In fact, accusations, by some Nandi politicians, of corruption amid the ongoing accumulation of already extensive landholdings in Uasin Gishu District and elsewhere were directed towards the political elites at the heart of the Moi regime, who were also Kalenjin. There were even some politicians who actively called for coexistence with Kikuyu settlers. In addition, even though large numbers of Nandi had been mobilised in a series of conflicts, it became clear that it was very difficult to totally expel the Kikuyu, who took flight temporarily from their settled territories, yet soon found they had nowhere else to go. For this reason, the (re-)acquisition of Nandi lands that had been promised by elites at the core of the regime during conflicts was in many cases never realised (Klopp 2002).

Moi's authority among the Kalenjin people was shaken with the result that many Kalenjin and Nandi politicians declined to support his nominated successor, Uhuru Kenyatta (son of the first President, and a Kikuyu) in the presidential election of 2002. Uhuru lost to the veteran politician, Mwai Kibaki, also a member of the Kikuyu. Kibaki's base of support included political leaders from almost all major ethnic groups of Kenya, such as Raila Odinga of the Luo people.

6.2.2. The Rift Valley Province and the Political Situation on the Eve of the PEV

The birth of the Kibaki regime heightened expectations of the end of the oligarchy promoted by influential politicians from specific ethnic groups. In the end, however, Kibaki did not honour his promise to Odinga to create the position of prime minister and allocate half the Cabinet positions to the Odinga faction, and instead the core of the regime was hardened with the president's Kikuyu confederates (CIPEV 2008, pp. 41–42; Tsuda 2009, pp. 95–96). This was regarded as a revival of the oligarchic political rule by the Kikuyu that had been practised under Jomo Kenyatta's regime, and generated fierce opposition, intensifying the antagonism between the Kikuyu and other ethnic groups both inside and outside the government. This antagonism was brought to a head by a constitutional amendment proposed by the Kibaki regime in 2005, and the national referendum that was to decide it (CIPEV 2008, p. 40).

The proposed amendment was taken to be far from appropriate to Kenya's constitutional democracy. Intersecting with criticisms against the Kikuyu monopoly of the regime, a growing movement against the amendment began to unfold whose leaders included Odinga, Uhuru and William Ruto, a Nandi, now leaders of the opposition. Anger intensified among factions, both in favour of and opposed to the national referendum, resulting in clashes that in some cases led to fatalities (CIPEV 2008, p. 52). Ultimately, while Kibaki's constitutional amendment was rejected by a wide margin in the national referendum, the antipathy towards Kikuyu that had gained traction among ordinary citizens was not so easily dispelled. In the Rift Valley, a discourse in which Kikuyu were seen as 'spots' and ancestral lands were to be taken back reportedly once again became widespread through radio broadcasts and other media in the Kalenjin language (CIPEV 2008, p. 52; Lynch 2011, p. 196). Immediately before the PEV, the social situation in areas where both Kalenjin and Kikuyu lived, such as Uasin Gishu, was fraught with impending disaster.

In 2007, anti-Kikuyu sentiment grew even stronger when Uhuru put his support behind Kibaki, who was seeking re-election in the coming presidential election, thereby unifying the Kikuyu political camp. On the other side, against this backdrop of strengthened anti-Kikuyu and anti-Kibaki sentiment, Odinga succeeded in bringing together the support of a coalition of influential politicians from across ethnic boundaries, and entered the presidential election as the most promising candidate to offer substantial opposition. Among the Kalenjin politicians, the most influential Nandi figure, William Ruto, also threw his support behind Odinga. While Odinga expressed a position of adopting Majimboist policies from the perspective of

174

strengthening decentralisation, this would effectively have attracted the support of the majority of Kalenjin, including the radical Majimboists (Lynch 2011, p. 198). In fact, as the presidential election and simultaneous parliamentary elections became imminent, some of the Nandi politicians, including Ruto, are believed to have advocated radical Majimboism among their own constituencies.

6.2.3. Uashin Gishu and the Progression of the PEV

The presidential and parliamentary elections held in 2007 were carried out, for the most part, peacefully despite some skirmishes and instances of intimidation against Kikuyu. On 30 December, when the Electoral Commission declared Kibaki's victory in the presidential election, Kibaki acted immediately to stage a ceremony to be sworn in for the second term of his presidency. Kibaki's victory upset not only the expectations of the citizens but, in truth, all forecasts as well. The advance polling, and large discrepancies in the number of votes for the ruling and opposition parties in the simultaneous parliamentary elections, as well as results that contradicted exit polls, convinced the majority of citizens of election fraud by the Kibaki administration. Immediately afterwards, protest demonstrations and fierce attacks began to be staged against the Kikuyu, not only by the Luo people to which Odinga belonged, but by the Kalenjin as well. In a flash, violence swept across major cities including Nairobi, Mombasa and Kisumu, as well as rural areas in the Rift Valley Province and others. This was especially true in the case of Uasin Gishu District, where the violence that unfolded was more intense than anywhere else in the rural districts. The Commission of Inquiry into Post-Election Violence (CIPEV), which was an official entity set up just after the conflict to explore causes and actions required for peace building consisting of Kenyan and international experts, found that of the 1,133 deaths resulting from the PEV across the country, just under 70 per cent took place in the Rift Valley Province. Of these, 230 took place in Uasin Gishu, which as a district, experienced the highest death toll in Kenya. In terms of casualties, as well, the situation was largely the same. There was also extensive evidence of sexual violence, especially against women (CIPEV 2008).

In Uasin Gishu District, mainly in the vicinity of Eldoret, groups of reportedly thousands of Kalenjin attacked homes and shops in Kikuyu residential areas. According to the official report, the principal means of attack was, apart from setting houses alight, to attack and kill or injure Kikuyu and other residents with weapons that included blades and blunt objects. From the data in the official report on the causes of deaths and injuries (CIPEV 2008, pp. 313, 316, 328), it may be inferred that casualties in the district were the result, not of attacks by people with heavy sophisticated weaponry, but rather of assaults carried out in close contact by lightly armed gangs carrying whatever weapons or fuel that came easily to hand. In addition, many of the victims reported witnessing, among their assailants, Kalenjin they knew as neighbours or acquaintances.[3] Given the extent of the mobilisation described above, what comes to mind is a situation in which Kalenjin, who usually lived quiet lives as ordinary citizens, not owning firearms or other such weapons, descended on the homes and neighbourhoods of Kikuyu in overwhelming numbers, engaging in acts of violence that included assaults, rapes and arson that produced numerous deaths and injuries.

The Kikuyu, and others targeted by this violence, in order to escape the assaults, sought refuge at the police stations, churches, as well as newly set-up camps becoming internally displaced persons (IDPs), if only temporarily. According to the official report, the Kenyan government originally estimated the number of IDPs to be approximately 350,000 individuals (CIPEV 2008, p. 272).[4] A considerable portion of these people were residents of the Rift Valley Province, and a large number presumed to be from the Uasin Gishu District.

The PEV afterwards saw counterattacks launched by the Kikuyu which also included a number of ordinary citizens. As the violence further intensified, it began to exhibit the character of an inter-ethnic struggle between the Kikuyu on one side and the Luo and Kalenjin on the other.[5] Uhuru, who supported Kibaki, mobilised the Mungiki sect – a criminal organisation comprising mainly Kikuyu – to lead the counterattack on behalf of the Kikuyu, which resulted in extensive deaths and casualties among the Luo and Kalenjin. This escalation prompted the international community to launch an attempt at mediation between the opposing sides. Eventually, mediation activities, chaired by Kofi Annan, former Secretary-General of the United Nations, proved successful with the establishment of the office of a Prime Minister and the launch of a 'Government of National Unity' (also known as the 'Grand Coalition') becoming the central pillars of a power-sharing agreement that was put in place at the end of February. The violence that had swept the country was finally brought under control.

Perhaps the most horrific of the series of violent incidents that took place occurred in the village of Kiambaa on the outskirts of Eldoret, one of the field sites for the research on which this chapter is based. On New Year's Day, 2008, a large number of Kikuyu, including many from nearby villages fleeing attacks that had broken out on 30 December, took refuge in the Assemblies of God Church located in the centre of the village. A combined group of upwards of 1,000 Kalenjin coming from all over, crowded around the church, and set the building on fire even with dozens of Kikuyu women and children trapped inside. This resulted in at least 35 people being burned to death, and many more suffered burn injuries. The events that took place in Kiambaa attracted considerable national and international attention, and came to serve as a symbol of the PEV.

According to the official report, police forces that had been aware of and tried to prevent the planned attacks on Kiambaa had been unable to arrive on the scene due to roadblocks that had been prepared in advance by the attackers (CIPEV 2008, p. 54). This suggested that a degree of planning and organisation had been involved in the staging of the attacks.

6.2.4. The Kalenjin People during and after the PEV

The official report, in light of circumstances immediately in the aftermath of the PEV, concluded that Kenyans' national consciousness had been undermined by these inter-ethnic conflicts, and that nation building of Kenya was itself on the verge of collapse (CIPEV 2008, pp. 35–36). The same report analysed the factors and processes that led to the PEV. This analysis suggested that these conflicts could not solely be explained as the result of antagonisms between the political elites who had competed in the election, or as being brought about by directions 'from above' (cf. Klopp 2008). While it is true that certain actions of the attackers, such as the preparation of roadblocks, indicate some degree of planning and organisation, the extremely large number of participants, many neighbours of those assaulted – in other words, people who up until then had been living normal, everyday lives – and the fact that the attackers were only lightly armed, suggests that the incident had arisen fairly spontaneously (Lynch 2011). It is also a fact that this conflict was in some aspects underpinned 'from below' by ordinary citizens. The official report points to matters relating to people's everyday lives, such as the marginalisation of those disadvantaged by ethnic inequality and unemployment that underlay the recruitment of youth into the conflict leading to the epidemic of violence as 'root causes' behind the conflict (CIPEV 2008, pp. 30–35).

In the wake of the PEV, it is surely important to explore the perceptions and ways of life of the ordinary people who were drawn into the conflict. The areas where the conflict took place have, on the surface, returned to a state of peace. In this regard, especially ordinary people's perceptions of the Kenyan nation, of inter-ethnic relations, of their land and of their own way of life surely offer a key to pursue the research questions posed by this chapter. We must pay attention to whether people still have a tendency toward inter-ethnic conflict and see failure in the project of nation building; in other words, whether and to what extent the influence of 'tribalism' or radical Majimboism will continue.

6.3. Tale of Two Villages

6.3.1. The Assaulting and the Assaulted: Field Survey and Field Site Overview

Developing the above ideas, this chapter is based on a study of residents' perceptions in the village of Kiambaa, where the brutal attacks took place, and the Village X, a nearby settlement inhabited by people widely regarded to have been involved in the attacks.

Prominent in the vicinity of both villages are large-scale farms that sprawl on lands cleared during the colonial period, once owned by Europeans but now belonging to Kalenjin political elites, which are in stark contrast with the inferior quality of the village infrastructure for ordinary citizens. Paths that connect the villages with the main highway become a quagmire when heavy rains turn the earth to mud, making the route impassable to regular automobile traffic. This is in direct contrast to the all-weather condition of the majority of rural roads in Kiambu District in the former Central Province, which accounts for the bulk of the Kikuyu population. This is likely due to the fact that, even under the Moi regime, the provision of public spending in this area was neglected.

One fact about the village of Kiambaa is that another place by the name of Kiambaa can be found in Kiambu District, and that this latter Kiambaa is the native constituency for many Kikuyu politicians who served central roles in the government of Jomo Kenyatta. Lynch points out that Kikuyu settlers had given names in the Kikuyu language to their farms and properties and this act of 'arrogance' had angered a number of Kalenjin (Lynch 2011, p. 200). This anger may well have been even stronger in cases where the sound of such names was reminiscent of the era of Kikuyu rule, as was the case in Kiambaa.

The village of Kiambaa was settled in 1964, primarily by settlers from Kiambu District. This was in the first year after independence, so the village settlement was comparatively early. Land that had been owned by Europeans was divided up into plots of 2.6 acres (just over one hectare) for purchase by settlers. At the time, no conditions were imposed on the settlers, and while the majority were Kikuyu, the history of the village shows that it included settlers from other ethnic groups as well. There were reportedly 150 households in the initial settlement. Kiambaa could be described as a typical example of settlement by ordinary people.

At the time of the 2013 field survey, the village population in Kiambaa consisted of 145 households, which, assuming this number to be accurate, suggests that the population had remained relatively stable since the initial settlement. The village population was reportedly 883 people, 86 per cent Kikuyu and 7 per cent Kalenjin. Most Kalenjin appeared to belong to the Nandi sub-group. A few members from ethnic groups other than these two were also included.

On the other hand, Village X was selected as a field site by virtue of its reputation as a village presumably inhabited by some of those who perpetrated the attacks. That is, due to the fact that it was an 'open secret' among villagers in Kiambaa and other local residents that individuals from Village X had staged the attack on the Assemblies of God Church, and moreover Village X was where these people had been trained for the attack.[6]

The origin of Village X differs considerably from that of Kiambaa. The village is located on the property of the former East African Tanning and Extract Co (EATEC), a large company founded in the colonial period. The company founded Village X in 1970 as a camp for Nandi labourers who worked on the plantation where tannins were extracted. Even though the settlement was founded 'for the Nandi', from the outset it was also home to people from other Kalenjin sub-groups, as well as two Kikuyu immigrants who were assimilated into Kalenjin ethnicity after settlement.

Many of the initial residents of Village X, as well as their parents during the colonial period, had been living there outside their designated reserves without official legal permission, as 'squatters.' Even after independence, their right to land had no official foundation, and one way to eke out a living was by working as day labourers at EATEC. Even when the village was first established, the homes (shacks) were cramped and subject to several rigid living restrictions; many recalled lives of frequent penury, due in part to the company's meagre wages.

When EATEC was dismantled in 2000, properties in Village X, mostly in parcels of about two acres, were distributed free of charge to the households of those who had worked for the company (subject to certain conditions).

At the time of the 2014 field survey, as far as could be determined, the village consisted of 129 households with a total population of 731 individuals. Among those who responded to a survey of ethnicity, 94 per cent answered that they were Kalenjin, and none claimed to be Kikuyu. The ratio of Kalenjin in Village X was thus far higher than the ratio of Kikuyu in Kiambaa. However, when these Kalenjin were asked to specify their ethnic affiliation more specifically, 66 per cent answered that they were Nandi (about 62 per cent of the entire village), while the rest belonged to various other Kalenjin sub-groups.

Our field surveys were conducted by visiting individual households to ask after the attributes of the household and its members, as well as solicit the views of the household head.[7] In questions about political awareness, we focused on questions relating to views on the responsibilities of politicians and national consciousness, through which we attempted to approach the question of how the image of nation and state was given shape in peoples' minds.

6.3.2. Ways of Life in the Two Villages

With regard to the realities of life in Kiambaa and Village X, one large difference in terms of first impressions is that whereas many residents in Village X could be seen to have nothing to do during the day, some wandering around inebriated while others whiled away their time in apparently shooting the breeze, such situations were more limited in Kiambaa. Except for this difference, however, both villages were, on the surface, equally peaceful whenever we visited. The sceneries of the two villages that we encountered made us feel as if the harsh violence that took place in this neighbourhood had been a historical anomaly.

However, Kiambaa was still home to survivors who were nonetheless physically and emotionally traumatised by the attack on the church and the village as a whole and mourned family members. It is also home to those who moved to the village when their families were killed elsewhere. Even so, it was difficult to find anyone who would openly admit a grudge against those who attacked Kiambaa. That being said, we did hear rumours from several individuals about specific Kalenjin residents who had been involved in the attack. Then again, there were also many inside and outside the village who mentioned cases in which Kalenjin youths, ostensibly associated with the attacks, who had experienced mental illness or committed suicide (interviews with a driver in Eldoret and a social worker living near Kiambaa, September 2012).

What stood out in Village X was the evident recognition by many that their village was particularly poor. When asked to rank their perception of their village's poverty on a 5-point scale, the combined proportion of villagers who responded that the village was 'somewhat poor' (32 per cent) or 'very poor' (44 per cent) accounted for almost three-quarters of the whole interviewees (about 83 per cent of those who responded to the question). This perception was shared by residents in neighbouring areas (confirmed in an interview with a social worker conducted near Village X in November 2014). One resident, who had recently moved to the village, admitted to concealing the move from friends and relatives (interview with Resident A at Village X, November 2014). Such a sense of inferiority is quite possibly related to the fact that Village X was originally formed as a camp of 'illegal squatters.'

On the other hand, we heard from some residents of Village X that it was originally supposed to be a *Nandi settlement*, and that other groups should leave, even if they were Kalenjin. In some cases, wealthy residents who were Kalenjin, but not Nandi, expressed a sense of anxiety about their residency conditions (interview with Resident B of Village X, November 2014). Indeed, cases had been reported of people being forcibly evicted by neighbours or local government authorities citing improprieties in the legal procedures by which their land plots were acquired (interview with Resident C in Village X, November 2014).

One issue in the series of conflicts that led up to the PEV had been the unequal distribution of land and eligibility for ownership of land. Let us examine the size of land owned, held, or rented by each household (in the following, we will simply use 'own' instead of 'own, hold, and rent').[8] The average land area owned per household in Kiambaa (based on responses from 130 households) was approximately 1.8 acres, as distinct from Village X (based on 126 responses) where the average was 1.1 acres. Dividing the land holdings of responding households into increments of 0.2 acres, the size of the most frequent landholding area in Kiambaa was around 2.6 acres (28 households), with only 15 households owning more. This suggests the lasting influence of the original land distribution at the time the village was founded, and that the concentration of land into the hands of only a few individuals had not taken place to any large degree. At the same time, those with marginal holdings of one acre or less remained limited to only 25 households.

On the other hand, the most frequent size of landholding in Village X was around 2 acres (36 households). While this similarly suggests the lasting influence of the initial distribution size of land plots, as many as 57 households owned land of smaller sizes. Of these, as many as 30 households held land at the minimal increment of 0.2 acres or less. While land ownership in Village X as a whole was on a smaller scale than in Kiambaa, it can be seen that a certain degree of polarisation was taking place in Village X.

Such differences in size and distribution of land ownership in the two villages seem to be related to the primary livelihoods of each. In Kiambaa, approximately 62 per cent of participants answered that this was agriculture, followed by informal and formal employment, which accounted for 17 per cent and 8 per cent respectively. In contrast, those who answered engaging in agriculture in Village X accounted for no more than about 18 per cent, while formal and informal employment accounted for 29 per cent and 27 per cent, respectively. The smaller landholding size in Village X, as residents readily admit to themselves and to outsiders, is likely correlated with the fact that it is a 'squatter' village, where the prevalence of impoverished residents is high. For a considerable number of residents, the size of land in Village X is too small, making agriculture difficult. The fact that employment is the primary means of subsistence for many people conceivably demonstrates the absence of any other reliable option.

Also, while we cannot elaborate in detail due to limitations of space in this paper, it should be noted that according to our survey there did not appear to be any significant differences in the level of education between the two villages.

6.3.3. Popular Awareness concerning the Security of Rights to Land

Having seen differences in the characteristics of the two villages ourselves, we should examine the perceptions of the residents with regard to their access or rights (hereafter rights) to lands. These are likely to relate to issues at the crux of the series of conflicts.

Household heads were therefore asked about the extent to which they felt that their personal land rights were secure.

Among participants in Kiambaa, 85 per cent of householders responded that their own land rights were 'very secure,' with a further 8 per cent responding 'secure.' Those who responded 'not very secure' or 'not secure at all' accounted for a mere 2 per cent and 5 per cent, respectively. On the other hand, in response to the same question in Village X, those who responded 'very secure' accounted for only approximately 40 per cent, 'secure' 5 per cent, 'not secure' 20 per cent, and 'not at all secure' 35 per cent. In other words, the majority of householders in Kiambaa felt little or no anxiety over security of their own rights to their land, yet more than half of those in Village X felt some or a great deal of anxiety. Given the circumstances of the PEV, this was different from our expectations since the Kikuyu people's entitlement to land property was challenged by radical Majimboism and thus one of the hottest issues underlying the PEV. It, therefore, seemed to require further careful examination.

This finding is perhaps related to drastic changes in the political situation after the PEV. Uhuru Kenyatta, a Kikuyu leader, and Ruto, a Kalenjin (Nandi), who bitterly opposed each other during the PEV, later reconciled and became allies. When the former became the president in 2013, he inaugurated a regime in which the latter served as the vice-president. Behind this dramatic development was the break-up between Ruto and Odinga triggered by Ruto's corruption scandal. There was also a concern that since Uhuru and Ruto were suspected to have been the ringleaders of the PEV, the two would have to face trials at the International Criminal Court. Kenyatta and Ruto both became increasingly isolated, and in order to stand against Odinga – the leading candidate to become the next president – they formed a political alliance that successfully won them control of the government in the 2013 election. For the Kikuyu people, continuing to have one of their members as national president and reconciled with the influential Nandi politician, who was once the most formidable advocate of eviction of Kikuyus from the Rift Valley, may have signified a reduction in the political threat to the security of their land rights.

Conversely, the fact that most residents in Village X remained anxious about the security of their own land rights requires a separate explanation. One notable difference between Kiambaa and Village X is that whereas 86 per cent (110 individuals) of responding householders in Kiambaa had registered title to their land, in Village X households with registered titles accounted for only about 32 per cent (37) of the respondents. Of the 70 householders (approximately 55 per cent) in Village X who responded that their land rights were 'not very secure' or 'not secure at all', 58 responded that their land had no registered title. Conversely, of the 37 who did have registered title, 29 responded that their rights were 'very secure.' The low ratio of title registration in Village X seems to demonstrate that the desire for land among those who had been 'squatters' since the colonial period had not been given adequate resolution in the sense of conferring official ownership. The differences between the two villages suggests that, quite apart from the political realities of rivalry and reconciliation among political elites at the national level, the circumstances of land market institution, i.e. in this case, land registration, had a significant impact on people's sense of security with regard to land.

6.3.4. Popular Awareness concerning the Responsibilities of Politicians and their Relationship to Ethnicity

Next, let us consider the awareness among household heads in Kiambaa and Village X with respect to politicians' responsibilities. As previously outlined, while conscious of the fact that these were formerly conflict-ridden localities, we tried asking multifaceted questions to learn what Kenya as a state meant to people (Table 1).

The first question, seeking to know people's conception of the proper relationship between the president's responsibility for resource allocation and ethnic groups, asked respondents to select the response that most matched their own ideas from among five possible answers to the question 'If the President of Kenya belongs to your ethnic group, what should be his/her attitude?' Detailed results are shown in Table 1. The assumption underlying this question was the hypothesis that if residents (i.e., householders) embraced a so-called 'tribalist' way of thinking that privileged their

185

own ethnic group over the state, most would choose the first option (i.e., resources such as roads, schools, electricity or employment, etc.

Table 1. Politicians' Responsibilities and Ethnic Relations in Post-Conflict Villages (Villagers' View)

Question[1]		Choices	The Number of Interviewees (proportion)	
			Kiambaa	Village X
Q1	If the President of Kenya belongs to your ethnic group, what should be his/her attitude?	1=Resources (roads, schools, electricity or employment, etc.) should be provided to his/her ethnic group as priority	2 (1%)	16 (13%)
		2=Resources should be provided as equitably as possible regardless of the difference of ethnic groups	129 (95%)	63 (49%)
		3=Resources should be provided to the ethnic group which is poorer than others	5 (4%)	10 (8%)
		4=Others (Would you tell us more in detail if you don't mind?)	0 (0%)	4 (3%)
		5=I don't know	1 (1%)	36 (28%)
Q2	If the member of parliament belongs to your ethnic group, what should be his/her attitude?	1=Resources (roads, schools, electricity or employment, etc.) should be provided to his/her ethnic group as priority	2 (3%)	26 (20%)
		2=Resources should be provided as equitably as possible regardless of the difference of ethnic groups	126 (93%)	60 (47%)
		3=Resources should be provided to the ethnic group which is poorer than others	6 (4%)	7 (5%)
		4=Others (Would you tell us more in detail if you don't mind?)	0 (0%)	4 (3%)
		5=I don't know	1 (1%)	32 (25%)

Q3	If the President of Kenya does not belong to your ethnic group and he/she provides resources to only his/her ethnic group as priority, what do you perceive it?	1=I think it is natural for him/her to do so	2 (3%)	4 (3%)
		2=It is unfair and he/she should stop it	130 (96%)	92 (71%)
		3=It is acceptable if that ethnic group is poorer than others	3 (2%)	6 (5%)
		4=Others (Would you tell us more in detail if you don't mind?)	0 (0%)	2 (2%)
		5=I don't know	1 (1%)	25 (20%)
Q4	If roads in your village are in trouble, who do you ask for maintenance or repair?	1=Village chief	14 (10%)	6 (5%)
		2=Other public official	9 (7%)	7 (5%)
		3=Local politician	84 (62%)	86 (67%)
		4=National politicians	9 (7%)	4 (3%)
		5=Village elders	8 (6%)	7 (5%)
		6=(Consult among) village members	5 (4%)	11 (9%)
		7=Others	10 (7%)	2 (2%)
		No answer	0 (0%)	6 (5%)

187

Q5	If schools in your village are in trouble, who do you ask for maintenance or repair?	1=Village chief	16 (12%)	4 (3%)
		2=Other public official	12 (9%)	5 (4%)
		3=Local politician	75 (55%)	56 (43%)
		4=National politicians	13 (10%)	11 (9%)
		5=Village elders	5 (4%)	6 (5%)
		6=(Consult among) village members	7 (5%)	38 (29%)
		7=Others	11 (8%)	2 (2%)
		No answer	7 (5%)	7 (5%)
Q6	What is the most important responsibility of the member of parliament from your district?	1=To contribute to the whole Kenyan nation	29 (21%)	38 (29%)
		2=To contribute to members of his/her own ethnic group	5 (4%)	1 (1%)
		3=To contribute to the constituency/local community	95 (70%)	82 (64%)
		4=Other (would you tell us more in detail if you don't mind?)	2 (1%)	1 (1%)
		5=I don't know	4 (3%)	7 (5%)

Q7	If the leaders of your ethnic group enrich themselves and their family through corruption, what do you perceive it?	1=I don't know	2 (1%)	9 (7%)
		2=The wealth should be distributed to his/her ethnic group	10 (7%)	4 (3%)
		3=The wealth should be returned to the Kenyan Government	105 (77%)	89 (69%)
		4=Only he/she should not be blamed because a large number of politicians do the same thing	2 (1%)	9 (7%)
		5=Corruption is not bad if the politicians distribute the wealth much more than he/she gets for him/herself	3 (2%)	11 (9%)
		6=Other (Would you tell me more in detail if you don't mind?)	15 (11%)	2 (2%)
		7=I don't feel anything particularly	1 (1%)	6 (5%)
		No answer	0 (0%)	1 (1%)
Q8	Do you think it is right to use the taxpayer's money to save victims from other ethnic groups suffering from natural disasters in Kenya?	1. Yes	129 (95%)	124 (96%)
		2. No	7 (5%)	2 (2%)
		No answer	0 (0%)	3 (2%)
Q9	Do you have a feeling to donate for the victims suffering from natural disasters?	1. Yes	129 (95%)	124 (96%)
		2. No	6 (4%)	2 (2%)

		No answer	1 (1%)	3 (2%)
Q10	Do you agree to pay more tax to save the victims from other ethnic groups suffering from natural disasters?	1. Yes	112 (82%)	124 (96%)
		2. No	23 (17%)	2 (2%)
		No answer	1 (1%)	3 (2%)

[1] Multiple answers are possible for Questions from 1 to 7.

Source: Created by the authors based on results of the field survey.

should be provided to his/her ethnic group as priority), while conversely fewer would choose the second option (i.e., resources should be provided as equitably as possible regardless of the difference of ethnic groups). The results found that, contrary to our expectations, the second option accounted for the most responses in both villages, while the first did not even come close. In addition, those who chose the third option (i.e., resources should be provided to the ethnic group which is poorer than others) remained in the minority in both villages.

However, there was a clear difference in the composition of answers between the two villages in that while those who chose the first option accounted for only a tiny proportion of respondents in Kiambaa, they accounted for approximately 13 per cent of respondents in Village X. In addition, whereas those who chose the second option accounted for the overwhelming majority in Kiambaa, those who did so in Village X accounted for fewer than half of respondents, even though it was the most popular answer. Furthermore, while there were very few in Kiambaa who chose the fifth option ('I don't know'), this was selected by almost 30 per cent of respondents in Village X.

Moreover, approximately identical results were obtained for Question 2, which asked about the responsibilities of the members of parliament in terms of resource distribution, offering the same optional responses as in Question 1. In Village X, a larger number of respondents (approximately 20 per cent) harboured the expectation that parliamentarians would prioritise resource allocation to members of their own ethnic group, while 'I don't know' also accounted for a considerable percentage of responses (almost 25 per cent).

In Question 3, respondents were asked about their views on a case in which a president, belonging to another ethnic group, gave priority to that group with regard to resource allocation. While it was expected that those who held to a 'tribalist' mentality would tend to choose the first option ('I think it is natural for him/her to do so'), only a few respondents chose this option in either village. Instead, the majority of responses chose the second option ('It is unfair and he/she should stop it'). While this response was essentially unanimous in Kiambaa, it surpassed 70 per cent even in Village X. However, a considerable proportion of respondents in Village X – almost one in five – also chose 'I don't know'.

While Questions 1 through 3 asked whether people followed what could be envisioned as a 'tribalist' mentality when forming opinions, the results showed meagre evidence of people expressing such opinions in either village. Nevertheless, all three questions did share a relatively high response rate to the option 'I don't know' in Village X.

Questions 4 referred to 'roads' and 5 to 'schools' in the village as concrete examples of resources provided by governments or other public institutions, asking who could be relied on for support in the event of some problem. The intention here was to clarify who people expected to play the most direct role in allocating these public goods, each of which were important in their daily lives. Despite our own perceptions about state-level 'tribalist' resource allocation by ethnic patrons, when consulted, respondents were more dubious about the idea of appealing to state-level politicians. This might be very natural, given that such figures would not normally have direct responsibility for, nor be easily accessible to, ordinary citizens.

Question 6 asked respondents about the roles and most important responsibilities of parliamentarians elected from their home districts. While it was expected that those who embraced a 'tribalist' mentality would tend to choose the second option ('To contribute to members of his/her own ethnic group'), as shown in Table 1, such a mind-set was found among only a very few respondents in either village. Conversely, while the first option ('To contribute to the whole Kenyan nation') accounted for a considerable proportion of respondents in both villages, it was not the most frequent answer. The most frequent answer in both villages was the third option ('To contribute to the constituency/local community').

Question 7, as the final question concerning politics, asked 'What would you think if a political leader from your own ethnic group were to engage in corrupt practices to enrich himself or his family (herself or her family)?' If the leaders of your ethnic group enrich themselves and their family through corruption, how would you perceive it?' While it was expected that those who had strong 'tribalist' tendencies were used to such practices, or treated them as a matter of course would tend to choose the second option ('The wealth should be distributed to his/her ethnic group'), it was expected that majority of respondents would choose the fourth option ('Only he/she should not be blamed because a large number of politicians do the same thing') or fifth option ('Corruption is not bad if the politicians distribute the wealth much more than he/she gets for him/herself'). And while, as shown on Table 1, these responses were somewhat more common in Village X, they were by no means popular in Kiambaa. The most frequent answer in both villages was the third option ('The wealth should be returned to the Kenyan Government'), with over three-quarters of respondents choosing this option in Kiambaa and more than two-thirds in Village X. If this finding were to be taken at face value, we could perhaps say that people are certainly not willing to forgive corruption on the part of elites, and that the popular image of the Kenyan state, though it has suffered from corruption, is that it is the legitimate owner of public resources.

6.3.5. Support for Other Ethnic Groups

Finally, in the next three questions a hypothetical situation was used to ask respondents what they thought of supporting people from other ethnic groups who fell victim to a natural disaster.

Question 8 asked 'Do you think it is right to use the taxpayer's money to save victims from other ethnic groups suffering from natural disasters in Kenya?' Question 9 asked, 'Do you have a feeling to donate for the victims suffering from natural disasters?' And question 10 asked 'Do you agree to pay more tax to save the victims from other ethnic groups suffering from natural disasters?' While views in favour of Question 10 were somewhat less common in Kiambaa, the overwhelming majority of respondents in both villages chose options that affirmed the provision of public and private funds for victims of natural disasters from other ethnic groups in all three questions. While it was thought that those who held to a simple 'tribalist' mentality would tend to hold negative views for all three questions, the findings proved the reverse.

6.4. Popular Views of the State, Ethnicity, and Conflict: A Preliminary Discussion

What can we say about the challenges posed by our study? In our field site, where groups of Kalenjin and Nandi are alleged to have attacked Kikuyu villages, the question of one's ethnic affiliation was apparent when death and injury were inflicted on one another. Here, with regard to the nature of the state, it was assumed at the outset of our research, that a large proportion of people would harbour views rooted in discrimination of other ethnic groups and affirm the idea of a state that is biased towards a particular ethnic group – in other words 'tribalism.'

However, after speaking with people in Kiambaa, the village where residents were assaulted, and in Village X, home to the alleged assailants, we found very few who openly expressed such 'tribalist' views. While respondents in Village X were somewhat more likely to be reserved in their responses – something that requires separate exploration – the majority of people in both villages felt that national politicians should allocate resources fairly among ethnic groups, and felt also that it was unjust for public resources to be appropriated by private individuals through corrupt means and that such resources should be turned over not to their own ethnic group but to 'the government of Kenya' as a public entity.

On the other hand, while people in both villages emphasised that contributions of members of parliament to their own communities and constituencies were more important than contributions to the country as a whole, they understood allocating resources for their own villages (such as schools and roads) to be the role of local politicians rather than something to expect from parliamentarians. Of course, contacting parliamentarians directly is unfeasible for most residents; moreover, if citizens understand the relationship between parliamentarians and local politicians as a vertical link (or as a relationship between patron and client), as is frequently pointed out in Kenyan society, this perhaps suggests an underlying expectation that by petitioning local politicians, they would be able to ensure that such parliamentarians would allocate resources in ways that the local people would find advantageous.[9] However, the demand for parliamentarians to prioritise contributions to their local community is a phenomenon that is frequently observed not only in Kenya, but also in advanced countries around the world, including Japan. Moreover, there are also many who deny that parliamentarians should make preferential allocations of resources *to their own ethnic groups*. From this, it cannot be argued that demanding preferential contributions *to their own constituencies* is unequivocally or directly linked to 'tribalism.'

Furthermore, an overwhelming majority of respondents in both villages expressed affirmative sentiment with regard to contributing public and private support to the victims of natural disasters who, although belonging to other ethnic groups, were also Kenyan compatriots.

To summarise, we found in the field sites for this study, which had been at the fore in the PEV widely regarded to have almost brought the Kenyan state to the brink of collapse, there are in fact shared thoughts that, quite unlike the 'tribalism' assumed at the outset of the study, are much more conducive to national integration – or else, at least, a shared awareness of how things should be in principle.

The absence of past studies makes it difficult to know precisely when people came to hold (or be aware of) such thoughts conducive to national integration. For example, it is conceivable that the momentum provided by Kenyans' remorse over the PEV inspired people to adopt new non-'tribalist' ways of thinking. However, newly learned or otherwise, the responses to our survey must be said to share much in common in terms of their being conducive to national integration. It should also be recalled that there were Nandi politicians who opposed Majimboism. And from the situation in our field sites, we did not get a sense that calls for ethnic reconciliation and national solidarity were being routinely or enthusiastically carried out in a manner that would completely change people's ways of thinking. Rather, it seems more natural to speculate that throughout Kenya's post-independence history, a perception conducive to national integration has gradually taken root in people's thinking, even before the period of the PEV.

However, if this was the case, why then did so many people (who likely included residents of Village X and their associates) become involved in the brutal assaults of the PEV? One explanation, already mentioned, is that the attacks were mobilised 'from above' in return for financial reward and allocations of land seized from the Kikuyu. However, as the findings of this study indicate, there was not actually any drastic reduction of Kikuyu residents in Kiambaa, nor were these replaced with large numbers of Kalenjin. If the acquisition of land owned by Kikuyu was a significant, non-negotiable goal, this area would still be experiencing the kind of antagonism espoused by Majimboism on a daily basis. Also, from information gleaned in Village X and elsewhere, the financial incentives paid at the time of the PEV amounted to little more than 50 shillings (approximately 0.80 US dollars). It is inconceivable that this would be sufficient to instigate masses of people aware of the idea of national integration into murderous action against neighbouring residents. Not to mention the fact that these people are also human beings who bear a sense of guilt at causing death or injury to others.

What Lynch suggests, quite apart from economic gain, is the strength of intrinsic social bonds based mainly on the age sets of Nandi society (Lynch 2011). It is not difficult to imagine how this strength, culminating at its apex with Ruto and other national politicians, coupled with vertical relationships overseen by local politicians and village elders, was able to exert pressure on subordinate youth that would have found it difficult to resist. This could be one factor that explains the organised character of the violence and series of attacks, as well as the continuing state of peace in the aftermath, once a compromise had been established between the political elites. However, if we consider that the Kalenjin (Nandi) are always living out their lives in the midst of such vertically organised peer pressure, it would seem unlikely that there could ever be sufficient room to engender thoughts of national integration.

Also, as mentioned earlier, the view of the official report points to inequalities between ethnic groups over land and other resources as factors. Certainly, there are differences between Kiambaa and Village X in terms of the degree of farming success and in the average land area owned by individual households. Even so, compared to the scale of the disparities, particularly apparent in Uasin Gishu District, between ordinary farmers and the large plantations owned by influential figures, the differences between the two villages are so minor as to be disregarded as a factor.

Rather, where the two villages differ significantly, as pointed out in Section 3(3) above, is in the proportion of people who feel secure in their rights to their own land. Whereas there are many in Kiambaa who enjoy a sense of security over their land rights, there are considerably fewer such residents in Village X, It is almost as though incidents such as the attacks instigated by the radical Majimboists had never happened. It was pointed out in Section 4(3) that this difference is likely related to the proportion of lands to which residents' titles to land are registered in each village.

Lynch suggests that many Kalenjin still, even if they do not support radical Majimboism, harbour a sense of injustice over the circumstances surrounding land issues from the colonial period which are the basis for the neighbouring Kikuyu people's success at farming even today, and this is likely connected to their sense of grievance (Lynch 2011, pp. 199–200). This sense of grievance seems to be closely related to their awareness that little has been done to ensure their land rights will be recognised, such as registration of their land titles. This is likely also compounded by their underlying sense of alienation as former 'squatters.'

In other words, this seems to imply that the importance of title registration, as the official system propping up the land market, has found its way into Kalenjin society. As already pointed out, under Kenya's current system, to become a registered title holder is to have one's right to ownership assured anywhere in the country, regardless of ethnicity. This was the system promoted by the Kikuyu-led regime of Jomo Kenyatta, and opposed by the Majimboists. It could also be said that among the Kalenjin, whether they liked it or not, and regardless of whether it was opposed by the Majimboists, registration was gradually coming to be accepted as the institutional basis of the nationally integrated land market.[10]

What our study suggests is that a conception of national integration and an institutional sense of an integrated land market were gradually finding their way into the consciousness of ordinary Kenyans, including those who launched themselves at the forefront of ethnic conflict. Such composition of consciousness seems to offer a rational explanation for several aspects of the PEV and the attack on Kiambaa village. Most important here is the sense of grievance among the Kalenjin, as well as their feelings of pressure and guilt. The sense of grievance that they bore towards the Kikuyu and other ethnic groups was nurtured and rooted in the fact of the necessity of their having to live in the same national territory alongside these other ethnic groups. Precisely because they were citizens of the same country, their dissatisfaction stemmed from the fact that they did not enjoy the same standard of living, nor were they guaranteed the same rights. If we assume that this disparity was brought about in part through abuses of political influence, the people would inevitably be sensitive regarding the locus of power. President Moi's behaviour must be seen as inappropriate, both in terms of his taking advantage of power to allocate resources in favour of the Kalenjin, and of making extensive use of violence in order to maintain that power. Lynch states that many Kalenjin felt that Moi's preferential policies towards them had gone too far, and they feared that they would be hated by other citizens as an ethnic group that had committed violence and this was precisely why they feared a Kikuyu monopoly on power (Lynch 2011, pp. 195, 197).

The abuse of state power sometimes provoked a sense of grievance among members of the same particular ethnic group, and sometimes a sense of fear through guilt by association with an ethnic group that collectively supported the abuse of state power. It is likely precisely because they were so cognisant of these facts that the largest number of people in Village X, as in Kiambaa, said that the proper stance for those in power was to be fair in the allocation of resources between ethnic groups.

In light of this, after the PEV, what does it mean that some of those who were involved in the attacks appear to have developed mental illness, or even been driven to suicide? Perhaps even those who committed themselves to radical Majimboism experienced a sense of remorse at having caused such hurt to neighbours who belonged to other ethnic groups. Put otherwise, this seems to suggest that these people came to think of themselves and their victims, not merely as enemies from different ethnic groups, but also as human beings, and perhaps as members of the same *nation*.

The frequency with which participants in Village X responded 'I don't know' about the responsibility of politicians as compared to those in Kiambaa may have been due to the fact that, at the same time that Nandi peer pressure gave individuals strong restraints on explicitly stating about their own personal opinions, it was also difficult to express the intricacy of the ideas described above in terms of a simplified formulaic response.

6.5. Conclusion: Contemporary Kenya and the Potential for Coexistence

The PEV that lasted from the end of 2007 into the following year exacerbated existing inter-ethnic tensions and is said to have brought Kenya to the brink of collapse. Even so, the idea of a Kenyan state is gradually putting down roots in people's minds. People already know how to answer questions about the kind of state and models of authority that are ideal for coexistence in ways that are conducive to national integration. It is for this very reason that people experience rage and fear in the face of state-related injustice; it is for this reason that they inflict death and injury, and that they suffer. Conversely, might it also be in this popular awareness that we will be able to discover a potential source for coexistence among

Kenyans who differ from each other in terms of their ethnicity and other attributes?

Nevertheless, whether or not the people of Kenya will be able to finally coexist and achieve a more desirable way of life remains to be seen. Serious problems still face the Kalenjin and Nandi. These include their notoriety as 'squatters,' carved out for them in the colonial period, their continued low socioeconomic status, and their alienation from markets underpinned by institutional guarantees and the sense of anxiety regarding rights that stems from this. As far as can be seen from the current situation in Village X, even now, with William Ruto, the top Nandi politician, enjoying the centre of state power, it cannot be said that these issues have found any significant resolution. It seems beyond doubt that residents of Village X were mobilised in the attacks that took place during the PEV, and it seems undeniable that many of the dimensions of the alienation within the Kenyan and Kalenjin/Nandi communities that facilitated such mobilisations to violence remain very much unchanged.

At present, Nandi from this research field site, under the governance of a Kikuyu president and Nandi vice-president, have shelved their radical Majimboism, accepting that their Kikuyu neighbours cannot be easily evicted even in the face of extreme violence. At the same time, they seem to have escaped the fear that their grievances will be compounded, which is likely precisely why day-to-day peace has been maintained in the region.

However, there are still those among the Nandi and other ethnic groups who are poor, still squatters and barred from finding opportunities in the market and society at large. The conversion of this anger into attacks on other ethnic groups has frequently been exploited in this country as a means of recruiting ordinary citizens for political advantage. While something like the PEV should never happen again, in order to prevent it, it will be important to foster a sense of shared community across society at large so that the misfortunes of one ethnic group will not be allowed to remain and fester as a problem for the members of that group in isolation. No matter the ethnicity, it is precisely the act of coming together to help each other as fellow citizens that is the path to once again approach the dream of national integration.

In this sense, it is important that in both villages, as the survey findings have shown, people tend to oppose corruption on the part of politicians even in cases where they may give an unfair advantage to their own ethnic group, to think that misappropriated funds should be returned to the Kenyan government and to provide positive support to other ethnic groups stricken by disaster. This all suggests the following: though Kenya's national integration continues to face many real obstacles on the path to coexistence among its various ethnicities, as well as to further development, while the road may yet be long, the Kenyan people have already begun their preparations to set out on this journey together.

Notes

[1] Provinces established under the old Constitution were abolished with the enactment of the new Constitution in 2010. However, since the names of the Rift Valley and other former provinces are still used to refer to these regions, they are used in this chapter as is.

[2] *Majimbo* is a Swahili word meaning 'regions' or 'provinces'.

[3] According to interviews conducted every year from 2012. Similar testimony from other districts is also referenced in the Waki Report (CIPEV 2008, p. 44).

[4] The government later revised its estimate of the number of IDPs to over 660,000 individuals (Lynch 2011, p. 2003).

[5] The Kikuyu who took part in the counterattack included not only those who had settled in Rift Valley Province, but also many living in Central Province, and these groups went on to stage raids on other ethnic groups as well as Kalenjin (CIPEV 2008, pp. 205–212).

[6] We refer to the village anonymously here out of consideration that evidence that could be tried in criminal proceedings is not available, as well as with the intention to avoid outside interference that may disrupt the lives of local residents who would rather that the conflict not be rekindled.

[7] The field surveys were conducted in Kiambaa in August 2013, and in Village X over October and November of 2014, using a variety of questions prepared in advance on topics such as living situation, economic activities, consciousness about land issues and political awareness. The

surveys were conducted by Japanese researchers accompanied by interpreters on visits to interview the heads of 142 households in Kiambaa and 129 households in Village X. Responses were obtained with some omissions, such as when householders elected not to respond to certain questions. In addition, our team visited the sites each year between 2011 and 2014, carrying out interviews on many related issues in addition to those listed above, generally conducting observations regarding villagers' daily lives, economic activities and ways of thinking,

[8] Although some households, in both villages, possessed and used lands rented from absentee owners and the like, we did not undertake to distinguish these here.

[9] Devolution of the power and financial resources from the centre to each county, introduced under the constitutional reform in 2010, may have complicated the picture of the vertical link between national leaders and local politicians by giving the latter more space for their own manipulation of public resources.

[10] While Yamano and Tanaka's analysis of the properties of people who became victims during the PEV suggests that the likelihood of being attacked was significantly lower in the case of registered owners, this fact may be interpreted in itself as evidence that an understanding of the importance of registration was gradually penetrating Kalenjin society, which is consistent with the claim being advanced here (Yamano and Tanaka 2010, p. 172).

References

CIPEV (The Commission of Inquiry into the Post-Election Violence) (2008) *Report of the Commission of Inquiry into the Post-Election Violence (the Waki Report)*, Nairobi: Government Printer.

HRW/AW (Human Rights Watch/Africa Watch) (1993) *Divide and Rule: State-Sponsored Ethnic Violence in Kenya*, New York: Human Rights Watch.

Huntingford, G.W.B. (1953) *Tribal Control in a Pastoral Society*, London: Routledge & Kegan Paul.

Klopp, J.M. (2002) 'Can moral ethnicity trump political tribalism? The Struggle for land and nation in Kenya', *African Studies*, Vol. 61,

No. 2, pp. 269–94.

----------(2008) 'The Real reason for Kenya's violence', *Christian Science Monitor* (14 January 2008), http://www.csmonitor.com/Commentary/Opinion/2008/01 14/p09s02-coop.html (Accessed 15 December 2015).

Lynch, G. (2011) *I Say to You: Ethnic Politics and the Kalenjin in Kenya*, Chicago: University of Chicago Press.

Tsuda, M. (2009) 'Kikuyu-phobia which turned into violence: Turmoil after the 2007 national election and multi-party politics', *Chiiki Kenkyu*, Vol. 9, No. 1, pp. 90–107 (in Japanese).

Yamano, T. and Tanaka, Y. (2010) 'Politico-economic analysis on the violence in Kenya', in K. Otsuka and T. Shiraishi (eds.) *Kokka to Keizai Hatten,* Toyo: Keizai-Shinpo-sha, pp. 153–179 (in Japanese).

Chapter 7

Human–Environment Relations in Gedeo Area, Ethiopia: Links between Worldviews, Environmental Values, and Livelihood Strategies

Senishaw Getachew

7.1. Introduction

Human–environment relations have been recognised in anthropological studies since the beginning of the discipline. Bronislaw Malinowski (1932), one of the earlier anthropologists, described the environment of the Trobriand Islands in his study on the Kula trading system. However, at the beginning of the 20th century, environment was viewed by environmental determinists and possibilists as key in shaping human behaviour (Rambo 1983). This makes human–environment relations central in anthropological studies. However, environmental determinism failed to explain the existence of different human behaviour in similar environmental and geographical settings. In the 1950s and 1960s, the classic studies of Julian Steward (1955) and Roy Rappaport (1967) hugely influenced anthropological interest and thinking in human–environment relations. In the 21st century, Fikret Berkes (2008) views human environment interactions in relation to local knowledge, practices and belief from a systems perspective.

The reciprocal relationship between humans and the environment varies in both time and space, based on the knowledge, production systems and culture of the society in question. Change in one of these elements could alter human–environment relations (Moran 2006). In addition, human–environment relations are influenced by the nexus between worldview, environmental values and livelihood practices. With this in mind, the present study focuses on the human–environment relations among the Gedeo people of southern Ethiopia. The paper intends to examine the relationship among multiple variables: the Gedeo worldview regarding human–environment relations, local environmental values, local ecological knowledge, livelihood practices and the implications of these complex links for both livelihood and environmental sustainability.

These issues have been considered in the context of diverse challenges (e.g., resource scarcity, population pressure, introduction of new religion, modern education and modern production system) that the Gedeo have recently been experiencing. Moreover, population pressure is a persistent and serious challenge in which the Gedeo respond in various ways that show African potentials of resilience in human–environment relations.

This article emerged from a year-long fieldwork (20 February 2012 to 1 March 2013) undertaken employing the mixed method approach. This approach is closely related to the pragmatic paradigm, which rationalises combined research methods, and which sees qualitative and quantitative methods as complementary (Hewson 2006). In this regard, qualitative approach was used to explore, describe and interpret major issues that require in-depth analysis and issues related to values, feelings and discourses. Participant observation was employed to observe everyday events and rituals, including agricultural activities. Unstructured and semi-structured interviews were held with interviewees drawn from diverse sections of the society. In order to generate data from different groups, nine focus group discussions were held with men, women and youth. A survey also was conducted to generate data from a sample population of 344 households, which were selected using a stratified sampling technique. The qualitative data were analysed concurrently with data collection. Descriptions, categorisation and interpretations of qualitative data were undertaken at different stages of the fieldwork. Data from the surveys were coded and the relationships between variables were analysed mainly using descriptive statistics.

This article has seven sections including the introduction. The second section describes the study area. Section three discusses Gedeo worldviews; section four is about the environmental values that relate to the worldview. Section five discusses livelihood activities and local knowledge. Section six analyses major challenges of human–environment relations and responses to respective challenges. The last section, conclusion, has remarks on human–environment relations as African potentials.

7.2. The Study Area

The Gedeo people belong to the Cushitic language family in Ethiopia and they live in the Gedeo Zone, Southern Nations, Nationalities and Peoples Regional State (SNNPRS), Ethiopia. According to the Central Statistics Agency (CSA 2012), the population of the Zone in 2012 was 990,185 of which the majority (87.3 per cent) were living in rural areas and the remaining 12.7 per cent were living in the urban areas. The estimated crude population density was 817.7 persons per square kilometer (CSA 2010; CSA 2012). This makes Gedeo one of the most densely populated areas in the country (SLUF 2006). The total area of the Zone is 1,210.89 square kilometers. The Zone is positioned 5°.84″–6°.43″ North Latitude and 38°.08″–38°.44″ East Longitude. It is bounded by Sidama Zone of SNNPRS in the north and Borena Zone of Oromia Regional State in the south, east and west. Dilla, the capital of the Zone, is situated 365 kilometers south of Addis Ababa.

Wonago *Woreda* (district), where the research was conducted, is one of six *woredas* of the Gedeo Zone. The total area of the *Woreda* is 141.55 square kilometers. According to the 2007 census, the population of Wonago *Woreda* was 116,921. However, the 2012 CSA projection estimates the population at 135,261. The *Woreda* is the most densely populated in the Zone where the crude density was 955.6 persons per square kilometer (CSA 2010; CSA 2012).

Mekonesa *Kebele* (the lowest administrative structure) is one of 18 *kebeles* of Wonago *Woreda* where this study was conducted and it is 380 kilometers south of Addis Ababa and eight kilometers from the *Woreda* capital, along the Ethio-Kenya road. According to the *Woreda* and *Kebele* office records, the *Kebele* was inhabited by 17,500 individuals in 2012, which is the highest in the *Woreda* and the Zone. The total area of the *Kebele* is 9.6 square kilometers. Thus, the crude density of the *Kebele* in 2012 was 1,823 persons per square kilometer.

The Gedeo Zone has three agro-ecological zones: highland, midland and lowland. However midland constitutes 67 per cent of the total area of the Zone. Wonago *Woreda* also has three agro-ecological categories but predominantly midland. Mekonesa *Kebele* is in the midland agro-ecology (Tadesse 2002). According to the information from the Gedeo Zone Statistics Office, in 2011 the mean annual temperature was 22.5C°. The Zone has two rainy seasons from March to May and from July to mid-October, and average annual rainfall varies from 760–1800 mm. The altitude, rainfall and temperature of the area are favourable for the agroforestry system especially in the predominant midland agro-ecology. Hence, the Gedeo local ecology is dominated by agroforestry (Bogale 2007; Mesele, Eshetu and Olavi 2012; Tadesse 2002).

As informants further explain, in addition to developing the natural forest into agroforestry, grasslands and open places have also been developed into agroforestry through the hard work of the local people. According to Tefere Bogale (2007) 95 per cent of the Gedeo Zone was covered with agroforestry in 2004. The agroforestry in the study area mainly consists of *enset* (*E. ventricosum*), coffee and trees. *Enset* is the main subsistence crop of high socio-cultural importance. It is related to the banana plant that produces large quantity of carbohydrate-rich food from the pseudo stem and corm. Coffee is the main source of cash income for the local farmers which necessitate the existence of trees on the farms for shade. There are annual crops like maize, cabbage, *boyena* (yam) and *godere* (taro) as part of the agroforestry system. The agroforestry coverage, which looks like a natural forest, is in the UNESCO World Heritage Tentative List as cultural landscape.

7.3. The Gedeo Worldviews

Human–nature relations are complex and relate to the worldview, environmental values, livelihood practices and local knowledge of a society. As Berkes (2008, p. 18) states, a worldview '... shapes environmental perceptions and gives meaning to observations of the environment'. Worldviews are deeply rooted in religion and include interpretations of observations in our world as well as environmental ethics (Berkes 2008). Jacinta Mwade (2011) also explains that variation in environmental perceptions, interactions and knowledge among different peoples in the world depends on divergence in worldviews and environmental ethics. As Sebastien Boillat (2007, p. 288) states:

> The ontological and epistemological principles are usually only partially perceived explicitly by the members in a community. However, they are expressed in their values, their practical norms, customs, rituals, beliefs and in the discourse of the community's members regarding their daily life. Just as social organization allowed identifying more clearly the normative principles valid within the communities, the religious universe of the peasants also allows a clearer knowledge of the philosophical principles that govern their worldview.

Likewise, ontological and epistemological principles in this study are not explicitly stated by informants, rather they are observed in the values and daily activities of the local community. As illustrated below in Figure 1, this study shows the interrelations between worldview, environmental values and livelihood practices, and local knowledge. The worldview prescribes environmental values, which in turn govern livelihood practices and local knowledge. However, as Berkes (2008) states these levels are not always distinct but rather closely coupled to the extent that the division seems artificial.

The Gedeo worldview is related to the indigenous religion. The local people believe that *Mageno* (God) is the creator of everything including the sky and the earth. He creates the hills, the mountains, rivers, plants, animals, humans and all other creatures. This basic idea does not seem to contradict the local version of Protestantism, which has been spreading fast. The ordinary Protestants and Orthodox Christians in Gedo refer to God as *Mageno*, although prayer services are conducted differently. Although they believe in the universality of God and his creations, Protestants in Gedeo do not find it contradictory to uphold the traditional worldviews about human–environment relationships. Boillat (2007) identifies similar developments in Bolivia where Catholic Christianity has been in harmony with the indigenous belief system for more than five centuries in terms of ideas related to worldviews.

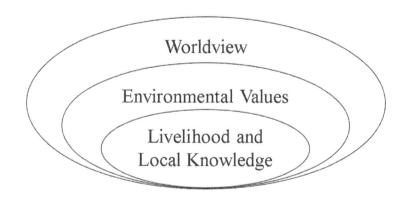

Figure 1. Levels of analysis in understanding the Gedeo human ecology

Source: Adapted from Berkes (2008, p. 17).

Ontology or what is being/existence, and relations among beings are fundamental to understand the Gedeo worldview. According to local informants, there are three beings: spirits, humans and natural beings. The relations among these beings are framed by religious beliefs. The natural community is perceived to include all living and non-living things like plants, animals, rivers and mountains. The spiritual community consists of *Mageno* (immanent divine) and ancestral spirits. The human interaction with the spiritual community is expressed through prayer, sacrifice, dreams and interpretations of phenomena.

The Gedeo perceive human being with social institutions that govern their relations among themselves and with the natural environment. They believe that the human community is between the 'natural community' and the 'spiritual community'. This perspective is consistent with the basic idea that humans are part of nature. This is because during their lifetime, humans are *Mageno's* creation and therefore part of the 'natural community', and when they pass away, they become part of the 'spiritual community' as ancestral spirits.

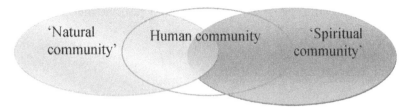

Figure 2. Interrelation of natural, human and spiritual communities

Source: Compiled from field data, 2012.

The relations among the beings are based on ontological principles of wholeness and relatedness. According to local perceptions, all the entities are interrelated and they depend on each other. Human beings depend on the natural community but by the will of the spiritual community. The spiritual community is believed to dwell in the natural environment such as mountains, trees and rivers that humans often encounter. Local farmers have respect for the natural community and they know that it is the basis of their livelihoods and survival.

Among the local community, all phenomena relate to the will of *Mageno*, whose power is manifested in climatic phenomena such as frost, drought and shortage of rain, among others. Ancestral spirits are also believed to have an important place in the lives of descendants. If a person has good relations with his ancestral spirits (doing what his father wanted him to do or behaving according to tradition), he could be successful in the pursuit of his livelihood. But if he is not on good terms with the ancestral spirits (doing what his father does not want him to do), he may not be successful in life. In addition, if someone is cursed by his father, they believe that he/she may face difficulties in life. This implies that the Gedeo daily activities are dictated by the will of God or spiritual community. However, it does not mean that the power of *Mageno* and ancestral spirits is acknowledged equally by all Gedeo people. The followers of the traditional belief systems show some sense of fundamentalism; while most others seem to be sentimentalists who remain sympathetic to the belief system. This is due to its positive contribution to their livelihood and provides a chance to preserve memories of their beloved ones.

7.4. Environmental Values

Gedeo environmental values, which are based on their worldview, are related to livelihood activities and local ecological knowledge. The major environmental values among the Gedeo people, which are observable from their everyday activities, include respect, reciprocity, balance and sustainability.

Respect: Respect is one of the most important values that relate to the local ecology, livelihood, local knowledge and social cohesion. Respect in the local community has broad aspects: respect for plants, respect for animals, respect for land, etc. Boillat (2007) explains that respect for plants and animals is based on the general normative dimensions of respect for life and fertility. Farmers in Gedeo are restrained from activities that negatively affect the natural community and natural processes. For instance, according to informants, cutting trees is discouraged in general and at the flowering stage in particular. It is considered as interrupting the reproduction process, which would annoy the spiritual power and deny human access to such resources. Besides, there are different trees which are not subject to cutting due to their socio-cultural values. For instance, as elderly informants explained, it is a taboo to cut the *adibaare* (sacred tree where sacrifices are offered) and *Songo* (ritual and public place at the village level) trees which are considered as heritage. A tree that grows on ancestral graves is not to be cut down or used as fuel wood. One can understand that religious, ecological and social values have a role in preserving certain types and species of trees in certain places.

The local people in the study area expressed their respect for animals in different ways. As one of my informants noted, all animals are considered as *Mageno's* creation. Wild animals are not supposed to be killed unless they become dangerous to human life. Female animals especially the pregnant ones are not supposed to be killed. Among the Cree of east James Bay in Canada respect is a base for the relationship between humans and animals in which they pay respect for animals from hunting to consumption (Berkes 2008).

Land is one of the respected natural resources. It is perceived as being a resource that needs continued input or nourishment to be productive. Improper utilisation, which leads to land exhaustion, is disapproved. Degraded land is likened to a necked person, and well-preserved land is equated with a well-dressed person. Hence, the owners of lands are respected or disrespected, appreciated or criticised based on the condition of their lands.

Reciprocity: The normative principle of reciprocity governs relations among human beings as well as human, nature and spiritual communities (Boillat 2007). Farmers in the local community are aware of the importance of reciprocity in human–nature relations. Agricultural productivity depends on soil fertility, which in turn depends on the farmers' efforts to keep their lands fertile. Hence, the Gedeo farmers use different types of soil fertility enhancement mechanisms. They firmly believe that the amount of the crop yields that the land gives depends on the amount of input that it receives. The human offer to the spiritual community (believed to regulate climatic phenomena and enhance production) includes festivity, prayers, rituals and appreciations that often follow major agricultural harvests. The natural community is believed to serve as resting place of the spiritual community, while receiving grace and nourishment (e.g., rainwater) from the latter. The belief in the reciprocal relationship between humans and nature, and humans and spirits has immensely contributed to the sustainability of the socio-ecological systems.

Balance: The Gedeo people have the tradition of keeping balance between all forms of relationships. For example, they keep balance between the production of *enset* for subsistence and coffee for generating cash income. Coffee plantations are not allowed to expand at the expense of *enset* crops. Though coffee generates sometimes better cash it is affected by market failure and crop failure. On the other hand *enset* is drought resistant with less chance of crop failure. Thus, higher dependency on coffee is associated with vulnerable for food insecurity which most farmers need to avoid. The farmer is also expected to keep balance between coffee plants and trees needed to provide shade. If the trees are thinly distributed, then the coffee production could decline due to the subsequent decline of soil fertility and lack of proper shade. If the trees are too dense, the canopy is likely to deprive the coffee plants of sunlight which leads to production decline. From the perspective of the local farmers, the existence of trees is inseparable from sustainable coffee production. Balancing conservation and use is perceived in the local community as using natural resources, especially land, by considering the use rights of the next generation. The Gedeo father is expected to give a plot with matured and immature *enset* and coffee plantations when his son(s) is about to marry. Balance among the Gedeo perceives as a state of mind in doing culturally just activity in human–environment relations.

Sustainability: The concept and principles of sustainability are central to the livelihood, activities and local ecological management. Sustainability is perceived from two perspectives: maintenance of the productive potentials of resources and an extended period of cultivation. Natural resources are managed with the view to ensuring long-term utilisation and conservation for the next generation. According to informants, the current generation is consuming the fruits of their parents' labour and the present generation is similarly expected to invest on land (plant trees and perennial crops) for the next generation.

Most informants frequently mentioned the culture of *baabo* (planting) rather than cutting. *Baabo* is a concept which includes planting and managing trees and other plantations. In the process, farmers hope that they and their children can use the products and maintain their livelihoods. The concepts of hope and patience are embedded in the *baabo* tradition because it is a long-term investment, unlike the annual crop production. It is common to find aged trees on the fields of the Gedeo farmers. Trees and *enset* are not planted with the current generation in mind. Therefore, the cultural value of *baabo* establishes inter-generational links and contributes to the sustainability of livelihood strategies and local ecology.

The value of respect was discussed above and relates to reciprocity and resultant environmental sustainability and inter-generational equality. Reciprocity also relates to the value of respect and balance that contribute to sustainability. Similarly, balance embedded in the idea of suitability relates to respect and reciprocity.

Sustainability is a cumulative effect of balance, reciprocity and respect. Hence, these environmental values are interrelated and complement each other in sustaining local ecological knowledge, livelihoods and local ecology. Livelihood practices among the Gedeo are highly dictated by these values.

7.5. Livelihood Practices and Local Ecological Knowledge

Frank Ellis and H. Ade Freeman (2005) and Lasse Krantz (2001) analysed livelihood activities in terms of resources that include human, physical, financial, natural and social capital. All these forms of capital are vital in the livelihoods of local farming households, though the degree of importance varies. Survey results of this study show that 57.6 per cent of respondents put land and 35.5 per cent respondents made knowledge their primary choice in the pursuit of their livelihoods. As Madhav Gadgil, Frikret Berkes and Carl Folk (1993) refer to knowledge as 'cultural capital', the local farmers also differentiate between knowledge and labour. They explain that knowledge makes a difference in production if individuals have equal labour power. Land is a critical resource for local farming livelihoods. According to the Gedeo Zone Finance Office, the zonal average household plot size in 2012 was less than 0.5 hectares. The survey results of this study show that in 2012 the average land size in Mekonesa *Kebele* was 0.4 hectares per household. The same survey shows that 82 per cent of respondents do not have sufficient land to use their household labour effectively and that resulted in the engagement of considerable numbers of members of the local community in off-farm activities and periodic labour migration into the neighboring Guji Oromo area.

Agroforestry is a primary source of livelihood for the local community that helps them to use the scarce land resource properly. The components of the agroforestry system, i.e, *enset*, coffee, trees, livestock and apiculture are interrelated, and help livelihood and local ecology to be sustainable. *Enset* is used as a shade for coffee, enhances soil fertility and is used as fodder for livestock. Coffee trees on the farm provide shade and also enhance soil fertility; the flowers from coffee trees are used for honey production; income from coffee is

213

used to purchase livestock and its fodder. Livestock is used to manure the soil for better *enset* and coffee production. Agricultural experts explain that bees are important for cross-pollination and good coffee production. Thus, Gedeo agroforestry accommodates natural resource conservation and human needs in a sustainable way. That is why Mesele et al. (2012) argue that agroforestry has ecological and economic advantages. Ecologically it controls soil erosion, diversifying crop production, maintaining indigenous tree species, minimising risk, increasing productivity and ecological sustainability (Bogale 2007).

The livelihood activities of the local farmers are guided by the well-developed local ecological knowledge. Boillat (2007) describes eco-cognition as a set of mental constructions in a specific ecology which includes soil, plants, animals, topography and climate. In Gedeo language (*Gede'uffa*), the concept of *Hujetixxa beekkuma* (literally, work knowledge) corresponds with agro-ecological knowledge. It is knowledge about plants, animals, soil, water, including rain, seasonality and others which are used to manage agroforestry. *Hujetixxa beekkuma* is an accumulated knowledge that has been handed down for generations and knowledge acquired in interaction with the natural environment and other societies. The Gedeo oral tradition shows that Derasso, the founding father of the Gedeo, inherited agro-ecological knowledge from his father to manage his livelihood and use natural resources in a sustainable way. As a result of their livelihood activities, the Gedeo have developed knowledge about soil fertility management, succession management and managing plants in agroforestry from the upper canopy to the lower ones.

7.5.1. Soil Fertility Management

Soil degradation has become a global problem. There are two opposite views on the relationship between population growth and soil degradation. Neo-Malthusians have argued that soil degradation is a result of population growth whereas Neo-Bosreupians have argued that population pressure under certain conditions particularly in the context of the private ownership of land results in more soil fertility enhancement (Saidou et al. 2004). A study in 1996 shows that the Gedeo was not only known as a food self-sufficient area but also as one of the most fertile areas in the country (Ayalew et al. 1996) despite the high population density. As informants explained, soil fertility maintenance and conservation are two of the major activities in the Gedeo's agricultural history. Gedeo farmers have a mechanism to identify soil fertility level and to maintain and conserve soil fertility for generations. Farmers in the study area are dependent on indigenous soil fertility enhancement mechanisms rather than on inorganic fertilisers. According to this study, 99.7 per cent of respondents did not use inorganic fertilisers in 2012. Of this, 93 per cent said that inorganic fertilisers were not applicable to the agroforestry system, while the remaining 7 per cent found the cost of inorganic fertilisers to be exorbitant.

The local farmers use different types of soil fertility enhancement mechanisms like animal manure, compost, household refuse, leaf litter and mulching. However, this study survey shows that household refuse, leaf litter and animal manure are the first three preferred soil fertility mechanisms. The choice is mainly dictated by the availability of livestock in the household. Those households who have livestock have better chance to have more and better quality household refuse by adding animal manure; so they prefer household refuse or animal manure as first choice. Local farmers use the above soil fertility management mechanisms separately or in combination in a complementary way for survival because productivity is directly related to soil fertility. In the process, women and children provide a greater contribution in collecting, carrying and spreading household refuse in the fields.

7.5.2. Succession Management

The Gedeo are working for their livelihoods as well as for the livelihoods of the next generation because *enset* and coffee are harvested after four to five years and trees require even more years. They are conscious of the succession management of *enset*, coffee and trees. According to informants, every year, a local farmer has to plant the number and type of *enset* clones based on the size of the plot and the number of harvested *enset* plantations. There are two major stages of *enset* plantation, matured and maturate stages, from propagation to harvest. According to informants, every year, a local farmer has to plant the number and type of *enset* clones based on the size of the plot and the number of harvested *enset* plantations. Although *enset* can be multiplied through seeds, local farmers prefer propagation that allows them to get 40–80 seedlings depending on the diameter of the *enset*. Then, there are multiple transplantations of seedlings. These result in the existence of *enset* crops at different growth and maturity stages that demonstrate succession management knowledge and balance are kept in mind.

Like *enset,* coffee has different stages of development, which they classified into four categories: *Golqqo* is newly growing coffee between one to two years old; *Gurbe* is about three years old coffee; *Geyabuno* is matured coffee at the age of more than four or five years; and *Aameessa* is 'mother' coffee which is more than twenty years old. Likewise, managing the types and number of trees on the farm is important for coffee and *enset* production, construction and household fuel consumption or for sale. Like the *enset* and coffee plantations, different stages of trees have different names; however, unlike coffee and *enset,* it is difficult to fix the ages of each stage due to species variations in the case of trees. In general the succession of trees in number and type is well managed in the locality.

7.5.3. Managing Ecological Processes at Multiple Stages

In addition to the succession management of specific plantations, as discussed above, managing overall plantations in agroforestry at multiple stages is central for the local ecology sustainability in general and the agroforestry systems in particular. Local farmers have the knowledge to manage interactions of plantations within the agroforestry system for the survival of plantations in the upper, middle and lower levels of plant height. They are selective in the planting and managing of trees in the upper level. There are trees which are favoured by the farmers due to their ecological and economic value.

Under the tree canopy, there is *enset*. As my informants explain, the height of *enset* should be managed to give enough space for the coffee tree to maximise coffee yields, if *enset* and coffee are intercropped. At the lower canopy there are crops like yam, taro, maize and cabbage that are planted in the existing open spaces and enhance efficient land utilisation. Farmers consider the depth and spread of roots in managing underground interactions, and avoiding competition for resources.

Thus, the farmers manage horizontal and vertical arrangements of their farmlands, which start from the tips of the trees to the ground roots. Such ecological processes management at multiple stages gives a chance for each farmer to develop unique spatial arrangements of agroforestry on their respective plots.

7.6. Challenges and Local Responses

7.6.1. Challenges

Human–environment relations among the Gedeo faces challenges from different directions. The most important ones are population pressure and land shortage, expansion of formal education, and modern production systems, and religious change.

Population Pressure and Land Shortage: Population pressure and land shortages are identified by all the focus group discussants as major challenges to the farming household livelihoods. Tadesse et al. (2008) argue that scarcity of labour and availability of land in Gedeo Zone encouraged population pressure in the past. Informants explain that during the imperial period, especially before the 1950s, population pressure was not a noticeable problem because most households had enough land for cultivation. The Gedeo experienced rapid population growth in the last half a century. This study survey shows that in 2012 89.2 per cent of respondents identified population pressure as a challenge and future threat to their livelihoods. The same survey result shows that the average household size in the study area was 5.8 individuals.[1]

Population pressure leads to shortages of land, which limits farmers' ability to cultivate a range of crops and keep livestock, which subsequently limits income sources. It also affects efficient labour utilisation by making some members of the household idle. In addition, most FGD discussants identified population pressure as one of the causes for the declining tendency of trees in the

217

agroforestry and the local ecology, since households' wood consumption increased from time to time.

Expansion of Formal Education: The introduction and expansion of modern education is not in itself a problem, rather it is an opportunity for the local community to obtain access to alternative sources of knowledge. However, its introduction and expansion which presents scientific and local knowledge as binary opposites often results in negative attitudes towards local knowledge. Okolie (2003) argues that African local knowledge and ways of knowing are marginalised and inferioritised in African higher education curriculums. Similarly, Risiro et al. (2013) argue that the introduction of Western education downgrades local knowledge. Akena (2012) explains that the introduction of missionary schools and subsequently the colonial education system in Uganda created inequality and caused the decline of local knowledge. Furthermore, Mwade (2011) argues that, in most cases, local ecological knowledge is considered as 'traditional and outdated' and is understood as the opposite of 'Western, scientific or modern education'. Viewing 'Western knowledge' and worldviews as the only solution for environmental problems contributes to the development of negative attitudes towards local ecological knowledge validity, status and sustainability. Nevertheless, such generalisation and a wrong attitude towards local knowledge have negative implications on the continuity of good practices in the local community.

Male FGD discussants noted that the lack of interest among the youth to learn local agro-ecological knowledge was a challenge to local ecological knowledge sustainability.[2] The reasons for the decline of interest vary but external influences are partly to blame. Viewing local ecological knowledge as an obstacle to formal education is the main one due to the perception of local knowledge as the binary opposite to scientific knowledge. According to the elderly informants, children and the youth are spending most of their time in school (rather than on the farm to acquire local ecological knowledge) and the elderly are passing away without properly transferring their knowledge to the next generation. As a result, the Gedeo youth is facing a serious local knowledge gap.

Modern Production System:[3] Similar to the introduction of formal education, the 'modern' production system has brought both opportunities and challenges to the local community. According to my informants, they have been advised by agricultural experts about the 'modern' production system since the period of Emperor Haile-Selassie (1930–1974). Government agricultural experts and NGOs intervene in the name of 'modernising' the agricultural sector. During the *Derg* period (1974–1991) government agricultural workers advised farmers to clear trees from the coffee fields to improve coffee production. Most local farmers resisted but a few accepted the advice. However, the advice negatively affected soil fertility and coffee production. Because the coffee fields lost leaf litter from the trees that enhance soil fertility and shade from strong sunlight and hail during the coffee flowering stage. It took a long time for those farmers who followed the experts' advice to recover from the negative setbacks they experienced. This event demonstrates that some interventions had a negative effect on local ecological knowledge sustainability. One of the general limitations of such intervention is that it does not consider the situation at a local level.

Introduction and Expansion of Christianity: The Gedeo were followers of their traditional religion until the end of the 19th century. Then Orthodox, Catholic and Protestant Christianity was introduced into the study area. As informants and focus group discussants pointed out, the introduction and expansion of Protestant Christianity since the 1940s, resulted the decline of the number of traditional religious followers, and the decline has been dramatic since the Ethiopian Peoples' Revolutionary Democratic Front (EPRDF) government came into power in 1991. This is because during the Derge (military rule) period (1974–1991) the government suppressed Protestant Christianity more than the traditional one. In the EPRDF period the coming into power of predominantly Protestant Christians in the local administration provided a favourable situation for the expansion of Protestant Christianity.

Protestant Christianity is the only religion which grew by 69.3 per cent from 1994 to 2007. On the other hand, Orthodox Christianity declined by more than half (51.7 per cent). Moreover, traditional religious followers were reduced by 67.6 per cent, which is a dramatic decline. Some cultural values and rituals, related to the indigenous belief systems, have been weakened due to the expansion of Protestant Christianity. In a 2012 survey, 78.5 per cent of respondents said that rituals related to ecology have declined. From all rituals, according to respondents, rituals for human, animal, coffee and *enset* health have declined the most. One of the elderly informants explains: Protestant Christians are against some rituals as they associate them with 'evil' spirits. In reality these are cultural practices performed by the traditional, Orthodox Christians or even some Protestants; which have nothing to do with 'evil'. As stated above Protestant Christians continued to use environmental values due to their importance for their livelihoods. However, most rejected rituals related to the traditional belief system. Such development results in the continuity of environmental values but changes in rituals. The change in rituals has implications for the reinforcement mechanisms of environmental values at the time of violation or against the traditions of human–environment relations. Another change that has come with Protestant Christianity is that the youth who can read the Bible and understand Christian teachings have become religious leaders, whereas in the indigenous belief system religious leadership is dominated by elders. This shift has weakened the values and power of the elders and has resulted in negative implications for the transfer of local ecological knowledge.

7.6.2. *Local Response to Challenges*

As Berkes (2008, p. 249) states '… adaptability is the key ingredient for developing sustainable local economies with which indigenous and other resource-dependent rural peoples of the world can make a living'. This view shows that adaptability depends on the ability to cope with the impacts of change. The local farmers in the study area respond to the above stated challenges in different and holistic ways to sustain local ecology, livelihood and local knowledge.

Response to Population Pressure and Land Shortage: The local community and government respond to population pressure in various ways. Some informants and most FGD discussants identified family planning as a coping mechanism for population pressure. Family planning has been addressed in the locality by the governmental and non-governmental organisations for more than a quarter of a century. However, according to the health officer in the *kebele*, the practical action is not yet effective and the numbers of users of family planning was 50 per cent below the expected 60 per cent users target in the Zone. The *kebele* record shows that, in 2012, family planning users were 30 per cent.

One of the coping mechanisms to land shortage is crop choice. Therefore, the shift from annual barley production to perennial *enset* plantation is an important response to population growth and shortages of land over a long period. Brandt et al. (1997) argue that the *enset*-based agriculture system has a higher carrying capacity than other cropping systems in the same agro-ecology. According to Tadesse (2002), 0.2 hectares is enough to cover the *enset* needs of a household of seven members, which is equal to 1.5 hectares of land for annual grain production. The field survey conducted for this study shows that the average annual household *enset* consumption of six members is 62 *daggicho* (an inflorescence *enset*). The average harvesting time with one meter spacing is five years. Thus, based on these figures, 0.31 hectares of land is enough to feed a household of six members for a year. In addition, as local farmers say, 'our farm is our bank'; *enset* could be harvested throughout the year and matured *enset* could stay in the field for years.

Even though the plot per household is very small, all households have at least *ansho* land (a plot given for married couple) and use different soil fertility mechanisms to maintain or enhance the potential of their plot to feed household members.

Diversification is another response to land shortage. Table 1 shows that smallholders cultivate an average of 5.02 different crops per 0.20 hectares of land, medium holders cultivate 5.03 crops per 0.62 hectares of land and large holders cultivate 5.69 crops per 1.42 hectares of land. The general trend shows that when plot size increases cultivated crop types also increase. However, smallholders cultivate more diversified crops per unit of land than medium or large holders. Smallholders cultivated an average of 5, medium holders 1.6 and large holders 0.8 crops per 0.20 hectares of land at a time. The diversification is important mainly to minimise the risk of crop failure, and to diversify products and income. In such a case the use of high fertility inputs is decisive to get better product.

Table 1. Plot size and numbers of crop cultivated by landholding categories

Land holding category	Average plot size in hectares	Average number of crop types cultivated	Average number of cultivated crops per 0.20 hectares
0.01–0.49 hectares	.20	5.02	5.02
0.50–0.99 hectares	.62	5.03	1.62
1 and above hectares	1.42	5.69	0.8
Average	.42	5.10	2.4

Source: Compiled from field survey, 2012.

Therefore, agricultural intensification is one major response to land shortage and population pressure. Intensification is viewed in this study in terms of using more soil fertility enhancement inputs and labour in cultivation per unit of land than in the past. SLUF (2006) explains that the Wonago farming system is an old intensified agricultural system, which might be attributed to population growth and limited possibilities for horizontal expansion. It is true that the production system is dynamic in the study area. Though there is no data which show intensification across time, one can understand from informants that intensification evolved dramatically when farmers replaced the annual barley production with *enset* production.

In addition, expansion of off-farm activities as an alternative livelihood activity is another response to land scarcity. According to this study survey in 70 per cent of respondents' households, at least one member has been engaged in off-farm activities that include engaging in different types of trade and daily labour. As informants explain, some members of the local community who face land shortage migrate temporary to the neighbouring Guji Oromo during the harvesting and planting seasons to work as daily labourers to minimise ecological stresses on natural resources and subsidise household incomes.

Promoting Local Knowledge: Local farmers are well aware of the challenges of transferring local ecological knowledge which is deeply rooted in their survival and identity. Therefore, they try their best to sustain the transfer of local ecological knowledge to the next generation. Mwade (2011) also explains that local ecological knowledge is increasingly recognised among academics and to some extent among policy makers. There is argument about the importance of promoting local ecological knowledge for biodiversity protection.

In the Gedeo tradition, knowledge is transferred through generations culturally. Some youth explained that they have recognised their weaknesses in acknowledging the importance of local ecological knowledge and have started to change their attitude towards local knowledge. In actual fact the complementarities of the scientific knowledge through formal education and local knowledge through socialisation are important for the sustainability of local ecological knowledge. Parents are trying to convince and advise the youth patiently and persistently to transmit and cope with the challenges of local ecological knowledge. There are some youth who listen to their parents and acquire the knowledge by understanding the importance of the knowledge in relation with their future livelihoods. Those who listen to their parents' advice and learn the knowledge are doing well in cultivating their land while the others who did not pay much attention to the knowledge due to their desire to engage in non-agricultural activities after the completion of their education are not. Thus, those who acquire the knowledge are being rewarded by their good harvest, and this started to motivate others to acquire the knowledge. Therefore, complementary to formal education that recognises the potential of local knowledge, reward and punishment, and the dynamic nature of the local ecological knowledge, promote the importance of the local ecological knowledge. In addition, local ecological knowledge has been used as a local response mechanism for the challenges, though the challenges are sometimes too strong to respond completely.

Religious Tolerance: Traditional religious followers in the local community used different mechanisms to resist the expansion of Protestant Christianity. Strengthening the traditional belief system was one response to the expansion. For instance, traditional religion believers merged four *Songos* (ritual and public places at the village level) into one to conduct weekly rituals by making the gathering larger and having better visibility. They also established a self-help association like that of the Protestants to help each other in times of difficulty. They tried to capitalise the link between traditional values with the sustainability of the *Baalle* system (Gedeo political and generation grade system). In addition to the efforts of the traditional religious followers to sustain their belief and the recognition of elderly indigenous belief followers by Protestant Christians has had a positive implication for the minority indigenous belief followers. For instance, in any public ceremony, the first blessings should be given by traditional religious leaders followed by Protestant Christian leaders. Moreover, most of the environmental values are accepted by Protestant Christians and sustained due to their importance for livelihoods. Traditional religious followers tried to use different mechanisms with the help of religious tolerance in the study area for the sustainability of the belief system and related rituals. Hence, environmental values that relate to traditional religion are able to sustain but religious change has had significant implications for the continuity of rituals which relate to the traditional belief system.

7.7. Conclusion

The Gedeo worldview framed environmental values, livelihood practices and local knowledge. The Gedeo have extensive and well-developed local ecological knowledge. The knowledge is both cumulative and dynamic that enables farmers to manage the local ecosystem in a sustainable way. The management is holistic and integrated in that it involves soil fertility management, succession management and managing agroforestry from top to bottom. The management of agroforestry requires not only diversified knowledge of every element in the agroforestry but also the relations of the elements to each other. Better land management is based on agro-ecological knowledge and labour utilisation which is a key to the Gedeo's ecological and livelihood sustainability. It is clear that local ecological systems are directly related to the survival of the local community. Yet, its sustainability is challenged by different factors.

Especially, population pressure is the major and persistent one. Nevertheless, it does not lead to degradation rather it results in more intensification and crop diversification. Environmental values are important for livelihood sustainability; conversely such importance results in environmental values' sustainability. These values are a source of environmental ethics for the local people. Furthermore, the Gedeo's worldview and environmental values ultimately shape the attitude and practices of the members of the local community in human–environment relations.

Therefore, perceiving human–environment relations in a holistic and integrative way is an area of African potential. Local ecological knowledge, livelihood activities, environmental values and worldview are highly intertwined and structure human–environment relations. The Gedeo agroforestry and cultural landscape that are considered as an identity and central to the Gedeo survival is the product of this nexus. This African potential plays a positive role in resolving local ecological problems.

Notes

[1] The national average household size in the 2007 census was 4.7 and SNNPRS was 4.8 individuals (CSA 2010, pp. 25, 28).

[2] Cristencho and Vining (2009) also identified lack of interest among the youth and the communication gap as challenges in the transmission of indigenous ecological knowledge among indigenous groups in Colombia and Guatemala.

[3] A modern production system is used in the sense that 'modern' inputs and technologies based on conventional science are used.

References

Akena, F.A. (2012) 'Critical analysis of the production of Western knowledge and its implications for indigenous knowledge and decolonization', *Journal of Black Studies*, Vol. 33, No. 6.

Ayalew, G., Abeje, B. and Amaha, K. (1996) *Ethiopian Village Studies:*

Adado Gedeo, unpublished research report.

Barnard, A. and Spencer, J. (2002) *Encyclopedia of Social and Cultural Anthropology*, London: Routledge.

Berkes, F. (2008) *Sacred Ecology*, 2nd edition, New York: Routledge.

Bernard, H.R. (1995) *Research Methods in Anthropology: Qualitative and Quantitative Approaches*, 2nd edition, London: Altamira Press.

Bogale T. (2007) *Agroforestry Practices in Gedeo Zone, Ethiopia: A Geographic Analysis*, unpublished Ph.D. dissertation, Panjab University.

Boillat, S. (2007) *Traditional Ecological Knowledge, Land Use and Ecosystem Diversity in the Tunari National Park (Bolivia): An Ethnoecological Approach to Dialogue between Traditional and Scientific Ecological Knowledge*, unpublished Ph.D. thesis, University of Bern.

Brandt, A.S., Spring, A., Hiebsch, C., McCabe, J.T., Tabogie, E., Diro, M., Wolde-Michael, G., Yntiso, G., Shigeta, M. and Tesfaye, S. (1997) *The 'Tree Against Hunger'; Enset-Based Agricultural Systems in Ethiopia*, Washington DC: American Association for the Advancement of Science.

Central Statistics Agency (CSA) (2010) *The 2007 Population and Housing Census of Ethiopia Result for Southern Nations, Nationalities and Peoples' Region*, Addis Ababa: Central Statistics Agency.

----------(2012) *Ethiopian Statistical Abstract 2011/2012*, Addis Ababa: Central Statistics Agency.

Cristancho, S. and Vining, J. (2009) 'Perceived intergenerational differences in the transmission of traditional ecological knowledge (TEK) in two indigenous groups from Colombia and Guatemala', *Culture and Psychology*, Vol. 15, No. 2.

Ellis, F. and Freeman, H.A. (2005) 'Conceptual framework and overview of themes', in F. Ellis and H.A. Freeman (eds.) *Rural Livelihoods and Poverty Reduction Policies*, London: Routledge.

Gadgil, M., Berkes, F. and Folk, C. (1993) 'Indigenous knowledge for biodiversity conservation', *Ambio*, Vol. 22, No. 2/3.

Hewson, C. (2006) 'Mixed methods research', in V. Jupp (ed.) *The Sage Dictionary of Social Research Methods*, London: SAGE Publications.

Krantz, L. (2001) *The Sustainable Livelihood Approach to Poverty Reduction, Sida: Division for Policy and Socio-Economic Analysis*, Stockholm: Swedish International Development cooperation Agency.

226

Mesele N., Eshetu, Y. and Olavi, L. (2012) 'Potential of indigenous multistrata agroforests for maintaining native floristic diversity in the South-eastern Rift Valley Escarpment, Ethiopia', *Agroforestry Systems*, Vol. 85, Issue 1.

Malinowski, B. (1932) *Argonauts of Western Pacific: An Account of Native Enterprise and Adventure in the Archipelagoes of Melanesian New Guinea*, London: George Routledge and Sons.

Moran, E. (2006) *People and Nature: An Introduction of Human Ecological Relations*, Oxford: Blackwell Publishing.

Maweu, J.M. (2011) 'Indigenous ecological knowledge and modern Western knowledge: Complementary, not contradictory', *Thought and Practice: A Journal of Philosophical Association of Kenya (PAK)*, New Series Vol. 3, No. 2.

Office of the Population and Housing Census Commission (OPHCC) (1989) *Population and Housing Census 1984 Analytical Report on Sidamo Region*, Addis Ababa: Central Statistics Agency.

Okolie, A.C. (2003) 'Producing knowledge for sustainable development in Africa: Implications for higher education', *Higher Education*, Vol. 46, No. 2.

O'Reilly, K. (2009) *Key Concepts in Ethnography*, London: SAGE Publications.

Rappaport, R.A. (1967) *Pigs for the Ancestors*, New Haven: Yale University Press.

Rambo, A.T. (1983) *Conceptual Approaches to Human Ecology*, Honolulu: East-West Environment and Policy Institute.

Risiro, J., Tshuma, D.T. and Basikiti, A. (2013) 'Indigenous knowledge systems and environmental management: A case study of Zaka District, Masvingo Province, Zimbabwe', *International Journal of Academic Research in Progressive Education and Development*, Vol. 2, No. 1.

Saidou, A., T.W. Kuyper, D.K. Kossou, R. Tossou and P. Richards (2004) 'Sustainable soil fertility management in Benin: Learning from farmers', *NJAS- Wageningen Journal of Life Sciences*, Vol. 52, Issue 3-4.

Steward, J. (1955) *The Concept and Method of Cultural Ecology: Theory of Cultural Change*, Urbana: University of Illinois Press.

Sustainable Land Use Forum (SLUF) (2006) *Indigenous Agroforestry*

Practices and Their Implications on Sustainable Land Use and Natural Resources Management: The Case of Wonago Woreda, Addis Ababa: SLUF.

Tadesse K. (2002) *Five Thousand Years of Sustainability? A Case Study of Gedeo Land Use (Southern Ethiopia)*, unpublished Ph.D. dissertation, Wageningen Agriculture University.

Tadesse K., Tilahun, E., Tsegay, T., Hayilu, B. and Shinitu, L. (2008) *Ye Gedeo Biher Tarek*, Addis Ababa: Berhanena Selam Printing Press.

Chapter 8

African Chiefs in the Global Era: Chieftaincy Titles and Igbo Migrants from Nigeria

Hisashi Matsumoto

8.1. Introduction

In many African countries, democratic governments protect traditional rulers of ethnic groups, and confer on them political power over local administrations (cf. Van Rouveroy van Nieuwaal and Rijk van Dijk, eds. 1999). Though it seems difficult to reconcile democratic states with monarchies such as kingships and chieftaincies, both 'selected chiefs and elected councilors' (Logan 2009) are expected to represent local communities and mediate between the people and the state (Eggen 2011). As grass-roots leaders, traditional rulers are considered to have potentials for peace making and community development. During decolonisation, many such rulers were kept in peripheral positions as 'agents of foreign colonial rule' or 'relics of the pre-modern era' and, later, returned to power, particularly in the period since the 1990s. Therefore, some scholars refer to these phenomena as the 'revival' (Van Binsbergen 1999, p.102), the 'resurgence' (Oomen 2005, p. 27; Eggen 2011, p. 319), or the 're-entry' (Geschiere 1993, p. 151) of traditional rulers.

This 'revival' has occurred not just in kingdoms and chiefdoms that have long histories; interestingly, the phenomenon can also be observed among societies in which a centralised authority did not exist before the colonial period. In these societies, people crown new 'traditional' rulers and seek recognition from the state. One example of such a society is that of the Igbo of Southeastern Nigeria. While many scholars have characterised traditional Igbo societies as lacking central authorities, today we can find many kings and chiefs in local communities throughout Igboland.

In African studies, scholars use the words 'king' and 'chief' to refer to a centralised authority in traditional societies. In particular, 'chief' has been used to denote various types of authority. On one hand, 'chief' often serves as a synonym for 'king' to designate the paramount ruler of a certain society; on the other hand, it may also refer to authority figures in local groups ruled by a single king. Moreover, there are examples from African history of the word 'chief' being used even for leaders of non-centralised societies. Michael Crowder and Obaro Ikime (1970, pp. ix-x) have observed that, 'It is only by accident that they have all been called "chiefs"', and, 'It is impossible to define "chief" in pre-colonial terms'.

In the present article, I analyse an important role that traditional rulers play in contemporary Africa. I use the Igbos as a case study, for whom traditional rulers are a relatively new occurrence in the colonial and postcolonial, socio-political environment. My focus is the relationship between these traditional rulers and transnational migrants, especially those living in East Asia, including Japan.

Regarding transnational migration from Africa, while some scholars are apprehensive of the potential for a 'brain drain', others expect migrants to financially support the development of their homeland (Duke 2010). Remittance inflow to sub-Saharan Africa reached over 20 billion US dollars in 2010, an amount equivalent to two-thirds of official aid. Remittance inflow to Nigeria accounted for approximately half of all officially recorded remittances to sub-Saharan African countries (Ratha et al. 2011, pp. 49–51).

Migrants who have made fortunes in foreign lands aspire to return home in glory. Migrants provide financial support to their homelands in order to gain recognition from the local population (Trager 2001). This phenomenon is related to a trend for migrants to seek traditional titles in their homelands. In the case of Igbo migrants, these titles are chieftaincy titles conferred by traditional rulers. The chieftaincy title is a symbol of honour that traditional rulers bestow on persons who have made significant contributions to the development of the town. Many wealthy Igbo migrants aspire to become chiefs in their homeland.

In the following sections, I review the conferral of chieftaincy titles by newly invented traditional rulers in contemporary Igbo societies. Using the example of Igbo migrants living in Japan, I assess the manner in which these titles attract the migrants and affect their relationship with the homeland. First, I explain the invention of traditional rulers in contemporary Igbo societies with reference to colonial and postcolonial administrative policy. Next, I summarise the migratory flow from Nigeria to Japan. Finally, I examine the phenomenon of title-taking among Igbo migrants, including those in Japan, focusing, in particular, upon their motivations and methods for obtaining chieftaincy titles. Through this process, I analyse a major role that traditional rulers play in contemporary globalised Africa.

8.2. The Invention of Kings and Chiefs in Contemporary Igbo Societies

In Nigeria, the Igbo constitute one of the three major ethnic groups, along with the Hausa and the Yoruba. While the other two groups are well known for their kingdoms, many scholars have described traditional Igbo societies as being decentralised and 'democratic'. Before British colonial rule, the area called Igboland was no more than a gathering of loosely linked local communities, the majority of which had no centralised authority. Though there were some cases in which a central authority existed (Henderson 1972; Nzimiro 1972; Onwuejeogwu 1981), scholars considered such communities as having 'exotic origin' (Meek 1937, p. 185) or 'intrusive cultural traits' (Uchendu 1965, p. 3) until around the 1970s.

Nevertheless, there are authorities called '*Eze*' (*Ndi-Eze* for plural) in each local community within contemporary Igboland. Eze is the Igbo word for 'king' or 'traditional ruler'. An Eze is crowned within each local community, which is composed of several villages. The Igbos call these communities 'towns', and choose Ezes based on local agreement among the townspeople. Since the Igbos usually consider towns to be based on patrilineal lineages descending from a common ancestor, the majority of towns choose Ezes from each subsection in turn.

Table 1. Legal status of Ezes in the Fourth Republic (1999–present)

Eze
A traditional or other head of an autonomous community who has been identified, selected, appointed and installed by his people according to their own tradition and usages, and presented to the Government for recognition.

Autonomous community
A group of people inhabiting an identifiable geographical area or areas, comprising one or more communities and bound by a historical heritage and recognised and approved as an autonomous community by the Government.

Source: I.S.N. (2000)

However, in order to acquire full recognition as an Eze, the chosen individual must obtain approval from the state government and receive the staff of office. A town recognised by the government is referred to as an 'autonomous community' (see Table 1). As we will discuss in detail later, motions for the creation of new communities and the recognition of their Ezes are commonplace throughout Igboland today. Consequently, the government has established rules for recognition and restricted the creation of Ezes. On the other hand, the townspeople themselves consider government approval to be indispensable for the legitimacy of an Eze. The Igbos distinguish between those who have been crowned by the people but not yet approved by the government, and call them the 'Eze-elect'. Thus, to be an Eze, one must obtain recognition both among the townspeople and the government.

The position of Eze originated from the Chieftaincy Edict, a law that was implemented in each state under military rule in the late 1970s. However, its origin can be traced back to colonial policy in the early 20th century. In order to enforce indirect rule in Southeastern Nigeria, the British government appointed the members of the Native Court and gave them vast administrative power. Since appointees were those whom the colonial government identified as 'chiefs', this colonial policy was later referred to as 'the warrant chief system'. This system brought serious confusion to Igbo societies, among which the majority of local communities had not previously had chief positions, and was one of the main causes of the Aba Women's Riot of 1929 (Afigbo 1972).

In spite of this confusion, since postcolonial ethnic politics made traditional rulers key political actors (Nwaubani 1994; Vaughan 2000), the Igbo people came to see the creation of new autonomous communities and their Ezes as a sort of political empowerment (Harneit-Sievers 1998; Matsumoto 2008). However, various types of conflict over the status of Ezes occurred throughout Igboland. Thus, in many cases, Ezes represented the source of conflict rather than the solution to conflict.

Nevertheless, contemporary Igbos are deeply interested in the institution of Ezes. Movements seeking the recognition of a new Eze, and conflicts over the succession of deceased Eze, are now common. One particularly controversial topic is the conferral of chieftaincy titles by Ezes.

In the 1970s, the word 'chief' was used to indicate the status of Ezes in the implementation of the Chieftaincy Edict. However, when this law was revised under the 2nd Republic (1979–1983), it was replaced with the title 'Eze' because 'the title Eze was more akin to Igbo tradition, usage and culture than 'Chief' (I.S.N. 1980, p. 2). After this change, it became customary for Ezes to confer chieftaincy titles to eminent individuals within their towns.

There are several titles conferred by Ezes. Among these, the title of 'Chief' is given to individuals who have significantly contributed to community development. Candidates for chief are not limited to indigenes living inside the town: Ezes can also confer this title on those outside the town, including non-indigenes.

The conferral of chieftaincy titles is an important aspect of the authority of Ezes (Oha 2009). It is a common complaint among townspeople that Ezes provide chieftaincy titles to unqualified persons who are wealthy but have not made any visible contribution to the town (Inyama 1993). Such individuals are rumoured to buy the title of chief. Harmeit-Sievers (1998, p. 70) described chieftaincy conferral as 'one important and much-deplored source' of Ezes' incomes.

This is an issue not just for the Igbos. In his study on traditional institutes and modern politics in Yorubaland, Olufemi Vaughan (1991, p. 319) mentioned 'the conferral of chieftaincy titles on influential dignitaries' as 'a sub-culture throughout the country':

> In the ideal situation, they reserve the right to award such titles as a mark of honor to those who have lived exemplary lives and made significant contributions to the community. In practice, however, some paramount chiefs have been known to confer these titles on their political allies and business associates (Vaughan 1991, pp. 319–320).

In the following sections, I analyse this custom from the viewpoint of migrants who, according to critics, 'buy' the title of chief.

8.3. Chiefs among Transnational Igbo Migrants

Compared with other regions, mass migration from Africa to East Asia is a relatively recent phenomenon. The total number of Africans with legal status in Japan is now about twelve thousand, representing only 0.6 per cent of all the foreign residents in Japan. Among them, Nigerians constitute the largest population. The Nigerian population increased dramatically in the early 1990s. While the number of Nigerians with legal status was only 44 at the end of 1984, it reached 2,730 in 2011. Of these 2,730 Nigerians, 91.0 per cent are male (Immigration Bureau of Japan, 1985–2012).[1]

The Japanese government does not provide work visas for unskilled labourers. While migrants may have professional skills and knowledge, their job opportunities are limited by language barriers and discrimination against foreigners. Consequently, the majority of Nigerians enters Japan with short-term visas and work as illegal labourers after the visas expire.

However, some Nigerians have acquired relatively stable legal status, particularly through marriage to Japanese women. In 2011, 1,277 Nigerians (46.8 per cent of legal immigrants) had permanent visas, while 702 (25.7 per cent) had spouse visas (Figure 1).[2] Today, it is no longer uncommon for Nigerian migrants to have lived in Japan for more than ten years and to have children attending a high school or a university.

The Igbos form the majority of this Nigerian population. In Nigeria, the Igbos are well-known as 'business-oriented people' and 'traders'. Igboland is a relatively populous area of Nigeria. Since the colonial period, the population density of Igboland has caused a steady flow of migration both locally and transnationally.

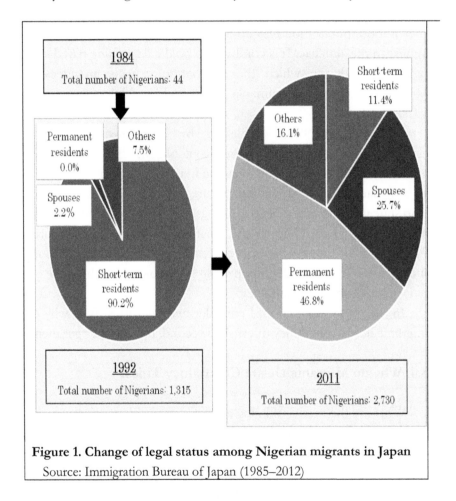

Figure 1. Change of legal status among Nigerian migrants in Japan
Source: Immigration Bureau of Japan (1985–2012)

The desire for chieftaincy titles can be observed even among Igbo migrants who live in Japan. For example, there are a number of chiefs among leaders of Igbo migrant associations. One of the largest

235

associations is that established by migrants from the Imo State of Nigeria, who live in the Kanto region of Japan. This association was founded in 2001, and now has about 180 active members who pay monthly dues. According to their membership list, 16 members hold a chieftaincy title. Many of these chiefs have been members of this association for over 10 years.

In Nigeria, the publication of almanacs is a common tactic for the promotion of associations. In an almanac, the association prints the pictures of executives and other major members with their social status. If the association needs to raise the funds for their activities, they impose publication fees upon those who want their pictures to appear in the almanac. It is common to hold a 'launching party' after publication, during which the association expects attendees to purchase a copy of the almanac and provide additional monetary gifts.

Almanacs are often published by hometown associations established by Igbo migrants outside of Nigeria. For instance, the abovementioned Imo state association in the Kanto region published an almanac in 2007, containing pictures of the Nigerian president, Imo state governor and Nigerian ambassador in Japan, along with the national flags of both Nigeria and Japan. Surrounding these pictures, 72 members of the association were featured in the almanac. Among them were 14 chiefs, including the Imo state governor, who wore the red cap, a symbol of chieftaincy.

In the following section, I consider two questions: first, why do migrants desire chieftaincy titles? And second, how do they get them?

8.4. Why do Migrants Desire Chieftaincy Titles?

What are the merits of being a chief, especially for migrants who live far away from their homelands? In Igboland, the holder of a chieftaincy title becomes a member of the Eze-in-Council. This group is one of the administrative bodies of a town, and is composed of titleholders and presided over by the Eze. Since the government recognises Ezes as leaders of local communities, the members of the Eze-in-Council exercise certain political influence within the community. In addition, some towns offer certain economic privileges for chiefs. For instance, when the town slaughters cows or goats, specific cuts of meat are allocated to the members of Eze-in-Council. Titleholders also receive special gifts when women in their lineages marry.

These merits would seem to have little meaning for migrants who live abroad and visit home less than once in a year. However, Igbo migrants regard chieftaincy titles as cultural capital, which lends their holders prestige and confidence. Chiefs are treated as eminent individuals not only in local towns of Igboland but also in urban settings within and outside Nigeria.

In Japan, Igbo migrants hold various yearly events through their associations. While it is common for hometown associations to hold an end-of-year party for their members, they host events which are common in their homeland. These include *Iriji*, the New Yam Festival and fund-raising parties for their activities. Igbo migrants organised a memorial service in Tokyo when Chukwuemeka O. Ojukwu, the former leader of the breakaway Republic of Biafra, died in 2011.

On these occasions, the host association prepares a 'high table' and invites influential individuals as special guests. At the beginning of the event, the master of ceremonies calls out the names and titles of guests and asks them to take a seat at the high table. Chiefs are usually among these guests.

Chiefs are also distinguished by their appearance and behaviour. For example, chiefs are expected to dress in traditional attire appropriate for their title, and greet each other using special handshakes (chiefs shake hands by clapping the backs of their hands together three times before shaking). In Japan, it is difficult to identify chiefs by their appearance, since many chiefs wear a suit or jeans as their regular attire. However, even without traditional dress, Igbos can be identified as chiefs by their handshakes.

Moreover, it is significant that a chieftaincy title can give its holder almost permanent prestige. Even if migrants achieve a certain degree of economic success, their opportunities to build their reputations are limited while they remain in Japan. Apart from chieftaincy titles, some successful Igbo migrants aspire to be the executives of hometown associations. Elections within large associations, such as chairmanship appointments in state-level organisations, are always major events for members, since the executives of large associations have great influence over the migrants. The Nigerian Embassy of Japan seeks the advice of these executives on migrant-related issues. When the Nigerian Union, Japan (the apex organisation for Nigerians living in Japan) was founded in 2014, some ambassadors of African countries attended its inauguration ceremony, and it was covered by the Japan Broadcasting Corporation. However, the executives of hometown associations have tenure of office under their constitutions. While the honour of these executives is temporary, a chieftaincy title can guarantee its holder lifelong social recognition. Furthermore, while chiefs do not have a great deal of power among migrants, they avoid the troublesome duties for which the executives of hometown associations are always expected to take responsibility.

Interestingly, some Igbo migrants believe that a chieftaincy title carries cultural capital even among non-Nigerians. One informant in Guangzhou, the largest city in Southeastern China, told me that a chieftaincy certificate can serve as a personal reference in the application for a visa to the United State of America. This informant knew one man who had been rejected twice, but finally acquired a visa after he had obtained a chieftaincy title and attached its certificate to his application form. Many Igbo migrants were sceptical of this story. However, the anecdote demonstrates that some migrants believe that chieftaincy titles are valuable outside the context of African culture.

In February of 2008, *SEARCHINA*, a Japanese website distributing China-related information, released the following news story:

Headline: 'A Chinese Businessman Became an Igbo Chief for the First Time'

Owing to his contribution to the development of Nigerian society and its economy, an Igbo chieftaincy title was conferred on Mr. Chen Xiao Xing, the vice-president of the China Civil Engineering Construction Corporation (CCECC). CCECC is in charge of Nigerian infrastructure improvement. This is the first case in which a Chinese citizen has become an Igbo chief. With his 10 years' experience in the country, Mr. Chen said, 'There are high expectations for our work. I'm feeling the weight of my responsibility'. The Chinese National Press Agency reported this story on the 18th of this month (Translated by the author).

This type of news story is uncommon in Japan. However, it is still significant that the Chinese national news agency saw fit to release this news and that a Japanese website also decided to translate it. Since the African continent is beginning to be considered 'the world's last market frontier', both China and Japan are eager to strengthen their relationships with African countries. This story was reported three months before the Fourth Tokyo International Conference on African Development (TICAD IV). The conferral of a chieftaincy title to a Chinese businessman was viewed as an indication of the grass-root partnership between Nigeria and China, and provided evidence that African chiefs can be newsworthy topics in East Asia.

8.5. How do Migrants Obtain Chieftaincy Titles?

There are three ways for a migrant to obtain a chieftaincy title: by getting a title from his hometown, by acquiring a title from another community and by creating a title for himself.

Many Igbos regard the first route as the most proper. If a successful migrant decides to make a contribution to his homeland, he will usually choose his hometown (the town of paternal origin) as the first site for his patronage. Among Igbo migrants in Japan, some have contributed to their hometowns by roofing the town hall, buying electrical equipment, donating money at fund-raising parties for various self-help development projects and similar gestures. A wealthy migrant can provide financial support for town meetings, churches and the Eze-in-Council whenever he returns to his hometown. If the people in his hometown recognise his philanthropy, the Eze will confer a chieftaincy title to him as 'a prominent son of the soil'.

Since chieftaincy titles are conferred at the town level, some Igbos have titles from more than one town. In such cases, many people emphasise the importance of taking the first chieftaincy title from one's hometown, since such a title provides its holder with a warrant for his family background.

In precolonial Igbo societies there were outcasts called *Osu*, cult slaves who were religiously dedicated to certain deities (Uchendu 1965, p. 89). *Osu* played a key role in ritual performances, but they were marginalised as aliens by others in the society. The status of *Osu* has been abolished with the spread of Christianity. However, the descendants of cult slaves are still called *Osu*, and discrimination against them exists even today. For example, many in society avoid marrying descendants of *Osu*. Owing to social mixing among people from different hometowns, it is difficult to determine who has *Osu* ancestry. However, before marriages, the families of the bride and groom usually investigate the family backgrounds of each partner.

As an example of this type of discrimination, an individual with an *Osu* family background cannot be a candidate for a chieftaincy title in his own hometown. However, the screening process for chieftaincy candidates is not as strict as for marriage partners. In some cases, individuals descended from outcasts have been granted chieftaincy titles outside of their own hometowns. Therefore, some migrants prefer to take their first chieftaincy titles from their hometowns in order to avoid malicious gossip regarding their family backgrounds.

Nevertheless, there are many chiefs who have obtained their titles from communities other than their hometowns. This is the second method by which migrants may take a chieftaincy title. Generally, chieftaincy titles are conferred upon those who have contributed to the town because they have some affinity to it – for example, because it is their maternal home or place of business. However, for some chiefs, townspeople are unable to remember any of their past achievements.

Among the Igbo migrants in Japan, one striking occurrence was a title-taking tour led by a wealthy Igbo migrant in the mid-2000s. This migrant was an influential leader among the Igbo living in the Kanto region, the metropolitan area of Japan. He had been in Japan for more than twenty years, and had become a successful entrepreneur. As a 'prominent son abroad', he often offered financial assistance to his hometown, and the Eze decided to confer a chieftaincy title upon him. When the title was granted he brought more than 10 Igbo friends from Japan to his hometown, and the Eze gave chieftaincy titles to each of these followers.

None of the followers had any connection to this town before their title taking. As such, this is a case in which we might make the critique that *Ezes* engage in business transactions, using chieftaincy titles to facilitate deals and relationships. However, it must be noted that some, but not all, of these followers began to make financial contributions to the town after they became chiefs there. Therefore, we can see this type of title conferral as a sort of 'sell on credit' – giving a title first, then collecting the debt later. Thus, chieftaincy titles play a role building in the relationship between wealthy outsiders and towns seeking financial aid.

Finally, the third route for Igbo migrants to obtain chieftaincy titles is by creating new communities and Ezes. Today, petitions to create new autonomous communities and Ezes occur regularly throughout Igboland. In Imo state, when the state government created the Chieftaincy Edict in 1978, the number of towns recognised as autonomous communities was 268. Now, however, that number has increased to 638 owing to a large number of petitions to create more autonomous communities. In 1991, Abia state was split off from Imo state, and the size of Imo state was reduced by half. In spite of this reduction in land area, the number of autonomous communities increased by 2.4 times that of 1978. While the average area of an autonomous community was 47.3 km^2 in 1978, it had decreased to 8.67 km^2 by 2012. It is clear that the average size of autonomous communities has decreased because of the creation of new autonomous communities and the recognition of new Ezes.

Petitions for the creation of new communities are often led by an aspiring new Eze and his supporters. Once the government approves a new autonomous community and the aspirant obtains the Eze certificate, he will confer chieftaincy titles on some of his supporters in recognition of their help regarding his coronation. Thus, by joining these petitions, migrants can obtain chieftaincy titles in new autonomous communities. Migrants may even aspire to be Ezes themselves, and gather supporters for their own coronations.

One interesting phenomenon related to this third method is the emergence of migrant kingships among Igbos living outside Igboland (Osaghae 1994, 1998). Today, some Igbo migrant communities within and outside Nigeria have a leader called *Eze-Igbo* or *Igwe*. These leaders are authorities, in the tradition of Ezes in their homeland, and are considered by their supporters to be the king of Igbo migrants in the area. For instance, '*Eze-Igbo, Lagos*' is the king of the Igbo migrants living in Lagos state, as '*Igwe Hong Kong*' is for those in Hong Kong. Like Ezes in Igboland, each Eze-Igbo confers chieftaincy titles and organises Eze-Igbo-in-Council events with his chiefs.

According to Osaghae (1994), the status of Eze-Igbo first emerged among Igbo migrants living in Northern Nigeria in the late 1980s. It then spread to areas in Southern Nigeria, such as Lagos, Oyo, Edo, Rivers and Cross-River State. Today Eze-Igbos can also be found in Igbo migrant communities outside Nigeria. In East Asia, the Igbo migrants in Honk Kong have *Igwe Hong Kong*, while those in Osaka have crowned *Igwe Osaka*. In South Korea, although the Igbos once selected *Eze-Igbo, Seoul*, the position was later abolished by *Ohaneze Ndigbo, South Korea*, an association for the Igbo in South Korea.

The creation of migrant kingships is controversial among the Igbos. Their supporters emphasise the notion that the Eze-Igbo is intended 'to 'import' the traditional system from home and implant traditional loyalties' (Osagae 1994, p. 57). However, this idea has been harshly criticised by detractors, especially non-migrant Igbos, including some Ezes. These critics regard Eze-Igbo as an example of the 'bastardization of Igbo culture'. While Ezes in Igboland are authorities, officially recognised under state law, Eze-Igbos are pseudo-kings chosen by certain migrants based on their own initiative. Although the individual in the position of Eze-Igbo is considered to be the 'king' in his place of residence, he is subordinate to the Eze in his hometown. In this way, migrant kingship creates tension between migrants and their hometowns. In 2008, the South East Council of Traditional Rulers, the organisation for all the Ezes in southeastern Nigeria, announced its decision to ban the institutions of Eze-Igbo (*allAfrica.com* 21 October 2008). This was one reason why the Igbo in South Korea abolished *Eze-Igbo Seoul*. However, *Igwe Honk Kong* still exists, and *Igwe Osaka* was crowned by the Igbo in Japan, even after the prohibition was announced by Ezes in their homelands.

8.6. Conclusion: African Chiefs in the Global Era

In past studies on African migration, scholars emphasised the persistent ties between migrants and their homeland (Gugler 1971, 1997). In fact, many migrants regard themselves as 'temporal sojourners' and often speak of their dreams to return home after retirement. However, for many migrants this dream goes unfulfilled (Plotnicov 1970 [1965], Peil et al. 1998).

The relationship between migrants and their homeland is no longer straightforward, especially for those who have founded a family and earned permanent residence outside their hometowns. However, financial support from 'sons abroad', the migrants living outside their communities, is growing increasingly important for development projects within their hometowns. Today, raising funds from migrants is a major concern for local communities. To aid these efforts, Ezes can bring the community to migrants' attention by conferring a chieftaincy title. This is a potential for traditional rulers in contemporary Igbo societies. By making migrants chiefs, the *Eze* reminds migrants that they are 'sons of the soil' of their home community.

However, the concept of 'home' differs among migrants. 'Home' does not necessarily mean the community of one's (paternal) origin. For some it can be the maternal community, or another community in the 'home' country. Others may decide to contribute to their 'home' at the state or federal level, rather than at the town level, through the government or support groups. Moreover, while some migrants are eager to support development projects in their homeland, others are more concerned about the welfare of fellow migrants from the same homeland. These various concepts of 'home' reflect the socio-cultural character of contemporary Africa, where, like other parts of the world, globalisation has diversified the relationship between people and place. This has also contributed to the variety of ways to access chieftaincy titles.

Among the three ways to obtain a chieftaincy title, the creation of migrant kingships has aroused much controversy among the Igbos, especially those in the homeland. There is little doubt that this, too, is one way in which migrants think about their homes. It must be remembered that, owing to the difficulty of acquiring permanent residency, migrants often overstay their visas. This prevents them from returning home and inevitably causes a loss of contact. For those who stay abroad for many years and lose substantial ties with their hometowns, the creation of migrant kingships provides an opportunity to recreate the kingship and chieftaincy institution, which is central to Igbo culture today. This said, migrant kingships are self-sufficient kingdoms outside the homeland. They deprive people in the homeland of the opportunity to reconstruct relationships with 'sons abroad' through the conferral of chieftaincy titles by Ezes.

Finally, it is interesting to note that the value of a chieftaincy title seems to differ between migrants and the people in their hometowns. Like the story about the application for a US visa, its value is deconstructed to accommodate a global context. The notion of 'African Chiefs' is associated with new meanings. This explains why some Igbo migrants do not care about criticism of their methods of acquiring chieftaincy titles; it is also a reason why the institution of traditional rulers can be revived in contemporary Africa.

Notes

[1] These data were obtained from *Zairyugaikokujin Tokei [Statistics on the Foreigners Resistered in Japan]* issued by Immigration Bureau of Japan. These statistics are based on the number of foreigners staying in Japan at the end of the previous year. With the introduction of a new residency management system in 2012, it began to exclude the foreigners with short-term visas and restricted to cover only those with medium-/long-term visas. I use the data

before 2012 in order to show the transition including those with short-term visas

2 Permanent Residents' refers to both 'Permanent Residents' and 'Special Permanent Residents'. 'Spouses' is the percentage of the persons staying as 'Spouse or Child of Japanese National' or 'Spouse or Child of Permanent Resident'

References

Afigbo, A.E. (1972) *The Warrant Chiefs: Indirect Rule in Southeastern Nigeria 1891–1929*, London: Longman.

AllAfrica.com (2008) *Nigeria: Ohaneze, South-East Monarchs Move against Diaspora's Eze Igbo*, http://allafrica.com/stories/200810210729.html.

Crowder, M., and Ikime, O. (1970) 'Introduction', in M. Crowder and O. Ikime (eds.), Translation from the French by Brenda Packman, *West African Chiefs: Their Changing Status under Colonial Rule and Independence*, Ife: University of Ife Press, pp. vi–xxix.

Duke, O.O. (2010) 'Remittances inflow into Nigeria', in A. Adepoju and A. van der Wiel (eds.) *Seeking Greener Pastures Abroad: A migration Profile of Nigeria*, Ibadan: Safari Books Ltd, pp. 341-74.

Eggen, Ø. (2011) 'Chiefs and everyday governance: Parallel state organizations in Malawi', *Journal of Southern African Studies*, Vol. 37, pp. 313–31.

Geschiere, P. (1993) 'Chiefs and colonial rule in Cameroon: Inventing chieftaincy, French and British style', *Africa*, Vol. 63, pp. 151–75.

Gugler, J. (1971) 'Life in a dual system: Eastern Nigerians in town, 1961', *Cahiers d'etudes Africanies*, Vol. 11, pp. 400–21.

----------(1997) 'Life in a dual system revisited: Urban-rural ties in Enugu, Nigeria, 1961-1987', in J. Gugler (ed.), *Cities in the Development World: Issues, Theory, and Policy*, Oxford: Oxford University Press, pp. 62–73.

Harneit-Sievers, A. (1998) 'Igbo "traditional rulers": Chieftaincy and the state in southeastern Nigeria', *Afrika Spectrum*, Vol. 33, pp. 57–79.

Henderson, R.N. (1972) *The King in Every Man: Evolutionary Trends in Onitsha Ibo Society and Culture*, New Heaven and London: Yale University Press.

I.S.N. (Imo State of Nigeria) (1980) *Government White Paper of the Chieftaincy / Autonomous Community Panel of Inquiry, 1980*, The Government Printer.

----------(2000) 'I.S.N. Law No. 3 of 1999: Traditional Rulers and Autonomous Communities Law, 1999', *Supplement to Imo State of Nigeria Gazette*, Vol. 1, No. 25, pp. 1–36.

Immigration Bureau of Japan (1985–2012) *Statistics on the Foreigners Registered in Japan*, Tokyo: Japan Immigration Association.

Inyama, E.O. (1993) 'Trends in traditional rulership in Igboland', in U.D. Anyanwu and J.C.U. Aguwa (eds.), *The Igbo and the Tradition of Politics*, Enugu: Fourth Dimension Publishing, pp. 216–31.

Logan, C. (2009) 'Selected chiefs, elected councilors and hybrid democrats: Popular perspectives on the co-existence of democracy and traditional authority', *Journal of Modern African Studies*, Vol. 47, pp. 101–28.

Matsumoto, H. (2008) *The Resilience of Chieftaincy in Postcolonial Africa*, Tokyo: Akashi Shoten (in Japanese).

Meek, C.K. (1937) *Law and Authority in a Nigerian Tribe*, London: Oxford University Press.

Nwaubani, E. (1994) 'Chieftaincy among the Igbo: A guest on the Center-Stage', *The International Journal of African Historical Studies*, Vol. 27, pp. 347–71.

Nzimiro, I. (1972) *Studies in Ibo Political Systems: Chieftaincy and Politics in Four Niger States*, Berkeley and Los Angeles: University of California Press.

Oha, O. (2009) 'Praise names and power de/constructions in contemporary Igbo chiefship', *Culture, Language, and Representation* Vol. 7, pp. 101–16.

Onwuejeogwu, M.A. (1981) *An Igbo Civilization: Nri Kingdom & Hegemony*, London: Ethnographica.

Oomen, B. (2005) *Chiefs in South Africa: Law, Power & Culture in the Post-Apartheid Era*, Oxford: James Currey.

Osaghae, E.E. (1994) *Trends in Migrant Political Organizations in Nigeria: The Igbo in Kano*, Ibadan: IFRA.

----------(1998) 'Hometown associations as shadow states: The case of Igbos and Yorubas', in R.H. Kano and S. Okafor (eds.), *Hometown Associations: Indigenous Knowledge and Development in Nigeria*, London: IT Publications, pp. 111–21.

Peil, M., Stephen, K.E. and Oyeneye, O.Y. (1998) 'Going home: Migration careers of southern Nigerians', *International Migration Review*, Vol. 22, pp. 563–85.

Plotnicov, L. (1970 [1965]) 'Nigerians: The dream is unfulfilled', in W. Mangin (ed.), *Peasants in Cities: Readings in The Anthropology of Urbanization*, Boston: Houghton Mifflin Company, pp. 170–4.

Ratha, D., Mohapatra, S., Ozden, C., Plaza, S., Shaw, W. and Shimeles, A. (2011) *Leveraging Migration for Africa: Remittances, Skills, and Investments*, Washington, DC: World Bank.

Searchina (2008) *A Chinese Businessman Became an Igbo Chief for the First Time*, http://news.searchina.ne.jp/disp.cgi?y=2008&d=0219&f=business_0219_004.shtml.

Trager, L. (2001) *Yoruba Hometown: Community, Identity and Development in Nigeria*, London: Lynne Rienner Publishers.

Uchendu, V.C. (1965) *The Igbo of Southeast Nigeria*, New York: Holt, Rinehart and Winston.

Van Binsbergen, W. (1999) 'Nkoya royal chiefs and the Kazanga cultural association in western central Xam', in E.A.B. Van Rouveroy van Nieuwaal and R. Van Dijk (eds.), *African Chieftaincy in a New Socio-Political Landscape*, pp. 97–133, Hamburg: LIT.

Van Rouveroy van Nieuwaal, E.A.B. and Van Dijk, R. (eds.) (1999) *African Chieftaincy in a New Socio-Political Landscape*, Hamburg: LIT.

Vaughan, O. (1991) 'Chieftaincy politics and social relations in Nigeria', *Journal of Commonwealth & Comparative Politics*, Vol. 29, pp. 308–26.

---------- (2000) *Nigerian Chiefs: Traditional Power in Modern Politics, 1890s–1990s*, New York: University of Rochester Press.

Chapter 9

The Power to Speak, Listen, and Negotiate in the Local Meetings of Africa:
The Palaver of the Bakongo, Clan Gathering of the Borana, and Bridewealth Negotiation of the Turkana

Itaru Ohta

9.1. Reaching Coexistence by Overcoming Contradictions

How do we overcome the mixed emotions, tension and antagonism that arise between the self and the 'other'? Our society is rife with all kinds of antipathy, conflict and disputes. There may be anger towards perceived infringements of our rights or position, competition for a piece of an estate, crime and imperilment to our wellbeing. The simplest solution to these may be to take the matter to the police and courts. These institutions are practical and able to bring a dispute to some conclusion. In other words, we would trust a third party whom we believe to have the authority to judge the disputes that we are not capable of resolving ourselves.

Of course, in Africa also, there are public institutions such as the police and the courts where disputes are settled. However, it is also true that many conflicts and confrontations are handled in meetings that the interested parties call forth by themselves to seek some resolution. This is to say that these meetings function to modulate various people's behaviours to maintain order or to prevent disputes, and if these arise, to mediate and resolve the issues, sometimes even making the violator of a promise or norm to pay compensation. Even in Japan, not all disputes are taken to the courts, and discussions may suffice to resolve an issue. But in comparison, it is much more common in African societies to deal with an issue through an informal meeting.

Such systems have been created and practised by the African people themselves, and we usually call them 'traditional', 'customary' or 'indigenous' knowledge and institutions. Where such a system exists, a set of norms and laws exist and function for the people to acknowledge and adhere to, and also to settle disputes. The academic field of legal anthropology, or the anthropology of law, has dealt with the questions of what set of disciplines people abide by in the various societies of the world, what is the authority that binds people's behaviour, which political systems make this possible, what is law, etc. Many questions have been explored, such as what system can punish the perpetrator of a crime, or order the perpetrator to pay monetary compensation, and ultimately, how conflicts are resolved.

These studies first started with the uncritical presupposition of a Western and modernistic paradigm (Hayden 1984). To put it succinctly, these studies held that law was a set of rules with enforcement power. Evans-Pritchard (1940, p. 162) was also uncritical of the paradigm, and so argued that the Nuer do not have law in the strict sense. However, it soon became clear that such thinking was inappropriate, and studies have been undertaken that are free from the paradigm. A model example is one by Comaroff and Roberts (1981). They analysed how the Tswana abide by a set of rules, and yet, at the same time, freely use the rules to fortify their demands and to negotiate. Comaroff and Roberts showed us how law could simultaneously be a set of rules to be adhered to and at the same time, subject to negotiation. In this sense, law is not at all absolute and exogenous to an individual, nor unequivocally definitive of behaviours that are 'correct anywhere, anytime' (Ohta 2001).

With the above said, the author will not discuss further as to 'what constitutes law'. This chapter is on how the African people behave in a local meeting with the goal of resolving some kind of contradictions. An issue on the agenda may be a difficult relationship between certain people, competition over a resource or estate, violation of norms, theft, or even physical harm. Any of these will be talked over in a meeting, where people will try and seek a resolution.

These meetings share certain qualities with our 'modern' courts and mediations. When we go to the courts, we have a stake over some kind of conflict, and as a matter of fact, will argue for ourselves for maximum benefit. Opposing parties will rather have their own benefit maximised, and to this end will proffer various evidence, seek flaws in the opponent's argument, and are not afraid to argue

250

incessantly. The opponents will need to eventually seek settlement at some point where the process will have resembled a discount negotiation, and having gone through with the process, the settlement will inevitably be a certain 'calculated compromise'. If the two sides choose to go through the court system for this purpose, there will be a judicial winner and a loser at the end of the process.

In contrast, the meetings the author submits in this chapter are markedly different from the above judicial and mediational process, although the meeting is a space where people come to engage in an 'earnest match', to resolve a conflict with perceived high stakes. This is true, because the process involved does not seek to decide which side is correct or wrong, nor label a winner and loser, but rather, the process aims to create order through the formation of an agreement between the interested and stakeholding other.

The author means the following by an 'earnest match': when people cannot accept a different viewpoint and come to an impasse in argument or conflict in stakes between the self and the other, they will try hard to realise what they deem necessary in life, strive to better their foothold in life and to break the impasse between the interest of oneself and the other. By this they try to reach a goal that they can rest easy with. Such an endeavour is what this author calls an 'earnest match'.

The other, the opponent, in such an earnest match is by no means someone that understands, or is empathetic without many words exchanged. In all practicality, that someone is to the contrary, so it is impossible to quickly enter into a stable and lasting relationship. Rather, ceaseless efforts are necessary to renew a mutually fair relationship with the other. In the sense that a relationship can be created through engagement and influence, the other is an open existence. Quick understanding is unattainable between the self and such an other, and it is no surprise that any such relationship is always in flux.

The case studies that the author submits here show how the African people energetically talk to and listen to the other so that they can try to build an agreement through mutual negotiations, because they know that understanding is only possible that way. People seek to accommodate, as well as punish antisocial behaviour. When a meeting is convened for such a purpose, people share the recognition that an issue will be dealt with so that conflict will be settled through talks and negotiations. To 'create an order through forging an agreement between the self and the other' is to behave in a 'cooperative' manner. That this involves an earnest match is a matter of fact, since two parties are never alike, and all relationships with the other are individual and specific, as well as inviolable.

The author in this chapter will describe the kinds of negotiations that take place where people acknowledge conflict, engage in an earnest match and, at the same time, behave in a collaborative manner with the opponent. For this, the author chooses the three cases of the palaver by the Bakongo, gatherings by the Borana and bridewealth negotiation by the Turkana. What is obvious is the practice for attaining coexistence, which the author believes to be one typical manifestation of the African potentials.[1]

9.2. Palaver: Techniques to Deal with Threats to the Community

9.2.1 Palaver Practised in Africa

When the Africans gather for discussion to decide on an issue or mediate a conflict, sometimes the occasion is called the 'palaver'. When one looks up the word in a dictionary (The Compact Oxford English Dictionary, 1991), it lists the following meanings:

1. A talk, parley, conference, discussion: chiefly applied to conferences, with much talk, between African or other tribes people, and traders or travellers.

2a. Applied contemptuously to (what is considered) unnecessary, profuse, or idle talk; 'jaw'.

2b. Talk intended to cajole, flatter, or wheedle.

2c. In West Africa: a dispute or contest.

2d. Business, concern.

2e. Jargon.

2f. In Africa: trouble

The dictionary also states that 'Palavra [palaver in Portuguese] appears to have been used by Portuguese traders on the coast of Africa for a talk or colloquy with the natives, to have been there picked up by English sailors, and to have passed from nautical slang into colloquial use' ([ ]: the author's annotation).

It follows that palaver is not only nebulous chattering, but also means negotiation and business talk in the African context, and more commonly denotes what we call discussion. In Africa, there has been a tradition for the people to gather, discuss matters that they face, and to resolve them.[2] These gatherings, categorised as palavers, who and where these are held, and what role they play are described in *Socio-Political Aspects of the Palaver in Some African Countries* (1979) published by UNESCO. The publication comes under the 8-volume series title, *Introduction to African Culture*. Palaver is chosen as one of the topics representing African culture. Meetings and gatherings comprise palaver, including those that are either open to all of the villagers, or exclusive to only some in the society, for example, the aristocracy and the elders. A variety of matters are talked over to ease tension and to reach some kind of a consensus.

African palaver has come to be known to the world by Wamba dia Wamba (1985).[3] He is a politician and a scholar of history and philosophy. He was born in the Democratic Republic of the Congo, finished middle school and studied in the United States where he earned his degree. He later taught there and in Tanzania. In 1998, Wamba dia Wamba returned to his mother country torn apart by the Second Congo War to join the antigovernment struggle. With the war over, he became an important political figure in the newly struggling political system.

Wamba dia Wamba's ideological foothold is Marxism, and he has struggled with the question of how a democratic political system can materialise in Africa. He has argued that uncritical, thoughtless introduction of Western thoughts and paradigms will not help democracy take root in Africa. He was critical of politics that put party interest ahead of the public, saying that it would only oppress the people. He sought the conditions for politics that emerged from people's political activities to ultimately liberate them. For this, he placed his hopes on palaver practised by the Bakongo he witnessed growing up in his home village.

9.2.2. *Palaver by the Bakongo*

The literature on palaver include Diong (1979) and Fu-Kiau (2007), besides Wamba dia Wamba. Here, the author will refer to them all. The Bakongo held various gatherings, different in character according to the where and the why of the location. Some gatherings were attended by all of the community, while some others were held for the elderly or particular professionals. Fu-Kiau (2007) called all of the gatherings, *mbongi*. This word refers to the simple hut seen in any village centre, where people gather and have all kinds of discussions. According to Fu-Kiau, the people themselves also called these gatherings '*mbongi*'. Topics ranged widely, including news from within and without daily life in the village or the city, some from the women who married out, as well as births, deaths, land disputes, and labour to be cooperated on.

Sometimes, a specific issue may be put on the table, while, at other times, a spontaneous gathering may come about at weddings and funerals, where people happened to assemble. Besides at *mbongi*, a gathering may take place at the market.

In the gatherings, there is a modulator called '*nzonzi*'. These professionals are quick-witted masters of rhetoric and well versed in sayings, songs and aphorisms, yet they never attack their opponents into silence. They let others talk, they listen and quickly grasp the core matter. They would not take sides, but keep the discussions from becoming agitated or confrontational, and help prod the palaver along to reach some kind of a conclusion.

However, Wamba dia Wamba has commented that since only the men of the same lineage can participate in *mbongi*, it is exclusive, and therefore not 'a real case of palaver' which is 'a public debate involving everybody' (1985, p. 3). Because a real palaver is open to all the villagers to speak up, man or woman, young or old, etc., Wamba dia Wamba's real palaver is distinctly different from other meetings and gatherings.

A real palaver starts with a specific incident such as an unexpected death of a villager or some elderly person beaten by a younger villager. Many villagers will demand for an occasion to proffer their opinions on the incident. The clan elder may call for the gathering to take place, and having pledged their loyalty to the ancestors, people will start talking. Men, women, young and old can all take part, as this is the rule. Villagers will verbally affirm how the ancestors must be respected, believing that because somebody did not follow the ways of the community, the community as a whole is imperilled.

The palaver is assembled in response to a specific event, but the topics may veer from this event, and touch upon people's frustrations and conflicts, which are made public so that the violators of norms and expected social behaviour are openly accused. The goal of the palaver is not to resolve specific issues. Rather, it is to make public the contradictions that torment the people. Through this endeavour, the sense of a united community and shared values is restored. According to Wamba dia Wamba, the ultimate goal of palaver is to reassemble the community, restore and preserve harmony, and to mend peoples' relationships.

At the end of the palaver, people will rejoice, express fervour and congratulate each other in a quite festive bliss. It is said that the ancestral spirits are present at the gathering to ultimately watch over their wellbeing. In a palaver, because everybody can speak up, the daily social relationships are temporarily suspended, and because there is festive rejoicing, it has a *communitas* element in that the rebuilding of the community is possible at the end.

To reiterate, everybody can participate and speak up in a palaver. Not only the *nzonzi* employs aphorisms and similes, jokes, song and dance, but everybody. There is value in eloquence. To summarise, this occasion for discussion is the occasion to express the skills in oratory. Something will be decided at a palaver with unanimous agreement by the participants. Some issues will be discussed in both such participatory palavers and the palavers open only to the elders. If this is the case, the former can reject a decision by the latter. Also, people of importance such as the clan leader may summarise the discussion of the villagers to move the talk along, but does not have the power to decide. According to Wamba dia Wamba, palavers can deal with the imperilled unity of a community, but also let the villagers rebel against the elders who may seek to oppress. In other words, villagers reestablish equity among the communal members through palavers.[4]

9.3. The Clan Gathering of the Borana: The Skills to Extract Forgiveness and Realise Reconciliation

9.3.1. The Borana

The author describes below the Borana who live in the semi-arid area between southern Ethiopia and northern Kenya. Legesse (1974) and Tagawa (1997, 1998, 2001, 2005) are referred to for greater understanding of their social structure. The Borana mainly conducted pastoralism as their livelihood, where recently, the importance of agriculture for them has increased. Their society has a complex age system called *gada*, which is composed of eight age-grades, through which a generation-set passes. Generation-sets are formed eight years apart, and all Borana men join the fifth generation-set junior to their father's. Each generation-set elects six official appointees, of which one is the *hayu*, described below. The official appointees carry out the ceremonies as well as resolve conflicts. The Borana comprise two exogenous moieties, and each moiety has numerous paternal clans. Members of each clan gather to talk over various issues, including conflict mediation, assistance to members in need, conducting ceremonies, selecting generation-set appointees, certifying marriage and divorce or livestock ownership, etc. Because the habitat is very dry, wells and ponds are important resources owned by the clans, and members of each clan cooperate and maintain the resource. In the gathering described below, one topic is the discussion on how to prepare the money to dig a new well.

9.3.2. Clan Gathering of the Borana

The following clan gathering took place in southern Ethiopia on 22 June 1990 (Bassi 1992, 2005). The people gathered to talk and decide on how to pool money for a new well. The well was to be used by all members of the clan, and to pay for digging it was a responsibility shared by all. However, as the discussion ensued, one *hayu* brought forth another issue. He said that he was asked to mediate a conflict between two men a few months before, and that the parties met for several days. It was then decided that one of the two men, X, should pay a fine. X was dissatisfied, and declined. The *hayu* brought up the matter in this gathering because X and his opponent Y were both present.

Many elders at the gathering accused X of not paying the fine at the time of the decision. After a pause, X said, 'There are two *hayu* presiding here, and I will follow any decision made at this meeting'. This was an insinuation that the original ruling by one specific *hayu* was unfair. To this, the elders admonished X even more, saying, 'What you say is all wrong'. The *hayu* that brought this matter up proceeded to give a long speech full of rhetoric referring to the origins of the authority he stood for as well as how richly versed he was in the traditional rules. This was the *hayu*'s way of expressing his indignation to X, and the will to regain the *hayu* authority challenged by X.

Suddenly X grabbed some grass from the ground where he was, ran to the *hayu*, and offered the grass to him. He repeatedly wailed, 'Father, forgive me'. The gathered men burst into laughter. But X grabbed even more grass from the ground, offered it to his opponent Y and the elders present, and repeated his wail, 'Forgive me'. X had admitted his wrong, and admitted what he said and had done was against the social order. He was ready to observe order.[5]

But a new ruling had to be made, of what new punishment befitted X's wrongdoing and how he would compensate for it. The *hayu* whose authority had been challenged argued that X had to pay with his 10 cows, as well as proffer one ox to the coffer for digging the well, which was, after all, the subject of the meeting. The ox was, so to speak, the 'court expense' to be paid by the violator of the social order. A discussion ensued as to how many cattle were to be paid by X. Eventually one elder said, 'X is now repentant and already declared he follows the ruling of this meeting. How about pardoning his fine?' To this, the *hayu* who was insulted was unflinching, saying, 'X should pay me two cows'.

All of a sudden, all the men there started to bless the *hayu*. They chanted, 'Let your life be fruitful always. May your family prosper, may your wealth grow!' The Borana often chant a formalised blessing by all present to a person or a group who is acknowledged to have made an unselfish deed or sacrifice. The chant is a prayer to the god as well as blessing towards a specific person or a group, whose renown is elevated being blessed this way.

It also follows to say that the collective blessing can pressure someone or some group to make a good contribution to the whole community. In the above, the *hayu* who was bestowed the blessing had not made any concession at that point. But to make him take back his demand for two cows from X, instead of telling the *hayu*, 'Your demand is unrealistic', the people were nudging him to take back his demand and pardon X, because that was self-sacrifice which amounted to a good contribution to the community. In other words, the people blessed the *hayu* preemptively. The *hayu* did annul his demand. All the men present repeated their chanting blessing to the *hayu* even more.

The issue of how to pool their resources for digging the well still remained. Eventually the *hayu* announced, 'X should give to the clan his ox, but the opponent Y needs to pay nothing' (even though he might have had to share the court expense), and the meeting came to a close.

What is the lesson in this Borana episode? First, note that the process is to make a violator admit his wrong, rather than penalise him with a fine. Sporadic social conflict and stress would be ameliorated, and peoples' minds would be put to rest. Through this process, the people carefully avoid aggression and overt anger. The conflict that was confined to a small group of people would be made open to many, and the ultimate understanding as to what happened would be shared by the community.

The second point of interest was that the process is always accompanied by ceremonial and institutional behaviour. In the case above, it was the actions of grabbing the grass from the ground and group chant of blessing through which the penalty was lessened. Bassi (1992) called such a process 'institutional forgiveness'.[6]

9.4. Bridewealth Negotiation among the Turkana: The Skills to Formulate Consensus through Negotiation

9.4.1. Overview of Turkana Society and Payment of the Bridewealth

There is a vast expanse of arid land in northern Kenya where annual rainfall is less than 500 ml. The people here live on livestock that include camel, cattle, goat, sheep and donkey, and conduct highly mobile pastoralism. The Turkana whom the author will describe in this section is among these pastoralists.

For a wedding to take place in the Turkana society, the groom's family transfers many heads of livestock to the bride's family as bridewealth. The question of how many heads of livestock will be determined by the negotiation between the two families. Generally, the more heads of livestock owned, the more will be paid as bridewealth. In some cases, the number may equal two thirds of all that are owned by the groom's family. On average, roughly 30 heads of large-sized livestock (camel, cattle and donkey) and about 110 heads of smaller-sized livestock (goat and sheep) are paid out. No other occasion calls for this many heads of livestock to be transferred. In sum, because the Turkana deem livestock as their sole asset, the bridewealth payment is the most important social event.[7]

The Turkana live scattered across a vast arid expanse, and may only gather in the rainy season, and even then, only if there is measurable rainfall. The author was indeed privileged to have sat in one case of bridewealth negotiation from beginning to the end. The author will describe here how the people mutually negotiate and come to decide the amount of bridewealth. As the meetings make the people face the issues to be resolved to formulate agreement, through speaking up, it shares characteristics common with the palaver of the Bakongo and the clan meeting of the Borana. Before delving into the case study, the author will briefly describe here the participants of the negotiation meetings, and what social relationships are found among the participants.

In Turkana society, small patrilineal descent groups and regional groups each make their own decisions on political, economic and religious matters. The Turkana have about 30 patrilineal clans, but the members of a clan have no occasion to act as a group. Each clan only functions as a unit of exogamy. There is an age system as the organisational principle, but age-set contemporaries have different names in different areas, and members never act as a group. In other words, neither clan nor age-set serves to bind the Turkana society.

To the Turkana, agnates, in-laws and friends with whom they have specific day-to-day interaction are the important relations. These people at times will co-manage the livestock, and will work for a smooth operation of life events of magnitude, such as weddings and funerals. These individuals that one maintains day-to-day social relationships with are the most valuable partners in life. The participants of the bridewealth negotiation meetings are such individuals that have a realistic social relationship with the bride and the groom's family. Gulliver (1955) called these individuals as 'stock associates'.

9.4.2. The Negotiation to Decide the Number of Livestock as Bridewealth

The meeting to seal the bridewealth negotiation at how much livestock to exchange hands is open to all of the villagers. But before this, the close agnates of both bride and groom need to have had numerous private meetings to exchange information on the specific network of binding social ties, etc., so that each can ascertain the marriage as suitable. Because the Turkana in-laws often become important as mutually supporting partners, the process of these private meetings to know each other is where various gifts are exchanged to increase 'closeness'. Each side also accumulates information on the number of livestock the other party has.

At the same time, the in-laws-to-be repeatedly meet in the above process, as the central family members of both sides talk about the bridewealth. The bride's father by then has general information on the number of livestock owned by the suitor and his close kin. In other words, how much bridewealth the groom's family can support. The bride-to-be's father will list the members of his 'stock associates', and will start suggesting how many heads of livestock each of them might receive. The groom's family will not commit to any specific number nor will there be an agreement. Rather, each side will feel each other out through the preliminary meetings and gift exchange, and if they feel comfortable enough, work together for the bridewealth agreement. The ultimate negotiation will be held with open participation. The open meeting comes in two stages.

(a) The First Stage at the Village of Bride-to-be's Father:

Open bridewealth negotiation must always be held in a clearing to the east of the village. The suitor's close agnates, in-laws and friends will travel to the village of the bride's father, settle down under a tree several tens of meters east from the village. The bride's father and brothers will settle down under another tree closer to the village. There will be 20–30 m between the two groups, and this space will be the centre stage for oratory concerning bridewealth negotiation. One by one, the men of each group take turns to step forward, and with much gesturing, will say aloud his opinion to the other group and neighbours. Only men participate in the oratory, one hundred of them including the on-lookers, but no woman.

At the village of the bride's father, negotiation ensues on the total number of camel paid by groom's side to bride's side, as well as the number of goats and sheep to be paid to the father of the bride, the mother, the mother's co-wives and the rest of close agnates. The author will call this stage the 'first stage of negotiation', for convenience, and this usually takes one to three days. In Turkana, it is called *eloto*. The next second stage is called '*akiuta*', meaning wedding (ceremony).

(b) The Second Stage at the Groom's Village:

When agreement is reached at the first stage, the groom's entourage returns to their village. As early as the next day, it is the turn of entourage of bride's father to visit. As in the first stage, they gather under the canopy of a tree to the east of the village. The groom's entourage settles down under a tree closer to their village. In the second stage of negotiation, the camels, goats and sheep whose numbers that had been agreed upon in the first stage are presented to the bride's entourage. Then, the negotiation ensues on the number as to goat and sheep for the already married sisters of the bride, grandmother, uncles and aunts, and paid out upon agreement. When this is over, the negotiation starts for the number of cattle to be paid to the bride's father, and when an agreement is reached, the cattle for him change hands. Then, the negotiation continues for the payment of cattle to the mother, the mother's co-wives, close agnates, and the rest of 'stock associates' of bride's father. The share of each person is paid separately.

The bride's entourage keeps all the livestock they gained close by as the negotiation takes place. Only when the process is over, do they return to their village. As early as the next day, the groom's entourage revisits, and this time the wedding ceremony will follow.

9.4.3. The Negotiation as an Earnest Match and Turkana Generosity

The above was a brief summary on the process from marriage proposal by the suitor, bridewealth negotiation and the wedding ceremony. Here, the author will focus on how people behave when the mutual negotiation of the bridewealth is under way, so that the commonalities may be found with the Bakongo's palaver and clan meetings of the Borana.

(a) The Earnest Match

The negotiation is nothing less than an earnest match. The bride's party expects to gain much, and will demand as much. For example, in the camel negotiation that the author sat in, they initially demanded 20 heads of camel. To this, the groom's party responded, 'We own no camel'. Much oratory ensued from both sides, and after 34 minutes, the groom's side yielded, saying, 'We shall pay you two heads of camel'. Again, much oratory ensued, during which time the number of camel increased three times: first, three heads were added, then two and then another three. The final number, 10, was agreed upon by the two sides, only after two hours and eight minutes during which 49 speeches were made totally.

At times the negotiation comes close to a breakdown because neither side yields. The author has witnessed a case where a groom was about to give up when one of his close kin spontaneously offered help, saying, 'You can pay with my livestock'. To this, the gallery all started to murmur, which grew into a roar, because they were impressed at the generosity shown by the man. The Turkana uses a verb, '*aekin*', to mean this kind of behaviour. When the author asked about the verb, the people usually said, 'When my brother is in a physical fight, for me to help him is to *aekin'*. The Turkana has another verb with the meaning 'to help, to assist', whereas *aekin* is more specific, 'to lend reinforcement to comrades in battle', as it were. This indicates how the bridewealth negotiation is akin to a combat, a true 'earnest match'.

(b) Rhetoric of Eloquence

One of the lasting impressions of the negotiations was that people had a striking command of oratory. All the men taking centre stage will make a speech, striding about with much gesturing, usually for one to three minutes, but at times 10 minutes long. They all resemble actors giving the performance of their lifetime. Of course, some are more eloquent than others, but any man can face 100 people or so and argue what he wants to, quite unperturbed. The men employ numerous expressions in persuasive logic and emotion, interspersed with rhetoric including rhymes and metaphor. Sometimes only the literal meaning is quite apparent, but not the figurative. In all speech making, the two sides always alternate.

(c) Show of Generosity

Another strong impression the author had was the excellent timing the people have for showing generosity. And they are proud of it. This is to say the negotiation is never simply for a measurable discount.

The bridewealth negotiation is an earnest match that at times heats up so much and requires reinforcement. Because the two sides argue with fervour and demand concessions from the other, the author became afraid that the people might be beyond mending their relationship afterward. Even if an agreement was possible, the author was unsure if the people would come out free of ill feelings and spite. The intensity of the bickering is such that there seems almost no end to the people's desire for livestock or discount thereof, and the negotiation seems full of utilitarian calculation.

However, the Turkana people do not believe that pursuing the maximum interest is selfish, but rather, they affirm this as a matter of fact for a person. Upon this understanding, the people proceed to an endpoint, which is a compromise. Generally speaking, a negotiation is understandable if it means 'the opponent's gain is my loss'. But the Turkana do not engage in such a zero-sum game. Kitamura (2002) has analysed the Turkana's seemingly contradictory interaction of pursuing maximum individual gain while at the same time seeking to resolve the confrontation with the other for maintaining social order. Kitamura's conclusion is that the Turkana principle is that 'people must cooperate'. The Turkana process may strike as zero-sum, if one looks at only the ultimate outcome. This view omits the joy the Turkana feels in engaging in an earnest match and this deep sense of satisfaction and accomplishment in working towards an agreement.

For example, the author has repeatedly seen a situation where a man who up to then had strongly demanded 'more livestock' for his share in bridewealth suddenly exclaim, 'I demand no more. Mind the number of livestock you pay to so-and-so who is next in turn'. There are abrupt displays of generosity. The author has also seen a man admonish another of his own entourage, 'Your demand was met. Enough'. The party giving out the bridewealth at times gives quite liberally and willingly. Both parties in negotiation are soon to be in-laws who will be important partners in life. The show of willing generosity works to win over the other's trust.

The bridewealth negotiations are always attended by the neighbours in the area, who enjoy the oratorical matches. They also will participate in the numerous rituals in the wedding ceremony and play important roles. They are keen to find cowardly acts such as where the groom's party tries to conceal the number of livestock they own to lower the number of the livestock to be paid, or the bride's party exhibits wanton greed. When the negotiation stalls because of these acts, the gallery voices their strong dissatisfaction, saying that the cowardly acts are insults to them. Thus, the two negotiating parties are under the watchful gaze of the gallery, and also because of this, they rise to give the best performance of their life, which in turn brings about great pride.

(d) Together Facing the Ordeal of the Bridewealth Negotiation

The author has described the way the people act at the bridewealth negotiation in Turkana society. Here, the essence of the social interaction will be reiterated to analyse what is at the core of the negotiation.

The negotiation is akin to a do-or-die match that needs reinforcement from comrades. It is indeed an earnest match, and no party will compromise half-heartedly. The occasion calls for up to two-thirds of the owned livestock exchanging ownership, and since livestock is the only asset for the Turkana, the bridewealth negotiation is indeed a big event. However, to emphasise only this aspect is to lose sight of what else is important in the whole picture.

The groom paying the bridewealth is not 'losing' his livestock through the process. The kinfolk of the bride and groom are soon in-laws, bound to offer help and cooperation to each other in day-to-day life from then on. They come to the negotiation prepared, with background information to size up the other side. Behind this is a strong determination to acknowledge the goodness in the marriage and to make it happen.

The people are capable of rescinding their strong demand with a show of magnanimous generosity. And the gallery, the villagers who watch over the theatrical negotiation, play a pivotal role. They are intolerant of excessive demands and nagging over the livestock. They cry out, 'We do not stand to be insulted!' So the directly involved parties are more than aware of their presence, and desire to proudly and honourably accomplish a good deal for the important event. For them to command eloquence and to be able to listen to the other are linked to their joyous pride.

If the negotiation is simply a battle for discount, frustration may linger on both sides at finalisation. However, this is not at all the case for the Turkana. The author happened to witness both parties congratulate each other for their 'good job done' at the end of the negotiation. This is to say they appreciate a fine, earnest match as well as the show of generosity by the other, indeed an occasion for congratulation. When the whirlwind days of the wedding ceremony are finally over and it is time for the both parties to part, they exchange words of blessing, chanting, 'Our father/son, farewell, take care, live happily'. These words are laden with the sense of accomplishment and satisfaction shared by the people who faced and cooperated in the ordeal of bridewealth negotiation.

9.5. Conclusion: The Power to Speak, the Power to Listen, the Power to Negotiate

9.5.1. The Power to Strive for Coexistence with the 'Other'

Having submitted the above three cases, the author will now focus on the commonalities among the three to contemplate what kinds of social relationships, and notions of the 'other', that are presupposed by the people when they partake in the interaction of the meetings.

The most apparent common factor among the three cases is the importance of the power to speak. People command aphorisms and metaphors to lend lively rhetoric to buttress their oratory in the meetings. At the same time, the people not only are skilful in speech, but in listening to others, so that they can encourage the other to speak up more. For the opposing parties to agree, the people must persuade themselves as well as the other. The people do not rely on an absolute standard of a legal system that they must always observe. There is no such convenient and omnipotent, fantastically recognisable authority. The reality being such as it is, people try to overcome the misconception that separates the two parties to formulate a consensus. They embrace the earnest match and employ the twin skills of the power to speak and the power to listen.

The people who participate in the gatherings and meetings described in this chapter all belong to one ethnic group, such as the Bakongo, Borana and Turkana. In other words, generally these people share a common culture and set of values. This, however, does not warrant that opposing parties are able to arrive at mutual consent. The above cases show that it does not follow that the 'self' and the 'other' are one with the group, nor can they understand each other without spoken words. They speak to each other precisely because they will not understand each other otherwise.

The fixed categories of gender, age or kinship relationships bind no party to a prescribed action and behaviour that will predetermine the outcome of the mutual negotiations. The 'other' to these people is always indeterminate and unforeseeable, and because they accept this as a matter of fact, they keep themselves open to the other to let their relationship flourish through the mutual negotiations. The other is a specific person or persons with names and faces. The people mutually acknowledge each other as individual beings, and never reduce each other to some category.

So the people take for granted that the other is unknowable in advance and that there will be conflicts and antipathy between the self and the 'other'. They face the other and use the powers to speak and listen in an effort to gain understanding and new ways for coexistence. The author will name the capacity for this mutual interaction 'the power to negotiate'. It is a power not to gain discount, nor to predetermine harmony, but to willingly negotiate in an earnest match so that coexistence is possible between undeterminable, unknowable 'others'.

9.5.2. Acknowledging the 'Other' in Negotiation

Wamba dia Wamba stressed that the palaver of the Bakongo was democratic. To this, there has been criticism that it does not help to idealise and romanticise past customs to tackle the contemporary issues that African societies face.[8] However, Wamba dia Wamba has not argued for bringing back palaver practised in the past or for returning to a practice of long-lost ancestry. His point was that palaver aside, to introduce democracy isolated from any familiar African practice is bound to fail, and that to utilise a transformed palaver was only one prescription for better politics (Wamba dia Wamba 1985).

It is understandable that some questions are inevitable here in the approach to apply a custom practised in one society to a larger context. For example, one may criticise that to arbitrarily single out one custom of one ethnicity and transplant it to another context is to technicalise, fragment and disembody the custom. There is no reason that palaver would work as well in mediating conflict among different sets of ethnicity. It is true that all of the cases above pertain to one ethnic group, where the people overcome conflict through negotiation. Therefore, the remaining pages will be devoted to trying to answer the question as to whether dialogue and negotiation are possible among people of different cultures.

Kurimoto (2016) has argued that the indigenous method for mediation after a murder, for example, will only function among the people who share the notion that the method is desirable. He called such a group of people 'the moral community'. One may deduce that because there are many ethnic groups in Africa with different values and beliefs, coexistence among such people may be difficult. The African people themselves insist at times that they are incommunicable with a neighbouring ethnic group or that different groups have different values.

However, Kurimoto (2016) points out that people in South Sudan survived the civil wars by the social and economic relationships with the neighbouring ethnic groups who in the past were sometimes antagonistic. Furthermore, he describes a case where, during the 2013 militant clashes in South Sudan between the Dinka and the Nuer, peace was maintained in some areas among ethnic groups under the leadership of prominent prophets. This is to say that the moral community can overcome the rift among different ethnic groups.

Matsuda (Chapter 10 in this volume) also reports on the Kikuyu, Luo and the Luhya in Nairobi, who protected their family and estate from harm through solidarity formed in spite of ethnic differences in the violence that ensued after the general election in 2007 in Kenya. This author also has reported that in a Kenyan refugee camp, serendipitous and impromptu friendship grew among many individuals from Sudan, Somalia and Ethiopia with the indigenous Turkana to support daily living (Ohta 2005).

Nyamnjoh (2015) has focused on the 'frontier qualities' of the Africans. The image of African communities as exclusive and strongly ethnic with an insurmountable barrier between each group is one that may have been overly stressed by anthropologists. In reality, people come and go freely across the ethnic divisions, living in a flexible and complex world. To demarcate the in from the out, or to think that there are numerous unyielding moral communities, is only a projection of our world cognition onto Africa.

Sagawa (2011) reported on the Daasanach and their neighbouring ethnic groups in southwest Ethiopia and pointed out that the former were very willing to coexist with others. The other cannot be managed or manipulated, and their behaviour is fraught with unpredictability. To build a relationship with such an other generally requires one of the two opposite approaches: First is to differentiate 'them' as alien to 'us', and categorise them as having 'such and such qualities', and rely on this image to interact. Sagawa has called such an approach 'preemption oriented' (2011, p. 355). This approach builds a wall between them and us, so that the specificity of persons disappears and social relationship is fragmented. Another approach will be to interact vis-à-vis the other and react to their speech and actions to build a relationship. This approach acknowledges the unmanageable and variegated other, to mutually relate to each other's actions and to create an order. Sagawa calls this second approach, 'coexistence oriented' (2011, pp. 355, 428). He reported that the Daasanach and their neighbouring groups share this latter orientation, which helped maintain order in the area with different ethnicities.

The orientation does not compartmentalise the other to particular categories of fixed properties as in the thinking, 'They are such and such kind of people', whose actions are foreseeable. But rather, it is to face 'now' and 'here' the other who is a specific person just as oneself is, to mutually respond to actions so that a relationship may be created anew.[9]

This chapter has described processes that overcome contradictions to formulate a consensus through negotiation. The people's actions in negotiation are but one part of malleable daily practices that extend in time and space. It is where people express how they view them and the other, and ultimately their human existence. They view the other as each different, unpredictable, unmanageable and uncontrollable being. With this as their starting point, they are open to the other whom they recognise as specific and individual so that they may work for consensus and coexistence.

Notes

[1] The argument of this chapter is particularly indebted to Neocosmos (2016), who highlighted 'a politics of peace' in Africa, taking 'a deliberate Afro-centric perspective'.

[2] The word, 'palaver', is found, for example, in *Things Fall Apart* of

Chinua Achebe (1994, p. 193), which described the tumultuous beginning of British colonialism in Nigeria. The second half of the novel is about social confusion with the arrival of the Christian missionaries and the impact brought on by the ruthless rule by the colonial government. A British regional governor in the novel uses the term 'palaver' for the gathering that he forces the local African leaders to partake. Achebe did not elaborate, but we can surmise the condescending British attitude toward the traditional African gathering. Contemporary media also use the word 'palaver' and in Ghana, an online newspaper is called *The Palaver*. The *Daily Standard* of Kenya has a column with the title, 'Palaver'. It can be found on the op-ed page where the reporters submit timely and short critiques on political and social events.

[3] Wamba dia Wamba was born in 1942 in Bas-Congo (Kongo Central) province, at a place called Sundi-Lutete. This introduction mostly follows Wamba dia Wamba (2004). His parents' generation already had been much influenced by the Western societies so that, on one hand, community values were very much intact, but on the other, Christian values already ran deep. Wamba dia Wamba's parents were devout Christians. Wamba dia Wamba grew to be a young man during the upheaval that led to the eventual independence of the Democratic Republic of the Congo in June 1960. He won a scholarship to the US, majoring in history, philosophy and African history, where he developed a keen interest in modern Western thought. Upon graduation he taught at, among others, Harvard University. In 1980, he was appointed professor of history at the University of Dar es Salaam, where he founded the Philosophy Club. From 1992 to 1995, he became the representative of the Council for the Development of Social Science Research in Africa (CODESRIA) and became active in both the academic and political arena (Wamba dia Wamba, 1991, 1992, 1995a, 1995b, 1996). In the political turmoil after the First Congo War, Wamba dia Wamba founded the Rally for Congolese Democracy (RCD) in 1988, became its representative and engaged in antigovernment activities during the Second Congo War. With this war over, he has remained influential, for example, as a member of the senate.

[4] Peter Geschiere (1982, pp. 210–227) who studied the Makaa in southeastern Cameroon has also described the palaver. In this society also, the 'all-important principle is that the decision-making must be arrived at democratically' (p. 211) and all villagers have 'right to speak' (p. 211) their

270

opinion. The 'intention [of a palaver] is, above all else, to affirm the unity and the mutual solidarity in the village' (p. 218, [ ] the author's annotation).

[5] Green grass, as well as green tree branches, symbolises peace among many ethnic groups in Ethiopia (Yntiso Gebre, personal information).

[6] Ruling processes that place more importance on mending social relationships rather than on punishing the violator has attracted academic attention as restorative justice (Zehr 2003), which the author will not discuss further here.

[7] See Ohta (2007) for details on the bridewealth negotiation and payment by the Turkana.

[8] See Depelchin (2005), Note 5.

[9] Refer to Lyotard (1998) for an in-depth contemplation on dialogue.

References

Achebe, C. (1994) *Things Fall Apart (50th Anniversary Edition)*, New York: Anchor Books.

Bassi, M. (1992) 'Institutional forgiveness in Borana assemblies', *Sociology-Ethnology Bulletin (Addis Ababa University)*, Vol. 1, No. 2, pp. 50–4.

----------(2005) *Decisions in the Shade*, (translation by C. Salvadori), Trenton: The Red Sea Press.

Comaroff, J. L. and Roberts, S. (1981) *Rules and Processes*, Chicago: University of Chicago Press.

Depelchin, J. (2005) *Silences in African History*, Dar es Salaam: Mkuki na Nyota Publishers.

Diong, B.K. (1979) 'The palaver in Zaire', in UNESCO (ed.), *Socio-Political Aspects of the Palaver in Some African Countries*, Paris, UNESCO, pp. 77–93.

Evans-Pritchard, E.E. (1940) *The Nuer*, Oxford: Clarendon Press.

Fu-Kiau, K.K.B. (2007) *Mbongi: An African Traditional Political Institution*, Atlanta: Afrikan Djeli Publishers.

Geschiere, P. (1982) *Village Communities and the State: Changing Relations among the Maka of Southeastern Cameroon since the Colonial Conquest* (translation by J. J. Ravell), London: Kegan Paul International Ltd.

Gulliver, P.H. (1955) *The Family Herds*, London: Routledge & Kegan Paul Ltd.

Hayden, R.M. (1984) 'Rules, processes, and interpretations: Geertz, Comaroff, and Roberts', *American Bar Foundation Research Journal*, Vol. 9, No. 2, pp. 469–78.

Kitamura, K. (2002) 'Epistemological uniqueness of pastoral peoples: The art of existence of the Turkana in northern Kenya', in S. Sato (ed.), *The World of the Nomadic Pastoral Peoples*, Kyoto: Kyoto University Press, pp. 87–125 (in Japanese).

Kurimoto, E. (2016) 'Several aspects of African potentials for conflict resolution and reconciliation', in M. Endo (ed.), *Overcoming Conflicts*, Kyoto: Kyoto University Press, pp. 79–111 (in Japanese).

Legesse, A. (1974) *Gada: Three Approaches to the Study of African Society*, New York: Free Press.

Lyotard, J.F. (1998) 'The other's rights', in S. Shute and S. Hurley (eds.), *On Human Rights*, Tokyo: Misuzu Shobo, pp. 167–82 (Japanese translation by H. Nakajima and M. Matsuda).

Neocosmos, M. (2016) 'Thinking an African politics of peace in an era of increasing violence', in S. Moyo, and Y. Mine (eds.), *What Colonialism Ignored: 'African Potentials' for Resolving Conflicts in Southern Africa*, Bamenda: Langaa RPCIG, pp. 317–59.

Nyamnjoh, F.B. (2015) 'Incompleteness: Frontier Africa and the currency of conviviality', *Journal of Asian and African Studies*, 0021909615580867, first published online on 23 April 2015.

Ohta, I. (2001) 'Motivations, negotiations, and animal individuality: Livestock exchange of the Turkana in northwestern Kenya', *Nilo-Ethiopian Studies*, No. 7, pp. 45–61.

----------(2005) 'Multiple socio-economic relationships improvised between the Turkana and refugees in Kakuma area, northwestern Kenya', in I. Ohta and Y. Gebre (eds.), *Displacement Risks in Africa*, Kyoto: Kyoto University Press, pp. 315–37.

----------(2007) 'Marriage and bridewealth negotiations among the Turkana in northwestern Kenya', *African Study Monographs, Supplementary Issue*, No. 37, pp. 3–26.

Sagawa, T. (2011) *Ethnography of Violence and Hospitality: War and Peace in*

East African Pastoralist Society, Kyoto: Showado (in Japanese).

Tagawa, G. (1997) 'Rituals of the *gada* system of the Borana: With special reference to late comers of a generation-set', in K. Fukui, E. Kurimoto and M. Shigeta (eds.), *Ethiopia in Broader Perspective*, Volume II, Kyoto: Shokado, pp. 616–31.

----------(1998) 'Age systems in oral history and ethnicism: A report on the Gumi/Gayo of the Borana-Oromo in southern Ethiopia', *Shakaijinruigaku Nenpou*, Vol. 24, pp. 99–122 (in Japanese).

----------(2001) 'Relationship between two age systems: Generation set and age set among the Borana-Oromo', *Minzokugaku Kenkyuu*, Vol. 66, No. 2, pp. 157–77 (in Japanese).

----------(2005) 'From folk time to the modern state space: The transformation of time and space of the gada system among the Borana-Oromo', in K. Fukui (ed.), *The Socialized Ecological Resources: Ethiopia and its Incessant Regeneration*, Kyoto: Kyoto University Press, pp. 295–322 (in Japanese).

The Compact Oxford English Dictionary (Second Edition) (1991) Oxford: Oxford University Press.

UNESCO (ed.) (1979) *Socio-Political Aspects of the Palaver in Some African Countries*, Paris: UNESCO.

Wamba dia Wamba, E. (1985) 'Experience of democracy in Africa: Reflections on practice of communal palaver as a social method of resolving contradictions among the people', *Philosophy and Social Action*, Vol. XI, No. 3. http://readingfanon.blogspot.jp/2011/06/experiences-of-democracy-in-africa.html (accessed 31 October 2016).

----------(1991) 'Philosophy and African intellectuals: Mimesis of Western classicism, ethnophilosophical romanticism or African self-mastery?', *Quest*, Vol. 5, No. 1, pp. 5–17.

----------(1992) 'Beyond elite politics or democracy in Africa', *Quest*, Vol. 6, No. 1, pp. 21–42.

----------(1995a) 'The place of Pan-Africanism in world history', *Quest*, Vol. 9, No. 1, pp. 3–18.

----------(1995b) 'Zaire: From the National Conference to the Federal Republic of the Congo?' *Development Dialogue*, Vol. 2, pp. 125–46.

----------(1996) 'Pan-Africanism, democracy, social movements and mass struggles', *African Journal of Political Science*, New Series, Vol. 1, pp. 9–20.

----------(2004) 'Harry Kreisler in conversation with Wamba dia Wamba', http:// globetrotter.berkeley.edu/people4/Wamba/wamba-con().html (accessed 30 October 2016).

Zehr, H. (2003) *Restorative Justice*, Tokyo: Shinsensha (Japanese translation by N. Nishimura, Y. Hosoi and N. Takahashi).

Chapter 10

Everyday Knowledge and Practices to Prevent Conflict:
How Community Policing Is Domesticated in Contemporary Kenya

Motoji Matsuda

10.1. Introduction

Infamously, for three months from the end of 2007, Kenya was brought to the brink of civil war amidst the confusion surrounding the results of a contested presidential election, a state of affairs that left over a thousand dead and produced hundreds of thousands of internally displaced citizens.[1] This incident, now generally known as Kenya's 'post-election violence' (PEV), anticipated a major shift in Kenyan society, particularly in the lives of the people living in the country's urban slum districts. In August of 2015, Kenya's largest daily newspaper, *Daily Nation*, pointed out this change while sounding a caution that 'in the slums of Nairobi … the re-organisation of settlement patterns along ethnic lines' signalled the growing entrenchment of an exclusive tribalism (Achuka 2015). Underlying this situation lay the sentiment among many Kenyan citizens that the state and, as an apparatus of state security, the police were no longer to be trusted, and that in times of emergency such as the PEV, the safety of property, as well as their own and their families' physical wellbeing would be better entrusted to a traditional consciousness based in ethnic solidarity.

When confronted with the extreme state of violence, where can people turn when the state or the police, as the state's 'apparatus of violence,' prove to be unhelpful? Can they turn to only 'tribal consciousness' that in many respects had been created to suit the needs of the white rulers in the colonial period? Might not the mechanisms that African society has itself devised to cope with conflict (and violence) prove useful in this context? When we

275

consider this problem from an 'African Potentials' point of view such as this, perhaps the first thing that comes to mind would be a solution based in the communities that the people themselves call home. A community initiative that utilises community resources in the attempt to safeguard people's lives, property, and social connections – this is precisely the kind of mechanism that one would expect to serve citizens as the most useful and pragmatic remedy. This is the idea of relying on the community for the maintenance of peace and security (i.e., policing).

This concept, known generally as community-based policing or community policing, finds expression worldwide in societies in both advanced and developing nation.[2] Of course, the diverse communities found in African societies have their own unique characteristics. Amongst community-specific organisations intended to prevent conflict, for example, there are those who claim disproportionately to be the legitimate successors of traditional ethnic culture, those who boldly advocate an African-style justice in contrast to Western justice, and yet others who seek to reorganise cultural customs to suit contemporary needs. And certainly amongst the community policing associations found in Kenya there are some whose characteristics might seem quite foreign to Western notions of democracy and human rights. Such characteristics have in some cases even been decried as 'pre-modern, anti-democratic patron-clientelism' by global human rights NGOs. How might we understand forms of community policing that have such characteristics from the point of view of African Potentials? Should we in fact evaluate these as being useful expressions of a potential to prevent conflict? Or should we reject them as simply endorsing illegal criminal organisations under the auspices of being 'African' and undermining the freedom of individuals and societies from within?

This chapter seeks answers to these questions from clues in the acceptance and creation of the wide variety of forms that community policing has taken in Kenyan society. Therefore, first of all, after ascertaining the deterioration of public order and the spread of violence that have become prominent in Kenyan society in the wake of the PEV, I examine several types of community policing that have been introduced as remedies for the mitigation and prevention of damage and the protection of property and the physical wellbeing of individuals and families from the threat of violence. On this basis, I attempt to follow a procedure whereby, through consideration of the risks and possibilities inherent within these cases of community policing, I can identify and extract ways in which community policing may be interpreted as a *potential* for conflict prevention produced by African societies.

Conflict, once it erupts, necessarily produces perpetrators and victims of violence. That is, acts of killing, destruction and looting result in the scars of trauma and the desire for revenge on the part of the victim, and a destruction of the spirit and terror of retaliation (and repeated attacks as a result) on the part of the aggressor. Such conflict, once it has erupted, produces an unending chain of mutual violence that it is extremely difficult to stop. Accordingly, it is safe to say that it is precisely the prevention and suppression of the very conflict (i.e., physical violence) that, once it has erupted, produces this unending chain of hatred and vengeance that is the most important remedy for resolving conflict and achieving coexistence. African society, as mentioned in the Introduction (Chapter 1), has seen the invention of cultural expedients for dealing with such extremely difficult problems. However, the spotlight in this chapter is on the *forces* that physically inhibit, prevent and suppress conflict. That is, in the kind of forces that can squarely confront and attempt to control the explosions of violence and fury that bring about conflict, this study is seeking the potential for conflict resolution that is produced by African society itself.

Such physical force, since the establishment of the modern nation-state system, has in principle been monopolised by the state. This is why all states maintain a police force and military; the presence of these overwhelming apparatuses of violence has deterred personal violence between citizens (whether individual or collective). There are systems in place to ensure that individuals and groups who resort to violence in spite of such measures are subject to prosecution in the courts on the basis of laws before being incarcerated in prisons if found guilty. Under such systems, the resolution of private grudges through private sanctions based in private justice becomes criminal and unlawful behaviour.

The same is true in the context of the international community. Conflicts that cut across national boundaries and hostilities between states are resolved by the violence apparatuses of regional coalitions of states, such as the African Union, or of international organisations that count states as individual members, such as the UN (i.e., Peace-Keeping Operations or Peace-Keeping Forces). Judgments relating to such conflicts are then carried out from the perspective of 'universal justice' by the International Court of Justice and the International Criminal Court.

In contrast, in Africa, there is a growing number of cases in which local communities have been forced to assume (or else actively encouraged to take on) the power to deter conflict inside the boundaries of nation-states. Certainly, the approval and commendation of such community initiatives has become a kind of accepted wisdom, as for example in the field of development in the 21st century. The current development industry has seen a trend towards the use of such terminology as 'citizen participation' 'participatory democracy' and 'ownership'. However, when the reality of what emerges as a force for deterring physical conflict is, for example, the creation of organisations emphasising their traditional ethnic culture and equipping themselves with traditional costume and weapons along with indigenous rituals and folk songs, who then band together as vigilante groups modelled on their own social organisations, many might be hesitant to regard these as being truly community-led.

Our questions, then, concern the manner of forces and systems that have emerged to prevent and deter conflict in Kenyan society in the wake of the PEV, how these have changed and how we might most appropriately evaluate them. I shall examine these points in the following sections.

10.2. The Violence Rampant in Kenyan Society

On 28 December 2007, Kenyans cast their votes in the national presidential election, held once every five years. In what was in effect a face-off between an incumbent president seeking re-election and the leader of the largest opposition party, the advance polls appeared to favour the leader of the opposition. In fact, as the ballots were being counted, the opposition candidate appeared indeed, at first, to be in the lead. Interim reports, however, began to describe the race as being very close, and when, after a long silence, the Electoral Commission of Kenya (ECK) declared victory for the incumbent, his inauguration ceremony was hastily arranged and carried out. From 30 December, all over Nairobi, fierce confrontations erupted between supporters of the incumbent president (particularly members of the Kikuyu to which he belonged) and supporters of the opposition leader (especially the Luo to which he belonged), with widespread attacks, arson, looting and rape that quickly spread across the entire country, plunging Kenya into a state of temporary anarchy. In Nairobi, the two parties clashed violently in slum districts such as Kibera, Mathare, Dandora, Kariobangi and Kawangware, resulting in significant casualties. In one example, a Kikuyu woman living in Mathare testified how she was forced to move from her house in Mathare 4A by a gang of Luo men who were evicting Kikuyu on the night of 30 December 2007 while another woman reported that on 29 December 2007, gangs of Luo youth went around the Mathare 4A area yelling that Kikuyu must leave. Fearing for her own and her family's safety they fled the next morning leaving all possessions behind (Waki 2008, p. 197). In the first case, the woman in question took refuge with her family at the Chief's Camp in Mathare, eventually fleeing to spend the night at the Chief's Camp in Huruma just to be safe. The next morning, when she returned home to fetch some necessities, she found that not only had all of her possessions been stolen, but another Luo family had already taken up residence in her house. Elsewhere, a young Luo man, also from Mathare 4A, reported that two of his family members in their rooms in his former home in Dandora were set upon and killed by members of the Mungiki, a nativist sect among the Kikuyu. On the night in question, the Mungiki were searching houses door to door, and upon finding either Luo or members of the or Kalenjin who constituted a support base for the opposition leader, cut them down with machetes one after another. The young man reported that when he first sought refuge in Huruma, he found the neighbourhood neatly divided into the Kikuyu-dominated settlement of Othaya and the Luo-dominated settlement of Bondo (both settlements named for the home villages of the government and opposition leaders, respectively), and that traffic between the two settlements had been disrupted. Out of fear, he then sought refuge by squatting in an abandoned house (in a room that had previously housed a Kikuyu family who had been chased off).

Such exchanges of naked violence lasted until the end of February 2008. In the face of such violence, the state's police forces were utterly helpless. Initially, while the police prohibited the 'One Million Protest', which the leader of the opposition had urged his supporters to stage in central Nairobi, and clamped down on those supporters who defied such prohibition, they could do nothing to address the everyday violence that was happening in the slums. Basically, the inhabitants of the slums were seen by the police more often than not as mere non-entities, their existence only recognised when they became 'perpetrators' in acts of violence against other residents. A woman selling vegetables on the streets of the Kibera slum was beaten when she resisted a police officer who kicked over her goods and implements, the officer stomping on her face as she fell to the ground. When a Christian priest who ran to her aid attempted to cover the woman, the police officer fired on the priest, causing grievous injury. Many such reports of police harassment are included among the testimonies of those who lived through the PEV.[3]

Such violence began to run rampant in Kenyan society in the wake of the PEV. And the police force, the modern state's exclusive agency for the enforcement of law and justice, remained powerless against it. The first to take the lead in violence in Kenya's post-PEV society were nativist ethnic sects whose influence expanded on the basis of the tendency, heavily exacerbated by the PEV, for respective ethnic groups in Nairobi's slums to form discrete residential enclaves. A typical example of such is Mungiki,[4] whose core membership consists primarily of unemployed Kikuyu youth. The Mungiki sect, a cultural and political organisation that emerged in the 1980s emphasising a return to traditional Kikuyu values, underwent a sudden transformation into violent radicalism from the 1990s to the 2000s.[5] The sect has gained notoriety for its raids on police stations in Nairobi and Kenya's former Central Province, its lynchings targeting individuals and groups it considers to be enemies, and extortionist behaviour that has included levying tolls and other taxes. Despite having been outlawed by the Kenyan Government in 2002, Mungiki staged a raid on a police station in Mathare just before the PEV, leaving over thirty dead after the confrontation became a firefight. In April of 2009, the sect massacred twenty-nine villagers who refused to conform to its tenets. Even now, however, some portions of Nairobi's slums remain under the group's control.

10.3. The Introduction of Western-Style Community Policing

The Kenyan state made a new attempt to guarantee the safety of the lives and wellbeing of its citizens in 2002, when an opposition coalition succeeded for the first time in wresting control of the government away from the KANU (Kenya African National Union), which had maintained its grip on the government since independence. The new administration quickly hammered out 'police reforms' that would serve as an important policy platform. The police, along with the army and court system, were widely regarded as one of the most seriously corrupt and venal organisations in Kenyan society (a reputation that has not changed). Thus, the new administration resolved to situate the introduction of 'community policing' as a key pillar of its police reforms and the restoration of public order. It established basic policies such as safeguarding public order through cooperation between the police and the local community, participation of the youth and women in this process, and promotion of peacebuilding and transparent governance. Then it subcontracted the planning to Saferworld, a global NGO with a track record of disseminating and applying its community policing model.[6] Founded in London in 1989, Saferworld has gained a wealth of experience through activities in more than twenty countries throughout Africa, Asia and the Middle East. A major organisation, it attracted enormous funding in excess of 11 million British Pound in 2014 alone. Approximately 25 per cent of this sum came from the European Commission, followed by substantial aid from the governments of the Netherlands, the UK, the USA, Finland, Sweden and Denmark. The organisation can thus be seen as a semi-public NGO, a kind of proxy agency for the EU.

Working together with the Kenyan NGO, Peace Net, Saferworld attempted to bring community policing to Kenya. In contrast to the pre-existing culture of the Kenyan police, the organisation held frequent training seminars and workshops to educate and advise police officers, government officials and community leaders under slogans such as, for example, relying on consent rather than coercion, becoming a member of the community and identifying community needs, cooperating with other organisations or individuals, and providing a high-quality service. The 'Community Policing Unit' was established in the Kenyan police force, and by 2006, 46 senior administration police officials, 40 county governors, 120 high-level local public servants and 60 police chiefs had been trained in the significance and operational methods of this new model of policing. And from among these students, for each of (what were at the time) Kenya's eight provinces, Community Policing Committees were set up consisting of representatives from the Kenya Police, the Administration Police and the civil sector. Thus a system for implementing community policing was put in place.

Saferworld, along with Peace Net and the Kenya Police, from 2003, launched trial community policing projects in communities across the country. As target areas for its own projects, Saferworld launched initiatives in Kibera, East Africa's largest slum and a hotbed of crime, violence and conflict (with a population at the time of approximately 800,000) and Kajiado, one of the central towns in Maasailand, about 80 km south-east of Nairobi. As a result, according to its own self-assessment, in Kibera's Makina village (settlement), the state police, Administration Police, business community (i.e., Nubian owners of commuter buses) and local residents (the majority of Makina's residents are the descendants of Nubian war veterans whose families have lived in the area since Kibera's establishment as a mercenary garrison for the British army at the start of the twentieth century) acted jointly towards the realisation of common goals.

Aside from Saferworld, there were other NGOs that had already implemented similar projects. While community policing originally emerged to safeguard community youth from local crime in the USA and the UK in the 1980s, in the African context, South Africa has famously been aggressively applying this model since the mid-1990s. Under the apartheid regime, the state police had been little more than a violent apparatus for oppressing the African people, and one of Nelson Mandela's first initiatives after his inauguration as president was to embark on fundamental police reforms. During this period, he had made use of community policing to carry out police activities in cooperation with citizens. Kenya's efforts to adopt the South African community policing model date back to 1999, long before Saferworld began to collaborate with the Kenyan government. At this time, two experimental community policing projects were put into practice with support from the New York-based Vera Institute of Justice.[7] The first of these was a project targeting the business community (shop owners) in Nairobi's Central Business District (CBD), where the breakdown of public order was growing worse, while the other was a plan for the Kangemi slum organised by the Kenya Human Rights Commission (KHRC).

The model of community policing that the Kenyan government aggressively attempted to introduce at the start of the 21st century ultimately had to be abandoned after it failed to take root in Kenyan society. Under the ostensible name of community policing, people who had been relegated to the fringes of society started being openly oppressed and excluded as elements considered 'disruptive' to public order. In the slums, originally the spaces where such 'disruptive' elements congregated and lived together, crackdowns were intensified, leading to increased tensions and antagonism against residents. This was one of the reasons for the initiative's failure. However, the overriding reason that the initiative failed to succeed was the deeply rooted lack of trust between the police and the community. Regarding the failure of the project in the Kangemi slum, the human rights group that had attempted the introduction found that the spirit of cooperation and collaboration with the police that represents the very essence of community policing was entirely absent from the lived experience of the residents of the slums, and that the police always adopted an uncooperative attitude towards initiatives by the local residents. Thus the community policing plan that the Kenyan government had envisioned as a national policy for preventing conflict and securing the safety of its citizens, and for which it had used a considerable amount of aid money, had essentially all but disappeared by 2010.

10.4. Imposition of the *Nyumba Kumi* Initiative

In the context of Kenya's post-PEV society, this situation of the state's inability to adequately guarantee the physical safety of its citizens continued unabated. The first presidential election under the new Constitution was held in 2012. Uhuru Kenyatta, the son of Kenya's first president Jomo Kenyatta was appointed as Kenya's fourth President, defeating the leader of the opposition party who had played a central role in the previous presidential election that had triggered the PEV (that is, the same man who had become prime minister in the subsequent Grand Coalition Government). Like his predecessor, in order to respond to the citizenry's needs, Uhuru undertook large-scale police reforms based on the new Constitution. Once again, at the core of this policy there was to be a community-led approach to the prevention of violence and restoration of peace and order. Having learned a lesson from the failure of the previous attempt to introduce a Western model of community policing on the basis of assistance from Western NGOs, Uhuru declared that this time he would adopt a community-led system of maintaining order that had been developed and implemented in Kenya's neighbouring country of Tanzania in the 1960s, adapting it for the needs of the contemporary era. This system was known as '*nyumba kumi*'.

The *nyumba kumi* system involves mutual surveillance by neighbours and reporting of outsiders. In the Swahili language widely spoken throughout East Africa, *nyumba* means 'household' and *kumi* means 'ten'. In a literal sense, clusters of ten households in local communities are reorganised into individual blocks, with a chairperson (i.e., representative) appointed in each block. Should suspicious persons or unknown guests stop at or spend the night at a house in the block, the system offered a mechanism for the chairperson to receive a report of the facts of the matter from other members, providing information to be passed from the village officer to the assistant chief, who then communicates with the chief or conveys this directly to the state police or Administration Police official stationed nearby.

When Tanzania first gained independence, it pursued a vision of state building grounded in the ideology of 'African socialism' under the direction of the country's first president, Julius Nyerere. With the proclamation of his famous 'Arusha Declaration' of 1967, Nyerere embarked on the implementation of the *ujamaa* (fraternity) policy whereby collective labour would be used to build farming villages in which small-scale communist societies could be realised, modelled on China's people's communes. Under this policy, the police and security sector would be in charge of the *nyumba kumi* system, which was to be responsible for the maintenance of order, working together with state police under the leadership of the community. In the Tanzanian context of the 1980s, however, Nyerere's successor officially abandoned the 'path of *ujamaa* socialism', and after the acceptance of economic policies that involved taking aid from the World Bank and IMF, the *nyumba kumi* system was similarly dismantled and consigned to a similar fate.

Nevertheless, Kenya's President Uhuru chose to set *nyumba kumi*, the creation of his father's sworn enemy – Nyerere had vehemently criticised the pro-Western capitalist course the elder Kenyatta had steered for Kenya – as one of the centrepieces of his police reforms. In October 2013, in response to the mass shooting by Al Shabaab at Nairobi's Westgate Shopping Mall the previous month, Uhuru directed the Interior Cabinet Secretary, Joseph Ole Lenku, to make *nyumba kumi* a strategic pillar for policing activities. In response to this directive, the Minister set up a Community Policing Committee in the state police, appointing members including powerful politicians, the directors of large corporations, NGO activists and others to develop a system that could be rapidly introduced. In 2014, in accordance with this framework, *nyumba kumi* was set to be launched and it began its activities across most parts of Kenya.

However, from the very outset there were many who harboured reservations about the introduction of *nyumba kumi* into Kenya, voicing their doubts about its effectiveness. The first thing that was pointed out was the fact that it had already been abandoned in

Tanzania, where it had originally been proposed. The initial introduction of *nyumba kumi* in Tanzania had taken place in the context of an attempt to build a socialist society, when the overwhelming majority of employment opportunities (over 70 per cent of the total) had been in the economic structures provided by the state. Critics pointed out that while *nyumba kumi* had been suited to these particular circumstances, it was not well matched to Kenyan society, which had no socialist aspirations, but was rather based on the free activities of private industry. Moreover, it was also pointed out that it would be impossible for a system like *nyumba kumi* to function effectively in the highly fluid and socially isolating urban slums, and that it would in any case be doomed to failure due to an overwhelming disinclination to cooperate with the police because of the deep-seated mutual distrust between the people and the police. Complaints also erupted from the chairpersons who were actually to be involved in the operation of the initiative, as well as the village officials who were to receive their reports. For example, one chairperson among those listed in the Community Development Plan that organised the *nyumba kumi* chairpersons in Kenya's second-largest city of Mombasa publicly raised the concern that 'although village elders will take up the post of *nyumba kumi* chairpersons and report to village officials, these worthies have their own and their families' lives, and it will be difficult for them to be seriously committed to taking on these hard tasks without pay. The optimal solution would be for the government to provide a salary for the elders and officials involved in *nyumba kumi*, thereby voicing the opinion that it was unlikely the cash-strapped government would be able to deliver.

Moreover, even human rights organisations and the general public raised doubts about the *nyumba kumi* initiative. The relationship between the *nyumba kumi* system and the police system was unclear in terms of lines of authority and powers of enforcement, and some pointed out that it would be difficult to mitigate the risks of *nyumba kumi* being used as a surveillance system for the government's convenience, or of the state's exploitation and abuse of the personal information and other data collected thereby.[8]

Thus while the Tanzanian model of community policing known

as *nyumba kumi* has now been launched in twenty-first century Kenyan society through the strength of a presidential initiative, in practice, there remain many challenges in terms of its effectiveness and operational format.

10.5. Two Currents in Community Policing: (1) External Hegemony

As we have seen so far, the orientation towards leveraging community initiatives rather than relying solely on police power to prevent conflict and to safeguard life, limb and property, although seemingly an effective solution in the context of contemporary African society, has nevertheless been accompanied by myriad difficulties in terms of its realisation in practice. Within this orientation, broadly speaking, we can ascertain two divergent currents. One such is the attempt, based on state hegemony, to realise community policing as an initiative inside the institutional state frameworks of police and administration, while the other is the current by which the hegemony of the community concretely manifests this idea even while transforming it to suit local contingencies. I would like to begin by considering the first of these currents.

Kenya's attempts at community-based policing thus far, as we have seen, may all be regarded as having involved the Kenyan government's adoption of extrinsic models that it has attempted to introduce across the country by incorporating them into the policing system of the Kenyan state. The first of these experiments was a Western model of community policing devised by a global NGO based in London and New York that had been put into practice elsewhere around the world. Despite being somewhat modified to suit the circumstances of the regions where it was introduced, basically, these implementations shared a common framework that was in line with a modern Western outlook on humanitarian and social values, including the protection of universal human rights, the equal and fair participation of all members of the community, female empowerment, transparent and democratic organisations, and the achievement of consensus through rational deliberation.

Conditional only on the acceptance of the basic principles of this modern Western model, substantial funding and the support of talented personnel would be provided. When the funding and educational systems provided by the global NGO proved effective for the Kenyan government that received them, the attempt was made to put this mechanism in place for utilisation inside the state's existing institutional frameworks of the police and administration.

However, this experiment failed to take root in Kenyan society, and was finally completely extinguished by the PEV. Despite the investment of huge amounts of funding and energy, the community policing initiative had already been on the wane prior to the 2007–2008 PEV. However, when the Kibera slum, which had been regarded to be a model example of the concept's successful application, became one of the worst affected regions in the context of the PEV, overrun by violence and chaos, it was clear that the initiative had failed.

The government, having perceived the incongruities between the principles and ideals of this first community policing model and the realities of Kenyan society, then attempted to introduce the *nyumba kumi* system as a new attempt at community policing for Kenya's post-PEV society. Here, again, inspiration was taken from a Tanzanian model, which was then grafted onto the institutional frameworks of Kenya's police and administration. And, once again, many claimed to predict that the new initiative would fail, pointing to discrepancies between the circumstances under which *nyumba kumi* had been practised in the Tanzania of the 1960s and the realities of contemporary Kenya.

In this context, there were also signs of an incipient movement in which agents in the state's police and administrative institutions, while leveraging their authority within these frameworks, began attempting to realise a community-led policing model tailored to the circumstances of individual communities and societies. We could describe this as the reconfiguration of community policing through the hegemony of state institutions. This is illustrated by the example of the 'Ten Ten' system that emerged in the Nairobi constituency of Makadara during the PEV.[9] The appearance of headlines on the Ten Ten initiative in the media occurred directly after President Uhuru's declaration that he would be introducing the Tanzanian '*nyumba kumi*' model of community policing. One community leader claimed that the core of the idea was nothing other than the Ten Ten system that he and his neighbours had created in Makadara, demanding that the government pay a fee for the originality and use of the idea. The idea for the Ten Ten system had emerged during the turbulent time of the PEV, when community leaders in Makadara, experiencing trouble with the distribution and allocation of food and relief supplies, had started working together with the local administrative chief. With his support and approval, they had organised residents into clusters of ten households, with each cluster nominating a representative, to create a mechanism for ensuring the fair distribution of supplies while distinguishing between local residents and temporary migrants from outside the community. Over 550 such clusters were organised throughout the district, weathering the disturbances of the PEV. Afterwards, the Ten Ten system became a semi-public governance agency under the control of the administrative chief, and began to serve the people in a supervisory and awareness-raising capacity.

The activities of the Ten Ten system were continued even after the PEV crisis. The range of its activities was expanded to include not only policing, but also finding solutions for a variety of other local problems. These efforts extended into many areas, including, for example, the conversion and rehabilitation of illegal bootleg distributors into purveyors of goods such as second-hand clothing, measures to combat delinquency and drug addiction among youths, and environmental clean-ups to protect the Nairobi River, which flows through the neighbourhood, from illegal waste disposal. As a result of these administrative activities, the administrative officials with jurisdiction over Makadara, respectively, received commendations as Best performing Locational Chief, Best Divisional Officer, and Best District Commissioner from the Office of the President. In this way, Makadara's Ten Ten initiative was organised and put into operation through the hegemony and needs of the agents (e.g., administrative chiefs) of the state institutions that governed the region. In this regard, a member of the state police's Community Policing Committee remarked wryly that the acronym CBP might rather stand for 'chief'-based policing instead of 'community'-based policing.

10.6. Two Currents in Community Policing: (2) Community Hegemony

Up to now, we have seen examples in which various activities, including community policing, while appearing to be community led, have in fact been carried out within the confines of hegemonic states (or else by making use of their institutions). However, in the context of Kenyan society during the PEV period and afterwards, we also find many examples of community policing and community activities that have been implemented in a different dimension than that of state hegemonies.

The PEV period saw an outpouring of disorder and violence, to the extent that the police officers who would normally have been tasked with containing the chaos were not only completely impotent in the face of it but, in fact, regularly became the perpetrators of harassment in their own right. Under these circumstances, organised gangs of unemployed and semi-employed youth emerged as ethnically homogeneous 'task forces' throughout Nairobi's slum districts. In addition to the aforementioned Mungiki sect, who advocated a return to the roots of Kikuyu tradition, and the groups of Luo youths who came together to oppose them, such as groups of 'Taliban,' other such armed groups shot up like weeds, assuming responsibility for maintaining their communities' safety and seeking vengeance for any injuries suffered by their members. Kibera, East Africa's largest slum, consists of thirteen distinct villages (settlements), each of which saw the formation of a different armed group for maintaining order.[10] In exchange for residents' payments of cash, these groups provided protection and security. For example, a small shop kiosk might pay 20 shillings a week, while after sundown a resident might pay a bodyguard a fee of between 50 and 100 shillings to provide protection from alighting at a bus stop until reaching home (at the time of the PEV, one US dollar was equivalent to about 65–70 Kenya shillings, and a construction labourer in Nairobi might have expected to earn a daily wage of 250 to 300 shillings). While such activities were one part of the 'community policing' being carried out by all of these groups, in each group there were some activities that were unique. For example, one gang in Kibera, Siafu, had a reputation for being adept at resolving 'hassles' among fellow residents, and was also known for its mass mobilisations of supporters for political rallies in support of the governmental opposition. They had also gone so far as to start supplying water and electricity to residents (though of course the water and electricity had been illegally pirated). Also in Kibera, the Kikuyu organisation known as the Kamukunji Pressure Group, collected taxes for every sheet of galvanised iron, which were used on houses as roofing material and television antennae, while the Nubian organisation known as Kibera Kanjo collected tolls of 150 shillings per round trip from commuter buses heading into the city centre.

Such violent organisations have also survived into the present time and continued similar activities in the increasingly ethnicized society of post-PEV Kenya. Even if we take just Kibera as an example, where each of the thirteen villages has displayed an increasing tendency to create an ethnically homogenous residential area (the Luo accounting for six settlements including Gatwekera, the Kikuyu, Luyia, Kamba and Kisii one settlement each, and the earlier settler Nubians four including Makina), counting only the principal actors, no less than six violent gangs continue to practise their own style of community policing today.

Community policing by these violent organisations is naturally fraught with many problems. In some cases, residents are subject to harassment from these groups, just as they once had been from the police, and especially for residents who belong to a different ethnicity from the gangs, these individuals are forced to live in a state of structural tension (not knowing when they might find themselves targeted). As well, residents who criticise or question their existence are met with unilateral, summary punishments based only in their own ideas of 'justice'. Certainly they are also community residents, and do turn their abilities toward protecting the safety of their own communities, but these endeavours have a strong tendency to be exclusive and dogmatic in the extreme.

In contrast, another phenomenon that has been widely discussed as a successful example of community policing that has worked towards easing such dogmatism and authoritarianism is that of *sungusungu* of Western Kenya.[11] While the name '*sungusungu*' refers to the Swahili term for 'army ants', the group was originally formed in the aftermath of the 1979 war in which Tanzanian forces invaded Uganda to depose the dictator Idi Amin. After the war, the influx of a significant volume of armaments and some of the retired soldiers into western Tanzania led to a rapid deterioration in public order when the veterans turned to banditry, forcing the people of the Nyamwezi and Sukuma to establish a community police force for self-defence and to arm themselves against the bandits. At the time, the Tanzanian government's state police were poorly armed and poorly equipped, and in the era of *ujamaa* socialism, local self-defence associations (i.e., vigilantes) could justify their actions as an expression of 'community power'. This was *sungusungu*, and after witnessing this example, the Kuria people in Tanzania's north-west also created a similar organisation. In the 1990s, a Kuria trader living in Kenya (about a third of the Kuria overall population lives in Kenya) learned of the group on a visit across the border. At the time, farmers in the Kuria lands on the Kenyan side of the border were experiencing bountiful cash crops of tobacco. However, the trucks transporting the crops from the farms and carrying fertilisers and farm supplies to the farms were being ambushed on the roads by armed gangs of robbers and tobacco traders had stopped coming into the Kuria territory. The Kurian farmers, despairing of this deterioration in public order, organised similar *sungusungu* groups, imitating the self-defence associations of Tanzania. In 1998, after receiving the endorsement of the district governor and police chief, they began to deal with the bandit gangs on their own terms, applying their own standards of justice. In this way, security could be maintained not only for the tobacco farmers, but also for the community's schools and churches

By incorporating traditional political organisations, *sungusungu* successfully acquired the recognition and approval of the community, as well as their cooperation and participation. A *sungusungu* committee consists of a single representative sent from each of the thirteen territorialised patrilineages, along with three representatives each from the various warrior age sets responsible for the core aspects of political and military life in Kuria society (Heald 2007). Committee members received a per diem allowance of 200 shillings. The committee formulated its own rules, which it sent to the governor for approval in order to prevent arrests by the police, and prosecution and punishment by the courts. Thus implemented, *sungusungu* dealt with 78 incidents over five months in 1998, the year in which it was launched, bringing 44 of these to successful resolution (by arresting the perpetrators of violence and imprisoning them within a stockade they had constructed themselves). Michael Fleisher, who carried out fieldwork with *sungusungu* in Kenya and Tanzania, praises the system as one of the 'most successful' examples of community policing (Fleisher 2000).

However, numerous people have levelled many criticisms at Kuria's *sungusungu* due to the application of arbitrary justice, which differs from the concept of justice enshrined in the Constitution and the laws of the Kenyan state, or for their exercise of summary punishment. In particular, the National Crime Research Centre, which studies violent criminal organisations in Kenya, has called on the government to strictly monitor and clamp down on *sungusungu* organised in 2003 by the Kisii people to the north, who had borrowed the concept from the Kuria, as one of six organised criminal organisations in contemporary Kenyan society (among others that include Al Shabaab, the Mombasa Republican Council and the Mungiki sect). In this context, the Kisii *sungusungu* has been accused of committing significant human rights violations that include ignoring the law, convening people's tribunals and carrying out executions in accordance with members' own views of justice.

10.7. Spontaneous Community Policing

In the foregoing, we have described several different types of community policing. In the context of a society where the state police system is ineffective and repressive, it is highly unlikely that the means of protecting life and property could be anything other than institutions that rely on the communities in which the people themselves live as residents. Moreover, in order to pre-emptively defend against violence or attacks and avoid potential damage, the only feasible strategy is to make use of the wisdom and strength that is grounded in community. However, the modern civil society model of community policing brought by Western NGOs has resulted in 'imposed ideals' that are far removed from the needs and realities of local communities. The Tanzanian model of the *nyumba kumi* initiative and the Ten Ten system, contrary to what was initially envisaged of their being community led and answering community needs, now seem to be prioritising the convenience and interests of the government as an instrument of the governing body of the state. This is the inevitable result of measures that are put into practice under the auspices of the state's hegemony.

However, even forms of community policing that do not rely on the state's hegemony, for ordinary people living in a community, these are no closer to something that they would voluntarily take part in or cooperate with, and have occasionally become authoritarian and oppressive apparatuses of violence similar to the police. The militarised gangs that control the village settlements that comprise the slums of Nairobi are even now gradually freeing themselves of the autonomy and independence of their communities, transforming into something far removed from the tolerance and rationality that are based in the lived logic provided by the community. A community policing system that has lost this openness and flexibility, this plurality and diversity, will do nothing more than recreate the state police in miniature. This point is also true for traditional political, social and cultural organisations assuming the function of community policing, like *sungusungu*. When we formulate newly codified rules for organisational management and systematically lock in committee-style organisation, the openness and flexibility, the plurality and diversity that once operated in people's day-to-day experience and which constitute the lived logic of community become dogma, collapsing into their opposites, and metamorphosing into the closure, fixedness, homogeneity and austerity of the organisational principles of the modern nation state. In that case, community policing descends to the level of exclusion and self-justification.

So might it be possible to avoid this metamorphosis and practise a form of community policing based in the logic of people's lived experiences? I believe that the seeds and perhaps the first sprouts of such a spontaneous and life-oriented form of community policing can be found in the experience of Nairobi's western slums during the PEV period and afterwards. It could be said that this is a manifestation of an African potential that could offer guidance on how to prevent and mitigate conflict (and violence). In selecting this example for discussion in the final section, I wish to consider community policing as an African potential in its own right.

10.8. Community Policing and the Experience of Post-Election Violence in Kangemi

Since the supporters of both parties in the elections, who were living in the slums throughout Nairobi, could be distinguished along more or less ethnic lines, 30 December 2007 saw the beginning of fierce clashes between the Kikuyu, who were then celebrating the victory of the incumbent president, and youths from the Luo (along with their allies the Luyia and Kalenjin) hailing the election of the opposition candidate, as well as between opposition supporters and armed police. With an eye toward the ethnic cleansing of each of the slum villages, these 'battles' to attack, despoil, and expel 'enemy peoples' became more intense as the days passed. The neighbourhood of Kangemi in western Nairobi had always been a stage for riots and mayhem in times of political upheaval in Kenya. Yet, curiously, Kangemi maintained a tranquil peace throughout the commotion of PEV. Previously, Kangemi had always appeared as a veritable battlefield in the history of Kenya's riots, from the rampage set off by the assassination of an influential Luo politician in the 1960s through anti-government demonstrations demanding democratisation in the 1990s. The slum was a notorious presence, its residents labelled 'drunks, addicts and layabout anti-social elements' by the then policy makers. While not a vast slum like Kibera, with over a million inhabitants, Kangemi was set into a narrow hilly area, a densely crowded settlement of more than 250,000 people, many of whom were indigent migrant labourers (cf. Matsuda 1996).

Kangemi was an area where the eruption of large-scale riots – of the same order as those in Kibera, Mathare or Kawangware, where the largest clashes occurred during the PEV – would not have been seen to be out of place. This was because the basic composition of the ethnic conflict during the PEV, which is to say between the Kikuyu, on one hand, and the Luo and Luyia, on the other, was precisely that of Kangemi's residential makeup. Up until the 1960s, Kangemi had been little more than a rural Kikuyu village whose inhabitants had cultivated sorghum and beans. However, after independence, the movement restrictions on Africans moving to Nairobi were lifted, resulting in the influx of a large pool of migrant labour into Nairobi, which experienced a population explosion of more than 7 per cent a year. Kangemi's Kikuyu peasants tore up their sorghum fields to set about building simple tenement housing to accommodate this influx of poor migrant labourers. Thus, by the mid-1970s, Kangemi had been transformed from a Kikuyu farming village into a suburban slum housing large numbers of migrant labourers. At this time, the overwhelming numbers of migrant labourers who had taken up residence in Kangemi were natives of Western Kenya. This was because Kangemi was located on the western fringes of Nairobi along the main road connecting Nairobi with hub cities in Western Kenya.

Since Western Kenya was the homeland of the Luo and Luyia, two of Kenya's largest ethnic groups, from the 1960s, Kangemi developed and expanded as an enclave for these groups. Therefore, Kangemi's basic social structure was centred on the relationship between the earlier settler Kikuyu landlords and property owners and the Luo and Luyia tenants who had arrived seeking employment. Their relationship was one that was fraught with underlying tension, since tenants who could not find work in Nairobi would not be able to cover their rent. In such cases, Kikuyu landlords would forcibly move tenants' belongings out of their rooms by employing guardsmen from other groups like the Maasai, then shut out the tenants by locking the door. Returning home in the early evening after a day of looking for employment to find one's entire kit of household goods piled in front of the door was a daily spectacle in Kangemi. There were also obvious economic disparities between the two groups. A Kikuyu landlord might divide a single row house into 10 to 16 back-to-back rooms of about seven square metres, for which the going rent at the time of the PEV would have been from 1,500 to 2,000 shillings per room. This alone would provide a landlord with a cash income of from 15,000 to 24,000 shillings. And since a landlord would usually build three to five tenements in a compound, we can presume that a landlord with five tenements might receive a monthly income amounting to the significant sum of 75,000 shillings or more. Since the daily wage at the time for unskilled labourers working at construction on building sites or roads ranged from 250 to 300 shillings, a monthly income that assumed 25 days of employment was still only a little over 6,000 shillings. Such a vast gap between the rich and the poor led to latent tensions developing in their relationship (as of 2 January 2008, 1 US dollar was equivalent to about 63 Kenya Shillings).

However, despite these potentially explosive tensions, there were no eruptions of violence over the course of the PEV. On the contrary, the two groups worked together to organise self-defence associations and began patrolling Kangemi. This spontaneous expression of community policing deserves to be considered in more detail.[12]

It started in the Kawangware slum adjacent to Kangemi, also a battleground during riots in the past. On 30 December 2007, arson and looting broke out when a battle began between Kikuyu youth and a gang of Luo and Luyia youth. While on previous occasions, this would have almost immediately touched off a war in Kangemi as well, this time it was different. Even in Kangemi, the Kikuyu landlords in the Gichagi neighbourhood on the boundary with Kawangware invited the most respected and venerable Luo and Luyia elders among their migrant tenants to their homes for consultation. The main purpose of this impromptu council was join forces to find a way to protect everyone's families and property as a small-scale war had already started in Kibera and Kawangware, and gangs of those who were semi-employed ('Nairobian'), both Kikuyu and Luo, were trying to bring the same mayhem to Kangemi. With regards to the 'Nairobian' element, as they described them, from whom these groups distinguished themselves, whereas the Kikuyu and Luo involved in this discussion were migrant workers or job-seekers that, while living in Kangemi, maintained farms and lived off the land in their home villages in Western Kenya, the Nairobians were those who had severed their connections to the land to live as a vagrant class in the cities. While there were some among the elders who remarked caustically that 'You folk have property, while we have none,' even the poorest migrant workers possessed something of importance in the form of household goods, be it a bed or mattress, table and chairs, sofa, radio, clothing, boots or something else, and more than anything their wives and young children were their most important treasures, and the overwhelming majority of voices agreed that these things should be protected at all costs, thereby evincing a shared 'community' consciousness.

The landlords and tenant elders contacted the youth leaders among their respective communities and worked out a method for joint patrol. Here, all of the participants had a particular referent in mind – namely, their experience of the failure of the community policing initiative that the New York NGO and the Kenya Human Rights Commission had sought to experimentally introduce in Kangemi in 2000. While the idea of members at every level of the community working together to maintain security and safeguard the lives and property of local residents had been natural enough for them *in theory*, it was their experience now that proved the utility of the idea *in practice*. Their experience also served them well in terms of specific patrolling strategies and organisational operation. What they came up with in this way was as follows. From each room in the tenements, an adult male was conscripted as a member of the patrol unit – households consisting of only women or the elderly were exempted from such service. Each patrol group was organised with 10 to 20 members. At first, the duration of the patrols was set from three in the afternoon until dawn, and was later modified to start at five after the situation had become calmer. In terms of weapons, the volunteers were to prepare their own (the most common weapons were clubs, but there were some on the late night patrols who also carried machetes). When a large group of outsiders made as though to enter Kangemi, off-duty patrol members were to be contacted immediately by mobile phone (this enabled patrols to rapidly summon more than forty men to come running if necessary). The core of the patrols was to consist of men in their twenties and thirties, while members aged forty and over were assigned to patrols only until midnight, when they were allowed to return home to remain on call. The patrols were each limited to the vicinity of their own homes, and prohibited from making 'excursions' outside these boundaries. In the event that they encountered a patrol from another region, a watchword was set (originally 'avocado').

In the event the violent Kikuyu or Luo gangs of the Mungiki or Taliban arrived in Kangemi with the intent of spreading mayhem, it is easy to imagine that there would have been victims among the patrol members. However, despite this underlying threat of mortal danger, most young men in Gichagi participated willingly in these neighbourhood patrols, and even though they did not receive any compensation in terms of meals or allowance, they continued to provide their time as a free service. Thus, in Kangemi, young members of the Kikuyu and Luo communities, whose members were killing each other elsewhere, came together to formulate activities that would allow them to protect their residential community and life-world. These patrols were ultimately continued until March 2008, when the government and opposition formed the Grand Coalition Government to restore order throughout Kenya.

10.9. Conclusion: Community Policing as African Potentials - The Wisdom of *Bricolage*

The community policing that was spontaneously devised in the Kangemi district has several characteristics that are clearly distinct from the various other types of community policing we have already described. First, there is the fact that they were organised as a form of community self-help group, utterly unrelated to the state's police or administrative institutions. In this regard, this was something fundamentally different in character from an idea premised on cooperation between the community and state police forces. This is also related to the fact that Kenya's clientelist politics had previously always seen the interests and goals of the entire society – matters on a different order entirely than residents' own life worlds, such as the security and peace of the entire country or else Nairobi's urban development and expansion – often somehow end up turning into the interests and objectives of a few politicians, to which end people were used and discarded as pawns. A style of community policing whereby community members drew on their own lived experience to enact their own ideas within the range of their own territory was in stark contrast to the more abstract world of rhetoric that aspired to encompass all of society, and was something more in keeping with the day-to-day experience of ordinary Kangemi residents.

The second characteristic is the lack of any clear rules or institutional organisations for exerting control over these activities. Although required for ensuring democratic and transparent organisational management, there are many precedents that show how, once brought into being, these elements often have the converse effect of limiting the freedom to think and operate, and lead to the formalism of orders and discipline (against violations), management and control. For example, in the event a young man scheduled to participate in a patrol according to the roster heard worrisome news concerning the safety of relatives in Kibera and withdrew his participation at short notice, rather than imposing some kind of penalty for breaking a promise or violating the rules, it was determined through discussions that he should be tasked with reconnoitring the situation in Kibera and putting out a request through acquaintances to gangs that shared his ethnicity (asking them not to come to Kangemi, as he and his fellows were free from persecution). Being able to respond flexibly to contingent situations was also effective in the sense that it encouraged the willing participation of community members.

Third, there is the fact that the association came into being not as a permanent institution or organisation, but in a temporary and limited fashion, according to the needs of the lives of the people living in the community. This is best seen by examining the social situation in Kangemi in post-PEV Nairobi. The community's spontaneous community policing activities had for the most part disappeared naturally by March 2008. There had been no grand wind-up party or ceremony with speeches by local worthies, rather the groups had automatically disbanded at the moment they were no longer necessary. Afterwards, such self-defence associations did not reappear. After the PEV, a station office for Kenya's Administration Police was set up for participants in Kangemi, too, and while keeping the usual peace, their relations of trust with the community remain as weak as ever. Also, despite having been launched with great fanfare by President Uhuru in 2013, the Tanzanian model of community policing represented by *nyumba kumi*, as of August 2015, has yet to even start being organised in Kangemi. An elder among the Luyia migrants who has lived in Kangemi since the 1980s points out that there are technical difficulties with introducing such a system to a highly fluid urban slum society in which migrants from Western Kenya as well as all over the country repeatedly move in and out of the community within a short space of time. Moreover, he says, 'there are few residents who feel any need to work up a sweat over *nyumba kumi*'.

In this context, in July 2015, an incident took place that for the first time in a long time resulted in the appearance of a community self-defence association. At this time, there were numerous cases of gangs of 'mothers' protesting against husbands who spent all day drinking liquor and neglecting their family and work responsibilities. These women took it on themselves to stage raids on taverns and destroyed the alcohol they discovered, both legal and illegal. After the President also voiced his approval of these actions, a similar raid was carried out in Kangemi. Originally, in Kangemi, fermented beer and spirits made from sorghum had been one of the chief sources of enjoyment for the migrant workers from Western Kenya, and many of the publicans who served such brews in drinking establishments were also natives of Western Kenya. In contrast, taverns that served beer and whisky had been the exclusive sphere of Kikuyu (such that if a tavern were opened by a non-Kikuyu, in most cases, the establishment would be sacked by robbers and forced to close). However, after the PEV (due to the risk of intensely violent exchanges), Luo and Luyia had been allowed to start managing such taverns as well. The gangs of mothers set their sights on these establishments. However, these were legitimate taverns that had legally applied for licences and obtained the necessary permissions. A Luyia man in his thirties who had served as the core member of the patrols at the time of the PEV attempted to set up patrols once again to defend the property belonging to the members of the same community and protect their own places of leisure. However, this time, only a few Luo and Luyia men answered the call, while the men of other groups, including the Kikuyu, Kamba, Maasai and Kisii, did not even express interest. In the end, the patrol units were organised with only a few men, and this group was successful in protecting the taverns from raids by the women. In this way, we can confirm that ideas and practices that tolerate participation by some and not by others, according to their perceived 'basic needs' are what lie at the base of the spontaneous style of community policing in Kangemi.

Depending on these perceived 'basic needs,' the residents of Kangemi employed the technique of *bricolage* to come up with their own mechanisms, picking and choosing as they saw fit from the techniques and principles of the New York model of community policing, from the institutions and ideas of the *nyumba kumi* initiative promoted by the government, as well as from the patrol methods of the state police and Administrative Police, and furthermore from the discipline and behavioural patterns of violent criminal gangs like Mungiki and the Taliban. Through such ingenuity, their own version of the ideas and practices inherent in the model of community policing guaranteed the autonomy and independence of their community, and enabled them to further develop the qualities of openness, flexibility, plurality and diversity.[12] The technique of *bricolage*, which is the essence of the interface function that bridges a wide variety of principles and ideas that belong to distinct dimensions, is arguably one of the most important qualities of African potentials. The community policing model created by the residents of Kangemi, in contrast to the characteristics of modern Western approaches that seek to compete with and eliminate difference – namely, closure, fixedness, homogeneity and austerity – is expressive of the potential that African society has created for the realisation of coexistence and resolution of conflict.

Notes

[1] For detailed accounts of the course of the post-election violence

(PEV) that scarred Kenyan society at the end of 2007 and beginning of 2008, the African Union mediation process led by Kofi Annan and the substance and implementation of the agreement, see Tsuda (2009) and Matsuda (2011). Influential politicians from the two opposing parties who were accused of 'crimes against humanity' during the PEV later reached a political accord, and although elected as president and vice-president in the 2013 elections, both were charged by the International Criminal Court (ICC). While the charges against President Uhuru Kenyatta were withdrawn due to lack of evidence, as of November 2015, proceedings against Vice President William Ruto remained ongoing at the ICC in The Hague in the Netherlands.

  [2] Oliver (2000) discusses the origins and development of the mechanisms of community policing, as well as their historical and political significance and ideological positioning. Also, Skolnick (1991) is particularly insightful with regard to the origins of their institutional practice. Community policing emerged in the context of the 'broken windows theory' to cope with security problems in the USA of the 1980s, and was later institutionalised under the Clinton administration in the mid-1990s. Since 2000, however, as well as finding itself in the limelight as a strategy for safety and security in emerging societies, it has also been criticised as a new type of government apparatus of surveillance and oppression (Cunneen 1991).

  [3] The Grand Coalition formed in the wake of the 2007–08 PEV (the two presidential candidates at the heart of the conflict were appointed to share power as president and prime minister, respectively) enacted legislation to reveal the truth and establish responsibility for the PEV. On this basis it established a commission chaired by Justice Philip Waki, a Judge of Kenya's Court of Appeal. The Commission undertook to collect witness testimonies and analyse evidence, and then submitted a report to the President, sealing the section of the report identifying the names of six individuals deemed to be chiefly responsible for instigating the PEV. After the Kenyan government determined that the problem of these perpetrators would be tried at the International Criminal Court (ICC) in The Hague rather than in the domestic court system, the list was handed over to a prosecutor at the ICC. It was later revealed that the six names identified were those of influential politicians and bureaucrats, three each on either side of the conflict. As a result of the ICC's investigation, three names went

forward to prosecution, while charges against the other three were dismissed. However, since these names also included those of the politicians elected president and vice-president in the 2013 elections (the case against the president was later dismissed, citing lack of evidence), calls have now been raised by Kenya's ruling party to condemn the Waki Report, demanding that the investigation be reopened.

[4] Mungiki is a strongly nativist sect that emerged in the late 1980s calling for restoration of the traditional values of the Kikuyu tribe, Kenya's largest ethnic group. The sect has found its main support among the underclass of unemployed Kikuyu youth who dropped out of elementary and middle school in Kenya's cities and farming districts. Its members emphasise the traditional body of aesthetic and folk culture of Kikuyu society, and have gone to violent extremes to bring about a return to tradition. Mungiki's recourse to violence escalated suddenly at the turn of the 21st century. In 2002, the group was outlawed by the government after its slaughter of a large number of African residents who opposed Mungiki in the living districts for Africans in Nairobi. On the other hand, a special task force has also been established by the police to exterminate the sect through extrajudicial 'executions'. The Mungiki sect may be said to be symbolic of the violent character of contemporary Kenyan society.

[5] In Kenyan society, the 1990s was an era characterised by the frequent occurrence of ethnic confrontations and conflicts of unprecedented viciousness. The immediate causes of this were a heightening of ethnic consciousness and the rapid sprouting of ethnically aligned political parties due to the abolition of the single-party state system and introduction of a pluralistic political system of multiple parties in 1991 in the face of international pressure from the West and elsewhere. Particularly in the Rift Valley Province, the centre of Kenya's agriculture and livestock industries, where members of many different ethnic groups live together, disputes over land rights have occurred frequently between the chiefly pastoralist indigenous ethnic groups and the agriculturally based ethnic groups that had legally purchased the land and immigrated after independence. The Akiwumi Commission, which was set up with the objectives of determining the actual situation and causes of the ethnic conflicts in the 1990s and restoring justice in their aftermath, submitted its report to the president in 1999 (Akiwumi 1999).

[6] Saferworld worked with Kenya's state police and local NGOs to

attempt the experimental introduction of community policing across the country. See Mbogo et al. (2008) for a detailed account of the lessons learned from the trials and errors of this engagement.

[7] Representatives of an NGO that had contributed to the introduction of community policing in the low-income Nairobi neighbourhood of Kangemi as a partner organisation, while speaking highly of this attempt, also attribute the failure to factors such as an Enlightenment mentality far removed from the endogenous needs or desires of residents (Ruteere and Pommerolle 2003).

[8] For example, in a 2013 post entitled 'Interrogating the *nyumba kumi* Initiative,' the influential Kenyan blogger Shitemi Khamadi worries that the system, devised for rural Tanzanian society in the socialist era of the 1960s, has little applicability in the context of 21st Kenyan society. Moreover, he expresses concern that the system may be even more conducive to police corruption and the culture of civic oppression (Khamadi 2013).

[9] A former administrative chief from the Nairobi neighbourhood of Makongeni, claiming precedence for having organised similar mutual aid activities under the name 'Ten Ten' prior to the introduction of *nyumba kumi*, took particular umbrage at the decision to honour the former Interior Cabinet Secretary with a commendation for helping to handle the PEV (that is, having achieved the suppression of the violence and distribution of emergency relief supplies by effectively organising neighbourhood mutual aid associations). The chief claimed that if anyone truly deserved an award it should be him (*Daily Nation* 2014).

[10] The Luo, for example, comprise the largest ethnic group in the six areas including Gatwekera, Raila, Soweto West, Kisumu Ndogo and Kianda, which were controlled by Luo ethnic gangs (e.g., J-10, Yes We Can and Siafu). Laini Saba became Kikuyu territory, Linda went to the Kamba and Silanga to the Luyia, with the remaining areas of Makina, Kambi Muru, Mashimoni and Kichinjio to the descendants of the Nubian slave soldiers of Sudanese heritage who had inhabited Kibera since before independence, and who accounted for the ethnic majorities in those neighbourhoods. In particular, Siafu had complete effective control of Gatwekera, the Mungiki sect of Laini Saba, and the Nubians of Makina.

[11] *Sungusungu*, which has taken root after its introduction to Kisii land in Western Kenya, is the most organised example of Kenya's ethnic gangs. At the time of their introduction, Kenya's administrative structure, moving

from the particular to the general, was categorised into villages, sub-locations, locations, divisions, districts and provinces (these categories are significantly different from those introduced by the 2010 decentralisation enacted under the new Constitution). At the time, assistant chiefs were elected at the sub-location level and chiefs at the location level, while the higher administrative levels were staffed with career civil servants appointed by Nairobi. *Sungusungu* were organised along the lines of these administrative units, each of which boasted a commander who vigorously worked to develop his activities (National Crime Research Centre 2012).

[12] I have elsewhere attempted a discussion of this spontaneous and emergent expression of community policing in Kangemi during the PEV using their 'embodied heart' as a key phrase (Matsuda 2013).

References

Achuka, V. (2015) 'In the city's Othaya and Bondo slums, tribe rules', *Daily Nation* (Nairobi), 2 August 2015,
http://www.nation.co.ke/counties/nairobi/city-Othaya-Bondo-   slums/-/1954174/2817136/-/q11v6x/-/index.html
(Accessed 27 February 2016).

Akiwumi, A.M. (1999*) Report of the Judicial Commission Appointed to Inquire into Tribal Clashes in Kenya (The Akiwumi Report)*, Nairobi: Government Printer.

Cunneen, C. (1991) 'Problems in the implementation of community policing strategies', in S. McKillop and J. Vernon (eds.) *The Police and the Community, Australian Institute of Criminology Conference Proceedings*, No. 5, Canberra, ACT: Australian Institute of Criminology, pp.161–72.

Daily Nation (2014) '*Nyumba kumi* my idea, says ex-chief', *Daily Nation* (Nairobi), 8 December 2014,
http://www.nation.co.ke/news/*nyumba   kumi*-my-idea-says-ex-chief/-/1056/2549506/-/woeqyxz/-/index.html
(Accessed 27 February 2016).

Fleisher, M. (2000) 'Sungusungu: State-sponsored village vigilante groups among the Kuria of Tanzania', *Africa*, Vol. 70, No. 2, pp. 209–28.

Heald, S. (2007) 'Controlling crime and corruption from below: Sungusungu in Kenya', *International Relations*, Vol. 21, No. 2, pp. 183–99.

Khamadi, S. (2013) 'Interrogating the *Nyumba kumi* initiative', *Brainstorm* [online blog], 26 November 2013, http://www.brainstorm.co.ke/2013/11/26/interrogating-the- *nyumba kumi*-initiative/ (Accessed 21 August 2016).

Matsuda, M. (1996) *Domesticating the City: African Urban Anthropology*, Tokyo: Kawade Shobo Shinsha (in Japanese).

----------(2011) 'How to heal a society riven by violence? Possibilities for social reconciliation after the genocide in Africa', *Gendai Shakaigaku Forum*, No. 33, pp. 37-49 (in Japanese with English abstract).

----------(2013) 'Bodies standing in the way of riot: Examples from the 2007–2008 post-election violence in Nairobi'', in K. Sugawara (ed.) *The Anthropology of Embodiment: Cognition, Memory, Language, and the Otherness*, Kyoto: Sekai Shisosha, pp. 397–419 (in Japanese).

----------(2014) 'Introduction: Learning from African potentials', in M. Matsuda (ed.) *Introduction to African Societies*, Kyoto: Sekai Shisosha, pp. 1-23 (in Japanese).

Mbogo, J., Ndung'u, J., Campbell, I. and Rai, S. (eds.) (2008) *Implementing Community-Based Policing in Kenya*, London: Saferworld.

National Crime Research Centre (2012) *Final Report: A Study of Organized Criminal Gangs in Kenya*, Nairobi: NCRC, http://ncia.or.ke/ncrc/phocadownload/ncrc%20-%20organized %20criminal%20gangs%20in%20kenya.pdf (Accessed 21 August 2016).

Njogu, K. (ed.) (2010) *Healing the Wound: Personal Narratives about the 2007 Post-Election Violence in Kenya*, Nairobi: Twaweza Communications.

Oliver, W.M. (ed.) (2000) *Community Policing: Classical Readings*, Upper Saddle River, NJ: Prentice Hall.

Ruteere, M. and Pommerolle, M.E. (2003) 'Democratizing security or decentralizing repression? The ambiguities of community policing in Kenya', *African Affairs*, Vol. 102, No. 409, pp. 587–604.

Skolnick, J.H. and Bayley, D.H. (1988) 'Theme and variation in community policing', *Crime and Justice*, Vol. 10, pp. 1-37.

Tsuda, M. (2009) 'Kenya's political crisis following the 2007 general elections,' *Africa Report* (Institute of Developing Economies), No. 47, pp. 3–8 (in Japanese).

UNHRC (Universal Periodic Review of the United Nations Human Rights Council) (2012) *National Midterm Report*, UNHRC.

Waki, P.N. (2008) *Report of the Commission of Inquiry into Post Election Violence (The Waki Report)*, Nairobi: Government Printer, http://www.kenyalaw.org/Downloads/Reports/Commission _of_Inquiry_into_Post_Election_Violence.pdf (Accessed 16 April 2009).

Part Three

Perspectives for the Future

Chapter 11

ZAIRAICHI (Local Knowledge) as the Manners of Co-existence: Encounters between the Aari Farmers in Southwestern Ethiopia and the 'Other'

Masayoshi Shigeta and Morie Kaneko

11.1. Using Life Histories to Examine the Encounter with the 'Other'

Over the years, the Aari people have encountered many different kinds of 'other'. Initially, this meant the ethnic groups that lived alongside them. In contrast to the neighbouring ethnic groups such as the Banna and Mursi who are called by their own particular ethnic names and who speak their own particular languages, the Aari have applied the name *gama* to all the 'settlers' who arrived from the north with Ethiopian Orthodox missionaries in the late 19th century.[1] The ethnic groups that were referred to as *gama* traditionally included those groups living in the northern highlands of Ethiopia, including the Amhara, Oromo and Tigre. Even today, the Aari people continue to use *gama* to refer to visitors from the north, and when they mention that someone is speaking in the *gama* language (*gama af*), what they really mean is that the person is speaking Amharic. However, the Aari, who have historically led very settled lives, were unaware until only recently that *gama af* was originally spoken by a separate ethnic group (the Amhara) that resided to the north.

The Aari have adopted two concepts of 'other' since the arrival of foreigners to their land. They have used the Amharic loanword *faranj* to describe foreigners such as protestant missionaries, anthropologists and tourists, who first entered the scene in the 1960s. The other concept, for which they use the term *gama*, refers to the many settlers who came from the north with the intent of controlling Aariland and its resources and at times resorted to violent means.

In 1974, Ethiopia's imperial government was toppled, and the country shifted toward socialist rule. This political change

311

transformed the relationship between the Aari and the *gama*. During the reign of the emperors, there was a ruler–ruled dynamic between the settlers from the north and the Aari. This dynamic produced tensions which sometimes erupted into violence. On the other hand, they also fought side by side against a common enemy that appeared in the form of the Italian army. Many of the wealthy *gama*, who had previously dominated the land and formed trading capital, were driven away by the socialist government, which touted land nationalisation and wealth redistribution. The *gama* that remained were small-scale subsistence farmers, and to this day they continue to live amongst the Aari (Shigeta 1993, p. 110). Relationships between *gama* and Aari have grown increasingly harmonious with each passing year, and intermarriage has become common recently, spanning the last few generations.

In the course of our fieldwork, which we started in 1986, we gained the insights of a man in his fifties regarding the encounters between the Aari and *gama*. The first insight he offered came by way of a discourse that details the extent to which his parents and grandparents were abused and controlled by the *gama*. The second is a recollection about how little his people knew until the *gama* entered into their land. When speaking about their encounters with the *gama*, the Aari do not only describe the painful experience of being invaded and subjugated. They also frequently mention that the arrival of the *gama* brought much knowledge from the outside world into their lives.

As to the context behind such an optimistic perspective, one could cite the fact that the ruler–ruled dynamic has changed, or that there are dwindling numbers of Aari who had the direct experience of being ruled by the *gama*.

The case that we explore in this paper is the account of an Aari elder and his son. During the time that the *gama* were ruling over the Aari, this man sent his son to the *gama* so that he could learn their language. What kind of thinking or experiences led this man to take the view that his son should learn something from the 'other' with whom his society was clearly at enmity? What impact did this experience have on the man's receptivity to the modern public education later implemented in Ethiopia?

We explored these questions by analysing relations from two approaches. For the first, we focused on the local concept of intentionality (Kaneko 2014; 2016) that the Aari have expressed using the Aari word *eskan*. Originally, *eskan* means 'to know for oneself', the implication being that the knower has practised and internalised the knowledge. In this paper, we will refer to this concept using the word *eskan* or the English word 'know', set in quotation marks. By focusing on this word and what it means for the Aari, we can understand Aari interactions with the *gama* as the manners of co-existence which can overcome conflict. However, the meaning of *eskan* is ever broadening, and the word is now used to refer to knowledge that is learned from books, media or teachers. The Aari now use the Amharic loanword *tamar*, which means learning, as an extension of *eskan*. For example, a common expression is, 'I managed to *tamar* it, but I could not *eskan* it'.

For the second approach, we focused on the concept of 'ZAIRAICHI (local knowledge)' (Shigeta 2013, p. 1). As used here, the adjective 'ZAIRAI (local)' is used to describe a situation in which the inter-relationship among subjects in a particular locale is reconfigured in relation to all research subjects, including all animate and inanimate creatures and human beings, as well as the actions, thoughts, knowledge, occupations, environments, institutions, customs and communities that they produce. Following this, 'localisation' refers to the processes through which the reconfiguration takes place. In many cases, every subject and the inter-relationship among subjects change through localisation. The knowledge people practise on a daily basis could be described as 'ZAIRAI (local)'; thus we might say that internal knowledge is practical or experiential knowledge (Shigeta 2014, p. 246), formed through people's daily interactions with their natural and social environments. Such being the case, 'knowledge' as in 'ZAIRAICHI (local knowledge)' has a high affinity with the Aari word *eskan* (Shigeta 2013, p. 1).

In what follows, we will explore the evolution of the relationships between the Aari people and the *gama* by focusing on the knowledge (*eskan*) that stems from the everyday experiences of the Aari. The *gama* have at times been the enemy and at other times, amicable

313

neighbours. Even as the ruler–ruled dynamic between the Aari and *gama* has changed in tandem with regime changes, the two groups have continued living together in the same community without hostility. In many cases, internalisation causes objects to transform and object relations to change. Thus, it may be effective to explain the Aari's relationship with the *gama* as an example of such internalisation.

The primary resource we rely on in this paper is a set of interviews with an Aari man (Mr. Y) and his adult son (Mr. G). We have conducted continuous anthropological research in the village in which these two informants have lived, and occasionally draw on background information that we acquired in the course of such research.

The interview records are Mr. Y and Mr. G's recollections of past events and experiences. According to psychological research on testimonies (such as in a court of law), when people give accounts about an event, the details of the event tend to vary from person to person, but the general characteristics or framing of the event will remain consistent (Neisser 1982, p. 158; Takagi 2006). We did not attempt to verify the details of each event recounted by Mr. Y and Mr. G. We were much more interested in finding out how these men recollected and verbalised their experience of the Aari's interactions with the 'other' (*gama*), and how their experience is connected to their present day lives.

Ethnographers have often resorted to life history as a technique to create ethnographies that are focused on the individuals (Davison 1989, p. 5). For example, Jean Davison collected life histories from seven Gikuyu women who witnessed developmental intervention in a rural community in Kenya. These seven life histories provide an account of how the women have perceived the various changes occurring around them and how their perceptions were informed by past experiences or their opinions about the necessity of the changes (Davison 1989). The changes brought by the *gama*, who came as domineering 'others,' and the Aari's response to these changes, resemble in some ways those of the Gikuyu women who encountered development.

One of the authors of this study, Shigeta, interviewed Mr. G in November 2003. The interview took place in Kyoto, Japan; it lasted a total of two hours, and it was conducted in English. Mr. G and Shigeta have been friends since graduate school, and they have spent much time as fellow researchers in Ethiopia's capital, Addis Ababa, Mr. G's birthplace (M Village, South Omo Zone, Ethiopia), and Japan. Meanwhile, author Kaneko, who has conducted lengthy fieldwork in M Village, interviewed Mr. Y at his home in February and March 2003. The interview was conducted in the Aari language, and it lasted a total of seven hours. Video and audio recordings were made of both interviews. At the time of the surveys, Mr. G was forty-two years old and Mr. Y's age was estimated to be seventy.

11.2. History of Aari-*Gama* Relations: Regional Background

11.2.1. Livelihood and the Role of Children

The Aari engage in sedentary agriculture in the highlands, where the altitude is between 1,500 and 3,000 meters. This region is relatively damp, with an annual rainfall of around 1,500 meters. Accordingly, the area has kitchen gardens (*tika-haami*), which grow root crops such as *ensete*, taro and yams, and other crops such as kale, beans and herbs. The residents also grow high-value cash crops such as coffee and corarima, *Aframomum corrarima*. On the peripheries of the kitchen gardens lie fields (*wooni-haami*), which primarily grow cereals such as corn, millet, barley, wheat and teff.

There are two main seasons: a dry season from October to March and a rainy season from April to September. Corn and barley are harvested twice a year, once in the dry season and once in the rainy season, while millet and wheat are harvested once a year, in the dry season. Yams are typically harvested in the dry season and taro in the rainy season. *Ensete* can be harvested all year, which enables the people to have a sedentary and autonomous livelihood (Shigeta 1993, p. 106). Coffee is harvested during the dry season.

When considering the role of children in Aari's livelihood, we cannot overlook the fact that cooperative work units (*molla*) once played an important role in agricultural production (Gebre 1995). During coffee harvesting, a *molla* comprised of around 10 to 20

315

children aged 5–12 who would work on their parents' coffee farms in rotation free of charge or undertake the harvest work for some farmers for payment. In the second context, up to half of the coffee beans collected were given to the farm owner, and the rest were shared among the *molla* members who had carried out the work. *Molla* had a considerable economic impact on households, as reflected in the expression 'as many storehouses as the number of children can be built'. But with the spread of modern education, *molla* activities have declined, and nowadays most children are in school.

Even so, children, regardless of the economic status of their family, still play important roles in the subsistence activities of their households. When girls reach the age of six, they start helping around the home, and when boys reach the age of six, they start undertaking the work of tethering and herding cows or sheep, or watering them. There is a notion among the adults that as children practise these tasks, they gradually come to 'know' (*eskan*) them, and thereby become 'fully developed adults' (*mata chaalta eed*) (Kaneko 2014).

11.2.2. Incursion from the North, and How This Was Experienced by the Aari

Since the late 19th century, Ethiopia, as an emerging nation state, has attempted to 'Ethiopianise' the peripheral peoples, a trend that has persisted through the various regime changes (Shigeta 1993, p. 104). The Aari first encountered the *gama* in the late 19th century. During that time, Ethiopia was in a rush to establish itself as a modern nation state. The government expanded its territory southward and dispatched troops and bureaucrats from the north. Around this time, Emperor Menelik II, who had recently increased his prestige on the world stage by winning the Battle of Adwa against Italy, was facing a domestic problem and a foreign relations problem. Domestically, a serious famine had broken out in the northern region. The foreign relations problem concerned the necessity of demonstrating the legitimacy of Ethiopia's territorial rule in the face of the partitioning of Africa by European powers. Menelik II believed that an invasion of the south was necessary in order to solve both problems (Donham 1986a, pp. 17-22; Bahru 1991). Many of the troops he dispatched, after subjugating the south, did not return to their homes in the north and continued living in the south together with their families because these soldiers were given the lands of numerous ethnic groups (including the Aari) in the occupied areas as a reward for their achievements.

The people living on the peripheral territory of the then Ethiopia have personally experienced the history of Ethiopianisation on a number of levels (Shigeta 1993, p. 105). The Aari people in particular were soon subsumed into the framework of the nation state both politically and economically. The Aari elders who experienced the subjugation of the *gama* say that they were obliged at the time to pay a tax (*gira* in *Araf* and *gibir* in Amharic) to their *gama* rulers. By contrast, many of the nomads dwelling in the same southwestern lowlands were not incorporated into a system of state rule through means such as taxation (Miyawaki and Ishihara, 2005).

Having become tenant farmers on *gama*-owned land, the Aari faced major changes which overturned their traditional customs. Aari society had hitherto been divided —culturally and occupationally — into two castes, namely, the farmers' caste (*kantsa*) and the artisans' caste (*mana*). However, the members of each caste would now have to work alongside each other because of *gama*'s intervention in the land allocation. Intermarriage between *kantsa* and *mana* had traditionally been taboo. The *mana* had been positioned on the cultural margins with, for example, a specific role to play in *kantsa* funeral ceremonies. This traditional hierarchical arrangement has also been challenged by the Protestant missionaries who began arriving in the 1950s (Naty 2005 pp. 124, 146–47). However, despite the efforts of the missionaries and the socialist government to disseminate human rights and equality, various discriminatory practices have persisted.

To this day, one will often hear anecdotes about how the Aari, working on feudal farms, had strained relations with the *gama* who owned the farms. For instance, the *gama* had brought with them the northern custom of inviting the farm workers to have coffee in their home after the day's work was done. In one anecdote, a tenant farmer picked up a cup filled to the brim with coffee and accidently dropped the cup and broke it having failed to anticipate the heat of the coffee. The farmer was reportedly forced to hand over his child as compensation for the damaged cup. There are in fact records in southern Ethiopia of cases where settlers from the north captured people in the south and kept them as 'slaves' (Donham 1986b, pp. 81–2).

However, according to a senior *mana*, the *gama* had very amicable relations with some of the *mana*. The settlers regarded the *mana*, who produced iron farm tools and earthenware, as highly skilled craftspeople, and had an affinity with them that was comparable to blood ties. There were cases where the *gama* would invite *mana* to participate in the mutual financing organisations they set up in towns. In addition, a *kantsa* male in his sixties reports that he, too, had a favourable experience with the *gama*. The man reported that he received teff seeds and herb seedlings from settlers, and he is still growing them today. Despite this example, however, the more common sentiment among the *kantsa* is a sense of inferiority to the *gama* expressed through words like 'they showed us how little we knew'.

11.2.3. School Education

Between 2008 and 2013, the overall school entrance rate in Ethiopia for grades 1–4 reached 100 per cent, while the rate for grades 5–8 remained in the range of 62–66 per cent (Ministry of Education 2013, p. 26). The percentage of people entering middle school and higher education is still low compared to that for primary education. The public elementary school that Mr. G attended reflects this trend. The schooling rate of those old enough to be in the first grade is nearly 100 per cent, but this trails off in successive grades (as of 2014). This phenomenon is probably the result of primary and secondary schools in Ethiopia tolerating leave and readmission for personal reasons or family circumstances (Arii 2015). Therefore, the ages of students in the same classroom can vary widely.

The high school enrolment rate in this region is closely related to the rise in employment opportunities. The Aari who proceed through the educational ranks and graduate beyond the primary level return to their home villages and begin working as local bureaucrats, public health officials and agriculture promotion workers. Seeing the graduates as role models, other villagers have started equating school

318

attendance with expanding job opportunities in areas other than agriculture. At the same time, it is becoming difficult to live on agriculture alone since farmland is being increasingly subdivided in tandem with the rising population and successions that divide inheritances.

After the socialist regime was established (1974), the Aari people encountered another 'other,' namely, modern school education. Whereas public primary and secondary schools were established relatively early on in the towns built by the settlers from the north, the best that schools could offer in farming communities where many Aari lived was four grades of primary education. Those villages where Ethiopian Orthodox churches had stood since the turn of the 19th Century had church schools, where priests taught Amharic reading and writing. At the time, it was rare for a child to receive schooling after the age of six. This was because children had vital roles to play on the farms and in the homes, and because many parents believed that children would grow lazy in their work if they went to school. In 1976, a primary school principal in the area regularly visited homes in an attempt to persuade parents to let their children go to school. A present-day primary school instructor in his thirties said that his parents were not willing to send him to school, so he brokered farm crops and used the profits to pay for his own school expenses.

11.3. Encountering the 'Other' and 'Knowing'

11.3.1. Mr. G's Experience with School

One of the subjects of this study, the male Aari (*kantsa*) we're calling Mr. Y, was born in M Village somewhere between 1920 and 1930, and grew up making a living from agriculture. Having married and divorced a number of women, he was married to Mrs. B (the birth mother of Mr. G). When Mrs. B married Mr. Y, she brought a daughter from her previous marriage. Mr. Y had two sons with Mrs. B. The oldest, Mr. G was born in the 1960s. As mentioned previously, children play an important in the household's livelihood activities. When Mr. G was born, it was believed that a boy's work was to carry out activities like changing tethers on livestock and chasing birds and monkeys away from fields. Before public primary

319

schools were established, the idea that children should be sent to school had not taken root among the Aari.

Nevertheless, when Mr. G was around four or five, Mr. Y sent him to a local male *gama* so that he would learn Amharic, the common tongue of the settlers. When the *gama* man went away on business, about a year later, Mr. Y sent Mr. G to board at the house of an Ethiopian Orthodox priest (*qes*). It was around this time that Mr. G was given his baptismal name. At the church, Mr. G studied Amharic letters in order to read the bible and other scriptures. He was also expected to help out with farm work and childcare. At the time, sending a child to a church typically meant that the child would be a member of the clergy in the future. It is unclear whether Mr. Y was fully aware of this when he sent his child there.

Sometime later, when a public primary school was established in M Village, Mr. Y enrolled his son in the school at the age of fourteen. Mr. G performed well at school. He skipped grades multiple times, and graduated from six-year primary school in four years. Likewise, he completed the two-year junior secondary school in one year. He advanced to lower and then upper secondary school, receiving both financial assistance and moral support from family members and teachers. At the time, it was rare for people from villages in southwestern Ethiopia to advance to universities. But Mr. G passed the standard entrance exam with flying colours, enrolled in Addis Ababa University, and later completed a master's programme at the university's graduate school. Mr. G also had the opportunity to go to a graduate school abroad, where he obtained a doctoral degree. He then returned to Ethiopia and began teaching social anthropology at a university.

The fact that Mr. G – born in the politically, socially and economically peripheral southwest – could study at a newly established public primary school, advance to secondary school and eventually become a university lecturer cannot be attributed to his exemplary academic performance alone. It is apparent that his success is owed in a large part to the physical and economic support he received from those around him. Another major influence on Mr. G's life was the parenting style of his father, who sent his young son to the house of a *gama*, then a priest, and consistently proclaimed that 'it is good to learn (*eskan*)'. Below, based on interviews, we describe the respective viewpoints of Mr. Y and Mr. G concerning the circumstances behind Mr. G's education by the priest and eventual enrolment at the primary school.

11.3.2. The Father Who Wanted His Son to Know the Language

Why did Mr. Y send his son to a priest to learn Amharic? We asked Mr. Y about the experiences that led him to make this decision. The interview with Mr. Y was also attended by his wife, daughter, grandchild, and, at times, by a male Aari farmhand. Most of the time, these persons listened to the interview in silence, but they also occasionally jumped in with side comments or when the interviewer, Kaneko, had problems understanding Mr. Y. Kaneko also asked them some questions to confirm the information that she had obtained from Mr. G and other people. During the interview, Kaneko and Mr. Y also discussed Mr. G's advancement to secondary and tertiary education and continuing education up to the present, but in view of space constraints, we will refrain from discussing this time period.

[Interview 1][2]

Kaneko (hereunder, K): Your son went to a church [Ethiopian Orthodox] school, didn't he?

Y: Yes.

K: Were there such things as schools when you were a child?

Y: (At the time), this village was not big. There were schools in Jinka, Arba Minch, Sawla, and Ubamer [towns in the southwest].

...

K: Did you never wish to go to school yourself?

Y: No, not myself. I worked with a *wali* [a sickle-shaped farming tool] and a *gosha* [a hoe]. I sent them [the children] to school because I didn't want them to do the same [farm] work. ... At the time, I did not have the idea that school would make a man of someone [empower one to earn a living]. ... When I realized that schools raised people to be upstanding adults, I felt like going to school myself. But at that time, I did not realize that schools raised people

321

in this way. I had the notion that one is raised to be an adult by the *gosha*, that one is raised to be an adult by the *wali*.

At this point in the interview, Mr. Y revealed that he, like many other Aari parents, did not initially regard schools in a positive light, because he thought of school as something that would deprive families of the labour force necessary to make a living. Mr. Y's case is notable for the fact that he sent Mr. G to school anyway, with the express intention of equipping him to learn a living outside of agriculture.

> Y: I worked with a *gosha* and *wali*, then G was born, and I sent him to school. I said, 'Go there and study'. ... In the past, we were *oya* (calabash). There are *oya* with no open mouth. That describes how we were. *Ufta* (processed calabash) has a mouth [for pouring]. The *oya* does not have a mouth [the seeds inside have not been removed]. If you make a mouth, you can pour out water. Or you could use it to drink a local brew. If there is no mouth, what use is it? That's what *oya* is like. I got the idea that it is good for children to learn, and so I sent G [to school]. That's the truth of it.

The closed, intact and unprocessed calabash in the natural state is equated with ignorance, while the processed calabash with a hole or mouth to pour something in or out is likened to sophistication. This kind of allegorical speech is not unique to Mr. Y. When the Aari explain something to children, they often use as metaphors things they have learned through their interactions with flora and fauna. In his interview, Mr. Y likened diligent study at school to toiling at a farm.

> Y: When there was a gathering,[3] the Aari and *gama* would mingle together. We got called to such a gathering around this time of the day [the interview took place in the afternoon], and so we went to their [the *gama*'s] house. We washed our hands, put on nice attire, and brought vessels for drinking local brew. We went to a *sergi* (Amharic word for wedding ceremony), and brought such vessels. Then, (the *gama* at the venue) looked at us, talked in

Amharic, and laughed at us. Seeing the grins on their faces, we also broke into laughter and smiles [without understanding]. We laughed, and then when I observed [the *gama*], it seemed that they were staring at [and laughing at] one member of our group. Looking at [the *gama* laughing], all [we] could do was laugh without understanding what was being said.

At the time, most of the Aari farmers did not understand Amharic, the language of the *gama*. On the other hand, various social relations were beginning to form between the *gama* and Aari. The Aari were forced to accept the settlers' dominance and exploitation after the superior imperial military force crushed their armed resistance early in the contact. This attitude of opting for peaceful coexistence continued when the socialist regime came to power, and it remains even to this day.

> Y: The next day, I was working together with my neighbors in a cooperative work unit. Then, [one of the members] started speaking, saying, 'Listen up everyone.' The member said, 'In the old says, *baabi* [traditional rulers of Aari territory] with names like Diksi and Kotsa sold Aari women and children [to the north]. My mother and father, instead of selling [their children] into slavery, raised them in secret. If only my mother and father had sold me!'
>
> [I asked,] 'What do you say that for? Yesterday, the *gama* looked at us and laughed. We didn't understand what they were saying, so when they laughed at us, baring their teeth; we could do nothing but laugh back. This is our foolishness.' When I said these words, half of my friends agreed, saying, 'You're right.' [Then I said,] 'If you are born in a *mana* family, you are a *mana*. [However,] *mana* are also human beings'. [In response], half agreed, saying, 'You're right.'
>
> Then my wife became pregnant with G and gave birth to him. Four months after his birth, my wife and son were secluded in the garden. After this period, they went to the house, and galta [the elder] came into our house and blessed [the child]. It occurred to me that it would be good if the child could speak [Amharic]. I already speak [remember] the language, but he was not yet starting

to speak [the language]. Therefore, I enrolled him [in school]. That's the truth of it.

An Aari had made a statement, which could be regarded as an obsequious attitude, that it would have been better to be a slave than to be laughed at. Mr. Y regarded the matter as a language issue. Rather than viewing the Aari's failure to understand the *gama*'s conversation as a product of the ruler–ruled dynamic between the groups, he instead saw it as an issue of not 'knowing' the language, and such a problem can be resolved. This line of thinking can also be considered the beginning of a new approach that the Aari took toward the *gama*. Mr. Y also connected Aari–*gama* relations to the *kantsas*' discriminatory attitudes toward the *mana*. The assertion that the *mana* are human beings just like the *kantsa* was revolutionary for Aari society at the time, before the socialist government launched an equality campaign in southwest Ethiopia under the slogan 'all people are equal'. We did not hear any Aari elder other than Mr. Y criticise the sociocultural marginalisation of the *mana*. It is uncertain as to why Mr. Y held this apparently unique, progressive view. The fact that he was open about his controversial opinions, and then made his son learn Amharic in the teeth of criticism from his neighbours, may have been related to the fact that he was the elder of a particularly powerful clan among the Aari.

> K: You sent your son Mr. G to a (church) school, didn't you? At the time, did you want your son to become something in particular, such as a policeman, a teacher, or a priest of the Ethiopian Orthodox Church?
>
> Y: No [this reply came instantly]. I just thought it would be good if he could write his name and my name in *Ha Hu* [Amharic letters], and remember the language.
>
> K: Just the language?
>
> Y: Just the language. If he can go so far as to learn the language, then what will be next? I did not know [what would be next].
>
> ...

I thought it would be great if he could write his name and his father's name. Anything beyond that would be his choice. That's what I thought.

K: Your son studied in school. He studied hard and then went to Addis Ababa. He even went abroad. He went to another land leaving you in your village.

Y: Yes. He went away.

K: Back then, when you sent him off to school, did you have any inkling of what was to happen?

Y: Is it my son asking this? No. I did not even entertain the notion of him becoming a priest. I just wanted him to know Amharic. We were *moini* [an Amharic word that means something like 'ignoramus']. That's why we were laughed at [during the gathering at a *gama* house]. I wanted him to learn Amharic. I wanted him to be able to write on paper.

A man next to Y [summarising Y's answer]: He felt we were *moini*, but he did not want his son to be *moini* too.

Moini refers to one who does not know what one should know. The equivalent word in Aari is *gada*, or the regional variant *joolta*. During the conversation with Mr. Y, there were frequent instances where he incorporated Amharic words into his speech. This may have been because he was conscious of the interviewer being a foreigner, but we cannot be certain of this. Regarding Mr. Y's allusion to 'what one should know', this might mean a plethora of things from social normative knowledge (or common sense) to the various things that a fully developed adult should know. While *moini* is often used as to criticise or insult, it is also sometimes used to excuse the behaviour of children. Mr. Y regarded the *gama* language as something that 'one should know'. The apparent implication is that the Aari people would henceforth have to incorporate new knowledge that would transcend what had hitherto been believed necessary for becoming an Aari adult.

11.3.3. The Son Who Kept on Learning

What was Mr. G's response to his father's desire that he [Mr. G] not to be *moini*? Though Mr. G's education experience ended well, his early experience in education was far from smooth.

Today, among the Aari who are aged fifty or older and did not go to a public school, there are many who cannot speak Amharic. Women in particular tend to know only enough basic Amharic to ask for prices and haggle at a market. Even the younger generation cannot speak Amharic with much fluency, save for those who advanced to higher education. In contrast to the neighbouring nomads, who have a command of multiple languages, the sedentary Aari have a high proportion of people who can only speak Aari. Mr. G, in addition to his mother tongue Aari, has fluent command of Amharic and English. Since his education was in Amharic, Mr. G has come to use Amharic as his everyday language. It has become the language he thinks in.

[Interview 2][4]

(The following exchanges were preceded by a discussion about whether the interview should be conducted in *Aaraf*, Amharic or English).

Shigeta (hereunder, S): What is your first language?

G: I learnt *Aaraf first*. I learnt Amharic starting at the age of six. According to the definition of language acquisition in the case of bilingualism, Amharic is also my first language.

S: When you were sent to an Ethiopian Orthodox church, what were your thoughts?

G: It was a shock at first. At the time, I knew hardly any Amharic. [Even so], I was also excited. Everything was a new experience. For an Aari like me, it was a real privilege to reside as a learner at an Amhara or Gurage home. The other Aari people who lived with Amhara were considered as servants.

S: It was only you? Weren't there any other children who studied with you?

G: There were others, but they soon left, and then it was just me. I was the teacher's second pupil. The first had left. Later on, people from the village started sending their children to the priest.

S: Did it become a trend to send one's children to a *gama* priest?

G: Yes it did. Unfortunately, however, few children stayed. I was the only one who did. I was the church's only pupil.

S: How long did you study there?

G: I can't quite remember. I was there for one or two years, I think. (…) The priest (hereunder, T) taught during the day, during the evening, and during holidays. I lived in the same place.

S: Did you board at the place?

G: Yes. T often taught there in the evening. I [converted to the Ethiopian Orthodox faith], and so he became my godfather. T was a very good man. … T passed away ten years ago. T was from Guraghe. He was called '*Mamur*' T.[5]. *Mamur* or *Memre* is a title for a priest. He was born in Addis Ababa and then he and his mother left the city when he was three or four years old. He was apparently five or six when he got to the village. He resided in the village since that time.

Mr. G's father sent Mr. G to the church school, and when word got out that Mr. G learned Amharic in the school, many people in the village started sending their children to the school. Ultimately, only Mr. G remained in the school, and only he continued in his education. Nonetheless, the fact that many of the villagers at the time sympathised with the idea of sending one's children to learn Amharic, and at least temporarily put this idea into practice, provided an important impetus for the changes that were to come.

S: So the other Aari boys dropped out, leaving only you. Why do you think they all left?

G: The first reason was the corporal punishment. The parents were not too pleased about it, and the children hated it. Another reason was that T made the children work at his home. The parents had sent their child there to learn not to work. So when they found out that the children were being made to work on the farm they must have thought, 'If my child is at home with us, then it should at least be working for us'. These were good reasons for pulling one's child out of the school.

However, my father bucked the trend. My mother said that since the other children had left, I should be pulled out as well, but my father replied that I should be in school. My father is the type of person who goes against the flow. I don't know quite how to

327

explain it, I have the utmost respect for my father, but at the time, I could not understand him.

He would always use a simple analogy to explain his thinking. 'If you are a farmer, you have to toil night and day. You have to carry out the appropriate farm work at the times that are right for seeds and grain. If you do this correctly, you will reap a good harvest. If you are a merchant, you have to work diligently and grapple with your horse [for carrying the load]. You must do so if you want to get a profit. Likewise, if you want to be an educated person, if you want to get smart brains, you've got to undergo tough experiences, and this will include punishments or [depending on the circumstances] physical labour. Whatever it is you do, you can't expect complete freedom'.

S: That's very impressive. When did he say this to you?

G: When I was small. The reason being that he had to justify taking a different decision to that of his friends who did not send their children to school. At the time, however, I did not understand. I thought that my father was not a good person. The other parents had pulled their children out of the school, but my father had not done the same thing. However, I am now grateful to him [for leaving me in school].

S: Generally speaking, are Aari parents strict with their children? Do they hit them for instance?

G: Yes, the parents hit their children. My neighbors do so in fact. It is accepted. The reason the parents could not countenance T's behavior was because they looked up to him as a priest and an educator and did not expect him to be someone who inflicts [physical] punishment. ...

The parents had the expectation that the church school would provide education based on methods that differed from the methods with which the Aari were already familiar. Mr. G's father, however, did not necessarily see the church school in the same way. In fact, Mr. Y regarded the education provided by this 'other' not as something special but rather an activity similar to what the Aari already know and do. As the interview with Mr. Y also reveals, he used allegory to express his strict views on generating one's own success. The thinking that he sought to inculcate in his son, namely – that one can only succeed in something after one has made efforts, studied diligently and undergone physical burdens such as punishments – is arguably the very essence of *eskan*. However, it is probably only natural that the young Mr. G could not understand his father's thinking at the time.

> G: Many boys had quit, and so I wanted to quit too. While T was a good person, he was also someone who beat me. I couldn't withstand the endless punishments. I sought help from my mother, but she just told me to go and convince my father. I didn't have the wherewithal to do that. I was supposed to return to my house as normal, and then go to the school in the evening to study. However, on that day, I decided to stay in the house without going to school.
>
> On the following day, my father brought me to the church school. He apologized to T, saying, 'I'm sorry. I couldn't get him to school yesterday, but I've brought him in today.' [After that], I did my studies and came back to the house.
>
> On the following day, I told my father that I didn't want to go to school. However, my father said that he would not come with me to apologize anymore, and he told me to go myself. He then left for work. I went to my mother and told her what my father said. My mother said she was sorry but that she could not do anything for me. Such being the case, I thought about what I myself could do. I headed toward the school but while I was walking, I decided that I should not go to the school and instead keep on walking right out of the village.

Mr. G started learning Amharic in accordance with his father's wishes, and then continued studying in accordance with his father's strong recommendation. However, at one point, unable to withstand the punishments, nor able to stand up to his father, Mr. G resolved to run away. While Mr. G's action may seem at first glance passive as escaping sometimes seems, it may actually have been the first dynamic action that Mr. G took. It should be noted that what Mr. G sought to do was simply to avoid the punishments; it was not the case that he resented learning something from a *gama*.

11.3.4. Running Away from Home and the Beginning of a New Journey

Running away from home was the first adventure of Mr. G's life and, as such, it was an unforgettable experience. As a highly settled people, the Aari have taken a dim view of leaving one's abode and moving elsewhere. Mr. G's decision to run away, which he made at the age of ten, would even today be considered beyond common sense. On the other hand, from the villagers' perspective, the act of running away was not just one family's problem; it might cause friction between the Aari and *gama*.

> S: Where did you go?
>
> G: I didn't care where I was going. I just wanted to get away. I did in fact disappear. I went to Berka town [which is about ten kilometers from the village]. I didn't know the way, but it happened to be market day in Tolta town, and so I followed people [to the market]. I knew that the people coming from Berka go to the market in Tolta, so I decided to go to Tolta and then go to Berka, where a relative I know well, called A, lives.
>
> My parents thought I was in school, and T thought I was in my parent's house. I don't know when they found out ...
>
> S: Was that the first time you'd gone so far away?
>
> G: Yes. I went to Berka, and I decided that if I couldn't find A, I would go to a church, stay the night there, and then return. With that in mind, I started walking in the town. I was in such a filthy state ...
>
> By 4:00 pm, I still could not find [A]. I then decided to go to the church. When I started walking toward the church, A walked into view. [At that moment] he had also found me. I started crying. He used to look after me when I was small, carrying me around on his shoulders. He always had a beaming smile. He was like a big brother to me.
>
> When he saw me, he cried as well. He must have thought that I had been sent to report a death [not only among the Aari but throughout Ethiopia, when someone dies, it is customary to dispatch a messenger to report the death to relatives living far away]. He expressed his surprise, saying, 'Why did they dispatch someone as small as you? I don't care who it was who died, that is just too

cruel'. I was crying, so I could not explain myself, but after a while, I managed to tell him that I was not sent as a messenger but had run away from home. He was shocked to hear this and asked, 'Why?' I told him that my father was forcing me to go to school, that I received corporal punishments whenever I went to school, and that the other children had all quit. He understood.

Tellingly, the Aari adult, A, rather than scolding Mr. G for his unimaginable behaviour, listened to what he had to say and respected his will. This was not the only incident where an adult listened to what a child had to say. During mealtimes for example, the parents of Aari households often ask their children for their opinions regarding livelihood activities that the children themselves carry out such as the procedure and timing of farm work or what to do about diseased livestock. This signifies that even if parents regard children as *moini* or ignorant, they are fully aware that their children have a key role to play in everyday livelihood tasks and often know more than the parents do about certain activities or changing situations. In settings where internal knowledge is formed, the old–young hierarchy itself is liable to reverse.

[Meanwhile], [my running away] was treated as a serious issue in my father's house. I heard that my father, thinking that he'd lost me, was going to kill T. This is because he thought that T was so cruel to have beaten me so. It seems that people thought that T had accidently killed me [during a punishment]. Apparently they went out to search T's house and farm. Some days later, my father decided to go to Berka. He didn't go to search [for me], but to tell A about my disappearance and to ask him to help find me.

[Of course], I was in fact there. My father was overjoyed to see me. However, I was sad and angry. I thought he would send me back to the school again. I therefore fled again.

In response, my father said he would not send me to the school. My father told me that we would live together, so please come back. When I fled from A's house, I decided to head off to the place of the Mursi [the Mursi are lowland nomads. They have often intruded into the Aari area and plundered] and die there. The reason being

331

that I had nowhere else to go. I told A everything, including this. A calmed me down and said that he would not make me return to my father. My father said that if I wanted to live with A, then I should. My father said that he loved me and so if I returned to him, he would not send me to the church school again. He then said, 'I made a big mistake. I have my own philosophy, and I thought that education was a good thing. However, I will make you a promise. I will not send you to school'.

S: Your father told you such a thing? What happened next?

G: I accepted what my father said. I spent the night at A's place and then returned home the next day. My father is a person who keeps his promises. He had resolved to stop sending me to school. For the next two years, I did not go to school [T's place]. After that, I went to the new public school in Metser.

The Aari people have lived through three different regimes: the imperial regime, the socialist regime and the present federal democratic regime. As such, the meaning of 'other' to the Aari has constantly undergone change. It is not the case that the Aari have simply let themselves be tossed about by change. Though their response may seem passive, it might rather be viewed as situational adaptation, whereby the Aari have flexed and adapted to the other. Such situational adaptation enabled Mr. G to make a bold choice that would alter the course of his life.

The story of Mr. G and Mr. Y's engagements and interaction with the 'other' did not end here. Mr. G ultimately became a symbolic presence as a successful Aari, and many young Aari started looking up to him as a role model. When Mr. Y passed away in 2005, Mr. G held a funeral ceremony that followed Aari convention. One notable feature of the funeral was that while the traditional funeral ceremony was taking place, Protestant Aari who had gathered around the other mourners sang a dirge and the Orthodox priest performed the Christian funeral rituals. Thus, co-existence with the 'other' continued even after Mr. Y's death.

11.4. *ZAIRAICHI* as the Manners of Co-existence with the 'Other'

The *gama* Mr. Y encountered as the 'other' were people who took the Aari's ancestral land, taxed them and assumed authority over them. Mr. Y recounted how at a dining event, someone in Mr. Y's group was laughed at (by the *gama*) and how everyone laughed having not understood what was being said. However, in reflecting on this incident, Mr. Y did not focus on the asymmetric power relationship between the *gama* and Aari and fall into despair. Instead, he was firmly convinced that if they had understood the *gama* language, they would not have all laughed together without understanding. Believing it necessary to engage with the *gama* in order to continue living on the land, Mr. Y believed that knowing the *gama*'s language and knowing what kind of people the *gama* were would alter the relationship between the two groups. One reason why he had no intention of opposing the 'other' (*gama*) with violence was his belief that one should not be *moini* (an ignoramus). Mr. Y equated 'not knowing' with being an immature person – something to be ashamed of. Such thinking can be regarded as the driving force that produced the internalisation process whereby the Aari people reconstituted their relationship with the *gama* within their community.

The *gama* that Mr. G encountered as the 'other' was, at first, a person – one who brought new experiences. As a result, Mr. G was stimulated by his new living environment and by his unique and privileged position. Mr. G listened to Amharic being spoken by a *gama*, gained an understanding of Amharic grammar, practised Amharic handwriting, and thereby came to know the Amharic language intimately. In the process, he received punishments, which sometimes lasted a long time, and he was trained in the basic acts of the settlers' everyday culture, including farm work and childcare. While he still lived very close to his Aari parents, the young Mr. G, in the process of studying Amharic, went so far as to internalise the customs and traditions of the Amhara. These unique circumstances came about because of Mr. Y's belief that one should not be *moini*. One aspect of these unique circumstances was the corporal punishment that Mr. G so detested. Early on, Mr. Y had lectured Mr.

G about his education using allegories based on his experience with farming. However, Mr. G failed to adequately understand these experiences and analogies, and continued in the circumstances only reluctantly. Mr. G's father himself may have been an 'other' to Mr. G at the time, considering the lack of understanding between them. Later on, Mr. G began to think that he could do something about his situation, and decided to run away from home. As a result, his relationship with his father was eventually reconstituted, and he stopped attending the church school. The experiences he gained at this time (studying at the church school and then managing, through his own volition, to stop going to school) led to Mr. G subsequently adopting the tenacious resolve to never abandon his hopes no matter how trials may persist, and he applied this attitude to a number of choices he faced (such as entering public school and advancing to lower/upper secondary school).

We can conclude that for the father and son, 'knowing' was the only identified method for continuing a relationship with the 'other'.

Soon after the father sent his son to the school, government officials denounced the region's hierarchical system, in which farmers and artisans led segregated lives. In addition, taxes were imposed, and conscription was enforced. Furthermore, the authorities made school education compulsory and established public health stations in villages, and posted many health workers there on a permanent basis. These changes occurred during the time of the socialist regime, which began in 1974. Shigeta, who conducted his first fieldwork in 1986 and was present during the regime change five years later, explained these circumstances as follows: 'It is easy to explain the driving force of the 'Ethiopianisation' that the Aari people of today are experiencing by relating it to the changes in the political system. However, such an explanation can only describe one side of the matter. The happiness of the Aari people is deeply related to the freedom that they, as individuals with agency, have to choose their own future regardless of whatever systems exist around them (Shigeta 1993, p. 112).' To base one's life on the knowledge that stems from accumulated experience and, at the same time, to continue seeking further knowledge – in other words, to always be thinking 'what should I be 'knowing' in order to not be ignorant?' – is a way of cultivating one's individuality and agency, which is an essential condition for people to live better lives.

Notes

[1] This paper has indicated Aari words in italics.

[2] The interview was conducted at Mr. Y's home on 21 February 2003.

[3] In the actual interview, Mr. Y explained his point using words like *diggis* (feasts) and *kurbaan* (memorial festivity). Both of these terms are derived from Amharic.

[4] The interview was conducted in a research room on 21 November 2003.

[5] *Mamur* or *memre* is derived from the Amharic word *membir* (teacher), which is also used to refer to a priest (*Qes*, in Amharic).

References

Arii, H. (2015) 'How women choose their schooling in their life course: The case of the Maale, southwestern Ethiopia', *Africa Kenkyu*, No. 88, pp. 1–12 (in Japanese).

Bahru, Z. (1991) *A History of Modern Ethiopia, 1855–1974*, Oxford: James Currey.

Davison, J. (1989) *Voices from Mutira: Lives of Rural Gikuyu Women*, Boulder & London: Lynne Rienner Publishers, Inc.

Donham, D.L. (1986a) 'Old Abyssinia and the new Ethiopian empire', in D.L. Donham and W. James (eds.), *Southern Marches of Imperial Ethiopia: Essays in History and Social Anthropology*, Cambridge: Cambridge University Press, pp. 3–48.

----------(1986b) 'From ritual kings to Ethiopian landlords', in D.L. Donham and W. James (eds.), *Southern Marches of Imperial Ethiopia: Essays in History and Social Anthropology*, Cambridge: Cambridge University Press, pp.69–95.

Gebre, Y. (1995) *The Ari of Southwestern Ethiopia: An Exploratory Study of Production Practices*, Social Anthropology Dissertation Series No. 2, Addis Ababa: Department of Sociology and Social

Anthropology.

Kaneko, M. (2014) "'I know how to make pots by myself": Special reference to local knowledge transmission in southwestern Ethiopia', *African Study Monographs, Supplementary Issue*, No. 48, pp. 59–75.

----------(2016) 'Variations in shape, local classification, and the establishment of a chaîne opératoire for pot making among female potters in southwestern Ethiopia', in H. Terashima and B. Hewlett (eds.), *Social Learning and Innovation in Contemporary Hunter-gatherers: Evolutionary and Ethnographic Perspectives,* Tokyo: Springer, pp. 217–27.

Ministry of Education (2013) *Education Statistics Annual Abstract 2005E.C.2012/2013*, Addis Ababa: EMIS, Planning and Resource Mobilization Directorate.

Miyawaki, Y. and Ishihara, M. (2005) 'Creating the peripheral area and constructing Ethiopia as nation', in K. Fukui (ed.) *Socialized Ecological Resources*, Kyoto: Kyoto University Press, pp. 1–32 (in Japanese).

Neisser, U. (1982) 'John Dean's memory: A case study', *Selections and Commentary, Memory Observed: Remembering in Natural Contexts*, San Francisco and Oxford: W.H. Freeman and Company, pp. 139–59.

Naty, A. (2005) 'Protestant Christianity among the Aari people of southwest Ethiopia, 1950–1990', in B. Verena, S. Kaplan, A. Martínez d'Alòs-Moner and E. Sokolinskaia (eds.), *Ethiopia and the Missions: Historical and Anthropological Insights*, Munster: Lit Verlag, pp. 141–52.

Shigeta, M. (1993) 'Aari people', in Shinano Mainichi Shinbunsha (ed.), *People in the World: Dark and Light Side, Vol. 2*, Tokyo: Akashi Shoten, pp. 103–12 (in Japanese).

----------(2013) 'Introduction', *ZAIRAICHI: Gender-Based Knowledge and Techniques in Africa*, p. 1 (in Japanese).

----------(2014) 'Local knowledge on Agriculture in Africa', in M. Matsuda (ed.) *Readers for Learning African Societies,* Kyoto: Sekaishisosha, pp. 240–53 (in Japanese).

Takagi, K. (2006) *Psychology on Testimony in Court*, Tokyo: Chuko Shinsho (in Japanese).

Photo 1: The *ensete* that is native to Ethiopia is a perennial crop that grows up to five meters tall. This crop is indispensable to the Aari people, who practise intensive agriculture, as it offers a stable supply of food. In the course of their daily activities, Aari children learn sophisticated techniques for cultivating *ensete* and the names of the varieties of *ensete*. Such ZAIRAICHI (local knowledge) is steadily spreading among outsiders who moved into the area.

Photo 2: Upon graduation with BA degree in 1988, the son returned to his village to rejoice his achievement that marked the realisation of his father's dream. The son started his life and career as a university lecturer in the capital Addis Ababa. Since his graduation, the son has been supporting his parents, inspiring the younger generation and promoting modern education in Aari. While the father did spend a short period of time recuperating in Addis Ababa where his son lives, he strongly desired to live in his village and subsist on the *ensete*, taro and other crops grown there.

Chapter 12

Incompleteness and Conviviality:
A Reflection on International Research Collaboration
from an African Perspective

Francis B. Nyamnjoh

12.1. Introduction

When I accepted the invitation to deliver a keynote address on conviviality and African potentials in Yaounde in December 2014, I was excited by the prospect of collaborative research between African and Japanese scholars. At the conference I was encouraged to see Japanese scholars doing joint research on various aspects of co-existence and conflict resolution with African colleagues and collaborators. I was struck by the seriousness with which Japanese scholars involved themselves in the various African villages, towns and cities where they worked, and was more than impressed by the richness of ethnological and ethnographic data meticulously harvested from such long and dedicated periods of immersion in fieldwork. In some instances there were attempts at researching Africans on the move – the case of a study of Igbo Nigerians in Japan and in Nigeria struck me in particular (see Chapter 8, this volume). A question arose in me, in view of all the exciting work Africans and Japanese social scientists are doing in various African countries, about how best to promote collaborative research in the interest of richer results and as a way of enhancing and sustaining a culture of maximising African potentials in the 21st century and beyond. Sitting through and following presentations at the conference left me in no doubt that such collaboration needed to be vigorously pursued, and that its success would depend very much on the model of collaboration adopted.

This chapter proposes a future Africa–Japan research collaboration grounded on the recognition of incompleteness as the normal order of things, and that draws on what I would like to call 'convivial scholarship'. I invite African and Japanese scholars to explore and draw on anthropological accounts on agency and subjectivity in Africa that point to the quest for accommodation and conviviality between the community and the individual as social agents. While cultural meanings of agency and subjectivity have been transformed remarkably by new political and economic developments on the continent, these meanings have themselves continued to influence such developments. There is much potential in ideas of domesticated agency and intersubjectivity informed by universes such as Tutuola's (1952, 1954) which have displayed remarkable dynamism, versatility and adaptability to new socio-economic and political developments, without becoming erased in the process. Adaptability and dynamism are displayed both in macro-level changes and in developments within the family among children. Continuity and change are similarly determined by concessional mutuality. The case for convivial scholarship is foregrounded by a discussion of how ordinary Africans have championed the middle ground of conviviality between modernities and traditions of various origins, to promote interdependence and interconnectedness among competing worldviews.

What do I mean by incompleteness and conviviality as used in this chapter? And what relationship do I seek to establish between these two concepts and the central concept of African potentials at the heart of this book?

Incompleteness touches on all aspects of being and becoming, at individual as well as collective levels, and applies to humans and their relationships with non-humans. Its dimensions include relatedness, openness, enrichment, humility and action. It is predisposed to and predisposes myriad interconnections, embeddedness and inextricable entanglements. The concept of incompleteness invites openness and reaching out across borders, to explore alternatives, and to build bridges as a mode of inclusionary existence. Recognising incompleteness opens the door for connectivity and interdependence, active participation, mutual fulfilment and enrichment. It compels us as humans to broaden our perspectives, embrace the unknown and the unknowable, and to be open-ended, open-minded and flexible in our identity claims and disclaimers.

Humility is the consequence of the awareness of incompleteness and the basis of a critical consciousness. To temper the feelings of inadequacy and despondency, and attitudes of passivity that could result from awareness of being incomplete, it is important to accentuate the dynamic nature of social action in awareness of incompleteness. The idea of incompleteness generates energy. It invites and compels people to reach out, to move beyond self-pity or victimhood, to be confident and courageous, even in the face of uncertainty, and to embrace the wider (and fuller) world and its complexity, nuance, messiness and the promise of resiliency.

Conviviality is recognition and provision for the fact or reality of being incomplete. If incompleteness is the normal order of things, natural or otherwise, conviviality invites us to celebrate and preserve incompleteness and mitigate the delusions of grandeur that come with ambitions and claims of completeness. Not only does conviviality encourage us to recognise our own incompleteness, it challenges us to be open-minded and open-ended in our claims and articulations of identities, being and belonging. Conviviality encourages us to reach out, encounter and explore ways of enhancing or complementing ourselves with the added possibilities of potency brought our way by the incompleteness of others (human, natural, superhuman and supernatural alike), never as a ploy to becoming complete (an extravagant illusion ultimately), but to make us more efficacious in our relationships and sociality. Drawing on Warnier (2009) who argues that: 'a subject is always a subject-with-its-embodied objects' and that: 'identifying with a subject entails identifying with its bodily *cum*-material culture', conviviality could be compared to 'techniques', defined as 'traditions *and* efficacious action' available to 'intimately interwoven' objects and subjects to draw on in the process of identification through mutual production, shaping and transformation (Warnier 2009, pp. 422–423). With conviviality, accommodation is the order of the day. Far from being a threat, other beings and ways of being are always a fascination to be embraced with open arms. Conversation is privileged over conversion, and ritual influences are more amenable to the logic of conviviality than is coercive violence to control others – mind, body

341

and soul – and resources with reckless abandon in a delusory quest for completeness.

I argue that an approach to research collaboration informed by a recognition of incompleteness as the normal order of being, would foreground conviviality in a manner that allows for Africans and Japanese involved in collaborative research to be more open to possible enrichment with creative, cultural, social and intellectual African potentials derailed or caricatured by the orgy of coercive colonial violence and impulse to monopolise humanity and the world's resources.

My perspective is crafted from the vantage point of an Africa-based researcher and scholar, in the hope that our Japan-based colleagues would contribute their insights and perspectives as well on the possibilities and challenges of collaborative research in and on a world that is perpetually on the move. If Africa is part of a nimble-footed world where things and people are permanently in circulation even in confinement, how do we provide for collaborative research that does justice to the reality of constant mobility of people and things African and Japanese? A Nigerian writer, Chinua Achebe, suggests a way forward in one of his proverbs as follows: 'The world is like a Mask dancing. If you want to see it well you do not stand in one place' (Achebe 1964, p. 46). In addition to a general introduction and conclusion, the chapter consists of two parts. Part one makes a case exploring African potentials through the lens of incompleteness and conviviality, and consists of: (a) the potentials of popular ideas of reality in Africa; (b) Africans as frontier beings; (c) African potentials in mediating frontier modes of existence; and (d) conviviality as a currency in African potentials. Part two discusses convivial scholarship and international research collaboration as follows: (e) convivial research collaboration; (f) convivial international research collaboration; and (g) African perspective.

Part One

12.2. The Potentials of Popular Ideas of Reality in Africa

At my keynote address at the African Potentials Conference in Yaounde in December 2014, I made a few claims about African potentials which I would like to reiterate in this contribution. First I argued that popular ideas of what constitutes reality in Africa are rich with ontologies of incompleteness and conviviality that could enrich our conceptualisation and practice of African potentials. I argued that despite their popularity with ordinary Africans and with elite Africans especially in settings away from the scrutinising prescriptive gaze of their western and westernised counterparts, endogenous epistemologies in Africa are mainly dormant or invisible in scholarly circles because they are often ignored, caricatured or misrepresented in the problematic western categories of 'magic', 'witchcraft', 'sorcery', 'superstition', 'primitivism', 'savagery' and 'animism'.

To explore the potentials of largely disparaged endogenous African epistemologies, the preponderantly Eurocentric modern intellectual elite in Africa would have to disabuse itself of the active and uncritical internalisation of the exogenously induced micro and macro problematic categories that have tended to systematically undermine African traditions of knowledge production and the knowledge generated under these traditions. Educated and steeped in the dualisms of colonial ways of knowing and producing knowledge, the Eurocentric intellectual elite in Africa are ill-prepared to oversee the renaissance of endogenous African ways of knowing and knowledge production. To achieve such an epistemological turn, such an elite would have to turn to and seek to be cultivated afresh by ordinary Africans immersed in popular traditions of meaning making – the very same Africans often denied the right to think and represent their realities in accordance with the civilisations and universes they know best.

This is all the more important as African elites schooled in western modernity are all too eager to label and dismiss (however hypocritically) as *traditional knowledge* the creative imagination of what their western counterparts love to term 'the African mind' – instead of creating space for the fruit of that mind as a *tradition of knowledge*. The full valorisation of African potentials in our future endeavours would depend on the extent to which African intellectual elite are able to (re)familiarise themselves with and encourage these popular modes of knowing and knowledge making in the production of relevant, inclusive, negotiated and nuanced social knowledge. They need to (re)immerse themselves and be grounded in endogenous African universes and the interconnecting of global and local hierarchies that shape and are shaped by these universes. In light of our recognition of incompleteness and conviviality, such reinsertion in African modes of thinking, meaning making and knowledge production must not be mistaken for an invitation to a bounded idea of Africa that is hostile to foreign ideas. Rather, it is an invitation to embrace and celebrate the different intellectual and epistemological traditions which Africa, through its rich histories of mobility and encounters with others has, in the spirit of incompleteness and conviviality, blended together into a nuance and complex idea and practice of itself and of being African.

As articulated in my Yaounde keynote, interested modern African intellectual elite would have to turn to popular narratives and accounts with comprehensive depictions of African endogenous universes for inspiration. Examples include the novels and short stories of the late Nigerian writer, Amos Tutuola. In *The Palm-Wine Drinkard* (Tutuola 1952), for example, reality is more than meets the eye and the world an experience of life beyond sensory perceptions. In Tutuola's universe, being and becoming materialise through the consciousness that gives it meaning. Consciousness matters more than the containers that house it. Consciousness can inhabit any container – human and non-human, animate and inanimate, visible and invisible – regardless of the state of completeness or incompleteness of the container in question. Both reality and the universe are imbued with endless possibilities of being and becoming, thanks to the multiplicity of consciousness available to inhabit them. Things, words, deeds and beings are always incomplete, not because of absences but because of their possibilities. Faced with inadequacies, we, every now and then, invest hope, interpretation and mediation in those claiming the status of seers and frontier beings, in those imbued with larger than life clairvoyance and capacity to straddle worlds, navigate, negotiate and reconcile chasms. With the potency with which they avail us, we are able to activate ourselves to mitigate the inadequacies of the five senses, so that we too might perceive what is ordinarily lost to us in terms of the fullness and complexity of reality. Mediators or interpreters are multidimensional in their perception, because of their capacity to see, feel, hear, smell and taste things that are ordinarily beyond sight, feeling, hearing, smelling and tasting.

Tutuola's is a universe where life is larger than logic, and where the logic and reality of sensory perception are constantly challenged. He invites us to perceive things as interlinked and to factor interconnections into how we relate to the world and the hierarchies we would like to claim or contest therein. No condition is permanent in this universe, not even the unity of being. Only the permanence of change is unconditional. Structures are just as subject to the whims and caprices of changing times and the shifting forms of the beings, things, words and deeds they seek to tame. Everyone and everything is malleable and flexible, from humans and their anatomies, to animals and plants, gods, ghosts and spirits. Anything can be anything. People and things adopt different forms and manifest themselves differently according to context and necessity. Something transformed can regain the state that preceded its transformation. A thing can double itself, and the double becomes the thing and the thing the double. Gods are humans and humans are gods. Spirits assume human forms, and humans can transform themselves into spirits, animals and plants. Sometimes a creature combines multiple forms of being – half-human and half-animal or half-plant, half-god, half-ghost, half-spirit, half-male or half-female, etc. – and assumes the consciousness akin to each form. It is a universe of agency ad infinitum, one in which structures exist only to the extent they can be humbled by the agency of those who make structures possible. Agency is not a birthmark or permanence, but something to be discovered, cultivated, nurtured, activated and reactivated to different degrees of potency through relationships with others, things and humans alike. Context matters and even nature and the supernatural are sensitive to context, and, like chameleons, are expected to collaborate with the consciousness that possesses it. Power is fluid, and so is weakness. Both change hands without warning. Woe betide those who invest too heavily on appearances in a nimble-footed world where signs are permanently scrambled and logic forever wrong-footed. Tutuola's universe of tales defies the currency of Cartesian rationalism and its dualistic ambitions of dominance.

In *The Palm-Wine Drinkard* (Tutuola 1952) the supernatural is quite simply natural. Gods, death, spirits and the curious and terrible creatures of the bushes and forests take on human nature, just as humans develop the supernatural attributes of these ordinarily invisible forces in their lives. The palm-wine drinkard himself is quite ordinarily extraordinary in his capacity to collapse the boundaries between nature and culture, village and town, home and bushes, human and supernatural, plausible and implausible, rational and superstitious, primitive and civilised, Africa and the West, etc. Not only is he a composite of the natural and supernatural, he and the world he inhabits provide for infinite shifts between categories through flexibility and fluidity in bodies and a capacity to be anything and to take any form, even the form of air. Something can come from nothing and nothing from something.

Just as there is more and less to bodies than meets the eye, and more and less to the eye than meets bodies, there is much more and much less to what strikes us in things or facets of things. When doubles mimic or parody in convincing ways, what reason is there to argue against a thing and its double being two sides of the same coin or cowry? While surfaces are obviously important and often suffice for many ends and purposes, delving beneath appearances and digging deep into the roots of things is critical for understanding eternally nuanced and ever-shifting complexities of being and becoming. Digging deep makes impossibilities possible, just as it makes the possible impossible. Being and becoming as works in progress require borrowings and enhancements to render them beautiful and acceptable. It is this capacity to enable and disable simultaneously that makes absence present and presence absent in certain places and spaces, private and public alike. Particular contexts challenge us in particular ways to heighten or lower the bar and threshold of acceptability and tolerability. This capacity, Mbembe

(2003) argues, is most unsettling to a fundamentally dualistic assumption in western thought that 'every life is singular'; hence: 'the impossibility for a single and same thing, or a single and same being, to have several different origins or to exist simultaneously in different places and under different signs' (Mbembe 2003, p. 3). Yet the science of grafting is there to prove otherwise.

Tutuola's bodies have meaning only to the extent that and in the manner in which they are harnessed, in full or as organs (Mbembe 2003, p. 17). As vehicles, containers or envelopes (Salpeteur and Warnier 2013; Warnier 2006, 2007, 2009), bodies are malleable, amenable to being compressed, contorted and extended, dissected, dismembered and remembered, and branded. Auras and essences are as much attributes of the parts as they are of the whole, just as the part is in the whole and the whole in the part. What seems more important than the forms bodies take is the consciousness which inhabits bodies and body parts. Even when a body is seemingly palpably the same and contiguous, the consciousness that inhabits it may be fluid and flexible, pointing to a reality that impoverishes fixations with permanence and stability. The human body can assume the consciousness of an ordinary human just as it can that of a god, a spirit, death, a curious creature from the wild bushes or the endless forests, as well as it can project its own consciousness onto a plant, an animal, air or whatever other element of nature is available and handy.

Tutuola's is a world in which being a hero requires being a composite – amenable to shifting bodily shapes and with the capacity for presence in simultaneous multiplicities, in familiar and unfamiliar ways. Bodies and forms are never complete; they are open-ended malleable vessels to be appropriated by consciousness in its multiplicity. Bodies provide for hearts and minds to intermingle, accommodating the dreams and hopes of both, and mitigating the propensity of the one to outrace the other. Bodies are melting pots of possibilities and amenable to being melted by possibilities. Similarly, sameness is emphasised through border crossing and unbounding and fusing identities.

To die in life and live in death is part of the flexibility characteristic of Tutuola's universe. Death is a form of circulation and not a matter of permanent severance of links with life and the living. One is dead to a particular context, as a way of becoming alive to prospective new contexts. Death is a form of adventure and exploration of the infinitudes of life. Death and dying are processes in gradations and by degree. There seems to be no end to dying, just as there is no end to living. People who die reappear elsewhere and are again available for death. There is no such thing as an ordinary mortal, just as there is no such thing as the fully dead. Death and dying are as much a reality for gods, spirits, ghosts and death itself, as they are for humans.

Tutuola's stories constitute an epistemological order where the sense of sight and physical evidence has not assumed the same centrality, dominance and dictatorship evident in the colonial epistemology and its hierarchies of perceptual faculties (Van Dijk and Pels 1996). In this epistemological order, one can be blinded by sight and sighted by blindness. Just as body organs can outsource their responsibilities to others, in the manner of the womb of the palm-wine drinkard's wife outsourcing a pregnancy to her thumb. The stories invite us to question dualistic assumptions about reality and scholarship, inspired by: 'the opposition between the affective and the cognitive, the subject and the object, appearance and essence, reason and passion, the corporeal and the ideal, the human and the animal, reality and representation, the one and the multiple', that tend to favour thinking which: 'privileges above all the ability to reason (*argumentation* and *deliberation*) and the will to power, giving short shrift to the ability to feel, to remember, and to imagine' (Mbembe 2003, p. 2, emphasis in original; see also Mbembe 1997, p. 152).

The real is not only what is observable or what makes cognitive sense; it is also the invisible, the emotional, the sentimental, the intuitive and the inexplicable (Nyamnjoh 2001). These popular ideas of knowing and knowledge challenge dualistic approaches to reality. They question the centrality accorded the mind and reason to the detriment of other modes of knowing. They suggest a world larger than its material realities, where matter is not as fixed as assumed in dualistic rationality. Instead, they focus on what is possible and not just on what exists made apparent by human sensory perception. Furthermore, they embrace the supernatural, and emphasise the interconnection of everyone and everything. We are introduced to a world of flux, where structure is a temporary manifestation of what is otherwise a flow of constant change. It is a universe of self-consciously incomplete beings, constantly in need of activation, potency and enhancement through relationships with incomplete others.

12.3. Africans as Frontier Beings

Guided by the concepts of incompleteness and conviviality, and in view of Africa's rich histories of encounters with worlds, cultures and intellectual traditions, I make the case for Africans as deeply uncomfortable with bounded identities and exclusionary ideas of being. They are more of frontier beings, not in terms of occupying geographical borderlands, but culturally and intellectually. If African realities are not steeped in dualisms, binaries, dichotomies and essences as Tutuola's stories of a universe of incompleteness and infinite possibilities suggest, then Africans – when not pretending, claiming identities in abstraction or being defined and confined by others – are frontier beings. Frontier Africans are those who contest taken-for-granted and often institutionalised and bounded ideas and practices of being, becoming, belonging, places and spaces. They are interested in conversations not conversions. They find abstract distinctions between nature and culture sterile, and seek to understand what cities have in common with towns and villages and bushes and forests or what interconnections hide underneath labels such as the civilised and the primitive, Europe and Africa, the Neolithic and the Bronze Age. With frontier Africans everyone and everything is malleable, flexible and blendable, from humans and their anatomies, to animals and plants, gods, ghosts and spirits. No boundary, wall or chasm is challenging enough to defy frontier Africans seeking conversations with and between divides. At the frontiers, anything can be anything. An understanding of African potentials inspired by Tutuola's universe would see the limitations or futility of continued insistence on defining and confining Africa and Africans through the illusions of completeness of others.

As frontier beings, Africans and the fruit of their creative imagination adopt different forms and manifest themselves differently according to context and necessity. And because frontier Africans do not insist on permanencies, any person or anything that transforms (or is activated and projected into something else) can regain the state that preceded the transformation. Frontier Africans thus straddle myriad identity margins and constantly seek to bridge various divides in the interest of the imperatives of living interconnections, nuances and complexities made possible or exacerbated by the evidence of mobilities and encounters. Through accelerated physical and social mobility afforded Africans and others by their creativity and technological innovations, such frontier Africans are able to navigate and negotiate myriad margins of identity and belonging. Their capacity to straddle physical and cultural geographies enables them to point attention to the possibility and reality of a world beyond neat dichotomies. Their world is characterised by flexibility in mobility, identity, citizenship and belonging. Myriad interconnections, inextricable entanglements and creative interdependencies, despite persistent hierarchies at global and local levels, afford Africans the opportunities to explore the fullness of their potentialities without unduly confining themselves with exclusionary identities. If civilisation means confinement to a narrow idea of reality characterised by dualisms and the primacy of the mind, the purportedly autonomous individuals and a world of sensory perceptions, then Africans (or any other race, class, gender, generation or social category) who feel unduly severed, dismembered, scarred, caricatured or savaged by such limited and limiting indicators, have every reason to disabuse themselves of civilisation and modernity. One is healthier and feels more wholesome saying farewell to such a bare, skeletal or streamlined notion of being human, civilised and modern. It is one's interest and the interest of others to acknowledge that being and becoming is an eternal process of incompleteness.

Anthropologist Igor Kopytoff (1987) recognises this frontier nature of Africans in their social formations. He argues that the largely frontier character of African societies has been ignored in the anthropological fixation on the elusive authentic insider firmly located in 'the unambiguous heartland', to the detriment of the 'uncertain peripheries' that represent histories of mobility, cultural encounters, negotiation and flux (Kopytoff 1987, pp. 3–17). Such a 'hierarchy of purity', informed by an uncritical mapping of 'difference', remains embedded in the professional practices of anthropologists (Gupta and Ferguson 1997, pp. 11–18). Straddling worlds the way nimble-footed and flexibly mobile Africans do in the capacity as 'frontier persons' (Kopytoff 1987, pp. 17–23; Nyamnjoh 2011, 2013a, 2013b, 2013c) is not always positively perceived by those who feel more embedded in either world, especially when mobile Africans behave in ways that translate into opportunism, dishonesty, lack of loyalty or impermanence in relationships with others (Alhaji 2014).

Fundamentalist and exclusionary claims and articulation of belonging are profoundly at odds with the frontier character of Africans and their societies. Such fundamentalism pays scant regard to the reality of those who inhabit borderlands, circulate and operate across borders or who seek to collapse the binaries, dualisms and teleologies as evidenced by both Tutuola (1952) and Kopytoff (1987). Being neither an insider nor an outsider in categorical terms might have its blessings, but it does not inspire confidence or trust among those who see the world and configurations of belonging purely in black and white and in very rigid and frozen ahistorical terms (Nyamnjoh 2006, 2010; Alhaji 2014). Many anthropologists have been just as rigid and categorical in distinguishing between insiders and outsiders, through a tendency to define and confine and to ignore the history of flexible mobility, encounters and fluidity of identities that make 'frontier' communities of African societies (Kopytoff 1987; MacGaffey 1995). The modern African intellectual elites must disabuse themselves of the policing of borders (whatever these are and wherever they are invoked) to realise and harness the full potentials of Africans as frontier beings and of Africa as frontier geography.

It is important for the modern African elites to see and relate to frontier Africa and frontier Africans, not as cheating or being unfaithful to their prescribed cultures and various other administered identities, but rather as people and places subverting the boundaries within which they are confined in the zero sum game of completeness. If the modern African elites appreciate the flexibility with which frontier Africans and frontier Africa are ready to claim and contest rigid modes of being and becoming, then the universe depicted by Tutuola (1952) is likely to make more sense than simply as a primitive world of magic, superstition, witchcraft and fantasies gone wild. They would appreciate the principle and value of a world where one can simultaneously belong and not belong, be a present absence and an absent presence, without the compulsion of the zero sum games of a regressive and stunted rationalism. If being and becoming are an eternal work-in-progress, it follows that identities and identifications are open to renegotiation in part by mobility and frontier encounters that enable purported outsiders to nibble away at the peripheries of host communities, even as they know and are constantly reminded of the prescribed aspiration to commit loyalties to cultures and communities to which they are purportedly wedded by birth and place. Such negotiation and renegotiation is only possible beyond the tokenism of tolerance (Brown 2006), if, as Fardon (2014, p. 2) argues, identification is about 'finding substantive sameness' rather than questing for 'similarity' in the worlds we encounter.

Naturally, such encounters and nibbling shape and are shaped by public opinion, and attitudes to frontier beings are varied and divided. It is not enough for frontier Africans to define themselves. They are often defined and confined by others who feel more embedded and entitled, hence the tensions and expectations of them to make a compelling case for inclusion on terms dictated by host communities. As with Tutuola's palm-wine drinkard (1952), the belonging and commitment of frontier Africans to their communities of origins may not be in doubt, but circumstances can bring them to explore other climes and chimes, notwithstanding the mountains and hurdles facing them in the process (Nyamnjoh 2010; Alhaji 2014). Frontier Africans make boundaries real by crossing and interlinking them, and are better able to contest these very same boundaries when activated to challenge their mobility as frontier beings. Operating at the margins, in conversation with those in their various homes, they challenge essentialisms, play with limits and expand possibilities for flexibility and inclusiveness. Their world is far from one of simple choices, even when they internalise and reproduce the rhetoric of flexible belonging in the ever-elusive quest for social visibility. Their determination to cross and subvert heavily policed borders is indicative of their discomfort with essentialisms and illusions of completeness (Nyamnjoh 2011, pp. 707–711).

12.4. African Potentials in Mediating Frontier Modes of Existence

Popular ideas of reality and the reality of frontier Africans suggest an approach to social action in which interconnections, interrelationships, interdependence, collaboration, coproduction and compassion are emphasised. Sameness, commonalities and possibilities ad infinitum, mean that everyone can act and be acted upon, just as anything can be subject and object of action, making power and weakness nimble-footed, fluid and situational, and giving life more a character of flux and interdependence than permanence. If hierarchies of social actors and actions exist, it is reassuring to know that nothing is permanent or singular about the nature, order and form of such hierarchies. Humans and non-humans, animate and inanimate, visible and invisible, are active agents in the manner depicted by Tutuola (1952) in *The Palm-Wine Drinkard*. Agency is available and affordable to humans as singular, plural and composite beings – whole or dis(re)membered – and in human or non-human forms, apparent or virtual.

Commitment to conversations across divides make Africans steeped in similar Tutuola-like universes express discomfort with the suggestion of autonomous action, that humans are the only actors or that the individual is the only unit of analysis for human action. In these universes where to be incomplete is normal and where dualisms are de-emphasised and frontier thinking, representation and practice recognised and championed, domesticated agency and subjectivity are prioritised and celebrated as the *modus vivendi*. In the absence of permanence, the freedom to pursue individual or group goals exists within a socially predetermined frame that emphasises collective interests at the same time that it allows for individual creativity and self-activation. Social visibility derives from (or is facilitated by) being interconnected with other humans and the wider world of nature, the supernatural and the imaginary in a communion of interests. Being social is not limited to familiar circles or to fellow humans, as it is expected that even the passing stranger (human or otherwise, natural or supernatural) from a distant land or from out of this world should benefit from the sociality that one has cultivated on familiar shores. The logic of collective action that underpins the privileging of interconnections and frontier beings is instructive in a situation where nothing but change is permanent. The tendency towards temporality, transience or impermanence calls for individuals to de-emphasise or domesticate personal success and maximise collective endeavours (Nyamnjoh 2002, pp. 115–116). Paradoxical as it may seem, individuals maximise their interests best when these are pursued in recognition and respect for the incompleteness of being and being interconnected with incomplete others and in communion with collective interests. This is something that does not depend simply on the goodwill of fellow social actors, but on a community or society providing an ordered environment in which all actors, in their incompleteness, can foster various ends, personal and/or otherwise.

12.5. Conviviality as a Currency in African Potentials

In my Yaounde keynote, I suggested that the future of African potentials could maximise or capitalise upon the currency of conviviality in popular African ideas of reality and social action. What exactly do I mean by conviviality?

Let us be generous to all those who claim that humans are, without exception, self-interested, calculating, manipulative creatures who toil selfishly and self-centredly night and day to maximise their interests – pursue, achieve and maintain completeness, so to speak – through making rational choices. What form does this take in a context of competing interests and unequal distribution of power, resources and opportunities? How do individuals maximise opportunities and minimise opportunisms in their interactions with one another? I suggest that conviviality as the recognition and celebration of incompleteness is needed to temper the quest for and opportunism in individual fulfilment. This is achievable with carefully negotiated collective interests through provision for the incompleteness of others, not as something negative but as a source of potency.

In rational choice circles, agency is often emphasised as being an individual navigation of social structures through the singular drive and confidence to act in self-fulfilment and unmitigated freedom. A less dualistic framework that recognises the sociality of being human through the normalcy of incompleteness calls for a consideration of intersubjective agency: 'how are individuals able to be who they are through relationships with others?' (Nyamnjoh 2002, p. 111). The group is more than just a composite of individual interests, selfishly pursued. Both group and individual are incomplete, as are individuals and groups. Conviviality allows for the empowerment of the individual and group alike, not the marginalisation of one by or for the other. It implies a sense of accommodating togetherness beyond mere *tolerance* (Brown 2016), where individuals can express themselves in a hospitable space but may also have to exercise restraint to maintain the comforts of being part of the full.

Callahan (2012) argues that conviviality is fundamental to being human – biologically and socially – and necessary for processes of social renewal and regeneration or, in particular contexts, reconstruction. To make his case for 'collective subjectivity', Callahan reiterates the importance of conviviality as a tool for activating human capacity to manage social transformation, drawing inspiration from anti-colonial, anti-capitalist and anti-state struggles inspired and facilitated by conviviality in the Americas. His case for conviviality as a tool for strategic mobilisation in the service of collective subjectivity draws on and enriches Illich's (1973) 'tools of conviviality' that afford individuals who employ them the fullest opportunities to enrich their environment with their vision and self-realisation. Conviviality is a popular concept across and even beyond the social sciences, with authors employing it to depict diversity, tolerance, trust, equality, inclusiveness, cohabitation, coexistence, mutual accommodation, interaction, interdependence, getting along, generosity, hospitality, congeniality, festivity, civility and privileging peace over conflict, among other forms of sociality (Caire and Van Der Torre 2010; Gilroy 2004; Karner and Parker 2011; Maitland 2008; Noble 2013; Vigneswaran 2014; Wessendorf 2014; Williams and Stroud 2013; Wise and Velayutham 2014).

Conviviality emphasises unrestrained sociality beyond its most familiar sense of festivity and hilarity. It involves more than the suggestion of good company where enmity and gloom have no place, and where an individual or group can legitimately afford to be merry, jolly, cheerful, hearty, genial, friendly and jovial. Conviviality tasks us to go beyond simply providing for a setting where one, like Tutuola's palm-wine drunkard, can risk a glass too many and be hilarious in the extreme, without fear of being taken advantage of. It works on the tacit or overt understanding that no one has the monopoly of incompleteness. Conviviality is a disposition that constantly challenges us to go beyond tolerance with accommodating processes, institutions and practices that enshrine and emphasise good-fellowship and feelings of security that one – in one's incompleteness – is part of a whole, imbued with the spirit of togetherness, interpenetration, interdependence and intersubjectivity. Conviviality stresses the pursuit of sameness and commonalities by bridging divides and facilitating interconnections.

In a context of recognised and well-represented incompleteness, there is a shared imperative for harmony and collective success, as everyone intuitively recognises the relevance and importance of interdependence. Maintained by and actively cultivating mechanisms for dealing with animosity, a convivial society prioritises: 'amiable, intimate sets of relationships which carry, as well, a notion of peace and equality' (Overing and Passes 2000, p. 14).

In a context where reality is more than meets the eye and matters are far from fixed, life becomes a process of negotiating and navigating possibilities of being and becoming. Being a constant work-in-progress, conviviality involves competing agentive forces which need a negotiated understanding of social reproduction and contestation. If the agents are states, interest blocs or universes, conviviality is about privileging dialogue and consensus over zero sum games through coercive violence. In cosmopolitan contexts (both urban and rural, given the frontier nature of African societies) and between communities (local, national, regional and global) tactical alliances informed by mutual needs and aspirations are the building blocks of conviviality. Frontier Africans are able to mediate with the truth of their circumstances and negotiate the limits of their conviviality with the state and, in turn, create new channels that contribute to their social networks of encounters and cooperation despite grand narratives of exclusion. Conviviality is maintained by a sense of community affirmation through network-based relationships. The strategic cultivation and maintenance of networks enhances conviviality in significant ways, especially in cosmopolitan settings where migrants from different backgrounds and origins are compelled to adapt to fit in, flourish or survive in their incompleteness. Conviviality is experienced in the very cramped nature of inner cities, emerging in the precariousness of living together under tense circumstances. Population density and diversity reflect the reality of cities as places and spaces of incompleteness, requiring trust, interdependence, solidarity and mutual support to get by (Brudvig 2014, pp. 38–72; Nyamnjoh and Brudvig 2014a, 2014b). In their call for a 'politics of conviviality', Hinchliffe and Whatmore (2006) see no reason why such negotiation and accommodation in the messy business of living together should be confined to humans, when urban spaces are home to all manner of inhabitants, human and non-human, natural and non-natural, visible and invisible. Caire and Van Der Torre (2010) make a similar argument for computer science and the development of ambient technologies.

Conviviality often emerges from the delusory and elusive search for autonomy and in contexts of dreams of completeness through violence, hostility and conflict. Far from denying or downplaying the existence of animosity, hostility, aversion and conflict, conviviality recognises that social life is a contested terrain of tensions and conflicts needing a careful balance of intimacy and distance in relationships between social categories and interests generated or informed by them (Karner and Parker 2011; Noble 2013; Vigneswaran 2014 Wessendorf 2014 Williams and Stroud 2013; Wise and Velayutham 2014). Conviviality as a negotiation of tensions between intimacy and distance, Luepnitz (2002) argues, entails a daily struggle by individuals and communities to: 'balance privacy and community, concern for self and others' (Luepnitz 2002, p. 53). In this regard, Schopenhauer's (see Farmer 1998; Luepnitz 2002) conviviality of the porcupines is instructive. Determined to keep from freezing by huddling together in winter, Schopenhauer (Farmer 1998; Luepnitz 2002) recounts the fable of porcupines compelled to negotiate just the right distance from one another, challenged to avoid poking one another with their quills. They had to be close enough to keep warm, but distant enough to avoid the pain of the quills (Farmer 1998, p. 422; Luepnitz 2002, p. 53). In such contexts of manifest incompleteness, meaning and belonging or conviviality are negotiated on the basis of a fine line of tolerance and respect, catalysed or imposed by necessity (Brudvig 2014, p. 74). Hay (2014) suggests we look for conviviality 'at the edge of conflict', where people avoid going over the precipice by: 'working out tensions positively' (Hay 2014, p. 4). In the case of the Bay Community Church in Cape Town, a church that brings together South African nationals and immigrants from various African countries, conviviality is an ongoing process that: 'depends both on the agency and aspirations of the individuals involved and on ways in which their subjectivity is governed, such as through religious rituals' (Hay 2014, p. 4). Where completeness is stubbornly pursued without sensitivity to the reality of full autonomy as an ultimate illusion: 'conviviality is not a constant state of relations but a process of building and remaking relationships in order to achieve a balance between intimacy and distance' (Hay 2014, p. 31) or: 'between getting close but not too close' (Hay 2014, p. 60).

Mobile encounters by and with incompleteness involve experiments with multiple, layered and shifting identities, which are tried and tested through convivial interactions. Urbanites desperately seeking (however misguided) completeness are like porcupines, their quills spanning out to protect against even the most warm-hearted neighbours. With defensive quills they aspire to create 'protective' barriers, reasserting notions of 'self' and distancing from the 'other'. Yet, every daily experience of the tensions and dangers of quills are subtle calls to recognise the normalcy of incompleteness, and detect and institutionalise ongoing strategies towards conviviality for all porcupines involved. Once the illusion of completeness is mitigated, the need to create space for one another to get by begins to be considered seriously by urban Africans. Their relationships as 'intimate strangers' in their incompleteness demonstrate the thorny paradoxes of intimacy and mutuality and are representative of contestations of regressive forms of belonging. Conviviality rests on the nuances inscribed and imbibed in everyday relations by individuals and communities at micro and macro levels, within and between societies. It involves cultivating and sustaining accommodating and interdependent styles of relating, of sociability and communality through careful and innovative negotiation of the constructive and destructive dimensions of being human. Providing for the reality of incompleteness as the norm, urban conviviality has little room for neat dichotomies emphasising distinct places and spaces for different social categories and hierarchies. Urbanites, like porcupines compelled to huddle together to keep warm in winter, can ill-afford to insist on rising above the messiness of everyday realities. Individuals learn to meander through the spatial and conceptual intricacies of everyday life in the city, accommodating one another socially, economically and otherwise, as the surest way of survival, getting by and aspiring for the good life. It is in this sense that conviviality is a frontier disposition *par excellence*, enabling social actors to delicately negotiate, navigate and balance the real or potential tensions, eruptions, outrage and violence of the various identity margins they straddle with conversations of unity in diversity (Brudvig 2014; Nyamnjoh 2002; Nyamnjoh and Brudvig 2014a, 2014b).

The entangled, interconnected or even mangled lives of urbanites suggest an approach at understanding conviviality as emerging from trends towards accommodation and hospitality for fluid identities learned in the face of uprootedness. Conviviality emerges out of the necessity to surmount tensions and divisions with attempts at flexibility propelled by the need to get by. Conviviality is fostered by the dynamics of mutual need and the prospects of mutual gain. In urban buses and other forms of public transportation, for example, conviviality is dependent upon a web of social and economic relations between drivers and passengers, whose differences (which are often confronted in public spaces of mobilities) must be put aside, if only momentarily, in order for individuals to continue to reap mutual benefit. For many trapped in crammed ghettos, conviviality provides rare occasions to fulfil their expectations of citizenship, which is otherwise confined to abstract statements in constitutions and public pronouncements by politicians. Conviviality may be a difficult force to cultivate and maintain, requiring vigilance and even suffering in order to collectively deter negativity and maintain accessibility of a service as critical as daily transportation. Conviviality may emerge from a resolution of frictions which, when turned into meaningful relationships, may actually facilitate mutual interests and mutual trust. The dynamics of social capital and forms of local governance that encourage notions of inclusion and belonging for people whose affiliations to a given country, city or town represent a spectrum of citizenship possibilities, facilitate conviviality in public places of transit such as bus and railway stations and in other public spaces such as markets and churches. Conviviality makes possible interdependence among humans whose tendency is to seek autonomy even at the risk of dependencies (Brudvig 2014; Nyamnjoh 2002; Nyamnjoh and Brudvig 2014a, 2014b).

Some spaces, dispositions and possibilities militate in favour of the emergence of conviviality more than others. Organised religion (churches, mosques, pilgrimages, rallies, etc.), public transportation (*kombis, matatus, car rapid, gbakas*, etc.), sports (football, rugby and wrestling competitions, etc.), public manifestations and festivities such as musical concerts, schools, communal water taps and marketplaces are among spaces likely to foster the emergence of conviviality. Not only do such spaces facilitate mingling and comingling among ethnic or national 'citizens', they are likely to welcome and accommodate ethnic and national 'strangers' beyond mere tolerance. The fact of incompleteness militates in favour of being open to other beings, other ways and other worlds not as questing for completeness but as seeking enhancement through the richness of encounters with incomplete others.

In her study of the Bay Community Church in Cape Town, where local South Africans and African immigrants co-worship, Hay (2014) argues that the church makes migrants feel at home away from home, and presents itself, to locals and migrants alike, as: 'a space in which it is possible to safely negotiate fears or misconceptions about the "other"' (Hay 2014, pp. 60–61). To Hay (2014): 'Conviviality at the Bay is facilitated by the spontaneous and expressive style of charismatic worship, which produces a sense of openness and intimacy' (Hay 2014, pp. 5–7). It is: 'expressed in physical interactions and bodily practices' (Hay 2014, p. 35), and: 'encourages free movement, spontaneity and intimate physical interaction such as hugging' (Hay 2014, p. 60). As: 'vessels for God's love and grace' (Hay 2014, p. 60), worshippers do not need to know each other outside of services to express physical intimacy during worship, especially through rituals and church activities that encourage indiscriminate: 'bridging and bonding' (Hay 2014, p. 60). 'The emphasis on being one Kingdom encourages a reconciliation of tensions towards convivial relations and religion ultimately becomes a greater criterion for inclusion than other differences' (Hay 2014, p. 60). The church is not simply a place of worship. It is also: 'the site of transnational and local networks which migrants draw on for social and spiritual capital, emphasizing a shared Christian identity and habitus' (Hay 2014, p. 61). Such flexibility beyond mere tolerance makes it possible for migrants not only 'to find belonging at the church' (Hay 2014, p. 63), but also: 'to forge relationships that allow them to belong in many places at once' (Hay 2014, p. 63). Migrants are also able to negotiate the obligations and reconcile conflicting expectations that belonging to many networks may imply (Hay 2014, p. 63).

In terms of change and continuity, conviviality is about negotiation between the incompleteness of the past and the present in the interest of a non-linear future. It is often about negotiating between and within animosity and friendship, being an insider and an outsider, desires and obligations at individual, family and societal levels, here and there, culture and nature, Africa and the rest. If all life and reality are ultimately socially shaped, then dichotomies that fail to recognise or deliberately downplay the power of the social in determining reality do conviviality a disservice with the tensions, conflicts and contradictions engendered by such exclusivity and exclusionary perspectives and practices. Conviviality offers spaces and opportunities for mutually edifying conversations across various divides, hierarchies and inequalities. It challenges us to desist from rigidities about what constitutes reality and identities, pointing us towards fertile fantasy spaces for social reinvention. It is in this sense that one can imagine and promote an infinite number of conviviality spaces – political, cultural, religious, economic, gender, class, generational, geographical, etc. – all stressing interconnections, dialogue, collaboration, interdependence and compassion. It is about building bridges and linking people, spaces and places, cross-fertilising ideas, and inspiring imagination and innovative ways of seeking and consolidating the good life for all and sundry. The trends towards increasingly global, flexible and mobile citizens advise the need for a new framework of citizenship that is flexible, informed by histories of relationships, interconnectedness, networks and conviviality rather than by rigid geographies and hierarchies (Isin 2012; Isin et al. 2008; McKinley 2009). Identities informed by the messy reality of entanglements occasioned by accelerated mobility, for long an inconvenience, may well be the indicators for the future direction of citizenship and what it means to belong in Africa and the world.

Part Two

12.6. Convivial Scholarship and International Research Collaboration

As I have noted elsewhere (Nyamnjoh 2012a, 2012b, 2015a, 2015b), although intended as convivial spaces *par excellence*, universities are not as convivial in practice as one would expect. Disciplines tend to encourage introversion and emphasise the exclusionary fundamentalism of the heartland rather than the inclusionary overtures of the borderland. Inter-, multi-and trans-disciplinary dispositions are more claimed than practised, as scholars stick to their spots like leopards and quills like porcupines. Despite our quest for distinction through science and reason, we *homoacademicus* are as much creatures of habit the *homoignoramus*. The scarcity of conviviality in universities and among the disciplines and scholars suggests, and rightly so, that the production, position in grand consumption of knowledge are far from a neutral, objective and disinterested process. It is socially and politically mediated by hierarchies of humanity and human agency imposed by particular relations of power (Bourdieu 2004, pp. 18–21). Far from being a 'liberating force' that celebrates 'achievement' over 'ascription', education, and thus universities, play: 'a critical role in the reproduction of the distribution of cultural capital and thus in the reproduction of the structure of social space' (Bourdieu 1996, p. 5). They are drawn upon by the elite to stake claims: 'in the struggle for the monopoly on dominant positions' and serve as a 'legitimating illusion' (Bourdieu 1996, p. :5). The elite are its primary victims and beneficiaries (Bourdieu 1996, p. 5). Given the resilience of colonial education in Africa, ordinary men and women and the endogenous alternatives on which they draw, do not receive the recognition and representation they deserve (Nyamnjoh 2012a, 2012b, 2015a, 2015b). Conviviality in knowledge production would entail not just seeking conversations and collaboration across disciplines in the conventional sense but also, and even more importantly, the integration of sidestepped popular epistemologies informed by popular universes and ideas of reality such as depicted in Tutuola's

The Palm-Wine Drinkard (1952) and *My Life in the Bush of Ghosts* (1954).

Granted the intricacies of popular conceptions of reality, and in view of the frontier reality of many an ordinary African, nothing short of convivial scholarship would do justice to the legitimate quest for activation of African potentialities. A truly convivial scholarship is one which does not seek *a priori* to define and confine Africans into particular territories or geographies, particular racial and ethnic categories, particular classes, genders, religions or whatever other identity marker. Convivial scholarship confronts and humbles the challenge of over-prescription and over-standardisation. It is critical and evidence based; it challenges problematic labels, especially those that seek to unduly oversimplify the social realities of the people and places it seeks to understand and explain. Convivial scholarship recognises the deep power of collective imagination and the importance of interconnections and nuanced complexities. It is a scholarship that sees the local in the global and the global in the local by bringing them into informed conversations, conscious of the hierarchies and power relations at play at both the micro and macro levels of being and becoming. Convivial scholarship is scholarship that neither dismisses *a priori* nor throws the baby out with the bathwater. It is a critical scholarship of recognition and reconciliation, one that has no permanent friends, enemies or alliances beyond the rigorous and committed quest for knowledge in its complexity and nuance, and using the results of systematic enquiry to challenge inequalities, foster justice and inspire popular visions, versions and aspirations for the good life. Convivial scholarship does not impose what it means to be human, just as it should not prescribe a single version of the good life in a world peopled by infinite possibilities. Rather, it encourages localised conversations of a truly global nature on competing and complementary processes of social cultivation through practice, performance and experience, without pre-empting or foreclosing particular units of analysis in a world in which the messiness of encounters and relationships frowns on binaries, dichotomies and dualisms. With convivial scholarship, there are no final answers, only permanent questions and questioning.

If we have not exhausted the nuanced complexities and fullness of being human, how can we be prescriptive and categorical about human agency? If being human is permanent work-in-progress (in the manner of Tutuola's (1952, 1954) universe of infinities and possibilities), where existence and consciousness matter more than essence, it is only scholarly to consider human agency as permanent work-in-progress. In a world where reality is more than meets the eye and existence defies containment, what scientific justification do we have for crowning an abstract, singular and individualised idea as the one best way of being human? Convivial scholarship provides instead for domesticated agency as interdependence between individuals and groups as autonomous (intersubjective) agents sharing common, consensual moral and ethical codes of conduct on what it means to be, become and sustain being human in multiple ways. This presentation draws on this understanding to reflect on international research collaboration from an African perspective.

12.7. Convivial Research Collaboration

What would convivial research collaboration entail? The mention of research collaboration immediately raises a number of questions, foregrounding issues that need to be interrogated when speaking of collaboration from an African perspective. These may be summarised as follows:

1. *The meaning of research collaboration.* One might ask what research collaboration actually entails, given that every research process involves conceptualisation, elaboration, implementation, analysis and interpretation, and dissemination of findings. The critical issue here is the amount of collaboration in this process that would qualify as genuine, equal or participatory.

2. *The weighting of a contribution.* If one is not involved from the very conceptualisation and elaboration of a given study, questions are raised about whether one's contribution can be weighted in the same way as the contribution of the initiator of the project, and/or of those who fund it.

3. *Position of research assistants and students.* Research assistants and students often get co-opted or involved primarily because they need the money. This raises the issue of whether they can or should be

considered part and parcel of the research in the same way as the principal researchers who see themselves as originators of the big idea(s) at the heart of the process.[1] This is a challenge, especially in the social sciences and humanities, where the tendency is for lone-ranger scholarship and single-authored publications.

4. *Negotiating interests in the collaborative process.* Many research projects involve collaborators from outside of the academy, whose interests may not always intersect or coincide with the academic interests and ambitions of scholars within universities and research institutions. How do they fit into the research process and the negotiation of the collaboration? How to provide for or contain their power and influence might require a careful balancing act, and prove challenging, particularly for researchers dependent on or desperate for the financial support of such collaborators.

5. *Decisions and democratisation.* When it comes to decision-making, tensions easily arise around the democratisation of the project. This often hinges on the willingness and readiness – or otherwise – of the grant winner or the funder to involve non-grant winning collaborators who are far more knowledgeable about the scientific issues and research questions than is he or she.

6. *Publications and the ordering of names.* When publications for legitimacy and credentials are part of the bargain as is usually the case, questions arise about the extent to which the ordering of authors' names reflects the actual work done. Situations arise where the head of the laboratory or the principal grant-holder insists on his or her name coming first and therefore being weighted more, merely because of their laboratory ownership or fundraising abilities. The situation is worse in institutions where well-placed academics who have sacrificed research for administration and management positions insist on being included as authors of publications without evidence of direct participation in the research process.

7. *Implications of co-production and co-publication.* A number of potentially contentious issues arise where collaborative work results in co-production or co-publication, among these being where copyright or patent lies (that is, with whom?). It also questions the meaning of co-production, co-publication and ownership in a

genuinely democratic or egalitarian participatory context – where paid pipers are, nonetheless, allowed to call their tunes.

8. *Hierarchies and collaborative work.* There are different hierarchies to be accommodated in collaborative work. First, given the hierarchies of disciplines within the same university institutions – ones where disciplines in the natural sciences often get weighted and valorised more than the social sciences and humanities – questions arise as to what form inter-, multi-, trans-disciplinary and faculty research collaboration takes. Second, we might ask who counts their luck more for being considered worthy to be collaborated with, and who takes for granted the superior value of their practice. Who is a natural winner and who is a perpetual runner up? Other factors that inform hierarchical relationships in collaborative work include race, place, class, gender and generation.

9. *Speaking and listening.* Who is ready, compelled or expected to listen to whom, and why? The success or failure of any collaboration might depend on the type of communication model adopted in the process by the institutions or scholars involved. If there is much *talking at, talking on, talking past, talking around and talking to, but little talking with* the one collaborator by the other, the collaboration in question is jeopardised. These same issues apply to collaboration between institutions within the same country, especially where such institutions are of unequal status – between the ivy and non-ivy league universities in the USA, for example, or in the case of South Africa, between the historically advantaged and the historically disadvantaged universities.

The questions raised are not to suggest that every collaboration should be at the same level, but rather to argue that where and how in the research process one is brought in as a collaborator speaks of how seriously one's contribution is weighted. In some cases certain collaborators are considered to be equipped only for data collection, and their contributions often earn little more than a token mention in the acknowledgements page or in a footnote on hired hands. Frequently the divisions between the mind and the body, the intellectual and the emotional, the rational and the irrational, the natural/hard sciences and the social/soft/human sciences are all too obvious and present in various disguises. Here, the power dynamics and hierarchies in the research process are also indicative of internalised hierarchies of humanity, and of the interconnections between the global and the local. Many researchers have been schooled in and are very much a part of these dynamics, often seeking to reproduce them even when their rhetoric is one of creative innovation.

It is important to keep in mind, as well, that an invitation to inter-, multi- and trans-disciplinary research and collaboration should not be taken to mean that one can afford to ignore the advantages of a thorough grounding in a discipline, its canons and practices. Many an interdisciplinary study is guilty of lacking depth, focus and scope, and of settling for bits of knowledge from different disciplines, instead of demonstrating compelling cohesion in conceptualisation, design and implementation. Genuine academic collaboration across disciplines should be firmly based within the disciplines which, in the spirit of incompleteness, should seek to enrich their potentials through conviviality as recognising and providing for interconnections and interdependences.

12.8. Convivial International Research Collaboration

International collaboration raises further questions as to what it presupposes or suggests, and whether its logic and challenges are different from the logic and challenges of research collaboration at the local and institutional levels. Beyond funding as an incentive, we need to ask about other factors that propel the need to collaborate internationally on matters of research, which may include the following:

1. The belief that different countries have different research cultures and traditions, and that interlinking cultures and traditions through international collaboration in research design and implementation would yield better results. International research collaboration on specific themes in different countries would allow for comparative analysis and scientific generalisation.

An underlying belief in human progress as a linear pursuit, in which those higher up the evolutionary ladder are necessarily superior to those lower down, and should serve as models to be adopted. That there are countries and regions of superior attainments and those with inferior achievements, and that the 'superior' partners are seeking to share their achievements or the fruits of superior intellects and technologies with their lesser counterparts, whose role in the collaboration is confined to learning, and not to teaching or questioning what they are taught.

2. Collaboration specifically with the Japanese scholars may be explained in relation to the growing interest of the Japanese researchers to work in partnership with African researchers and the former's demonstrated respect for African perspectives. These are evidenced by the 10-year project called the 'African potentials'.

Given the ever growing interconnections and interdependences in today's world, international research collaboration may contribute to mutual understanding and recognition, constructive engagement and revitalisation of the African potentials. In the long run, it could also reverse the on-way traffic of researchers from the North to the South, where the South has been the subject of inquiry by scholars from affluent societies.

If the *modus operandi* of the collaboration were to be otherwise informed and not based purely on conventional wisdom with its evolutionary logic of hierarchies of humanity, then collaboration could be something that does not presuppose, take for granted or define *a priori* who is who in the process and how. Such collaboration would have a number of features. It would be open-ended, democratic and participatory, underpinned by the belief that in research and science no single race, place, culture, gender or generation has the monopoly of innovative ideas and wisdom, and everyone learns from everyone else; a model of research and science as an exercise in humility founded by collective efforts with an open and genuine quest for the truth.

If one accepts that few cultures, races and geographies have escaped the entanglements and co-mingling brought about by imperial and colonial encounters and by global consumer capitalism, then all dreams and aspirations for pure and unbiased work are illusory. This suggests that international research collaboration that takes difference in research culture and tradition in a given context for granted is problematic from the outset. And if indeed there is no such thing as 'purity', and differences in research tradition or culture are more imagined than real, what could be the justification for research collaboration of an international nature?

It is important to contemplate these issues, in order to know exactly what we mean by and seek from international research collaboration. Unless we approach international research collaboration with this presence of mind, we run the risk of re-hatching outdated and contested evolutionary thinking – the type of thinking that pushes us to explain differences with assumptions and stereotypes rather than employ science to open up possibilities for deeper understanding of our world and of humanity.

African Perspective

Considering international collaboration through an African lens brings a range of additional issues into focus. We would need, for example, to interrogate the following:

- What added value is provided by an African perspective?
- What makes a perspective African?
- Is the perspective sensitive to predicaments, experiences, aspirations or ambitions that are African, or is it a perspective by someone who identifies or is identified with a particular racial category or geography?
- What is the identity of those doing the qualifying, and their rationale behind it?
- Is there a possibility that a perspective projected as 'African' may not be taken seriously by those who contest the 'Africanity' that supposedly informs such a perspective?
- The ideas of 'being African' that carry the day raise questions about with whom and why, where and when international research collaboration is being discussed, considered or contemplated.
- Is the capacity to carry the day empirically substantiated or ethnographically grounded in lived experiences, histories and realities of being and becoming African, or informed by a stubborn insistence on the conveniences of contested encounters and unequal relationships?

There is the risk that those seeking international collaboration may be in an all-powerful position – having both the yam and the knife as Chinua Achebe would put it (1964)[2] – able to call the shots both financially and in setting research agendas. And what if they were, in addition, to adopt age-old and long discredited evolutionary perspectives of humanity and progress in which Africa is confined to a particular geography peopled by the black race – a geography and people that could never outgrow nature, and that could be claimed by others without these others being necessarily claimed by Africa and Africans? What would collaboration entail, with a continent and people trapped in the state of nature, and governed more by raw emotions, superstitions, traditions and the forces of darkness of which civilisation is meant to free humanity? Civilisation here is seen as the progression away from raw nature and its unpredictabilities, as well as from raw emotions and its dangerous irrationalities.

What form would such collaboration take? Even if the collaboration were initiated by the African partner, the tendency would be for the supposedly superior collaborators, in the purportedly more civilised (often Western, increasingly Chinese) non-African institution and country to dictate the terms of the collaboration. This would be on the assumption that s/he who pays the piper calls the tune. Or, if indeed nothing good comes from darkness – albeit as a continent and as humans – the non-African partner could assume for her/himself, almost uncritically the role of harbinger and bringer of enlightenment. It is these unfounded assumptions underpinning international research collaboration that many a scholar and research institution within the geography of Africa have attempted to challenge (Costello and Zumla 2000).[3] Those who embrace collaboration without scrutinising the underlying assumptions of their collaborating partners are, even as Africans with Africa's best interests at heart, likely to continue perpetuating the same evolutionary fallacies, which are detrimental to Africa and Africans.

The Council for the Development of Social Science Research in Africa (CODESRIA), headquartered in Dakar, is one of the leading institutions in the struggle against unequal partnerships in research collaboration involving Africa. Since its creation in 1973, CODESRIA has served as the mouthpiece for many universities and intellectuals throughout the continent. It insists on those desirous of collaborating with African researchers and research institutions to channel core funding either directly to the individuals and institutions involved, or through CODESRIA as a pan-African enabler or facilitator of predicament-oriented scholarly conversations. In core funding, African institutions and individual researchers have the advantage of elaborating research projects in tune with a local sense of priorities. It is CODESRIA's preferred form of collaboration, as opposed to the more common practice of a non-African individual or research institution elaborating their own research agenda often without consultation, and then seeking to co-opt African collaborators, with money as the main enticer. How can this be fulfilling as research collaboration when the research agenda is set before the collaboration is established? One fallacy in international collaboration involving African institutions is the claim that Africa lacks capacity, and that capacity building should thus be privileged in various collaboration initiatives.

If the idea of research collaboration at local and global levels is to be informed not by fixations with binaries and evolutionary ideas of race, place, cultures and humans, but by histories of mobility and interconnections, then such collaboration should be founded on a permanent investment in challenging hierarchies and inequalities at every level of the research process. This entails, among other things, thinking of research as an ongoing conversation (among researchers and between researchers and research participants or subjects) in which people opt in, opt out or re-join from different vantage points; a conversation that is not linear, but circular in the way it unfolds. Could we consider research as a marketplace of ideas, truly open and receptive to all that come questing, and where practices such as protectionism are embargoed? Such a marketplace allows for all sensitivities and sensibilities, and for the importance of context, without the impulse to import and impose a hierarchy or a sort of Jacob's ladder of contexts. That, to me, is the sort of international research collaboration to which we should aspire.

12.9. Conclusion

If my experience at the Yaounde conference and subsequent visit to Kyoto University are anything to go by, it is evident that the African and Japanese colleagues involved in this research network are deeply committed to working together in the interest of maximising African potentials for co-existence and conflict resolution through quality collaborative research. The framework suggested in this chapter should hopefully guide us in our future research endeavours. I believe that through collaborative research conducted along these lines, we as members of this network will be able to achieve greater efficacy in our research actions and interactions. The model provides creative ways to activate ourselves to commensurate levels of potency, through the relationships of interdependence and conviviality it prioritises. Working together on common research in Africa and Japan, and promoting staff and student exchanges between Japanese and African universities and research centres, we, as members of the African potentials network, would be better able, I believe, to challenge a social science founded narrowly on dichotomies, dualisms and bounded identities. We would also be contributing, through the insights garnered, to the reconstruction of a decolonised social science in Africa and Japan.

Notes

[1] It should be noted that usually paid assistance for research does not require acknowledgement, but should this continue to be the case under our conviviality scholarship model?

[2] See also Nadine Gordimer's review of Chinua Achebe's *Anthills of the Savannah*.http://www.nytimes.com/1988/02/21/books/a-tyranny-of-clowns.html. Accessed 07 October 2015; Jayalakshmi V. Rao and A.V.N.College (n.d.), "Culture through Language in the Novels of Chinua Achebe" in African Postcolonial Literature in English: In the Postcolonial Web.

http://www.postcolonialweb.org/achebe/jrao1.html, accessed 07 October 2015.

³ See also www.bmj.com/contents/321/7264/827, accessed 07 October 2015.

References

Achebe, C. (1964) *Arrow of God,* Oxford: Heinemann (African Writers Series).

Alhaji, J.J. (as told to F.B. Nyamnjoh) (2014) *A Sweet-Footed African: James Jibraeel Alhaji,* Bamenda, Cameroon: Langaa.

Bourdieu, P. (1996) *The State Nobility,* Cambridge, UK: Polity Press.

---------- (2004) *Science of Science and Reflexivity,* Chicago, IL: University of Chicago Press.

Brown, W. (2006) *Regulating Aversion: Tolerance in the Age of Identity and Empire,* Princeton, NJ: Princeton University.

Brudvig, I. (2014) *Conviviality in Bellville: An Ethnography of Space, Place, Mobility and Being in Urban South Africa,* Bamenda, Cameroon: Langaa.

Caire, P., and Van Der Torre, L. (2010) 'Convivial ambient technologies: Requirements, ontology and design', *The Computer Journal,* Vol. 53, No. 8, pp. 1229–56.

Callahan, M. (2012) 'In defense of conviviality and the collective subject', *Polis, Revista de la Universidad Bolivariana,* Vol. 11, No. 33, pp. 59–90.

Costello, A. and Zumla, A. (2000) 'Moving to research partnerships in developing countries', *British Medical Journal,* No. 321, pp. 827–29.

Fardon, R. (2014) *Tiger in an African Palace and Other Thoughts about Identification and Transformation,* Bamenda, Cameroon: Langaa.

Farmer, D.J. (1998) 'Schopenhauer's porcupines: Hegemonic change in context', *Administrative Theory & Praxis,* Vol. 20, No. 4, pp. 422–33.

Giddens, A. (1993) *Sociology,* Cambridge, UK: Polity Press.

Gilroy, P. (2004) *After Empire: Melancholia or Convivial Culture?,* London, UK: Routledge.

Gupta, A. and Ferguson, J. (1997) 'Discipline and practice: "The field" as site, method, and location in anthropology', in A. Gupta and

J. Ferguson (eds.), *Anthropological Locations: Boundaries and Grounds of a Field Science*, Berkeley, CA: University of California Press, pp.1–46.

Hay, P.L. (2014) *Negotiating Conviviality: The Use of Information and Communication Technologies by Migrant Members of the Bay Community Church in Cape Town*, Bamenda, Cameroon: Langaa.

Hinchliffe, S. and Whatmore, S. (2006) 'Living in cities: Towards a politics of conviviality', *Science as Culture*, Vol.15, No. 2, pp. 123–38.

Illich, I. (1973) *Tools for Conviviality*, New York, NY: Harper & Row.

Isin, E.F. (2012) *Citizens without Frontiers*, London, UK: Continuum.

Isin, E.F., Nyers, P. and Turner, B.S. (eds.) (2008) *Citizenship between Past and Future*, London, UK: Routledge.

Karner, C. and Parker, D. (2011) 'Conviviality and conflict: Pluralism, resilience and hope in inner-city Birmingham', *Journal of Ethnic and Migration Studies*, Vol. 37, No. 3, pp. 355–72.

Kopytoff, I. (1987) *The African Frontier: The Reproduction of Traditional African Societies*, Bloomington, IN: Indiana University Press.

Luepnitz, D.A. (2002) *Schopenhauer's Porcupines: Dilemmas of Intimacy and the Talking Cure: Five Stories of Psychotherapy*, New York, NY: Basic.

MacGaffey, W. (1995) 'Kongo identity, 1483–1993', *The South Atlantic Quarterly*, Vol. 94, No. 4, pp. 1025–37 (Special issue on Nations, Identities, Cultures, edited by V.Y. Mudimbe).

Maitland, R. (2008) 'Conviviality and everyday life: The appeal of new areas of London for visitors', *International Journal of Tourism Research*, Vol. 10, pp. 15–25.

Mbembe, A. (1997) 'The "thing" and its double in Cameroonian cartoons', in K. Barber (ed.), *Readings in African Popular Culture*, Oxford, UK: James Currey, pp.151–63.

---------- (2003) 'Life, sovereignty, and terror in the fiction of Amos Tutuola', *Research in African Literatures*, Vol. 34, No. 4, pp. 1–26.

McKinley, M.A. (2009) 'Conviviality, cosmopolitan citizenship, and hospitality', *Unbound*, Vol. 5, No. 55, pp. 55–87.

Noble, G. (2013) 'Cosmopolitan habits: The capacities and habitats of intercultural conviviality', *Body & Society*, Vol. 19, No. 2/3, pp.

162–85.

Nyamnjoh, F.B. (2001) 'Delusions of development and the enrichment of witchcraft discourses in Cameroon', in H.L. Moore and T. Sanders (eds.), *Magical Interpretations, Material Realities: Modernity, Witchcraft and the Occult in Postcolonial Africa,* London, UK: Routledge, pp.28–49.

----------(2002) 'A child is one person's only in the womb: Domestication, agency and subjectivity in the Cameroonian grassfields', in R. Werbner (ed.), *Postcolonial Subjectivities in Africa,* London, UK: Zed, pp. 111–38.

----------(2006) *Insiders and Outsiders: Citizenship and Xenophobia in Contemporary Southern Africa,* London, UK: Zed Books.

----------(2010) *Intimate Strangers.* Bamenda, Cameroon: Langaa.

----------(2011) 'Cameroonian bushfalling: Negotiation of identity and belonging in fiction and ethnography', *American Ethnologist,* Vol. 38, No. 4, pp. 701–13.

----------(2012a) 'Potted plants in greenhouses: A critical reflection on the resilience of colonial education in Africa', *Journal of Asian and African Studies,* Vol. 47, No. 2, pp. 129–54.

----------(2012b) 'Blinded by sight: Divining the future of anthropology in Africa', *Africa Spectrum,* Vol. 47, No. 2–3, pp. 63-92.

----------(2013a) 'Fiction and reality of mobility in Africa', *Citizenship Studies,* Vol. 17, No. 6–7, pp. 653–80.

----------(2013b) 'The nimbleness of being Fulani', *Africa Today,* Vol. 59, No. 3, pp. 105–34.

----------(2015a) 'Beyond an evangelising public anthropology: Science, theory and commitment', *Journal of Contemporary African Studies,* Vol. 33, No. 1, pp. 48–63.

----------(2015b) 'Incompleteness: Frontier Africa and the currency of conviviality', *Journal of Asian and African Studies,* DOI: 10.1177/0021909615580867, pp.1–18.

Nyamnjoh, F.B. and Brudvig, I. (2014a) 'Conviviality and negotiations with belonging in urban Africa', in E.F. Isin and P. Nyers (eds.), *The Routledge Handbook of Global Citizenship Studies,* New York, NY: Routledge, pp.217–29.

----------(2014b) 'Conviviality and the boundaries of citizenship in urban Africa', in S. Parnell and S. Oldfield (eds.), *The Routledge*

Handbook on Cities of the Global South, New York, NY: Routledge, pp. 341–55.

Overing, J. and Passes, A. (2000) The Anthropology of Love and Anger: The Aesthetics of Conviviality in Native Amazonia, New York, NY: Routledge.

Rowlands, M. (forthcoming) Neolithicities: From Africa to Eurasia and Beyond.

Salpeteur, M. and Warnier, J-P. (2013) 'Looking for the effects of bodily organs and substances through vernacular public autopsy in Cameroon', Critical African Studies, Vol. 5, No. 3, pp. 153–74.

Tutuola, A. (1952) The Palm-Wine Drinkard, London, UK: Faber and Faber.

----------(1954) My Life in the Bush of Ghosts, London, UK: Faber and Faber.

Van Dijk, R. and Pels, P. (1996) 'Contested authorities and the politics of perception: Deconstructing the study of religion in Africa', in R. Werbner and T. Ranger (eds.), Postcolonial Identities in Africa, London, UK: Zed, pp. 245–70.

Vigneswaran, D. (2014) 'Protection and conviviality: Community policing in Johannesburg', European Journal of Cultural Studies, Vol. 17, No. 4, pp. 471-86.

Warnier, J-P. (2006) 'Inside and outside, surfaces and containers', in C. Tilley, W. Keane, S. Kuechler, M. Rowlands and P. Spyer (eds.), Handbook of Material Culture, London, UK: Sage, pp. 186–95.

----------(2007) The Pot-King: The Body and Technologies of Power, Leiden, The Netherlands: Brill.

----------(2009) 'Technology as efficacious action on objects ... and subjects', Journal of Material Culture, Vol. 14, No. 4, pp. 413–24.

Wessendorf, S. (2014) 'Being open, but sometimes closed: Conviviality in a super-diverse London neighbourhood', European Journal of Cultural Studies, Vol. 17, No. 4, pp. 392-405.

Williams, Q.E. and Stroud, C. (2013) 'Multilingualism in transformative spaces: Contact and conviviality', Language Policy, Vol. 12, pp. 289–311.

Wise, A. and Velayutham, S. (2014) 'Conviviality in everyday multiculturalism: Some brief comparisons between Singapore and Sydney', *European Journal of Cultural Studies*, Vol. 17, No. 4, pp. 406–30.

Chapter 13

Revisiting Indigeneity:
African Potentials as a Discourse for Sustainable
Development in Africa

Edward K. Kirumira

13.1. Introduction

In 2007, while making opening remarks for the Symposium on 'Toward a "Humanics" based on Anthropology: Perspectives from Africa', I reflected on the theme of 'Going global, glocal or local: a Humanics of alternative social vision'. I argued then – and this is still pertinent today – that the hiatus between development theory as a national project and as an international or global dynamic is not only characteristic of the political domain but also of the African scholarly project. Scholars like Rosser (2006) in *Achieving Turnaround in Fragile States*, Adésiná, Graham and Olukoshi (2006) on the New Partnership for African Development (NEPAD) debate on Africa's development challenges in the new millennium and Andreasson (2010) speak to these sentiments at greater length including possibilities for post-development alternatives. The 2012 NEPAD Annual Report adds to this debate by highlighting the importance of exploring innovative approaches in sustainably addressing Africa's development, echoing earlier debates on foreign aid and national development (NEPAD 2012; Kirumira 1992). The history, critique and practice of African anthropologies in Ntarangwi, Mills and Babiker (2006), and more recently in the works of Nyamnjoh (2015a) present interesting and challenging perspectives.

Through this exposé, a need to re-read the development trajectory and conflict resolution, and to go beyond 'an evangelising public anthropology' becomes not only apparent but critical. This calls on Africanist scholars, be they African or otherwise, to examine humans in their 'actual historical situation' and to seek to transcend the developmentalist and peace-building frameworks (Nkurayija

2011; Meja 2011; ECA-AUC 2013). We should inherit a critical attitude toward an otherwise dominant (Western-oriented) ideology without setting ourselves on the platform of judgment of what then is the alternative and correct way. We observe that African countries are in the midst of the continent's turbulence of modernisation and globalisation. Reductive explanation of those changes, however, fails in understanding the fertile and vivid dynamism of reality, the inner tension within the society, and social mobility and plasticity. It is in this context that the critique rather than adoption of the discourse of African potentials and the journey to construct and de-construct a conceptual underpinning presents a fresh breeze in Africanist scholarship.

It is important that we build a critical multi-disciplinary network of scholars keenly interested in shaping the debate and interventions related to coexistence and conflict resolution but most especially a new perspective to scholarly engagement with national, continental and global agendas. Among these are the National Development Plans of African states and regional blocks and continental pacts that speak to the social, economic, cultural and political milieu of African peoples. For example, the African Union (AU) Agenda 2062 builds on, and seeks to accelerate the implementation of past and existing continental initiatives for growth and sustainable development. Some of the past and current initiatives it builds on include: the Lagos Plan of Action, The Abuja Treaty, The Minimum Integration Programme, the Programme for Infrastructural Development in Africa (PIDA), the Comprehensive Africa Agricultural Development Programme (CAADP), The New Partnership for Africa's Development (NEPAD), Regional Plans and Programmes and National Plans. It is also built on national, regional and continental best practices in its formulation.[1] These are juxtaposed with the Sustainable Development Goals agenda as espoused in May 2013 by the High Level Panel of Eminent Persons on Post-2015 Development Agenda (United Nations 2013; Evans and Steven 2013).

Suffice it to note that there is a whole conversation around this process of Visions and Agendas development at state, regional, continental and global level and the trajectory of the successes and failures of the African continent's experiences, be they social, economic or political. One example of such concerted conversation is the effort by the forum of the Annual Meetings of the African Academies of Sciences (AMASA). Through this Forum, the African Academies of Sciences, under the auspices of the Uganda National Academy of Sciences (UNAS) commissioned a Consensus Study to examine the transitioning of millennium development goals (MDGs) and what really the sustainable development goals (SDGs) meant for Africa's thematic of Ensuring Country Ownership of the Post-2015 Agenda. To ensure ownership of the development agenda, the Consensus Committee identified and focused on five levers (drivers) of development, namely, the role of traditional communities, capacity-building strategies focused on education and health, capital broadly defined, and the culture and policies of national institutions (Uganda National Academy of Sciences 2014). The Study Report argues that all of these levers are interconnected, both overlapping with and reinforcing each other. Other reflections on the subject include Mukandawire and Soludo (2003) who argue for the broadening of the development policy dialogue for Africa, Jerven (2013) who raises the question of how do we even come up with these numbers on economic development on the African continent, and Nchube (2013) on *why governance and country ownership is critical to development progress.*

Of particular interest for this chapter are the assumptions of an African peoples' driven developmental pathway especially espoused in the African Union's Agenda 2063 Aspirations Number 1 to Number 7. The Agenda enjoins a continent with a culture of peace and tolerance, relying on the potential of African people, a strong cultural identity, respect of person and good governance, inclusive growth and sustainable development, and a resilient and influential global player. It is a conviction in African potentials with an intra-continental and global perspective(s).

13.2. Evolving the Concept of the 'African Potentials'

In 2011, a group of African and Japanese scholars convened in Nairobi to start a rather unstructured scholarly agenda at the time. What they had in common was that all of them, anthropologists, sociologists and political scientists, were active researchers on the African continent with field sites in Eastern, Southern and Central Africa where they have been working for as long as 20 years. The meeting was based on the premise of emphasising the knowledge and institutions that African societies have themselves developed and utilised in resolving conflicts and maintaining co-existence. It sought to provide a platform for understanding how this existing body of indigenous knowledge and institutions – which we termed 'African potentials' – might most effectively be employed in settling conflicts, bringing about reconciliation and healing post-conflict societies in Africa today. The Nairobi Forum was followed by Harare (2012), Juba (2013), Yaoundé (2014), Addis Ababa (2015) and Kyoto (2016) characterised by keynote addresses by African scholars including Moyo,[2] Nyamnjoh[3] and Kirumira.[4] The plot has become thicker and wider, collecting along the way an interesting and engaging group of mainly African and Japanese scholars, increasing the number of research and academic institutions in the process. It has been an intellectually stimulating journey. The promise of an inter-continental and inter-disciplinary network on the move has been operationalised that has had a veiled but strong call for accountability of and on our reflection as scholars in/on Africa, of what we are doing with regard to our contribution to the debates raging on Africa's development and, indeed, its history.

The scholars involved have sought to put to the centre-stage contextualised and 'from below' hitherto underrated values of African potentials in consideration of conflict resolutions and constantly emphasising the importance of avoiding the pitfall of far from romanticising, technicising (compartmentalising), and essentialising the debate. The Forums have provided an opportunity and challenged presenters to reflect on what is it that is inherent in African society(ies) that for example has created for resilience, how do we document or critique the structure and process of these potentials, and how do we mainstream them in scholarly discourse and perhaps more importantly in practice, especially in the political and globalised arena. We were especially aware that both governmental and non-governmental international bodies have intervened in these African conflict situations in various ways, such as peace-keeping missions, supporting the establishment of post-war political institutions and prosecuting violations of human rights and war crimes. These interventions have, however, achieved limited success, because they are based on ideologies, values and processes that are fundamentally external to the conflicting societies or states. Domesticating (if you will) the development debate through the eyes of conflict resolution and coexistence offered an approach for creating for an interrogative and comparative discourse in African potentials and Africa's sustainable development.

The introduction, written by Matsuda, Gebre and Ohta, to this publication gives extensive coverage on the first five African Forums. Suffice it to note that evolving the concept of the 'African potentials' has provided an opportunity to go beyond an essentially anthropological discourse and in turn broadening the scope of exchange and inquiry as well as situating the critique of that that is potentially 'African' in its historical, current and future perspective. Was it a formulation of a research project or creation of a Forum for exchange and inquiry? It begs the question of whether we as Africanist scholars can work together across disciplines, across institutions and across continents, and in the process support and give meaning to a grounded scholarship milieu for the African New Generation of Researchers and Academics.

The concept of the 'African potentials' evolves from a backdrop of global optimism about Africa's future growth including rising consumerism and business on the one hand and on the other, the tendency to assume that Africans are inherently conflictual/violent. The latter is informed by the insensate conflicts characteristic of the African continent. One can argue though that this to a great extent is reductionist perspective. Moyo (2016) points to the fact that while powers in global capitalism regard Africa as the land of opportunity, their interventions produce and aggravate contradictions across society, leading to renewed pessimism. He mentioned that the call for African solutions to African problems has seen various new initiatives to address violence and poverty, although these are not yet sufficient. Sam Moyo's keynote[5] address interrogating Southern Africa's conflict regimes highlights the abstracted framings of the African conflict regime(s) and reminds us of the dominant discourse on conflict tending to be disconnected from local and national struggles over land and resources within the context 'globalisation', ignoring the multi-layered politics which frame such conflicts. The challenge for Africa thus is to release potentials of people's agency to solve Africa's problems, transcending parochial identities and going beyond the dichotomy of 'tradition/modernity'.

What we learn from this is that as we evolve the concept of 'African potentials', it begins to make sense if it is grounded or rooted into hugely African contested spaces such as land and 'sense of belonging'. It is also a call to direct the concept of African potentials as in part an opportunity to challenge and shift the centre of gravity from the Euro-American scholarship to deepen intellectual collaboration in an alternative 'East-South' frame. Such other African contested space is that of the peace-building process. Such grounding of the concept allows us to interrogate what (or if) Africa had anything to offer from within herself to the 'above-and-below' interventions, in other words, looking at African potentials as a harmonising opportunity rather than necessarily an alternative approach/discourse. It calls for us to pay attention to societal cleavages and not leaving them to an essentially international and externally driven frame of/for Africa's development, be it conflict resolution or broader socio-economic development.

A case is made that in African potentials we are not simply coming up with a new concept but that indeed elements of African potentials are found in long historical processes. The historical mobility, flexibility and openness of African society contributed to the everyday practice of conflict resolution, which persists even today despite colonial and post-colonial distortions. We were reminded that according to Julius Nyerere (2000, p. xiv): the 'surprising thing is not that there has been so much political instability in Africa but that there has been so much stability, although this fact is less publicised internationally.' However as we dig deeper into the notion of African potentials and Africa's sustainable development a blanket notion of Africa is problematic, as Africa is extremely diverse in terms of not only ecosystems, cultures, religions and languages but also economic structures and political systems. Secondly, African potentials must be examined in the context of multi-ethnic societies, from a micro

384

perspective as well as examining 'traditional' authorities as potential. Seen from this perspective theorising democracy and accountability in Africa ought to emphasise networking and creative domestication of encounters with others. This focus should check the application of misleading labels, and draw attention to the various pressures exerted on the state and private corporate entities by various groups in various ways for various reasons of empowerment. No institution illustrates this accommodation of influences better than chieftaincy, which unfortunately is often wrongly reduced by scholars to the chief as an individual and credited with far more might than right, and with a frozen idea of tradition (Nyamnjoh 2014). Overall, we start a journey of bringing the conversation of African potentials together, to begin to crystallise and share/create a new understanding of African potentials, which will be a great gift from Africa to the rest of the world fraught with violent conflicts and deep animosities between groups and also to Africa herself in contributing to shaping the discourse around sustainable development as espoused in the new SDGs. Such perspective fits very well in the conversation around country ownership as a projected force in the operationalisation of the new sustainable development goals agenda.

As we concluded the first phase of the African Potentials Forums in January 2016 in Kyoto Japan, I proposed three vantage points, among several, that present an opportunity and a framework for interrogating and putting to test African potentials and sustainable development. First, in terms of ensuring country ownership and the sustainable development goals asking the question of whether and to what extent do African potentials present an opportunity for the implementation of indigenised or/and contextualised national development plans and strategic framework documents. Secondly, emphasising or being conscious of an ever-increasing youthful continental Africa, how we harness this into a demographic dividend. But perhaps more critical, if African potentials are an opportunity, how will they or do they play out with the new generation to assure Africa's sustainable development? This particular concern and vantage point is informed with the observation that estimates place the African continent's current population at 1.1 billion, and project that it will more than double to 2.4 billion by 2050 (Pflanz 2013). To

385

put this number in a global context, by 2050, well before the end of Agenda 2063, one quarter of the world's population will be African. Rapid population growth is driven by an average continental birth rate of 5.2 children per woman, and improved health care services that increase lifespans and decrease child mortality (Bongaarts and Casterline 2012; Pflanz 2013).

The third vantage point is from the position of Resilient Africa, historicising and contextualising the discourse of African potentials and sustainable development. In many cases, strong community networks are credited with making significant contributions to resilience capacity, particularly where they promote communal practices (Cooke 2015). Going back to the 2011 Nairobi Forum case studies were presented indicating local communities as agency and therefore African potentials not as an alternative discourse but as an engaging discourse in international conflict conciliation frameworks and more specifically in Africa's sustainable development agenda.

13.3. The Past, Present and Future

Over the years, the question keeps coming back of *'what is, or is there something* inherently African that permeates the socio-cultural, politico-economic domains' and can be a basis for interrogating and indeed comparing more post-modernistic and neo-liberal discourses that have otherwise informed Africa's development debates and indeed interventions in areas such conflict resolution and peace building, democratic governance and also the flavour of the day climate change and environmental management? There has been a tendency for most development theory to equate development with national economic growth and see the state as its primary agent; consequently, one of its central concerns is to understand and explain the role of the state in development and the nature of government–market relations. It is important however that the African states pay attention to practices and/or solutions from within; otherwise the African states will not only appear alienated but also appear irrelevant. We may also miss opportunity of taking advantage of and learning from coping mechanisms that are all around us but we brand them indigenous or 'local', missing their potential for broadening the conceptual and methodological frames for addressing state and global issues.

I propose a twofold conversation: a conversation that on the one hand is ensconced in a historic-anthropological tradition of systematic documentation or encounter with a cultural interpretative on the one hand, and on the other a conversation that focuses on the present and the future to forge ahead in charting pathways for co-existence, conflict resolution and beyond, emphasising or searching to understand and/or appreciate lived experiences of individuals and African societies. This conversation re-emphasises the need to guard against the danger of romanticising African potentials, and also seeking a necessarily alternative discourse to addressing global issues which usually is packaged in the adage of 'the call for African solutions to African problems'.

13.4. Indigeneity Revisited

The term 'indigenous' has long been used as a designation distinguishing those who are 'native' from their 'others' in specific locales and with varying scope. In recent decades, this concept has become internationalised, and 'indigeneity' has come to also presuppose a sphere of commonality among those who form a world collectivity of 'indigenous peoples' in contrast to their various others (Merlan 2009). This body of knowledge presupposes the concept 'indigeneity' to imply first-order connections (usually at small scale) between group and locality and connotes belonging and 'originariness' and deeply felt processes of attachment and identification, and thus it distinguishes 'natives' from others. Development practitioners have co-opted this line of thought and in turn external development aid especially in Africa being informed by the idea or philosophy of the idea of changing existing practices into something presumed to be better and safer and developmental. In this regard, development practitioners have often been on a collision course with traditional cultural practices presuming them to be non-developmental. Such ideology has often been a strong motivation for NGOs' work on the HIV/AIDS epidemic in sub-Saharan Africa where so-called 'traditional' practices are associated with the spread of HIV and AIDS (Kirumira 1992; Atuyambe et al. 2009). At the same time however development practice has sought recourse to localised social support as safety nets in times of crisis and in resource=constrained nation states' programme interventions. Community support systems ranging from 10-cell household systems, village health teams and community development groups/initiatives like *omugando* and *bulungibwansi* in Rwanda and Uganda, draw a lot on the assumption of the existence of traditional or 'indigenous' African systems of organising and development ethos. Reference to indigeneity from both of these perspectives – one of indigenous relationships and the other of development practice – can signify claims of a high moral order but also susceptible to arguments for greater or lesser inclusiveness, with a variety of possible (and often contested) implications (Merlan 2009, p. 304).

As we go the pathway of African potentials to alternative methods of addressing global issues and embracing the call for African solutions to African problems one needs to reflect on the concept of indigeneity more broadly as an empowering and historicised dynamic of African systems of value and practice, and how therefore this may play out in the context of the contemporary world. I invite researchers of the African potentials to reflect on, explore and indeed interrogate how indigeneity is expressed and understood in our complex globalising world. We need to interrogate and compare almost alternative discourses of/on what indigeneity has come to mean in particular places and at key moments; what kind of cultural, political, ethical and indeed aesthetic issues are negotiated within its canvas. For now, I propose three levels of the interrogative and comparative discourse from the perspective of a revisited and broader concept of indigeneity that have the potential of taking African potentials beyond conflict resolution.

First, we have to examine how the concept of indigeneity is used to negotiate with social, philosophical, cultural and environmental issues. We are reminded of how deeply embedded indigeneity is in the constitution of modern subjectivity and sovereignty and in modern conceptions and practices of politics and, if I may, in the economic sphere (Shaw 2008; Merlan 2009). In this way African potentials as an embodiment of indigeneity provide (potentially) rich insight into the practices, processes, limitations and possibilities of modern politics as well as the contemporary social and political conditions. For instance the Gandhian *satyagraha*, usually translated as 'truth force' that represents power as a moral energy, the ability to transform minds and relationships, rather than the capacity to control or dominate through the use or threat of violence. The emergent conversation is one of 'people's power'. But in doing so it is important to caution that the production, positioning and consumption of knowledge are far from a neutral, objective and disinterested process. It is socially and politically mediated by hierarchies of humanity and human agency imposed by particular relations of power.[6]

Second, the concept of indigeneity lends itself to negotiating translocal systems of power and knowledge. In much of the conflict resolution literature, negotiation is discussed from a third-party perspective. The popular image of conflict resolution is that of the tireless, resourceful mediator who somehow persuades the warring parties to see sense and averts or halts the worst of human tragedy. In the world of *realpolitik*, mediation usually means 'power mediation', in which someone acting for a powerful state or coalition of states 'persuades' the parties to accept an agreement with a tendency to assume a universalistic frame. However in this process of negotiating what often presents itself as translocal systems of power and knowledge it is important to observe that peace is too important to be left to outsiders (Deng 1991; Francis 2002; Nhema and Zeleza 2008).

Both governmental and non-governmental international bodies have intervened in these conflicts in various ways, such as, peace-keeping missions, supporting the establishment of post-war political institutions, and prosecuting violations of human rights and war crimes. These interventions have, however, achieved limited success, because they are based on ideologies, values and processes that are fundamentally external to the local actors. In the same vein, contemporary conflict conciliation has oftentimes invented or laid claim to 'best practices'. It has assumed that solutions (must) come from external to the conflictual context, be it community or geopolitical domain. There have also been instances where institutions and nations have appointed themselves as the arbitrators and reference for conflicting parties, especially in Africa. The role of foreign powers, the International Criminal Court and the United Nations Peace-keeping Forces are a case in point. The discourse of externalities continues to be central to national, regional and international conflict conciliation interventions. Almost invariably international conflict conciliation frameworks prescribe, and even dictate to African communities how to solve conflicts – the communities must be told or guided to what is good for them.

The question of objectivity and subjectivity, let alone agency, is often relegated consciously or unconsciously to the background in mainstream contemporary scholarly debates, in terms of not only directly observable aspects but also to the deeper invisible realities (Smith 1998). For instance in the debate of rituals as African potential(s) for conflict resolution, for healing and for resilience, that have been variously addressed through the five African Potentials Forums that we have held. Even in extreme cases we see in agrarian reforms in Zimbabwe and Burundi where the politics of indigeneity has been at the fore of translocal systems of locus of power replacement (Moyo and Chambati 2013; Bangerezako 2016). Land reforms and restitution processes are used as a way of asserting indigeneity, to compensate for past injustices but more importantly seeing material capital as defining belonging and indigeneity.

The concept of indigeneity lending itself to negotiating translocal systems of power and knowledge proposes that, without necessarily re-inventing tradition, African folklore, ritual and rights, point to the fact that communities are agency – they are actors not recipients – both individually and collectively in solving conflicts across cultures (Augsburger 1992; Larsson et.al. 2009). It is important to understand, or investigate, how local knowledge can be brought to bear not as an alternative discourse but as an engaging discourse in international conflict conciliation frameworks (Daley 2006). The concept also acknowledges the fact that case studies and scholarship abound in the African continent and it is worth taking stock of what is known, what African potentials 'related interventions have been tried and how these help to enrich or re-direct (rather than replace) existing international conflict conciliation frameworks. It is essential to the stability and growth of African societies to find effective means to ameliorate the varied problems these conflicts cause.

Third, there is the argument that identity and self-representation are vital elements of the political platform that a conversation on indigeneity must embrace. By inference, we can argue that African potentials are a vital window through which we launch into the political exigencies of the African societies.

We observe that with the recent and growing emphasis on globalisation of economic and social life, and the collapse of many state socialist societies especially in Eastern Europe, the notion of what constitutes a developing society has, in effect, widened (De Beer and Swanepoel 2000, p. 31). Development theory discourse runs between theory and ideology, on the one hand, and policy and practice on the other. Re-reading indigeneity provides a level of engagement in constructive reconstruction of knowledge production through discussion on its potential as a 'Humanics of alternative social vision' that takes into consideration the problem of politics of representation as well as the risk of blind belief in a given ideal world. The actor, be it the individual or the state, must of necessity take into consideration the problem of politics of representation as well as the risk of blind belief in a given ideal world. Revisiting indigeneity seeks to demonstrate the possibility of an alternative world or worldview and provide a key to make the concept for imaging the ideal society as a bundle of the world of possibilities.

Let us take a case of the revival on 'traditional authority' – the kingships or chieftaincy in several parts of Africa, almost creating states within states. They are often embraced by young people who did not even experience their presence and opposition leaderships and governments trying hard to co-opt traditional authorities as a way of appealing to people's sensitivities, but also from the position of 'the people' as a way of shielding themselves from the vagaries of modern-day state power. We see cases of the creation or recreation of 'African potentials' in the form of real or assumed cultural leadership as a uniting factor but also with potential for a divisiveness that can (and does) serve political expedience – social engineering of identity and self-representation with a great flavour of indigeneity. Case studies abound where such forms of identity and self-representation have been put to powerful development practice, for instance in immunisation campaigns and in the promotion of the girl-child in Uganda where the institution of kingship has been co-opted by the state. The *Gacaca* system of community justice that derives from a Rwandan tradition of grassroots self-representation is another case in point. On the other hand, Africa is witnessing a wave of political appeal to identity and self-representation framed in the context of indigeneity – the 'we against or oppressed by the others'. The African leadership's affront on the International Criminal Court is a case in point. African potentials and indeed the concept of indigeneity begin to play out in the words of Chinua Achebe namely that 'the world is like a Mask dancing. If you want to see it well you do not stand in one place'[7]. This calls for us to make an objective analysis of these revivalist movements that are fast becoming future research themes. In doing so we should be able to tell the whole story without value judgement and self-censorship.

13.5. Conclusion

If African potentials are tentatively defined as capabilities of Africans to bring solutions to contradictions among the people, utilising indigenous knowledge on human relations that has constantly transformed and accumulated at the level of people's everyday life[8], I would argue that the above three levels of interpretation to indigeneity act as a sufficiently robust platform for beginning to deal with the nexus of worldview and the African potentials, *creating for an interrogative and comparative discourse beyond conflict resolution*. Revisiting the concept of indigeneity allows for a renewed appreciation of studies on human–environmental relations and discussion of personhood that extends into the conversation around *ubuntu*. We can begin to deal with more transient phenomena in the Africa continent and to contextualise globalisation or globalising currencies, looking at African potentials in time and space. We appreciate in a more nuanced way African peoples as highly mobile but at the same time anchored, reflecting on the African phenomenon of 'burial ground' and the perpetuation of a mono-ethic settlement tendency wherever they go especially in the contemporary urban space and transnational dynamics.

Two points perhaps aptly provide useful footnotes to the argument of indigeneity. First with words from Francis Nyamnjoh (2016) 'what if we consider knowledge production as a never-ending process of the negotiation of mean?' Indigeneity becomes a dynamic, socially constructed and re-constructed African worldview. Secondly we may argue (therefore) that in the contemporary world, where imposed displacements and diasporas, volatile borders and coerced exiles confuse and obliterate human perspectives, a broader application of the concept 'indigeneity' holds the promise of illuminating and reframing questions of place, space, movement and belonging. How does, for example, indigeneity function as a political, geographical or theoretical category and how does bringing indigeneity to the fore as a vehicle for interrogating African potentials in fields such as anthropology, communications studies, literary studies, gender and women's studies, history, landscape architecture, law, philosophy, political science, psychology, racialised communities studies and sociology allow for new intellectual relationships in the humanities and social sciences? The cumulative effect of all these trends is to continuously interrogate African potentials in a way that demands a connectedness to the local, regional and international community. To do this demands a different kind of capacity of the Africanist scholar.

Notes

[1] African Union's Agenda 2063 (www.au.int/en/agenda2063).

[2] Sam Moyo *African Potentials: Southern Africa's Conflict Regime*, keynote address at the International Forum on Conflict Resolution and Coexistence through Reassessment and Utilisation of African Potentials, 27 and 28 November 2012, Harare, Zimbabwe.

[3] Francis B. Nyamnjoh *Incompleteness: Frontier Africa and the Currency of Conviviality*, keynote address at the International Forum on Comprehensive Area Studies on coexistence and Conflict Resolution Realizing 'African Potentials, 5 and 6 December 2014, Yaounde, Cameroon.

⁴ Edward K. Kirumira *African Potentials and Sustainable Development*. keynote address at the African Potentials 2016: International Symposium on Conflict Resolution and Coexistence, 23 and 24 January 2016, Kyoto, Japan.

⁵ Sam Moyo, keynote address: *African Potentials:* Southern Africa's Conflict Regimes.

⁶ P. Bourdieu (2004), *Science of Science and Reflexivity*. Translated by Richard Nice. Chicago, IL: University of Chicago Press, pp. 18–21.

⁷ C. Achebe (1969) *Arrow of God*, New York: Anchor Books, p. 55.

⁸ See Moyo and Mine (2016).

References

Achebe C. (1969) *Arrow of God*, New York: Anchor Books.

Adésiná J.O., Graham, Y. and Olukoshi, A. (2006) *Africa and Development Challenges in the New Millennium: The NEPAD Debate*, London: Zed Press.

Andreasson, S. (2010) *Africa's Development Impasse: Rethinking the Political Economy of Transformation*, London: Zed Press.

Atuyambe, L., Mirembe, F., Johansson, A., Kirumira, E.K. and Faxelid, E. (2009) 'Seeking safety and empathy: Adolescent health seeking behavior during pregnancy and early motherhood in central Uganda', *Journal of Adolescence*, Vol. 32, Issue 4, pp. 781–96.

Augsburger, D.W. (1992) *Conflict Mediation across Cultures: Pathways and Patterns*, Louiseville: Westminster John Knox Press.

Bangerezaho, H. (2016) 'The politics of indigeneity: Land restitution in Burundi' *The MISR Review*, Issue 1, pp. 12–43.

Bongaarts, J. and Casterline, J. (2012) 'Fertility decline: Is sub-Saharan Africa different?', *Population and Development Review* (Supplement), Vol. 38, pp. 153–68.

Bourdieu, P. (2004) *Science of Science and Reflexivity* (translated by Richard Nice), Chicago, IL: University of Chicago Press.

Cooke, J. G. (2015) *The State of African Resilience: Understanding Dimensions of Vulnerability and Adaptation*, Lowman & Littlefield: Centre for Strategic and International Studies.

Daley, P. (2006) 'Challenges to peace: Conflict resolution in the Great Lakes Region of Africa', *Third World Quarterly*, Vol. 27, No. 2, pp. 303–19.

De Beer, F. and Swanepoel, H. (2000) *Introduction to Development Studies*, Oxford: Oxford University Press.

Deng, F.M. and Zartman, I.W. (eds.) (1991) *Conflict Resolution in Africa*, Washington DC: The Brookings Institute.

ECA-AUC (2013) *Creating and Capitalizing on the Demographic Dividend for Africa*, Economic Commission for Africa and the African Union Commission.

Evans, A. and Steven, D. (2013) *What Happens Now? The Post-2015 Agenda after the High-Level Panel*, Centre on International Cooperation, New York University.

Francis, D. (2002) *People, Peace and Power: Conflict Transformation in Action*, London: Pluto Press.

Jerven, M. (2013) *Poor Numbers: How We are Misled by African Development Statistics and What to Do about It*, Ithaca: Cornell University Press.

Kirumira, E.K. (1992) 'Uganda; Foreign aid and national development: A quest for alternatives', in *CASA, Development Aid and Alternatives: North/South Cooperation in the Nineties*, Copenhagen: CASA.

----------(2004) 'Community construction of strategies for poverty eradication and integrated rural development in Uganda', in SUA Centre for Sustainable Rural Development, *Perspectives and Approaches for Sustainable Rural Development in Africa; Proceedings of the International Conference (18-20 Feb. 2004)*, pp. 32–40.

Larsson, P., Kirumira, E.K., Steigen, A.L. and Miyingo-Kezimbira, A. (2009) *Sharing Water: Problems, Conflicts and Possible Solutions: The Case of Kampala*, Bergen: UiB Press.

Meja, V. (2011) 'Entrenching democratic ownership in Africa: Opportunities and challenges', in *State of Civil Society Report*, CIVICUS – World Alliance for Citizen Participation.

Merlan, F. (2009) 'Indigeneity: Global and local', *Current Anthropology*, Vol. 50, No. 3, pp. 303–33.

Moyo, S. and Chambati, W. (eds.) (2013) *Land and Agrarian Reform in Zimbabwe: Beyond White-Settler Capitalism*, Dakar: CODESRIA & AIAS.

Moyo, S. and Mine, Y. (eds.) (2016) *What Colonialism Ignored: 'African Potentials' for Resolving Conflicts in Southern Africa*, Bamenda, Cameroon: Langaa.

Mugeere, A.B., Atekyereza, P., Kirumira, E.K. and Hojer, S. (2015) 'Deaf identities in a multicultural setting: The Uganda context', *African Journal of Disability*, Vol. 4, No. 1, 9 pages, doi: 10.4102/ajod.v4i1.69.

Mukandawire, T. and Soludo, C.C. (eds.) (2003) *African Voices on Structural Adjustment: A Companion to Our Continent, Our Future*, Ottawa: Africa World Press, Inc.

NEPAD (2012) *Africa's Decade of Change: Reflections on Ten Years of NEPAD*, NEPAD Agency, UNECA and UN-OSAA.

Nhema A.G. and Zeleza, P.T. (eds.) (2008) *The Resolution of African Conflicts: The Management of Conflict Resolution & Post-conflict Reconstruction*, Ohio: Ohio University Press.

Nkurayija, J. (2011) *The Requirements for the African Continent's Development: Linking Peace, Governance, Economic Growth and Global Interdependence*,
http://www.culturaldiplomacy.org/academy/content/pdf/p articipant-papers/africa/Jean-De-La-Croix-Nkurayija-The-Requirements-For-The-African-Continent's-Development-Linking-Economic-Growth.pdf.

Ntarangwi, M., Mills, D. and Babiker, M. (eds.) (2006) *African Anthropologies: History, Critique and Practice*, New York: Zed Books.

Nyamnjoh, F.B. (2014) '"Our traditions are modern, our modernities traditional": Chieftaincy and democracy in contemporary Cameroon and Botswana', *Modern Africa: Politics, History and Society*, Vol. 2, Issue 2, pp. 13–62.

---------- (2015a) 'Beyond an evangelising public anthropology: Science, theory and commitment', *Journal of Contemporary African Studies*, Vol. 33, No. 1, pp. 48–63.

---------- (2015b) 'Incompleteness: Frontier Africa and the currency of conviviality', *Journal of Asian and African Studies*, DOI: 10.1177/0021909615580867, pp. 1–18.

----------(2016) 'Communication and cultural identity: An anthropological perspective', in O. Hemer and T. Tufte (eds.), *Voice & Matter: Communication, Development and the Cultural Return*, Gothenburg: Nordicom.

Nyerere, J. (2000) 'Foreword', in Y.K. Museveni (ed.), *What Is Africa's Problem?*, Minneapolis, MN: University of Minnesota Press, pp. ix–xvi.

Pflanz, M. (2013) 'Africa's population to double to 2.4 Billion by 2050', *The Telegraph*.

Rosser, A. (2006) *Achieving Turnaround in Fragile States*, IDS Bulletin 37.2, Institute of Development Studies, University of Sussex.

Shaw, K. (2008) *Indigeneity and Political Theory: Sovereignty and the Limits of the Political*. London: Routledge.

Smith, J.Z. (1998) 'Religion, religions, religious', in M.C. Tylor (ed.), *Critical Terms of Religious Studies*, Chicago: University of Chicago.

Theron, L.C., Theron, A.M.C. and Malindi, M.J. (2013) 'Toward an African definition of resilience: A rural South African community's view of resilient Basotho youth', *Journal of Black Psychology*, Vol. 39, No. 1, pp. 63–87.

Uganda National Academy of Sciences (2014) *Mindset Shifts for Ownership of Our Continent's Development Agenda*, UNAS, Kampala.

United Nations (2013) *A New Global Partnership: Eradicate Poverty and Transform Economies through Sustainable Development*, The Report of the High-Level Panel of Eminent Persons on the Post-2015 Development Agenda, United Nations Publications.

Chapter 14

The Universality of Humanity as an African Political Potential[1]

Michael Neocosmos

Toute vie (humaine) est une vie ['Every (human) life is a life'] [The Hunters' Oath or Mandé Charter, 1222] [Ancient African egalitarian exception].

Tout moun se moun men ce pas memn moun ['Every person is a person even if they are not the same person'] [Haitian popular egalitarian exception, 1809].

Unyawo alunampumulo ['A person is a person wherever they may come from'] [*Abahlali baseMjondolo* 2008] [Current egalitarian exception in South Africa].

14.1. Introduction: The 'Immanent Exception' and Emancipatory Politics

The Western liberal conception of humanity has been deficient from birth but it now appears to be so in a more obvious way. Although the ideas of reason, liberty, individual freedom, democracy and rights were said by Enlightenment thinkers to be the central attributes of 'civilized Man', they were not applicable to those considered 'uncivilized'. For John Stuart Mill for example, in his famous essay *On Liberty*, 'despotism is a legitimate mode of government in dealing with barbarians ... liberty, as a principle, has no application to any state of things anterior to the time when mankind have become capable of being improved by free and equal discussion' (Mill 2002, p. 12).[2] This conception has without doubt been the core ideological feature of global capitalism since its inception; given that the colonised were barbarians, colonial capitalism could always justify their humiliation. Today liberalism's association with colonial capitalism and thus its ultimate dependence on exploitation, oppression and racism for its existence has become more evident than during previous historical epochs. This is because it exercises its dominance over the whole globe in a manner which is manifestly inhuman. The increasing levels of inequality and poverty, the greater incidence of wars worldwide, the destruction of whole states and the frankly fascistic turn taken by mainstream politics in Europe and some parts of Asia are only some of the symptoms of this crisis of liberalism. Given that liberalism, contrary to its own prescriptions regarding human rights, has been characterised by colonial domination and racism from its inception, one should not be surprised that this continues today (Badiou, 2016). In fact as Aime Césaire was to note, human rights were systematically trampled on in relation to the colonised so that the West undermined its own ideals: 'at the very time when it most often mouths the word, the West has never been further from being able to live a true humanism – a humanism made to the measure of the world' (Césaire 1972, p. 56).

Today, the contradiction between a liberal conception which restricts freedom, equality and justice to a minority while denying it systematically to the overwhelming majority of the world's population is becoming more and more obvious. Colonial racism has yet to be overcome, not least in post-apartheid South Africa. In this context, the search for a true universal which does not exclude supposed 'barbarians' is becoming more urgent.[3] Domenico Losurdo has shown clearly in his history of liberalism that colonial domination was inherent in the idea of liberalism itself. This was made possible by the fact that the idea of freedom and the universality of humanity which it embraced were applicable only to some. The core distinction drawn by liberalism, Losurdo notes in his detailed history of liberalism, was between what he calls the 'sacred space' and the 'profane space' (Losurdo 2014, p. 297ff.). It was only within the former that the power of the state over the individual was to be restricted. He argues that from its inception 'liberalism was the intellectual tradition which most rigorously circumscribed a sacred space wherein the rules of the limitation of power obtained. It was an intellectual tradition characterized more by celebration of the community of free individuals that defined a sacred space than by celebration of liberty of the individual' (Losurdo 2014, p. 309). In contrast to the small 'sacred space' populated by free individuals, the 'profane space' was populated by the majority of the 'unenlightened' 'where the distinction between man and nature does not seem to emerge, or does not play a prominent role' (Losurdo 2014, p. 310). Of course the latter space was composed of slaves, Amerindians, Africans and other colonised peoples whose systematic oppression even to the extent of extermination was thereby easily justified. These two spaces, although they remain continuous in liberal discourse, are flexible enough to adapt to changing circumstances so that under colonial conditions they are easily altered into racial spaces.

Oppression and exploitation justified by racism were therefore not only fundamental to colonial capitalism; racism was also inherent in liberal thought because the idea of freedom did not apply to the profane space which was too close to nature to allow for such a concept. Freedom was therefore identified with distance from natural constraints; the latter required despotic interventions to overcome them. Hegel's comments (for example) which deny a history to Africans are notorious. Although not usually associated with a narrowly conceived liberalism, Hegel provides a useful illustration of a widely held set of assumptions among Enlightenment thinkers. They are worth repeating briefly here even though they are reasonably well known. Hegel maintains that the 'Negro ... exhibits the natural man in his completely wild and untamed state ... there is nothing harmonious with humanity to be found in this type of character' (Hegel 1952, pp. 196, 197). He concludes: 'Africa ... is no historical part of the world; it has no movement or development to exhibit ... What we properly understand by Africa is the unhistorical undeveloped spirit, still involved in the conditions of mere nature, and which has to be presented ... only as on the threshold of the world's history' (Hegel 1952, p. 199). His comments are based on the crudest racist prejudices of his times (1820s–30s).

Interestingly Hegel dismisses Africa in a section entitled 'Geographical Basis of History' where he sees geographical location (place) as fundamental to the growth of 'spirit'. This argument is thus one of the most important formal assertions of the location of subjectivity in place. He maintains that Africa's natural state is a consequence of its 'isolated character [and] originates ... in its geographical condition' (Hegel 1952, p. 196) while he also states that native Americans 'gradually vanished at the breath of European activity' and were 'passionless' and of a 'crouching submissiveness ... towards a European' (Hegel 1952, p. 190), while mentioning that they were treated with violence, although not by any means illegitimately, it seems. It appears that, for Hegel, the accounts by travellers he used came in handy for his exposition as they enabled him to illustrate what his time saw as a fanciful 'natural condition' which was 'one of absolute and thorough injustice' (Hegel 1952, p. 199). It would have been extremely useful for him to show that the 'history of spirit' could obviously not germinate in such peoples and therefore that a 'civilising mission' was clearly legitimate. He notes for example when he refers to Egypt that 'this part ... *must* be attached to Europe; the French have lately made a successful effort in this direction' (Hegel, 1952, p. 196, *emphasis in original*). The reference is to Napoleon's invasion of Egypt; if that part of Africa was to be beneficially colonised by Europe, how much more could this be said to have applied to the rest of the continent. Hegel was not only a 'man of his times' but thought like the European racist state of his times. For Hegel, universal freedom (which he equated with reason) was a notion which could not be applicable to 'Negroes' for in his eyes they did not belong to humanity, 'for the essence of humanity is freedom' and 'slavery is and for itself injustice' this being the condition of nature; yet he goes so far as to 'conclude [that] *slavery* ... [was] the occasion of the increase in human feelings among the Negroes' (Hegel 1952, p. 199, *emphasis in original*); in other words European slavery and colonialism were justified by Hegel as ways of turning the inhuman and barbaric 'Negroes' into humans.[4] For those who may be tempted to believe that Hegel's views of Africans may no longer be in vogue, I can only refer to the outrageously patronising speech which ex-President Sarkozy of France delivered on 26 July 2007 in Dakar, Senegal, and the reactions which followed.[5] Inter alia he said: 'The drama of Africa consists in the fact that African Man did not sufficiently enter history' (i.e. the history of humanity) (Ndiaye 2008, p. 80, *my translation*).

It should be apparent then that liberal universalism is flawed in its very foundations. However, the conceptions proposed since the collapse of the Marxist alternative to liberalism have consisted overwhelmingly in an insistence on identity politics as metanarratives have gone out of academic fashion. Identities, however, cannot help us think 'humanity' and propose a universal alternative, but simply lead more and more to the dominance of particularisms. As a result we experience today continuous conflicts as narrow interests are seen as paramount: whether ethnic, national, religious, age, gender or whatever form they may take, interests in Africa – as embodied in identity politics located within social places and studied *ad nauseam* by cultural studies – have not helped us to think the universality of humanity. Thinking the latter is imperative if we are to begin to overcome the current limitations and problems which the world is currently facing. We must follow Fanon's injunction to 'work out new concepts' and not rely on dominant liberal precepts if we are to think the universality of humanity (Fanon 1990, p. 255).

How then are we to begin to think a true human universal? I think we can begin to do so by emphasising 'displacement' rather than place and also by looking precisely where liberalism does not look, among those who have been and are still oppressed; as they struggled together for their emancipation they sometimes invoked humanity by 'exceeding' in their thinking their social location or place precisely because they were regularly excluded from it. The African experience is of course central here. However, I do not think this true idea of universal humanity is to be found already given in African culture waiting to be 'discovered' and simply adhered to. In fact it is possible for it to arise in any human culture. However, I do think it may exist 'in potential' within African cultures, or even better within what Jacques Rancière refers to as a specific 'distribution of the sensible' regularly available in Africa namely a 'system of self-evident facts of sense perception that simultaneously discloses the existence of something in common and the delimitations that define the respective parts and positions within it' (Rancière 2004, p. 14). For me then the notion of an 'African potential' refers precisely to the exceptional reference to universal humanity made possible by a politics immanent in African experience which allows for a thought of displacement.

I would therefore like now to comment briefly on the idea of the potential or the possible, i.e. something that could exist but does not yet do so but which is also, in a sense, inscribed in the present. This 'something' for me is a way of thinking (i.e. a subjectivity) which is both particular, inherent in a given social situation and which at the same time is able to express something universal regarding humanity which is absent in the current situation. It is 'political' simply in the sense that it refers to a collective thought-practice i.e. to collective agency – it exists in collective struggle. Politics in this sense refers to the actions which people undertake collectively. In particular, by so doing, they become a collective subject through affirming their existence vis-à-vis their exclusion by power. This is very much what Fanon talks about when he refers to the nation being formed by the actions of ordinary men and women in *The Wretched of the Earth*. For example: 'The living expression of the nation is the moving consciousness of the whole of the people; it is the coherent and enlightened praxis of men and women. The collective construction of a destiny is the assumption of responsibility on a historical scale' (Fanon 1990, p. 165, *translation modified*).

The philosophical underpinnings I use here are provided by the French philosopher Alain Badiou. I follow him in speaking of a potential as enabling an 'immanent exception'. The latter is a subjectivity immanent to the situation (it does not emanate from beyond the particular situation so that it is invariably marked by it) and it is also exceptional to the situation (it exceeds or transgresses its regularity or habitual expression studied by the social sciences – e.g. as in the notion of *habitus* in Pierre Bourdieu's work). Badiou maintains that if particular subjectivities are able to have a *universal* value, it is 'because they are not entirely reducible to the particular conditions of their creation but are also an immanent exception within these conditions' (Badiou 2015, p. 63).

> The subject's potential is this, the immanent exception, the possibility for an individual to participate in an immanent exception

and consequently no longer to be a pure and simple product of his/her own concrete conditions, his/her own family, background, education. S/he is all of those things. In a sense, s/he is really all of those things, but s/he also has the possibility, from within them all, to become involved in a process that's a little different ... there's also the idea of a beginning in the immanent exception ... That beginning may not last, but it's not just a result of the past; it's also a pure present, a radical beginning, a beginning that can't be inferred from the past (Badiou 2015, pp. 65, 66).

Let me expand a little. This concept of the 'immanent exception' encapsulates the dialetic linking of the world as lived with the asocial thought of universal equality that prevails to a greater or lesser extent within any emancipatory thought of politics. One way of understanding this idea is to grasp emancipatory politics as exceptional, in other words as 'excessive' of the social; in Badiou's terms 'from an emancipatory perspective, there is always a moment when one is obliged to say that a possibility results from an active confrontation between the state of the world on the one hand and principles on the other; a moment when one can declare to be possible something which the weight of the world declares to be impossible' (Badiou 2012, 9th November, *my translation*).

It is this declaring of the possibility of what the state of the world deems to be impossible which lies at the core of the excessive subjectivity characteristic of emancipatory politics. This excessive subjectivity is not defined by a negative critique, rather 'any [emancipatory] politics is constructed by what it affirms and proposes and not by what it negates or rejects' (Badiou 2014b, pp. 215–6, *my translation*). Yet what it affirms and proposes is always tainted by what it rejects; this is why excessive thought is always in a dialectical relation with expressive political thought, in other words that thought which represents the social, which dominates today in the form of political interests and identities. Excessive thought is what Badiou refers to as 'disinterested interest'. This disinterested interest cannot be represented in the state, i.e. in state thinking for its universality is simply asocial whereas the state simply represents and regulates the social. In fact the notion of an egalitarian state is an oxymoron. As soon as the universal is represented it loses its universality.

Jacques Rancière (1995, p. 60, *my translation*) also makes a similar point: 'any subjectivation is a dis-identification, a tearing-away from the naturalness of place, the opening of a subject space where anyone can be counted'. It is this process that can be referred to as 'displacement'. Emancipatory political thought therefore is never 'pure' as that 'tearing away' is always influenced by the specific context, by that from which it tears itself away. It is thus the excessive-expressive dialectic in its specific form which identifies a singularity as well as the reasons for its eventual 'saturation' in Lazarus' (2015) terms, namely its eventual reaching of a point when it is no longer able to sustain itself and to maintain its capacity for excess. The most common occurrence of this saturation is its reverting to a state politics of representation. Politics then reverts to being exclusively expressive, it becomes overwhelmingly understood as representing class, nation, ethnicity, religious belonging and any number of social entities with the result that all politics is now visualised in one way or another as identity politics. Everyone returns to their allotted place in the social hierarchy.

An immanent exception, sometimes equated with an event in Badiou's thought, gives rise to new possibilities that were previously considered simply impossible; it is that which is not conceivable from within the knowledges of the world as it exists. Badiou puts it in this way: 'It is that which is not there which is important. The appearing of that which is not there; this is the origin of every real subjective power!' (Badiou 2006, p. 3, *my translation*). For example, it was quite impossible for the European Enlightenment thinkers to comprehend that slaves could be fully human, that they could reason, organise and be victorious over the armies of the imperial powers of the time. The slaves' affirmation that they were human in Saint Domingue/Haiti from 1791 was precisely a subjective power which indicated the void of Enlightenment thought for which only some were fully human. Today it is impossible to conceive an emancipatory politics from within the subjective parameters of liberalism and state democracy. An event which opens new possibilities is something which is both located within the extant and which points to alternatives to what exists, to the possibility of something different. It is thus a singularity before it becomes a universal or eternal truth – 'an immanent exception in the world where it arises' (Badiou 2013) – with the result that 'truth is the absolute condition of freedom' (Badiou 2014a). In Žižek's somewhat Hegelian but easily recognisable formulation:

> The authentic moment of discovery, the breakthrough, occurs when a properly universal dimension *explodes from within a particular context and becomes 'for-itself', and is directly experienced as universal.* The universality-for-itself is not simply external to or above its particular context: it is inscribed within it. It perturbs and affects it from within, so that the identity of the particular is split into its particular and universal aspects (Žižek 2008, p.129, *emphasis in original*).

In politics today, and in Africa in particular, which is what concerns me here, a political event would be expected to point us towards a different way of engaging in and thinking about politics, beyond the one-way thinking of neo-liberalism and its form of democracy. For outside of hegemonic political liberalism today all that exists is a void; in other words alternative modes of politics are considered to be impossible, utopian, impracticable. When events happen, they force us, for a while at least, to think of the situation differently. Popular upsurges, however brief, if they are indeed powerful enough, force new issues onto the agenda, for example, they enable changes in thought in the so-called 'public sphere'. However, I do not think it absolutely necessary for an immanent exception to be reduced to an unpredictable aleatory event. This is the case because, in Africa, different forms of the social, different domains of subjective politics can exist at the same time more or less intertwined.[6] As a result, a subjective exception to social identity and difference may emanate from beyond the limits of the hegemonic state liberal subjectivity; it may result from the political activation of a potentiality imbedded in tradition.

The interesting feature present to a greater or lesser extent in thought in Africa consists in the fact that liberalism has not become completely dominant, in popular thought in particular. This is a point which Amílcar Cabral for one had recognised: 'The people ... have kept their culture alive and vigorous despite the relentless and organized repression of their cultural life ... The influence of the culture of the colonial is almost nonexistent in the ... dominated society outside of the capital and other urban centers ... Its impact is significant only ... and affects, in particular, a group we may call the "native petite bourgeoisie"" (Cabral 1972 p. 162–3). Given the fact that the state in Africa has and continues to be an imposition on people and is far from imbedded in popular culture and life, it is possible to encounter exceptions to liberal thought which exist within popular life (to various extents) while being completely inexistent within what counts as the hegemonic discourses and practices in (civil) society, i.e. within the society of sovereign relations. In other words the issue of concern should be thought of not as a matter of closeness or distance from nature (as with the Enlightenment and the consequent notion of 'modernity'), but rather as a matter of distance from the civil realm constituted in dominance by the liberal state, i.e. the realm of relations of sovereignty known in the classical literature as 'civil society'.[7] The immanent exception here concerns a politics made possible by excluded traditions; a potentiality then often already exists within such exclusion which can be activated by struggle. I want to show through three examples separated by long periods of time, that Africans – or more accurately some Africans – have successfully activated existing potentials into immanent exceptions by thinking against and beyond the oppressive particularities of interests, place and identity embedded in dominant culture (and typical of civil society today) in order to emphasise the centrality of universal humanity in any idea of emancipation.

The idea of 'potential' here therefore refers to much more than a slogan, it refers in fact to an immanent potential for collective action guided by a universal conception of humanity. Africans are not exceptional to the rest of humanity in exhibiting such potentials of course. Humans have been able to express an idea of the universal throughout human history. What is important arguably is that such potentials for universality in Africa have not emanated from conceptions usually associated with modernity, although they are not simple leftovers either. Rather it is within what is usually referred to as 'tradition', always transformed to suit the present of course, that the potential has existed, not as a given but as an enabling of the transcendence of Western conceptions of modernity through political struggle. The category of the potential here therefore refers to the enabling of alternative politics (agency) that stress the universality of humanity as opposed to particular interests. This possibility is crucially important today precisely because a universal idea of human emancipation has largely disappeared from the thought of politics worldwide. It is thus not a matter of finding in a given culture a ready-made alternative as in the South African notion of *ubuntu* for example, but rather of providing the possibility – the potential in fact – for a thought of universal humanity beyond the identity determined by place.[8] This thought has been struggled for in Africa over centuries.

14.2. African Political Potentials as Immanent Exceptions

There have been many examples of resistance against oppression – particularly colonial oppression – by Africans. Not all have clearly evoked a concept of universal humanity; many affirmed ethnic identities and the formation of particular states. Below I discuss three distinct examples of a politics of universality located within African cultures. In all three cases it is a politics of universality which is affirmed against the dominant emphases on social location and identity. In all three cases these politics are expressed in a very unique statement which emphasises the universality of humanity. Of course other similar statements exist in the form of proverbs for example. The following statements can be linked directly to a popular political process not simply to a culturally transmitted proverb.

14.2.1. 'Every Life is a Life' – the Oath of the Manden: Fighting a Culture of Slavery

Popular struggles against slavery by Africans have a long history. One of the earliest statements against slavery on the continent itself dates (as far as can be established) from 1222 and is known as *The Hunters' Oath of the Manden, the Donsolu Kalikan* or the *Mandé Charter*.[9] This affirmation is based on the oral traditions of the Mandinka hunters in the area covering parts of modern Mali, Senegal and

Guinea and is said to date back to the reign of King Sunjata of the Mandinka. Statements from the Charter read like an 18th century European human rights document and are replete with the recognition of the truth of the universal nature of humanity. For example:

> The hunters declare that ... war will no longer destroy villages for the capture of slaves ... from now on no one will place the bit in the mouth of his fellow man in order to sell him ... The hunters declare that the essence of slavery is abolished from this day forth from one wall to the other, from one frontier to the other of the Mandé ... The hunters declare that each person is free to use his own person as he sees fit, each person is free and responsible for his own actions, each person is free to dispose of the fruits of his own labour (Cissé and Kamissoko 1991, p. 39, *my translation*).

Interestingly this is not a statement emanating from a state and seems to have inaugurated an event for a world in which slavery was an accepted practice. By 1236, another Mandinka document much more clearly of state origin – known as the Kurukan Fuga Charter – had rubbed out all traces of human equality and freedom and replaced them with a statement regarding the hierarchical stratification of society and the rights and duties of each social group.[10] It states inter alia: 'Do not ill-treat your slaves. You should allow them to rest one day per week and to end their working day at a reasonable time. You are the master of the slaves but not of the bag they carry' (article 20). Apart from stressing the obvious fact that Africans had been thinking along the lines of a universal conception of humanity long before it had occurred to European Enlightenment to do so, it seems important to note that the singularity of the subjective affirmation of the *Mandé Charter* evidently asserted a universal and eternal truth of the universality of the human. The fact that this episode has been occluded in the history books does not lessen this truth.

At the same time it should be noted that the second statement amounted to a subjective reaction by power to the first as it recognised and legitimised the practice of slavery. It thus adapted and moderated the new situation arising from the effects of the universal singularity – and hence the truth – of the *Mandé Charter* by simply ensuring and reasserting that slavery should continue, but now in a 'reasonable way' for 'reasonable' slave owners. We now have a new world in which the consequences of the truth of the universality of humanity are undermined and extinguished but in which the slave system is apparently 'moderated'. This, it could be argued following Badiou (2009, p. 72), constitutes a clear example of the essence of reactive reformist state subjectivity faced with the revolutionising effects of a truth. Moreover it is this latter document that is ironically seen today as an authentic expression of African culture. The *Oath of the Manden*, on the other hand, being an obviously excessive affirmation, has been quite simply effaced from the history books.

It is important to briefly compare the two texts and to note the clear distinction between a conception of culture underpinned by power and one which is purely affirmative. While the Kurukan Fuga Charter is organised around place, hierarchy and the rights and duties ascribed to each social group, the Oath of the Hunters is simply concerned with affirming life over death. It is the universality of life associated with the possession of a soul and the need to fight against death which here provides the essence of universal humanity. Foucault and Agamben would say that the issue here concerns 'biopolitics'. Life had to be affirmed in order to overcome the violence of hunger and the evils of slavery, both of which were closely connected with war and death; its language is that of an affirmation regarding what must be done to avoid hunger, war and death, namely the abolition of slavery itself. The Kurukan Fuga Charter on the other hand is a detailed analysis of social structure, in other words of hierarchies, rights and duties attached to social place. It tells us how the system must function according to established culture in order to ensure 'social cohesion'. Transgression of these cultural prescriptions brings about punishment by power. The statement is written in the language of power, of the state in fact. The Oath of the Hunters is not written in the language of power but in the language of freedom and equality, of the universality of humanity. It is politically prescriptive, not a statement of power.[11]

14.2.2. 'Every Person is a Person' – Freedom and Equality: Haiti 1809

The second statement to be considered refers to the freed ex-slaves in Haiti after 1804, the year the country became independent. A society and nation develops at that time which places itself in opposition to the post-colonial state. Independence opened a new historical sequence in Haiti – that of the struggle for the formation of a peasantry through what is known in the development literature as an 'agrarian reform'. In this literature this issue is treated as a problem of political economy and the state. Here, however, it must be understood fundamentally as a question of politics. The politics of the supposed necessity of maintaining the plantation system was proposed on the basis of its technical superiority, of its 'obviousness'. This probably constituted the first time in which this kind of argument, which was to become the core of a predominant statist approach to development in post-independence economies of 'Third World' countries and a constantly recurring theme in 20th century politics, was deployed. It regularly took the form of an argument for the primacy of 'economic growth', 'technical progress' or of the 'development of the productive forces'. Yet central to this debate in newly independent Haiti was the actualisation of freedom and its consequent extension into equality:

> Permanent freedom had been won through independence. But the masses had not yet won the freedom to till their own soil. And this perhaps more than anything else, sums up what the peasant masses expected out of freedom. A personal claim to the land upon which one laboured and from which to derive and express one's individuality was, for the black labourers, a necessary and an essential element in their vision of freedom. For without this concrete economic and social reality, freedom for the ex-slaves was little more than a legal abstraction. To continue to be forced into labouring for others, bound by property relations that afforded few benefits and no real alternatives for themselves, meant that they were not entirely free (Fick 1992 p. 249).

According to Barthélemy (1990 p. 28), it is precisely the exceptional character of a society of freed ex-slaves which explains

412

the 'egalitarian system without a state' which gradually emerged in rural Haiti. The African-born *bossales* managed to acquire ownership of peasant parcels and the plantation estate system was largely destroyed. The process began in 1809 and was initiated by Pétion who ruled the south of the country while (King) Christophe ruled the north. The forced labour system was abandoned and large private estates were broken up and leased to peasant sharecroppers (Lundhal 1979, p. 262). As a result no *Latifundia* developed in Haiti, unlike in most of post-independence Latin America and the Caribbean. The masses of Haitians insisted on establishing a parcel-owning peasantry to anchor their political independence in economic independence, successfully as it turns out so that the new bourgeoisie was deprived of direct access to surplus labour. A merchant bourgeoisie then developed which extracted surplus from beyond the peasant system and it is on this class that the state was founded which used taxation for the same purpose (Trouillot 1980). Within peasant society itself, a number of methods of self-regulation – largely of African origin – enabled the restriction of differentiation and the dominance of a system of equality which remained at an objective distance from the state power. These included unpaid collective forms of work, witchcraft and secret societies, a common religious ideology, family socialisation and so on (Barthélemy 1990, pp. 30–44). In fact Barthélemy (1990, p. 84) makes the point that from 1804 onwards, it gradually becomes understood by the masses of the *bossales* that 'the only alternative to the colonial hierarchical system is that of equality, more so than that of liberty, as while the latter enables freedom from external oppression, it is not able to take on board the ideological content of the system. Only equality is able to put into place an anti-system' (*my translation*).

A society and nation develops which therefore places itself in opposition to the post-colonial state.[12] Barthélemy (2000, p. 379, *my translation*) refers to this kind of politics as a new form of 'marronage, a counter-culture, a structural and collective reaction of escape'. We can also understand it as a singular form of politics which attempts to distance its thinking from that of the state and which is simultaneously rooted in local traditions of resistance to oppression. Commonly, this subjectivity was expressed in proverbs or sayings,

413

the most important of which was '*Tout moun se moun, men ce pa memn moun*' which loosely translated means 'every person is a person even though they are not the same person'.[13] Barthélemy (2000, pp. 293–94) explains this as a statement governing the world view of the Haitian rural people, for it is more than a simple proverb but reflects a fought for rule of social and political practice. The point is that equality cannot exist without difference and that, correspondingly, difference makes no sense without equality: 'In order to be different, not to be *memn moun* each man must begin by identifying what he has in common with others; what is the basic identity from which variations can be felt, interpreted and used' (Barthélemy 2000, p. 293, *my translation*).

While these variations obviously exist, they are restricted from becoming hierarchical through group reactions which limit the entrenchment of these forms of behaviour; these reactions include the attribution to one person of various statuses in different contexts so that all status is relativised. 'A good reputation, [social] behaviour, personal relations all contribute to balancing out the purely quantitative [differences]' so that identification is sought with an ideal of a 'middle peasant' (*moun mouayen*) (Barthélemy 2000, p. 303, *my translation*). Barthélemy insists that while Haitian rural society is generally understood as a failure, as wedded to traditions and poverty, it is in fact a highly organised social system that is self-regulating without an institutionalised state structure. In order to achieve this, it had to maintain hierarchical Creole society and the formal state at a distance, to block all attempts at individual enrichment and power-seeking, and to harmonise the group through a kind of automatic regulation of individual behaviour; 'all this outside any "political" dimension' of state control' (Barthélemy 1990, p. 29, *my translation*). In this way the Haitian nation (if by 'nation' we mean the subjectively constituted unity of the people) constituted itself in a manner which distanced it from the state. Nesbitt (2008, p. 171) notes that this egalitarian system, 'a legacy of the Haitian revolution, functioned in such a state of dynamic equilibrium from the late 1790s to the 1960s until the destruction of the Haitian (natural and social) environment under the regime of Papa Doc (Duvalier) undermined its viability' inter alia through the systematic use of terror. It should also be

414

recalled that Jean-Bertrand Aristide and Fanmi Lavalas, the mass popular movement with which he was associated, resuscitated the popular prescription '*tout moun se moun*' in their politics during the 1990s (Aristide 1992, and Hallward 2007).

14.2.3. 'Each Person is a Person' – Fighting Xenophobia in South Africa today

The third statement emanates from South Africa. It was uttered by Abahlali baseMjondolo, the movement of shackdwellers in Durban, and was explicitly geared against xenophobic attacks. In fact it was made in 2008 after such attacks. Abahlali base Mjondolo (AbM) contested the reference to migrants as 'illegal immigrants': 'There is only one human race. Our struggle and every struggle is to put the human being at the centre of society, starting with the worst off (sic). An action can be illegal. A person cannot be illegal. A person is a person wherever they may find themselves. If you live in a settlement you are from that settlement and you are a neighbour and a comrade in that settlement.'[14]

Apparent 'foreigners' then should not be treated differently from anyone else, as people have been living side by side for years and faced the same problems; only in this way can a nation of human beings be conceived. Abahlali have been organising systematically against xenophobic violence in the communities in which they have a presence and have been engaging in joint political actions with and organisation of Congolese migrants in Durban. We have in the statement above a complete rethinking of rights as applicable to all and not only to some, to formal citizens. In fact Abahlali attempt to maintain in their politics the axiom which Badiou (2008) has consistently stressed: 'There is One World Only'. In this manner they are rethinking and providing new political content to both democracy and nation in South Africa. Their statement re-affirms the universality of humanity in the contemporary context and attempts to build a political practice on this principle. In fact, during the major outbreak of xenophobic violence in 2008, the areas where Abahlali had political influence did not experience xenophobic violence (Neocosmos 2010). This was because Abahlali had already engaged in anti-xenophobic politics as a matter of principle and also because specific measures were taken to avoid such violence. Today Abahlali organise political events with the Congolese Solidarity Campaign which organises African migrants in Durban.[15] In their own words Abahlali note that this kind of principled politics has resulted in oppression:

We have been working to build a politic (sic) from below that accepts each person as a person and each comrade as a comrade without regard to where they were born or what language they speak. In this struggle we have faced constant attack from the state, the ruling party and others. We have been attacked for having members from the Eastern Cape, members born in other countries and Indian members. We have always stood firm against these attacks. Our movement has survived almost ten years of repression. On the 8th of April we supported a march against xenophobia organised by our comrades in the Congolese Solidarity Campaign together with the Somali Association of South African and other migrant organisations. There was a permit for the march and yet the police would not allow it to go ahead. They stopped people from leaving their communities to travel to the march. They attacked the march with tear gas, water cannons and rubber bullets. One Congolese man was severely beaten by the police with a plank. One of our members, from the Marikana Land Occupation in Cato Crest, had her leg broken during the assault by the police. We also noted senior police officers accusing Abahlali: 'What do you have to do with this march? Why are you supporting them?' One of our comrades from the Eastern Cape was told by the police that: 'You are from the Eastern Cape, you will cause a war here and then run away to Eastern Cape. Keep quiet.' We do not know who will be the next. Some of the people who are now attacking people born in other African countries are saying that they will attack the Indians next. (http://abahlali.org/node/14685/ #more-14685)

Nevertheless despite the predictable violence of identity politics unleashed by the state (which is a regular occurrence in Durban in particular), the fight against the scourge of xenophobia wherever it may exist requires a principled statement of the kind proposed by Abahlali to guide political action.

14.3. Conclusions: Thinking the Universality of Humanity in South Africa Today

A number of comments can be made on all three of these statements. Firstly, these statements are politically prescriptive in the sense that they affirm what needs to be done by collective agency; they are not descriptive or even an analysis of a given situation or world. This point should be clear. All three statements are stressing that in order to confront the exploitation and oppression based on the inequalities and identities backed by power and prevailing in each particular context, a politics should be developed which treats everybody in the same way. Whether we are dealing with confronting slavery, a counter-culture distancing itself from the state or a political opposition to xenophobia, the stress in each case is placed on the universality of humanity and not on identity. All three statements are political prescriptions or affirmations; they define political thought-practice. These attempts to think universality are unequivocally political; they are founded on a particular thought to be fought for and not on the searching for an ideal culture.

Secondly, these statements are separated in time and space but say the same thing in essence. It is actually uncanny the way that these statements are so similarly expressed. That each person is a person, that every human life is worth the same as any other irrespective of whether one is a master or a slave, a man or a woman; in each case the statements propose a fundamental understanding of the universally human despite reference to differences. Everybody is worthy of respect because everyone possesses the capacity precisely to practise this thought of universality.

Thirdly these statements cannot be understood to reflect a common African culture, but rather refer to the potential inherent in African culture for exceeding that culture, i.e. to the possibility of an 'immanent exception'. The idea that every person or human life must be treated equally is not to be understood as a habitual feature of African culture, for it is quite apparent that within African cultures people were (and are) not treated equally; past African societies were not usually egalitarian (with exceptions of course) because states were widespread by the 18th century, for example. This is fully apparent

417

as early as the 13th century in the Kurukan Fuga Charter, for example, which is indeed seen today by the authority of UNESCO as an authentic expression of African culture. Therefore the point here does not so much concern the cultural unity of Africa, but rather the fact that the potential is provided for such culture to be exceeded. It can be exceeded because the thought of the truly universal is existent in African cultures 'in potential' so to speak. There is no necessity for this potential to be 'realised' in any particular case, but the point is that it does not need re-inventing although it must be actively struggled for to ensure its existence. Should such a struggle not be present it is likely to be smothered by hegemonic liberal precepts.[16]

To put the same point in another way, the universality of humanity is thinkable from within African cultures; it is possible for it to enter the parameters of thought, something which is not so easy from within Western liberalism which assumes such universality while being founded on the exclusion of those in the 'profane space' as Losurdo shows. Liberalism therefore would tend to produce resistance in the form of identity politics as a matter of course, at least initially while a category of the universal would not usually be an immediate response to it. Social struggles, in the West – from feminist struggles, to civil rights and social movements – overwhelmingly concern the inclusion of excluded groups within the liberal capitalist system. They therefore fundamentally emphasise particular identities, not universal humanity. To move beyond identity politics one would have to contest and critique the whole basis of liberal thought itself in order to affirm the universality of humanity, which is of course precisely what Marxism did in the 19th century in Europe. Interestingly enough the Marxist response was also founded on an identity – that of the proletariat – which was itself supposed to combine its particular interests with universal ones. For Marx there was a crucial idea of universality inherent in the objective position in production of the proletariat itself – and manifested subjectively in communists – so that its insurrectionary movements would speed up the objective course of history itself towards the abolition of the class system as such. Its political form, he argued, was to be found in the Paris Commune of 1871 'the political form at last discovered under which to work out the economic emancipation of labour ... The Commune was therefore to serve as a lever for uprooting ... class rule' as such (Marx 1871/1970, p. 72). During the 20th century the mistake was made to assume that the universal could be represented in a state with the result that people had to be coerced to conform to this universality (Badiou 2015). In Africa, on the other hand, it seems that the possibility for thinking the universal may already be immanent beyond state thinking, it may exist 'in potential' and 'only' require a process of political activation.

Even though there are clear cultural similarities on the continent, the search for a common African identity would simply end up being another form of cultural essentialism which ultimately ends in nativism. *At issue is not the essence of culture but rather a political struggle for equality made possible through the use of cultural idioms which provide the potential for a thought of equality.* To repeat, the point is not to emphasise the social as such, but the exceeding of the social. It is such excess, emphasised here in prescriptions regarding the universality of humanity, which has defined such a universal politics in Africa, whether in the kingdom of the Mandé in 1222, among the Haitian *Bossales* in the 19th century or in South Africa today. None of these universal prescriptions deny differences; on the contrary they propose to accept that differences are simply given and to fight their elevation into identity politics by insisting on what is common to all humanity.

These prescriptions, it is apparent, were not made by the guardians of cultural orthodoxy, the powerful and the wealthy, but rather by the excluded in each historical sequence. All three of these statements are therefore not systemic but anti-systemic; the fact that such anti-systemic thought is possible, however, is precisely what potentiality is all about. It is then not a question of re-discovering 'subjugated knowledges' in Foucault's sense for example, but rather of a political struggle for a rediscovery of human universality. There exists a difficulty however in that these excessive subjectivities will tend to be limited to the domain of traditional society within which they arise. They do not enter the domain of civil society today, at least not automatically. In fact the egalitarianism of the Haitian Bossales remained largely restricted to the rural peasantry, while the practices of Abahlali have not extended to the rest of South Africa. This would require a collective political intervention in order to occur.

The statements I have discussed are thus not to be understood as part of an African culture to be taught (as proverbs) to children and to those who have forgotten their ancestry by experts assigned by power to do so as with the idea of *ubuntu* in South Africa. If any teaching is to be done, it should emphasise the struggles of our ancestors from all walks of life for an equal and just society and a dignified life. In other words these statements exceed ethnophilosophical thinking – in the sense used by Hountondji (1983, 1997) – and perforce any state-sponsored culturalism such as *ubuntu* discourse in South Africa. These statements are in fact all immanent exceptions to African culture. Such exceptions can exist because after all, culture – in the sociological sense used here – is primarily a politics whose practices have become habitual due to it being underpinned by hegemonic power; it therefore takes the form of self-evident facts. Exceptions are ruptures in habitual modes of thought and practice; they are the activation of potentials which contest the factual. Thus it is possible for these statements to be culturally located in the particular while at the same time being of universal relevance.

It should thus be evident that one does not have to live exclusively within the modernity of a 'civil' society for the human universal to be thinkable. Neither are the statements simply concerned with deploring the destruction unleashed onto black bodies; they do not stress victimhood but the struggle against oppression and for universal dignity. The three statements from the 13th century to the present express the continuing struggle of Africans to affirm the universality of humanity and their place within it. They express the truth that no one can be free unless everyone is free and do so at completely different periods of the continent's history. The truth of the prescriptions emphasised by the Mandé Charter, the *Bossales* in Haiti and Abahlali in South Africa today has been resurrected throughout the ages in a literally extra-ordinary manner. This truth is thus made possible by African political potentials after they have been activated through struggle. It is indeed conceivable that a different modernity could be constructed on this basis.

Perhaps there is no better place to end this discussion than with a re-statement of a politics of universality in the world. In one of his books published during his lifetime, Frantz Fanon – who incidentally chose to be an Algerian African during its people's upsurge against colonialism – makes a well-known statement which puts my point succinctly: 'It is the white man who creates the Negro. But it is the Negro who creates negritude' (1989, p. 47). This statement is clear: 'the black' is a creation of whites, but as a way of resisting, blacks will tend to emphasise and idealise their distinctive identity with the result that the idea of human universality is eschewed. In actual fact Fanon's statement here is incomplete because by creating the black, whites also create themselves as white, something which they were not prior to this act. Fanon makes this specific point elsewhere: 'the disaster and inhumanity of the white is to have killed man somewhere' (1986, p. 231, *translation modified*). In other words human universality was destroyed by the forced elevation of a European particularity into a human universality (by liberalism), through the racial distinction between whites and blacks which was made possible by a specific politics – a politics of whiteness which excluded non-Europeans, most obviously those deemed to be black (see Gordon 2013). 'Whiteness' must be understood as a form of (state) politics which is irreducible to skin colour but which accompanies and reproduces colonial domination in its various avatars. Races do not exist apart from within racist oppressive relations inherent in liberalism itself. It is racism that creates race not the other way around. How then are we to think human universality from within a context defined by such racist parameters?

It is clear that in a society such as South Africa, governed by liberal norms, for anyone to talk in terms of the irrelevance or absence of colour distinctions in favour of a liberal notion of universality ('multiculturalism' or 'diversity' in today's parlance or 'rainbowism' in South Africa) is simply to take for granted and to 'universalise' racial dominance. Blacks must then 'become' white, assimilate culturally and intellectually and alienate themselves from their own social existence. We are then within a colonial process of

421

assimilation and the dissolution of identity into a dominant whiteness. Here the idea of 'universality' is a false one for it remains within the liberal parameters so clearly analysed by Losurdo; it acts as a mechanism of exclusion. In fact the true universality emphasised by the African potentials discussed above can become the object of thought only on the basis of the vanquishing of a politics of whiteness through a principled politics of the universal so that the racially in-existant can think beyond racial resistance and all can relate exclusively as humans. It is not possible to say in advance what forms the struggle against the politics of whiteness will take in any context, but only through the latter's overcoming could a universal thought of humanity become dominant in which we could then truly maintain along with Fanon (1986, p. 231, *translation modified*): 'The black is not, any more than the white'.

Annex

The Mandé Charter or Oath of the Manden of 1222

1. The hunters declare:
Every (human) life is a life.
It is true that a life comes into existence before another life
But no life is more 'ancient', more respectable than any other
In the same way no one life is superior to any other

2. The hunters declare:
As each life is a life,
Any wrong done unto a life requires reparation.
Consequently,
No one should gratuitously attack his neighbour
No one should wrong his neighbour
No one should torment his fellow man

3. The hunters declare:
That each person should watch over their neighbour
That each person should venerate their progenitors

That each person should educate their children as it should be done
That each person should provide for the needs of their family

4. The hunters declare:
That each person should watch over the country of their fathers
By country, or motherland, or 'faso' one must understand also people
For 'any country, any land which were to see people disappear
Would soon become nostalgic'

5. The hunters declare:
Hunger is not a good thing
There is nothing worse than this on this earth
As long as we hold the quiver and the bow
Hunger will no longer kill anyone in the Manden
If by chance hunger were to arrive,
War will no longer destroy any village for the purpose of acquiring slaves
That is to say that no one will from now on
place the bit in the mouth of his fellow
In order to sell him.
Furthermore no one will be beaten
And all the more so put to death because he is the son of a slave

6. The hunters declare
The essence of slavery is today extinguished
'from one wall to the other' from one border to the other of the Manden
Raids are banned from this day onward in the Manden
The torments born of these horrors
have ended from this day onward in the Manden
What an ordeal this torment is!
Especially when the oppressed has no recourse
The slave does not benefit from any consideration
Anywhere in the world.

7. People from the old days tell us:
'Man as an individual

423

Made of flesh and bone
Of marrow and nerves
Of skin covered in hair
Eats food and drink
But his 'soul', his spirit lives on three things:
He must see what he wishes to see
He must say what he wishes to say
And do what he wishes to do
If one of these things were to be missing from the human soul
It would suffer and would surely become sick
In consequence the hunters declare:
Each person from now on is free to dispose of his or her own self
Each person is free to act in the way they wish
Each person disposes of the fruit of their labour from now on
This is the oath of the Manden
For the ears of the whole world.

(Source : Cissé, Youssouf Tata and Kamissoko, Wâ 1991. *La grande geste du Mali. Vol. 2 Soundjata ou la gloire du Mali*, Paris : Karthala-ARSAN, p. 39, *my translation from the French*)

The Charter of Kurukan Fuga, 1236

[1] The Great Mandé Society is divided into sixteen clans of quiver carriers, five clans of marabouts, four groups of "nyamakalas" and one group of slaves. Each one has a specific activity and role.

[2] The "nyamakalas" have to devote themselves to tell the truth to the chiefs, to be their counsellors and to defend by the speech the established rulers and the order upon the whole territory.

[3] The five clans of marabouts are our teachers and our educators in Islam. Everyone has to hold them in respect and consideration.

[4] The society is divided into age groups. Belong to the some age-group the people (men or women) who are born during a period of three years in succession.

The members of the intermediary class between young and old people, should be invited to take part in taking important decisions concerning the society.

5 Every body has a right to life and to the preservation of its physical integrity. Accordingly, any attempt to deprive one's fellow being of life is punished with death.

6 To win the battle of prosperity, the general system of supervision has been established in order to fight against laziness and idleness.

7 It has been established among the Mandenkas, the sanankunya (joking relationship) and the tanamannyonya (blood pact). Consequently any contention that occurs among these groups should not degenerate, the respect for one another being the rule.

Between brothers-in-low and sisters-in-law, between grandparents and grand-children, tolerance and rag should be the principle.

8 The Keïta's family is nominated reigning family upon the empire.

9 The children's education behoves the entire society. The paternal authority in consequence falls to everyone.

10 We should offer condolences mutually.

11 When your wife or your child runs away stop running after her/him in the neighbour's house.

12 The succession being patrilineal, do never give up the power to a son when one of his fathers is still alive. Do never give up the power to a minor just because he has goods.

13 Do never offend the Nyaras.

14 Do never offend women, our mothers.

15 Do never beat a married woman before having her husband interfere unsuccessfully.

16 Women, apart from their everyday occupations, should be associated with all our management.

17 Lies that have lived for 40 years should be considered like truths.

18 We should respect the law of primogeniture.

19 Any man has two parents-in-law: the parents of the girl we failed to have and the speech we deliver without any constraint. We have to hold them in respect and consideration.

20 Do not ill treat the slaves. We are the master of the slave but not of the bag he carries.

²¹ Do not follow up with your constant attentions the wives of the chief, of the neighbour, of the marabout, of the priest, of the friend and of the partner.

²² Vanity if the token of weakness and humility is the one of nobility.

²³ Do never betray one another. Respect your word of honour.

²⁴ In Mandé do never wrong foreigners.

²⁵ The ambassador does not risk anything in Mandé.

²⁶ The bull confided to your care should not lead the cattle-pen.

²⁷ The young lady can get married early as she is pubescent.

²⁸ The young man can get married from 20 years old.

²⁹ The amount of the dowry is 3 bovines: one for the girl, two for her father and mother.

³⁰ In Mandé, the divorce is tolerated for one of the following reasons: the impotence of the husband, the madness of one of the spouses, the husband's incapability of assuming the obligations due to the marriage. The divorce should occur out of the village.

³¹ We should help those who are in need.

³² There are five ways to acquire the property: the buying, the donation, the exchange, the work and the inheriting. Any other form without convincing testimony is doubtful.

³³ Any object found without known owner becomes common property only after four years.

³⁴ The fourth bringing forth of a heifer confided is the property of the guardian.

One egg out of four is the property of the guardian of the laying hen.

³⁵ One bovine should be exchanged for four sheep or four goats.

³⁶ To satisfy one's hunger is not a robbery if you don't take away anything in your bag or your pocket.

³⁷ Fakombè is nominated chief of hunters.

³⁸ Before setting fire to the bush, don't look at the ground, rise your head in the direction of the top of the trees to see if they don't bear fruits or flowers.

³⁹ Domestic animals should be tied during cultivation moment and freed after the harvest. The dog, the cat, the duck and poultry are not bound by the measure.

⁴⁰ Respect the kinship, the marriage and the neighbourhood.

⁴¹ You can kill the enemy, but not humiliate him.

In big assemblies, be satisfied with your lawful representatives.

Balla Fassèkè Kouyaté is nominated big chief of ceremonies and main mediator in Mandé. He is allowed to joke with all groups, in priority with the royal family.

All those who will transgress these rules will be punished. Everyone is bound to make effective their implementation.

(Source: http://www.oecd.org/dataoecd/47/36/38515935.pdf)

Notes

[1] I would like to dedicate this article to the memory of Sam Moyo with whom I had been discussing some of its arguments before his untimely death.

[2] The Eurocentric myth that the West invented 'free and equal discussion' at a certain stage of the development of its civilisation while elsewhere despotism was prevalent is made obvious here.

[3] After the November 2015 mass killings in Paris, the French state consensus has systematically opposed in discourse the (French) civilized to the (Muslim) barbarians. The state has declared a state of emergency which seems to be acquiring a permanent status. For a detailed discussion see Badiou (2016).

[4] To seek in Hegel, as Susan Buck-Morss does, a positive assessment of the struggle for freedom against slavery in Haiti is a fanciful idea of our own times, for which the universality of humanity has been rediscovered in the form of an imperial conception of 'human rights' (see Buck-Morss 2000 and also Nesbitt 2008). For a good critical assessment of Buck-Morss's argument see Stephanson (2010).

[5] For the details of which, see Ndiaye (ed.) 2008.

[6] Domains of politics are identified by distinct modes of state rule. As a result emancipatory or 'excessive politics' take different forms in each domain. For a detailed elucidation of the concept of 'domain of politics', see Neocosmos 2016, Chapters 10, 11 and 12.

[7] The reader is referred to the distinction between domains of politics drawn by Chatterjee (2004) following on from Foucault's (1978) distinction between sovereignty and governmentality. See Neocosmos, 2016 op.cit.

[8] The notion of *ubuntu* refers to the much celebrated idea of social interdependence (I exist because you exist) in African cultures. As it is predominantly understood, *ubuntu* is reduced to a cultural ethnophilosophical practice more or less undermined by colonialism/apartheid and more or less adhered to. It follows that in circumstances where this practice has been reduced, if it is to revive it has to be taught, like all cultures. See, for example, Praeg and Magadla (2014, p. 101). The reduction of complex African conceptions to a ethnophilosophical notion that 'I exist *because* of others' (p .96) effaces the centrality of political agency in African thought (i.e. that such a conception of mutual interdependence must be struggled for by a political practice) in favour of an anthropological notion of culture. It thus becomes compatible with communitarian identity politics.

[9] See the annex to this chapter for the full text in English. The Charter was orally transmitted within the hunters' guild. For a useful account of the transmission of knowledge by the hunters of Mali see Sidebé (2001).

[10] The Kurukan-Fuga Charter has recently been revived as a supposed authentic expression of African culture which is said to provide the basis for locating within ancient tradition such current concerns as conflict resolution, decentralisation and environmental sustainability in contemporary Africa, and has been promoted by various West African states and multistate agencies. In fact UNESCO has inscribed it on the 'Representative List of the Intangible Cultural Heritage of Humanity'. See the annex for the full text. I maintain that it is rather the Hunter's Oath which makes the obvious statement of a true universal humanity which ought to be given that status.

[11] Nesbitt rightly notes the important distinctions between the two statements arguing quite correctly that the Hunters' Oath 'asserts for perhaps the first time ... that a different organization of society is possible, one of universal equality ...' (2014, p. 19) yet at the same time he insists that it amounts to a human rights document which to my mind is false. The point is not so much that the Hunters' Oath anticipates modernity; claims for universal equality are historical invariants in rebellions against state power. Rather, this document must be understood as purely politically prescriptive, as a principled guide to action. I am grateful to Chika Mba for this reference.

[12] The opposition between state and society seems to be the central motif of radical analyses of Haiti. Trouillot (1995) sees state and nation as opposed in Haiti, Barthélemy (1990, 2000) sees Bossale rural equality as being opposed to Creole hierarchy, and Lundhal (1979) sees the 'government' as exploiting the peasantry. Nesbitt (2008, pp. 170–76) largely follows Barthélemy's argument. Barthélemy is himself heavily influenced by the work of the anthropologist Pierre Clastres (1974) who researched the purposeful opposition of society to the state.

[13] The first part of the statement '*tout moun se moun*' was resurrected politically by Jean-Bertrand Aristide as a guide to action for the Lavalas party in the 1980s and 90s (see Hallward 2007). The term *moun* is clearly derived etymologically from the Bantu word *(u)muntu* for a person.

[14] Abahlali baseMjondolo (2008). See also http://abahlali.org/node/14454/ accessed 4 April 2016.

[15] See http://abahlali.org/taxonomy/term/xenophobia/xenophobia/ accessed 4 April 2016.

[16] It would be important to develop further research which would make visible past or present occurrences of the thought of universal humanity in popular struggles for emancipation on the African continent. See Neocosmos (2016).

References

Abahlali baseMjondolo (2008) 'Statement on the xenophobic attacks in Johannesburg, 21/05/2008', http://abahlali.org/node/3582.

Aristide, J-B. (1992) *Tout Moun se Moun – Tout Homme est un Homme*, Paris: Seuil.

Badiou, A. (2006) 'Politique et Vérité: Entretien avec Daniel Bensaid', *Contretemps*, No. 15, http://www.contretemps.eu/alain-badiou-politique-verite/.

---------- (2008) 'The Communist Hypothesis', *New Left Review*, No. 49, Jan–Feb.

---------- (2009) *Logics of Worlds*, London: Continuum.

---------- (2012) Séminaire 2011–2012 : *Que signifie changer le monde ? 2, Notes de Daniel Fischer,* http://www.entretemps.asso.fr/Badiou/seminaire.htm

---------- (2013) Séminaire 2012–2013 : *L'Immanence des Vérités 1, Notes de Daniel Fischer*, http://www.entretemps.asso.fr/Badiou/seminaire.htm.

---------- (2014a) Séminaire 2013–2014 : *L'immanence des Vérités 2, Notes de Daniel Fischer* http://www.entretemps.asso.fr/Badiou/13-14.htm.

---------- (2014b) 'L'impuissance Contemporaine', in A. Badiou et al. *Le Symptôma Grec*, Paris: Lignes.

---------- (with Engelmann, P.) (2015) *Philosophy and the Idea of Communism*, Cambridge: Polity Press.

---------- (2016) *Notre mal vient de plus loin: penser les tueries du 13 novembre*, Paris: fayard.

Barthélémy, G. (1990) *L'Univers Rural Haïtien : le pays en dehors*, Paris: L'Harmattan.

---------- (2000) *Créoles – Bossales: Conflit en Haïti*, Petit Bourg, Guadeloupe: Ibis Rouge Editions.

Buck-Morss, S. (2000) 'Hegel and Haiti', *Critical Inquiry*, Vol. 26, No. 4 (Summer), pp. 821–65.

Cabral, A. (1972) 'The role of culture in the struggle for independence', in A. Cabral, *Resistance and Decolonization,* London & New York: Rowman & Littlefield, 2016.

Césaire, A. (1972) *Discourse on Colonialism*, New York: Monthly Review Press.

Chatterjee, P. (2004) *The Politics of the Governed: Reflections on Popular Politics in Most of the World*, New York: Columbia University Press.

Cissé, Y.T. and Kamissoko, W. (1991) *La grande geste du Mali. Vol. 2 Soundjata ou la gloire du Mali*, Paris: Karthala-ARSAN.

Clastres, P. (1974) *La Société Contre L'État*, Paris: Éditions de Minuit.

Fanon, F. (1986) *Black Skin, White Masks*, London: Pluto Press.

---------- (1989) *Studies in a Dying Colonialism,* London: Earthscan.

---------- (1990) *The Wretched of the Earth*, London: Penguin Books.

Fick, C. (1992) *The Making of Haiti: The Saint Domingue Revolution from Below,* Knoxville: The University of Tennessee Press.

Foucault, M. (1978) 'Governmentality', in M. Foucault, 2000, *Power: Essential Works of Foucault 1954–1984, Vol. 3*, London: Penguin, pp. 201–22.

Gordon, L. (2013) 'Race, theodicy, and the normative emancipatory challenges of blackness', *The South Atlantic Quarterly*, Vol. 112, No. 4, Fall.

Hallward, P. (2007) *Damming the Flood: Aristide and the Politics of Containment*, London: Verso.

Hegel, G.W.F. (1952) *The Philosophy of Right and the Philosophy of History*, London: Encyclopaedia Britannica.

Hountondji, P. (1983) *African Philosophy: Myth and Reality*, Bloomington: Indiana University Press.

----------. (1997) 'African philosophy, myth and reality' in R.R. Grinker and C.B. Steiner (eds.) *Perspectives on Africa*, Oxford: Blackwell.

Lazarus, S. (2015) *Anthropology of the Name*, London, New York, Calcutta: Seagull.

Losurdo, D. (2014) *Liberalism: A Counter History*, London: Verso.

Lundhal, M. (1979) *Peasants and Poverty: A Study of Haiti*, London: St Martin's Press.

Marx, K. (1871) *The Civil War in France*, Peking: Foreign Languages Press, 1970.

Mill, J.-S. (2002) 'On liberty' in *The Basic Writings of John Stuart Mill*, New York: The Modern Library.

Ndiaye, M. (ed.) (2008) *Sarkozy, la controverse de Dakar : contexte enjeux et non-dits*, Cours Nouveau Revue africaine trimestrielle de stratégie et de prospective, Numéro 1-2 Mai-Octobre.

Neocosmos, M. (2010) *From 'Foreign Natives' to 'Native Foreigners': Explaining Xenophobia in Post-Apartheid South Africa*, Dakar: CODESRIA. http://www.codesria.org/IMG/pdf/Neocosmos_From_Foreign_Native_to-2.pdf.

---------- (2016) *Thinking Freedom in Africa: Toward a Theory of Emancipatory Politics*, Johannesburg: Wits University Press.

Nesbitt, N. (2008) *Universal Emancipation: The Haitian Revolution and the Radical Enlightenment*, Charlottesville and London: University of Virginia Press.

------------ (2014) 'Resolutely modern: Politics and human rights in the Mandingue Charter', *The Savannah Review*, Vol. 4, November.

Praeg, L. and Magadla, S. (eds.) (2014) *Ubuntu: Curating the Archive*, Pietermaritzburg: UKZN Press.

Rancière, J. (1995) *La Mésentente: politique et philosophie*, Paris: Galilée.

[English translation *Dis-agreement: Politics and Philosophy,* Minneapolis: University of Minnesota Press 1999].

---------- (2004) *The Politics of Aesthetics: The Distribution of the Sensible,* London: Continuum.

Sedibé, F.M. (2001) 'Transmission des Savoirs: le cas de la confrérie des chasseurs au Mali', http://www.geophile.net/IMG/pdf/DOZO_TRANSMISS ION_DES_ SAVOIRS.pdf (accessed 14 November 2014).

Stephanson, A. (2010) 'The philosopher's island', *New Left Review,* Vol. 61, Jan–Feb.

Trouillot, M.-R. (1980) 'Review of M. Lundhal, *Peasants and Poverty: A Study of Haiti', Journal of Peasant Studies,* Vol. 8, No. 1 (October).

---------- (1995) *Silencing the Past: Power and the Production of History,* Boston: Beacon Press.

Žižek, S. (2008) *Violence,* London: Profile Books.

INDEX

S

CPSIA information can be obtained
at www.ICGtesting.com
Printed in the USA
BVOW11s0715240417
482063BV00017B/521/P